Charles Carleton Coffin

Old Times in the Colonies

Charles Carleton Coffin

Old Times in the Colonies

ISBN/EAN: 9783337151249

Printed in Europe, USA, Canada, Australia, Japan

Cover: Foto ©ninafisch / pixelio.de

More available books at **www.hansebooks.com**

OLD TIMES IN THE COLONIES

BY

CHARLES CARLETON COFFIN
AUTHOR OF "THE BOYS OF '76" "THE STORY OF LIBERTY" &c.

Illustrated

NEW YORK
HARPER & BROTHERS, FRANKLIN SQUARE

Entered according to Act of Congress, in the year 1880, by
HARPER & BROTHERS,
In the Office of the Librarian of Congress, at Washington.

All rights reserved.

PREFACE.

To the Boys and Girls of America:

THE settlement of our country was the beginning of a new era in human affairs. The people of England, ever since the days of King John, when the barons compelled him to sign the Magna Charta in the meadow of Runnymede, had struggled against tyranny; and when the emigrants sailed across the Atlantic to rear their homes in Virginia and New England, it was the transplanting of liberty to a continent where everything was new, and where the conditions that surrounded them were wholly unlike those of the Old World.

This volume is an outline of some of the principal events that transpired during the colonial period of our country, and portrays the hardships and sufferings of those who laid the foundations of a new empire. It will show how the Old World laws, habits, and customs were gradually changed; how the grand ideas of Freedom and the Rights of Man took root and flourished. It covers the period from the discovery and settlement of America to the Revolutionary War. In 1876 I wrote a volume entitled "The Boys of '76"—a narrative of the battles of the Revolution, and of the trials and devotion of our fathers in establishing the independence of the United States. While preparing that work, I discovered that there was no volume in existence that would give the young people of our country an idea of the struggles of men in England and Europe against the tyranny of emperors, kings, popes, archbishops, bishops, and inquisitors; to supply that want, I wrote a second volume, entitled "The Story of Liberty," which traced a chain of events through a period of five hundred years, from the signing of the Magna Charta to the settlement of Jamestown and Plymouth. This volume, therefore, fills the gap between the others in time, and together they make a series, not of general history, but an outline history of the progress of ideas.

PREFACE.

I desire to call your attention to a few things which will be made plain in this volume. You will notice that the beginning of the history of our country is clear and distinct, while the beginnings of the histories of other countries are obscured by tradition or made doubtful by fable. Our early history is definite; the early history of other lands uncertain.

The history of a nation is like the flowing of a river; there are many rivulets starting wide apart, which unite to swell the ever-deepening stream. Many of the fountain-heads of American history are in England and Europe; and in order to obtain a correct view of what transpired in the colonies, we must cross the Atlantic and follow the rivulets to their sources. The tracing of the relationship of one event to another, and showing their effect upon the human race, is the philosophy of history, and by studying the philosophy we are able to arrive at some conclusion as to its meaning.

You will notice how, through priority of discovery, Spain, France, and England claimed various sections of this continent, and how conflicting claims led to a great struggle between England and France for supremacy; that it was a conflict between two races, two languages, two religions, two systems of laws, two distinct civilizations; that great ideas were behind the struggle. In the opening chapter you will read how John and Sebastian Cabot sailed along the northern coasts, how Jacques Cartier sailed up the St. Lawrence; the closing pages will picture a battle on the Plains of Abraham. It was an engagement which lasted only a few minutes, yet it was one of the great decisive battles of the world—momentous in its results. John and Sebastian Cabot, Cartier, Champlain, the Kings of France and England, the Pope, Ignatius Loyola, the Jesuits, Oliver Cromwell, the Pilgrims of the *Mayflower*, the Puritans, are as inseparably connected with that battle as William Pitt, James Wolfe, and the Marquis de Montcalm. The history of the entire colonial period leads up to it.

You will notice that the forces of Nature—the turning of the earth upon its axis, the flowing of the Gulf Stream, the contour of mountain ranges, the courses of the rivers, have had a far-reaching influence upon the history of our country. The rivers were the highways along which the Indians paddled their canoes to fall upon the settlers—along which the armies of England and France marched to engage in battle. Mountains were barriers, stopping awhile the progress of civilization, and also shielding the colonies from attack. Not only these, but the order of the Pope forbidding people to eat meat on Fridays, saints' days, and during Lent, but granting permission to eat fish, the desire of the people of Europe to wear hats made from the glossy fur of the beaver, the love for tobacco, their ideas of holding men in slavery, are forces that have had much to do in shaping the history of our country.

The longing for adventure, the hunger for gold, led to the settlement of Virginia. Through convictions of duty and obligations to God, the Pilgrims were driven from England to Holland, and across the Atlantic, to begin self-government, and to give to the world the ideal of a written constitution. The hatred of the Puritans to the ritual of the Church of England, the determination of the bishops and archbishops to compel them to conform to it, are great fountain-heads of history. The inner light which illumined the soul of George Fox, the stern convictions of Roger Williams, of his obligation to conscience, are forces which give direction to the course of events. All the motives by which men are actuated— their passions, affections, religious convictions, the selfish ends—are part and parcel of the grand drama of Time.

I have spoken of the meaning of history. Surely it has a meaning, else what are we living for? Whichever way we turn in the material world we find things needful for our use, and we think of them as God's forethoughts, and as designed for our welfare. If there is design in the material world, there must be some meaning to history, some ultimate end to be accomplished. In "The Story of Liberty," and in this volume, you will see how Tyranny and Wrong have fought against Liberty and Justice; how that banner which the barons flung to the breeze at Runnymede, inscribed with the rights of man, which Cromwell bore amidst the carnage of Marston Moor, which waved from the mast-head of the *Mayflower* when that lone vessel crossed the Atlantic, has never been trailed in the dust in this Western World; but Tyranny and Wrong have gone down before it. Through the colonial period there was an advance of principles which are eternal in their nature. All through those years conditions and influences were preparing men for self-government. Men die, generations come and go, but ideas live on. When the world was ready for it, and not before, the American Revolution came, with the aunouncement that all men are created free and equal, and endowed with inalienable rights.

Through all the narratives of wars, massacres, and bloodshed, you will see Right, Justice, and Liberty ever advancing. "Old Times in the Colonies," therefore, is not an unmeaning record of events, but the story of the rise of a great nation, the growth of individual liberty, the coming in of constitutional government in this Western World—the history of the first period in the new era in human affairs.

As you peruse these pages, the conviction, I trust, will come that, under the power of great ideas, our country is leading the human race in its march toward a state of society inexpressibly grand and glorious.

CHARLES CARLETON COFFIN.

CONTENTS.

CHAPTER I.
DISCOVERY OF SAN SALVADOR... 17

CHAPTER II.
FORCES OF CIVILIZATION.. 37

CHAPTER III.
FIRST SETTLEMENTS... 54

CHAPTER IV.
THE WISE FOOL OF ENGLAND AND HIS TIMES................................ 72

CHAPTER V.
THE BEGINNING OF TWO CIVILIZATIONS.. 87

CHAPTER VI.
HOW BEAVER-SKINS AND TOBACCO HELPED ON CIVILIZATION........ 97

CHAPTER VII.
THE PILGRIMS... 111

CHAPTER VIII.
FIRST YEARS AT PLYMOUTH... 129

CHAPTER IX.
SETTLEMENT OF NEW HAMPSHIRE, NEW YORK, AND CANADA......... 141

CHAPTER X.
THE PURITAN BEGINNING.. 152

CHAPTER XI.
THE PURITANS TAKE POSSESSION OF NEW ENGLAND...................... 171

CHAPTER XII.
RHODE ISLAND AND NEW HAMPSHIRE.. 184

CONTENTS.

CHAPTER XIII.
Affairs at Manhattan 195

CHAPTER XIV.
The Struggle for Liberty in England, and How it Affected America 206

CHAPTER XV.
The Quakers 216

CHAPTER XVI.
The End of Dutch Rule in America 224

CHAPTER XVII.
The Times of Charles II 234

CHAPTER XVIII.
King Philip's War 241

CHAPTER XIX.
Louis Frontenac in Canada 251

CHAPTER XX.
Governor Berkeley and the Virginians 259

CHAPTER XXI.
How the King took away the Charters of the Colonies 265

CHAPTER XXII.
King William's War 271

CHAPTER XXIII.
New Jersey and Maryland 291

CHAPTER XXIV.
Settlement of Pennsylvania 297

CHAPTER XXV.
Witches 303

CHAPTER
The Legacy of Blood 318

CHAPTER XXVII.
Maine and New Hampshire 326

CHAPTER XXVIII.
The Carolinas 337

CHAPTER XXIX.
GEORGIA 350

CHAPTER XXX.
THE NEGRO TRAGEDY 357

CHAPTER XXXI.
THE BEGINNING OF A GREAT STRUGGLE 363

CHAPTER XXXII.
DEFEAT OF GENERAL BRADDOCK 374

CHAPTER XXXIII.
THE EMPEROR OF AUSTRIA'S WILL 389

CHAPTER XXXIV.
INCOMPETENT AND COWARDLY GENERALS 408

CHAPTER XXXV.
TWO CIVILIZATIONS 421

CHAPTER XXXVI.
THE DESTINY OF AN EMPIRE 437

INDEX 455

ILLUSTRATIONS.

	PAGE		PAGE
Battle of the Plains of Abraham....*Frontispiece*		De Monts	59
Icebergs between Europe and America	18	Cape Cod	60
Food for Fishes	19	Monhegan	61
What John and Sebastian Cabot Saw	20	Pemmaquid	62
Columbus's Spring	22	Captain John Smith	62
Foliage of Florida	23	Arrival at Jamestown	63
Church Built by Cortez	24	Holland	64
Spanish Discoveries	25	Samuel Champlain	65
John Verrazano	25	Tadousac	66
The Gloomy Solitudes	26	Quebec to the Saguenay	67
Where Cartier passed the Winter	28	The Beginning of Trade on the Hudson	68
De Soto	29	"They see a lightning flash, and hear a	
Burial of De Soto	30	roar"	70
St. Augustine	31	The Rocky Cliffs	73
Palms on the St. John's	32	Ledge of the Orkneys	74
Sir Humphrey Gilbert	33	The Bell-ringers Rung out their Joyful	
English and French Discoveries	34	Peals	75
Chair made from Wood of the Ship of Sir		Street Leading to Parliament-house	76
Francis Drake	35	Tobacco-shop. (From an Old Print.)	78
St. Malo	37	The Dinner	79
Street in Morlaix	38	Globe Theatre	80
Homes of the Fishermen of Brittany	39	House in which Shakspeare was Born	81
Fish-house and Boats	40	Holy Trinity Church, Stratford	82
The Beaver and its Home	42	Stratford Portrait of Shakspeare	83
The Trapper	43	Bear-garden	84
After a Moose	44	Medal of James I	86
Tobacco	45	Birthplace of Henry IV	87
The Slave-ship	46	The Indians at Home	88
"To be sold as slaves"	48	Nun Taking the Veil	93
The Tomahawk and Scalping-knife doing		Mount Desert	94
Bloody Work	50	Penobscot Bay	95
Dining-room in a Puritan Manor-house	52	Smutty-nose	97
Riding out a Gale on the Banks	54	Captain John Smith's Monument, Isles of	
Running for Shelter	55	Shoals	98
Strait of Canso	56	Captain Block building the "Onrust"	99
Cape Ann	57	View at the Hague	100
Portsmouth, New Hampshire	58	John of Barneveld	101

ILLUSTRATIONS.

	PAGE
Going to Fight the Iroquois	103
Agreement between the Dutch and Iroquois	104
A Huron War-dance	105
Cultivation of Tobacco	108
First Settlements on the Chesapeake and Delaware	109
Dutch Revel. (From an Old Picture.)	112
Execution of Barneveld. (From Motley's "Life and Death of John of Barneveld.")	113
Dartmouth	117
Provincetown	118
Map	119
Plymouth	121
Where they were Buried	124
Plymouth Rock	125
"With tearful eyes they saw the white sails fade away"	127
Governor Bradford's House	130
Edward Winslow	131
Plymouth Wilderness	132
Wampum	133
Kitchen of Standish House	135
Captain Standish stirring the Punch	136
Standish's Sword, and the Barrel of the Gun with which Philip was killed	137
Autographs of some of the Pilgrims	139
The Pilgrim Monument, Plymouth	140
Mouth of the Piscataqua — Whale's-back Light	141
Landing of the Walloons	143
Manhattan	144
On the Delaware	144
Esplanade Hill, Quebec	145
Falls of Montmorenci	147
Court of the White Horse, Fontainebleau	149
Christmas	154
Puritan Settlements in New England	155
Gloucester, Massachusetts	156
John Endicott	157
Entrance to Salem Harbor	158
Endicott's Pear-tree	159
Charles I.	160
Old-fashioned Washing-machines	161
Cosy the Homes they left behind them	163
John Winthrop	165
Groton Church	166
"Norman's Woe"	167
The Cliffs	168
Blackstone's House	169
First Meeting-house in Boston	169
Statue of Governor Winthrop	170
Nantucket	171
Cohasset Harbor	173
Old Meeting-house, Hingham	174
Emigrants at Night	175
Lady Fenwick's Tomb	176
Wild Turkeys	177
Indian Rock, Narragansett	178
Where they Landed	180
New Haven	182
Harvard College, 1720	184
General View of the University Buildings, Cambridge	185
Where Roger Williams landed	189
Residence of Governor Coddington, Newport, 1641	190
Old-time Houses, Newport	191
Newport, from Fort Adams	192
Map	193
Manhattan	195
Wouter Van Twiller swearing Great Dutch Oaths	196
Paying Tribute	198
Gustavus Adolphus	199
The First Church in Philadelphia	200
Old Swedes' Church, Philadelphia	201
The American Colonies in 1640	202
The Massacre of the Indians	204
Strafford on his Way to Execution	208
The Battle-fields	211
The Washington House, Little Brington	212
Brington Church	213
Church in which Sir John Washington worshipped	214
George Fox	216
Quakers doing their Duty	220
Old Town Church, Newbury	221
Peter Stuyvesant, the Last Governor of New Amsterdam	224
Anna Merica Bayard, Wife of Peter Stuyvesant	225
Old Tiled Fireplace, Winthrop House	227
The Dutchman at Home	228
The Van Cortlandt Manor-house	229

ILLUSTRATIONS.

	PAGE
His Lips were White	232
A Cavalier, Time of Charles II	235
Patches, in the Time of Charles II	236
Nell Gwynne. (From a Painting by Sir Peter Lely.)	237
New Haven	238
Under this Bridge the Judges were concealed	239
The Judges' Cave	240
Mount Hope	242
King Philip	243
Fight at Tiverton	245
Only One Entrance across a Log	246
Death of Philip	248
Colbert	251
A Trapper going his Rounds	252
Louis XIV	253
The Rival Companies soliciting Trade	255
Berkeley, near Harrison's Landing	259
"All travel was by boats on the river"	260
Indian Massacre	261
Discussing the Charter	266
The Charter Oak	267
Where William Landed	272
Major Waldron's Terrible Fight	275
Schenectady	278
"He staggers with him through the woods"	283
Women Standing Guard	287
"A few strokes of the paddle bring them back to the island"	289
Middle Colonies	291
First Church in Newark	292
The Old Schuyler Mansion	292
Peter Schuyler	293
Arms of the Calvert Family	293
First Mass in Maryland	294
Laying out Baltimore	296
William Penn	297
Landing of William Penn at Philadelphia	299
First Brick Building erected in Philadelphia—Given by Mr. Penn to his Daughter	300
James Logan, Secretary to William Penn	301
Penn's House	301
The Penn Seal	302
Lake Geneva	304
Stories were Told of what the Witches were doing	306
Their Hearts Leaping up their Throats	307
The Idea was abroad that she had a "malignant touch"	308
Thomas Beadle's Tavern, 1692	311
Rebecca Nurse's Home	313
Shattuck's House	315
The Hill on which they were Hung	316
Palace of St. Germain	319
Garrison House, York	321
In Ambush	323
View from Fort George	330
Map	332
Death of the Medicine-man	333
Building Ships	335
Family of Bishop Berkeley	336
Carolina Home	338
On the Ashley	339
Yeamans Hall, Goose Creek	340
Drayton Hall, Western Front	341
Picking Figs	342
Orange Fruit and Flowers	343
St. Michael's Church	344
Landgrave Smith's Back River Residence	345
Old Meeting-house, Dorchester	346
Oglethorpe	351
John Wesley	353
Charles Wesley	354
The French Forts	364
"Crack! crack! went the guns of the Indians"	365
Arms and Crest of the Washington Family	368
Mount Vernon	369
Washington Surveying Lord Fairfax's Land	371
The Land in Dispute	374
Braddock's Head-quarters	378
Washington's Talk with Braddock	379
"They saw puffs of smoke, but few of the enemy"	381
Braddock's Grave	383
Lake George	384
Joseph Brant	385
Sir William Johnson	386
Hendrick	386
Site of Fort Number Four	389
Cape Breton	390
Following a Trail	391

ILLUSTRATIONS.

	PAGE
Governor Benning Wentworth	393
Wentworth House, Little Harbor	394
Sir William Pepperell's House	395
Navy-yard, Kittery, Maine	396
Sir William Pepperell	397
Stockbridge	398
"Guarding their wives and children"	400
The Indians Aiming at the Loop-holes	406
The Expedition	409
Oswego in 1755	410
Fort at Oswego	410
Fort William Henry	412
John Stark	414
Paradise Bay	417
Plan of Fort William Henry	418
Bloody Pond	419
Dragging the Boats	423
Lake George, from the Top of Rogers's Rock	424
Earl of Bute	425
Southern End of Lake George	426
"The great flotilla moves away"	427
Sabbath-day Point	428
The Northern End of Lake George	429
Plan of Attack by General Abercrombie at Ticonderoga, July 8th, 1758	431
"The Highlanders are brave"	432
Fort George	433
Taking Possession of Fort Du Quesne	435
William Pitt	437
Montreal, 1760. (From an Old Print.)	438
Wolfe	441
Montcalm	442
Montcalm's Head-quarters	443
St. John's Gate, Quebec	444
The Place where Wolfe Landed	445
Battle of Quebec	446
Burning the Prisoners	448
A Scalp-dance	450
Wolfe and Montcalm's Monument	452

OLD TIMES IN THE COLONIES.

CHAPTER I.
DISCOVERY OF SAN SALVADOR.

THERE it was, a green and sunny island. Christopher Columbus beheld it in the dawning light of October 12, 1492; an earthly paradise with stately trees, fragrant flowers, groves of oranges and bananas, hanging vines, birds of bright plumage, and groups of dusky men, women, and children.

It was San Salvador, one of the Bahama Islands. A few days later Columbus discovered Cuba and Hispaniola, now known as St. Domingo, and returned to Spain with the wonderful news.

Who owned the islands? They were occupied by Indians; but the Pope, Alexander VI., Roderick Borgia, wicked and cruel, a murderer, claiming to be God's agent on earth and endowed with all power, gave all lands that might be discovered west of an imaginary line, drawn north and south one hundred leagues west of the Azores, to Ferdinand and Isabella, king and queen of Spain. So, by priority of discovery, and by the decree of the Pope, Spain entered upon the possession of what Columbus had discovered.

The news reached England. The merchants of Bristol who were sending their ships to France, the Mediterranean, and the North Sea, applied to the king, Henry VII., for leave to send out an expedition for the discovery of new lands.

"If you discover any countries, they shall be mine," he said, asserting his right to hold or give away lands, against that claimed by the Pope.

"If you make any money by the expedition, one-fifth of it shall be mine," he added.

The merchants accepted the conditions, fitted out two vessels commanded by John and Sebastian Cabot, father and son, two Venetians in their employ as sea-captains. In May, 1497, the ships sailed down the river Severn, and steered west for a voyage over unknown seas, where vessels had not sailed since the days of the old Northmen.

In June they found themselves on soundings, and the sea around swarming with codfish. The water was warm, and dense fogs arose. A little farther on the water was colder, and filled with icebergs. They had reached a place where two great currents of the ocean meet. They did not know, nor was it till many years later that anybody knew, what caused the flowing of these currents; that the earth was whirling around the sun, and also turning on its own axis; that the speed at the equator was eighteen miles a minute.

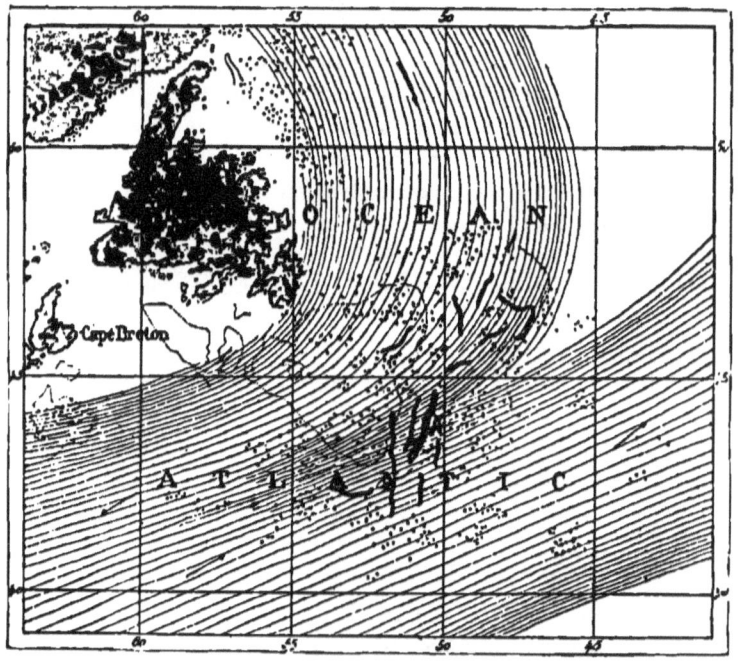

ICEBERGS BETWEEN EUROPE AND AMERICA.

We now know that the revolution of the earth upon its axis sets the water between Africa and South America to flowing westward, and that when the current strikes the coast of South America it is divided, a part flowing south and part north. The northern section, carrying with it the fresh water brought down the Amazon and Orinoco from the Andes and the plains of South America, sweeps into the Caribbean Sea, and whirls onward to the Gulf of Mexico, being heated by the sun to a temperature of eighty-six degrees. The Mississippi pours in its mighty flood, bringing minute particles of soil from the far distant prairies and mountains.

FOOD FOR FISHES.

Having no other outlet, the waters rush through the passage between Florida and Cuba, tearing great masses of sea-weed from the beds of white coral, which the coralline insects are building beneath the waves. This river of hot water, one thousand feet deep and fifty miles wide, sweeps on at the rate of five miles an hour, bearing the soil of two continents, the sea-weed, and myriads of marine insects—polyps, star and jellyfish, in infinite variety. East of Newfoundland it meets a current of cold water flowing south, from the frozen region of the North, bringing great icebergs; but the warm current whirls them north-east, speedily

WHAT JOHN AND SEBASTIAN CABOT SAW.

melting them, dropping the stones and gravel torn from the shore of Greenland beneath the sea. The fine particles of sand brought down from the Andes by the Amazon, and from the prairies of the West by the Mississippi, also settle to the bottom of the sea, thus making that portion of the sea a great dumping-place—building up the bank of Newfoundland. The hot river supplies the codfish with food, gives a mild climate to England, and makes it possible for men to live in Iceland and Northern Norway.

John and Sebastian Cabot caught all the fish they needed, and, sailing still west, on June 24th beheld the waves breaking against the rocky shore of Labrador.

Since the days of the old Northmen, no European eye had seen the main-land of the Western World. The Cabots sailed northward along a bleak and forbidding coast, with dense forests beyond the white granite ledges. They saw white-bears, floating on cakes of ice, plunge into the sea and catch fish in their paws. Walruses and seals frequented the shores, and myriads of birds reared their young upon the rocky cliffs; but their provisions failing, they returned to England.

What a year for discovery was 1498! Stimulated by what he had seen, Sebastian Cabot—young sagacious, bold—sailed once more westward. He coasted along the southern shore of Newfoundland, entered the Bay of Fundy, gazed upon the cliffs of Mount Desert, the majestic pines of Maine, the sandy beaches of Cape Cod, sailing southward to Virginia—thus, by priority of discovery, enabling England to claim the continent from Labrador to Cape Hatteras.

Christopher Columbus, at the same time, was making his third voyage; discovering the island of Trinidad, the coast of South America and Orinoco. He landed, and drank from a spring that still bears his name.

There was another brave sailor on the seas, Vasco da Gama, of Portugal, who was sailing south along the west coast of Africa, doubling the Cape of Good Hope; sailing on till, through the ocean haze, he beheld the mountains of Hindostan, thus opening a long sought for route to India. There was still another voyager on the seas, Amerigo Vespucci, a merchant of Florence, engaged in trade at Seville, in Spain, who, animated by a spirit of adventure, sailed to the West Indies with Captain Ojeda, and from thence to the coasts of South and Central America. He wrote interesting accounts of what he saw, which were published in 1507—probably the first printed narrative given to the public of the discoveries in the West. The pamphlet fell into the hands of Martin Waldseemuller, of Freibourg, in Germany, who translated it into German. People spoke of the new world as Amerigo's country, and thus the name became attached to the Western Continent, though the honor of discovery belongs to John and Sebastian Cabot.

The King of Portugal, desiring a share in the new world, sent Gasper Cortereal upon a voyage of discovery, who sailed along the coast of

COLUMBUS'S SPRING.

North America, from Virginia northward to Newfoundland. He enticed a number of Indians on board his ships, and treacherously carried them to Portugal and sold them into slavery.

Men do not like to grow old. How gladly would they ever retain the freshness of youth! The longing to be young again became a passion with Ponce de Leon, Governor of Porto Rico. The gray hairs had come, and there were furrows in his cheeks. Poets had written of a fountain of perpetual youth—a stream so clear, and pure, and life-giving, that those who drank of it would be forever young and fair. De Leon resolved to go in quest of it, that, tasting its refreshing waters, he might ever be young.

DISCOVERY OF SAN SALVADOR.

He sailed from Porto Rico, with three vessels, in 1513. On Easter-Sunday, which the Spaniards call Pasqua de Flores, he sighted land a few miles north of St. Augustine, and took possession of the country for the King of Spain, naming it Florida. He was charmed by its scenery—the wide-spreading live-oaks, the fan-leaved palmettos, the tangle of jessamine and honeysuckle, filling the air with fragrance; but vain his search for the fabled Fountain of Eternal Youth; and, after coasting along the shores, landing here and there and exploring the country, he returned to Porto Rico.

The Spaniards in the West Indies heard of the wonderful land of Mexico, inhabited by millions of people—a land of cities and villages, cultivated fields and gardens, abounding in silver and gold, advanced in arts and architecture, with schools, courts of justice, and great stone temples.

FOLIAGE OF FLORIDA.

On the 15th of February, 1519, an expedition, commanded by Hernando Cortez, sailed from Ravenna to conquer the empire of the West, landing first in Yucatan; again at the mouth of the river Tobasco, in the Bay of Campeachy, fighting a battle on the banks of that stream, sweeping the Indians down like grain before the reaper by his cannon and volleys of musketry, beginning a series of conquests that made him master of the empire of the Montezumas, and extending the authority and dominion of Spain westward to the Pacific, and northward to the Colorado and the Rio Grande; establishing the religion of the Roman Catholic Church, and the language and civilization of Spain over that vast section of North America.

CHURCH BUILT BY CORTEZ.

The Spaniards were in need of more slaves to work in their mines and cane-fields, and to obtain them Vasquez D'Ayllon visited the coast of South Carolina in 1520. He called the country Chicora, and entered the Combahee River, which he named the Jordan, and gave the name of St. Helen to the cape which bounds St. Helen's Sound on the south. The Indians received him kindly, accepted his trinkets, flocked in great numbers on board the ships, when he treacherously seized them, hoisted his sails, and carried them away. But it was to little profit; for, knowing nothing of the Gulf Stream, one of his vessels was borne upon rocks by the current, and wrecked, while upon the other the captives sickened and died. D'Ayllon made his second appearance in St. Helen's Sound in 1525, where one of his vessels was wrecked. The Indians attacked him, and drove him on board his ships, mortally wounding him. Instead of conquering them, and establishing the Spanish language and the Catholic religion in Carolina, as Cortez was doing in Mexico, he returned to Cuba to die.

Francis I. was King of France. He had desired to be Emperor of Germany, but his rival, Charles V. of Spain, had been elected instead; besides this, the Pope had given the whole Western Continent to Spain.

"I should like to be shown the clause in the will of Adam which disinherits me in the New World!" he bitterly exclaimed.

Francis despatched John Verrazano on a voyage of discovery in the ship *Dolphin* from Dieppe, January 24th, 1524. He reached South Carolina in March, and sailed northward along the coast, entering Narragansett Bay and the harbor of Newport, R. I., passing around Cape Cod to the coast of Maine. He landed in many places, and had interviews with the Indians.

In January, 1525, Stephen Gomez sailed from Corunna, in Spain, entered the Hudson River on St. Anthony's day, June 13th, named it St. Anthony. He seized some of the Indians, taking them to Spain and sell-

SPANISH DISCOVERIES.

ing them. The country was cold, and he reported that Spaniards could not live there.

Hunger for gold, desire for conquest, zeal for the establishment of religion, thirst for adventure—are there any stronger motives than these to lead men to brave danger or endure hardships? Moved by such motives, Pamphilio Narvaez, Cabez de Vaca, and several hundred young men from the rich and noble families of Spain, sailed from the Guadalquiver for America, landing in Tampa Bay, on the west coast of Florida, April 14th, 1528, taking possession of the country for the King of Spain. The

JOHN VERRAZANO.

THE GLOOMY SOLITUDES.

Indians that flocked around them were in possession of gold ornaments. When asked where they obtained them, they pointed to the north.

Narvaez marched in that direction. There were three hundred in the party, with horses and small cannon. Never before had the eyes of the adventurers beheld such gloomy solitudes—dense forests of pine, dark groves of cypress, wide-spreading oaks with long trails of gray moss drooping from the branches, magnolias filling the air with their overpowering fragrance. They toiled through swamps; bays, inlets, and rivers impeded their progress, and their way was blocked by decaying trees torn up by whirlwinds and blasted by lightning. They saw strange animals —the opossum, that carried its young in a pocket; panthers prowled around them, and bears. At every stream they were compelled to construct rafts. They had little to eat. They expected to find rich and populous Indian towns, but only beheld clusters of wigwams.

JACQUES CARTIER.

In August they were at St. Mark's, on Appolodree Bay; but their ships had not arrived, nor did they ever see them again. They began the construction of boats, making their swords into saws and axes, their stirrups and the bits of their bridles into nails. They plundered the Indian corn-fields to obtain food, and ate their horses. They twisted the film of the palmetto and the hair of their horses' manes and tails into ropes; calked the seams of the boats with grass, and smeared them with pitch; sewed their shirts together for sails; made water-bottles of the

WHERE CARTIER PASSED THE WINTER.

skins of their horses; and on the 2d of September embarked, two hundred and fifty in number, in five frail vessels, so deeply loaded that the gunwales were hardly six inches above the water. They seized some Indian canoes, split them in pieces, and built up the sides of their boats. Slowly they crept along the shore westward. On the 30th of October they reached the Mississippi, and tried to enter it, but the current swept them back. On the 5th of November two of their boats were wrecked not far from Galveston, and the others were driven out to sea. Of the company all but four—De Vasca, Dorantes, Castillo, and Estevarrico—perished. They made themselves at home among the Indians, learned their language, passed from tribe to tribe, travelled northward through Texas to the Canadian River and westward to the Rio Grande, and from thence to San Miguel, in Sonora, which they reached in 1536, where they found some of the soldiers of Cortez, who conducted them to the city of Mexico.

Jacques Cartier, a Frenchman, entered the Gulf of St. Lawrence in 1534, and set up a cross at Gaspé, claiming the country for France. The next year he made a second voyage up the St. Lawrence, beheld the gloomy gorges of the Saguenay, and dropped anchor in the Bay of Orleans. Upon the northern shore, under a rocky cliff, was a cluster of wigwams; the Indians called the place Stadacone. Little did Cartier think that on the plateau behind the town the last decisive battle between France and England for supremacy in America would be fought; that upon the site of the wigwams would rise the city of Quebec. Cartier sailed up the river in a boat, to a town which the Indians called Hochelaga. A hill which overlooked the town and all the surrounding country he named Mont Royal—which time has changed to Montreal. The ice closed around Cartier's ship before he could get away, and he spent the long winter at Stadacone, returning to France in the spring.

Cabeza de Vaca, who had experienced such hardships in his journey from Florida through Texas to Mexico, reached Cuba. His accounts of what he had seen fired the ardor of Ferdinand de Soto, Governor of the island, who had been with Pizarro in Peru. He resolved to conquer Florida, and landed on its western coast, near Hillsborough River, with six hundred men; marched north through Georgia, Alabama, Mississippi, crossing the Mississippi near the boundary of Tennessee, exploring the country north to New Madrid, in Missouri, and west to the western boundary of Arkansas. At the mouth of the Red River, De Soto died, and was buried beneath the waters of the Mississippi. The survivors of the party wandered in Louisiana till July, 1543, when they constructed boats, descended the Mississippi, reached the Gulf, and made their way west to the Spanish settlements in Mexico.

DE SOTO.

Cabeza de Vaca and his companions, while in Texas and Mexico, heard of a country still farther north which the Indians called Cibola.

BURIAL OF DE SOTO.

The Governor of Western Mexico, Coronado, resolved to conquer it. He despatched two vessels up the Gulf of California, which ascended the Colorado River about eighty-five miles beyond the present boundary between Mexico and the United States. Coronado himself with an army marched to Central Arizona, and eastward to Santa Fé, on the Rio Grande, claiming the country for the King of Spain.

While Coronado was marching through Arizona, Francis de la Roque and Cartier were planning the colonization of Canada. They made a settlement at Quebec, but the winter was cold, the emigrants pined for home, and they went back to France.

The Dominican priests in Cuba and Spain had set their hearts on converting the Indians of Florida, and, in 1549, Louis Cancella and several other priests endeavored to establish a mission. The Indians had not forgotten the cruelties of D'Ayllon, Narvaez, and De Soto, and in revenge killed several of the priests, and compelled the others to leave the country.

The Huguenots of France were heretics, and the Catholics were hunting them down. John Ribault, of Dieppe, turned his eyes to America as a place of refuge for himself and friends. He sailed to Carolina, and left twenty-six men to begin a settlement at Port Royal. When he returned to France civil war was raging, and he could send no supplies. The men at

DISCOVERY OF SAN SALVADOR.

Port Royal were homesick. Their provisions failed. They built a small vessel and set sail. Some died, but the others were picked up by an English vessel and saved. Two years passed. There was a lull in the strife between Catholics and Protestants in France, and Ribault began another settlement, on the St. John's River, in Florida. Several hundred Huguenots, with their families, weary of the strife in France, emigrated to Florida.

The news reached Spain. French heretics on Spanish soil! What an outrage! They were Frenchmen, and must be driven out: heretics—and must be exterminated. A heretic—one who did not recognize the Pope as head of the Church—must be put to the sword, as an enemy of God and man.

Philip Melendez, fired with zeal for the Church, stimulated by the preaching of the Jesuit priests and bishops, quickly gathered an army. The high-born sons of Spain enlisted under his banner to wipe out the insult to Spain and to the holy Catholic Church. A great company of priests joined in the enterprise. With twenty-five hundred men he made his appearance on the coast of Florida. It was St. Augustine's day, and he discovered a beautiful harbor to which he gave the name of the saint.

ST. AUGUSTINE.

He approached Fort Carolina. Ribault's vessels went out to meet him. A storm came on, and the French vessels were wrecked; but Melendez reached the harbor at St. Augustine. Fort Carolina was defenceless, and he marched overland, entered it without opposition, and massacred men, women, and children, old and young, sick and helpless, alike. A few men only escaped on two little vessels.

Upon the smouldering ruins of the fort, amidst the ghastly forms of mangled corpses, Melendez reared a cross, with this inscription:

"NOT AS TO FRENCHMEN, BUT AS LUTHERANS."

The Jesuit priests chanted a *Te Deum*, and, laden with the spoil, the army returned to St. Augustine.

PALMS ON THE ST. JOHN'S.

The shipwrecked sailors of the French fleet, living on roots, frogs, and alligators, gave themselves up as prisoners. Their hands were tied behind them, and then the work of death began. Those who were Catholics were spared to become slaves; the others were inhumanly butchered.

Beneath the palmettos, on the banks where the alligators lay basking in the sun of the St. John's, and on the beach of the St. Augustine, lay the mangled bodies of nine hundred men, women, and children, murdered through bigotry and hate; while over the gloomy scene priestly hands held the cross, emblem of love and peace, amidst the chantings of a *Gloria* to Almighty God.

The work of death done, the work of colonization began. Forts were built at St. Augustine, a town laid out, a chapel and houses erected. It was the first permanent settlement within the present boundaries of the United States, begun in 1565.

Intelligence of the horrible massacre reached the ears of Dominic de Gourges in France. He was a Huguenot and wealthy, but of what value was wealth with so terrible a crime unavenged? He sold his estates, purchased ships, enlisted one hundred and fifty men, sailed secretly, captured the garrison in a fort on the St. John's, hung the captives upon the wide-spreading branches of the surrounding trees, with this inscription above them:
"NOT AS UNTO SPANIARDS, BUT AS TO MURDERERS."

He was too weak to attack St. Augustine, and sailed for France, having only in part accomplished his purpose.

Sir Francis Drake, with three ships, had passed through the Straits of Magellan to wage war upon the Spaniards in Peru. One of his ships had been wrecked; the others had sailed he knew not where; but in the *Pelican* he carried havoc to the Spanish towns. In June, 1579, he was so far north off the coast of Oregon that his crew complained of the cold. In a spacious harbor—possibly in the Bay of San Francisco—he refitted his ships, made a map of the coast, and gave the name of New Albion to the country. From thence he sailed west across the Pacific, returning to England by the Cape of Good Hope.

Sir Humphrey Gilbert sailed from England in 1583, with five small vessels, on a voyage of discovery. On the 3d of August he dropped anchor in the harbor of St. John's, Newfoundland, where he found thirty-six vessels. The crews were catching fish and drying them on the rocks. Sir Humphrey informed the fishermen that the island belonged to Queen Elizabeth, and that they must obey the laws of England. If any one said

SIR HUMPHREY GILBERT.

anything against it he was to have his ears cropped off, and lose his goods. The fishermen for many years had been drying their fish on the rocks, but now they were informed that they must pay for the privilege. It was the beginning of a controversy about fish which has lasted three hundred years, and which is not yet settled.

Having set up the authority of Elizabeth, Sir Humphrey sailed for

ENGLISH AND FRENCH DISCOVERIES.

DISCOVERY OF SAN SALVADOR.

England, but his vessel went down in a storm with all on board; the other vessel reached England in safety.

Sir Walter Raleigh had large ideas in regard to America, and greatly desired to have England obtain a foothold in the New World. He sent two vessels, commanded by Philip Amadas and Arthur Barlow, to explore the coast. They sailed south-west, and on the 3d of July, 1584, found themselves off the coast of North Carolina. They were kindly received by the Indians, and, upon their return to England, gave such a satisfactory account of the country that Sir Walter Raleigh sent a few men to establish a colony.

CHAIR MADE FROM WOOD OF THE SHIP OF SIR FRANCIS DRAKE.

Sir Francis Drake was ranging the seas, destroying the ships, and plundering towns in the West Indies, which he called "singeing the beard of the King of Spain." He plundered Porto Rico and St. Augustine, then sailed along the coast and discovered Sir Walter's colony. The settlers longed to see England once more, and sailed with him for their old home. They had but just gone, however, when Sir Richard Grenville arrived at the abandoned settlement with supplies, which Sir Walter had sent. The houses were there, and the fields of wheat ready for the sickle. Sir Richard, not willing to give up the enterprise, landed fifteen men on Roanoke Island, with two years' provisions, to hold the country against Spain; but the men quarrelled with the Indians, and were destroyed.

Sir Walter Raleigh, instead of being disheartened, sent out one hundred and fifty colonists to found the city of Raleigh. John White was governor; he laid out a town on Roanoke Island.

On the 18th of August, 1587, Mrs. Dare gave birth to a daughter, who was named Virginia — the first child of English parents born in America.

The ships departed for England, and when they again returned to America the colonists had disappeared. The houses were there, but weeds were growing in the yards. What became of the settlers no one ever knew.

From these voyages and discoveries, covering a period of one hundred years, it came about that Spain, England, and France, by priority of discovery, could lay claim to various sections of the New World.

CHAPTER II.
FORCES OF CIVILIZATION.

"FISH! fish! the sea swarming with fish!"
That was the news carried to England, in 1497, by John and Sebastian Cabot. The people across the Channel, in Brittany and Normandy, heard of the discovery; they were accustomed to brave the dangers of the sea; to make hazardous voyages in their little fishing-boats; and it was not long before the sailors of St. Malo, Honfleur, Morlaix, and other

ST. MALO.

quaint old towns along the coast, were bidding good-bye to their friends, leaving their humble homes, and spreading their sails for a trip to a region all unknown till traversed by the Cabots.

The fishermen of Honfleur steered west, past the Jersey Islands, till they came to the wonderful fishing-ground, where they soon filled their boats, and returned to spread the welcome news.

No one knows exactly how it came about, but many years before the discovery of the New World the Pope decreed that it was wicked to eat meat on Fridays, saints' days, or during Lent, but that it was not wrong to eat fish. There were so many saints to be honored that on more than one hundred days during the year no meat could be eaten, and in consequence there was a great demand for fish.

The people of Brittany were all good Catholics, and, for that matter, there were no Protestants anywhere; everybody accepted the Pope as the head of the Church. The people in the old towns counted their beads,.

STREET IN MORLAIX.

said their prayers devoutly, and sailed boldly out upon the stormy ocean, enduring great hardships. They reached the Banks of Newfoundland, moored their frail vessels in the harbor of St. John's, dried their fish upon the rocks, and then, with full cargoes, sailed away to find a market in the seaports of Portugal, Spain, France, England, and Holland.

In 1527 the captain of an English vessel wrote to the King of England that the French were occupying the fishing-ground that belonged to the English; that he found twelve vessels from Brittany in one of the harbors of Newfoundland; that the Bretons were dressing and drying their fish upon the rocks, and taking possession of the country; that one of the islands was named Cape Breton.

HOMES OF THE FISHERMEN OF BRITTANY.

After awhile the question arose as to who owned the fishing-ground. England claimed it because John and Sebastian Cabot had discovered it. France claimed that the ocean was free, and that England could not set up any boundaries on the water; that fishermen of France had just as much right as Englishmen to catch codfish on the Banks of Newfoundland.

The question involved the dominion of the seas. We shall see, as this narrative goes on, that this controversy, in connection with the establishment of fish-houses on shore, led to the settlement of Canada, Nova Scotia, Maine, New Hampshire, and Massachusetts in part, and the planting of two races, two languages, two religions in the northern section of this Western world.

When the crusaders marched to the Holy Land to rescue Jerusalem, and the holy sepulchres from the Saracens, they wore caps made from cat-skins. The French word for cat is *chat*, and for skins *peau*, and so they called a cap a *chapeau*. Somewhere in the East they learned the art of making felt.

When the fishermen of Brittany built their huts upon the shores of Newfoundland and Cape Breton, they saw the beavers constructing their dams along the streams, felling trees, gnawing them into logs, floating the timber in the current, placing the logs in proper position, piling stones upon them, interweaving them with sticks, stopping the crevices with grass, plastering the structure with mud, curving the dam against the current to give it strength, and building their mud-houses in the ponds of still water thus created.

FISH-HOUSE AND BOATS.

Quite likely the hatters of France had already discovered that furs could be felted; but when the fishermen of Brittany carried home some skins of the beaver, they saw that hats manufactured from its fur would be far more beautiful than those felted from wool: there was soon a great demand for them; and not only the beaver, but other furs—the sable, fox, and marten—were wanted. To supply the ever-increasing demand, companies were organized in France, England, and Holland, with charters to carry on the fur trade; with power to hold lands, make settlements, and establish governments.

This desire to obtain furs became a mighty force. Emigrants bade

THE BEAVER AND ITS HOME.

FORCES OF CIVILIZATION.

THE TRAPPER.

farewell to friends, home, and the dear old things of the past, crossed the ocean, and reared their log-huts in the forest.

The demand for furs gave a new stimulus to the Indian tribes on the northern half of the continent. The knives, tinkling bells, and shining bits of tin, the glass beads, gunpowder, and rum, which the white men gave in exchange for furs, awakened desires all unknown before.

Canada was settled by emigrants from France, through this demand for furs, planting on the St. Lawrence the religion of Rome and the ideas of the Feudal age, that allowed the people no rights, nor any voice in government. The same desire to obtain furs led the Dutch to New York, to lay the foundations of a State and of a city which time has made the metropolis of the Western World.

Among the plants which Christopher Columbus beheld on the morning of October 12th, 1492, was one with broad, green lanceolate leaves, and rose-colored flowers, native not only to San Salvador and the West Indies, but growing in luxuriance in the soil of Virginia. Columbus saw the Indians roll up a dry leaf of the plant, light one end, and inhale the smoke at the other. They called it tobacco, and used it not only for pleasure, but believed that the odor was a fragrance that gave delight to the Great Spirit. Whenever they made a treaty, or transacted important business affecting them as a tribe, they smoked a pipe, making the act an oath of confirmation.

The Spaniards learned to smoke, and the French, who visited the North American shores, acquired the habit. Jules Nicot carried some of the dried leaves to France, and the plant became known to botanists as Nicot's plant, or *Nicotiana tabacum*. Its introduction to France was about the year 1560, and it was soon in great demand. People not only smoked it but chewed it, and ground it into dust and snuffed it.

AFTER A MOOSE.

Ralph Lane carried some tobacco to London, in 1586, where it was used first as a medicine, but soon became a luxury, and was made fashionable by Sir Walter Raleigh. He and his friends often met at the Pied Bull tavern to smoke their pipes. King James I. hated tobacco, and wrote a book against its use. Pope Urban VIII. and Innocent XI. issued bulls against smoking. The priests of the Mohammedan religion cried out against it, and the sultan, Amuret IV., cut off the noses of those who used it. Vain the prohibition! The love for tobacco increased. All nations acquired the habit of smoking. The first settlers of Virginia grew rich through the cultivation of the plant. It became their exclusive occupation. The colony was founded upon it. Laws, customs, habits, social relations, the progress of the state, all were affected by it. Tobacco became the currency of the colony; all values were reckoned by it. Far-reaching has been its influence.

TOBACCO.

Through all past ages the strong have enslaved the weak. Prisoners taken in war were held as slaves. Barbaric people were reduced to bondage by those more civilized.

When Christopher Columbus landed on San Salvador and Cuba he was kindly treated by the Indians; but the men of Spain were cruel and enslaved them, compelling them to work in mines and in the cultivation of the sugar-cane. They gave them hard tasks, with little to eat; cut off their ears, noses, hands and feet upon the slightest provocation. Under such cruel treatment the Indians died in great numbers, and, to supply their places, expeditions were made to Mexico and South America. Vasquez D'Allyon visited South Carolina in 1520 to obtain slaves, enticing the confiding Indians on board his ship, and carrying them to Cuba. The Indians were feeble, but the negroes of Africa were strong; and Bishop Las Casas, of Chiopia, in Mexico, who was a friend to the Indians, petitioned the emperor, Charles V., to permit the enslavement of negroes in Africa, instead of allowing the slavers to rob him of his flock. The emperor gave his consent, and the enslavement of negroes began.

Captain John Hawkins, of England, visited the West Indies, and the thought came to him that he might make it profitable to bring slaves from Africa. He returned to England, laid his plan before Sir Lionel Duchet, Sir Thomas Dodge, Mr. Gunnison, Mr. Winter, Mr. Bromfield, and other gentlemen, who joined in fitting out the ships *Solomon*, *Swallow*, and *Jonas*. Sir John sailed in December, 1562, to Teneriffe, and from there to Sierra Leone, in Africa, where three hundred negroes were captured or purchased from the chiefs, taken to Cuba and sold. Captain Hawkins returned to England with a great quantity of gold, besides a cargo of hides, sugar, and ginger. It was so profitable a trade that the following year he sailed with four ships, and captured five hundred negroes. It is not probable that Captain Hawkins or any one else connected with the enterprise thought for a moment that it was wrong.

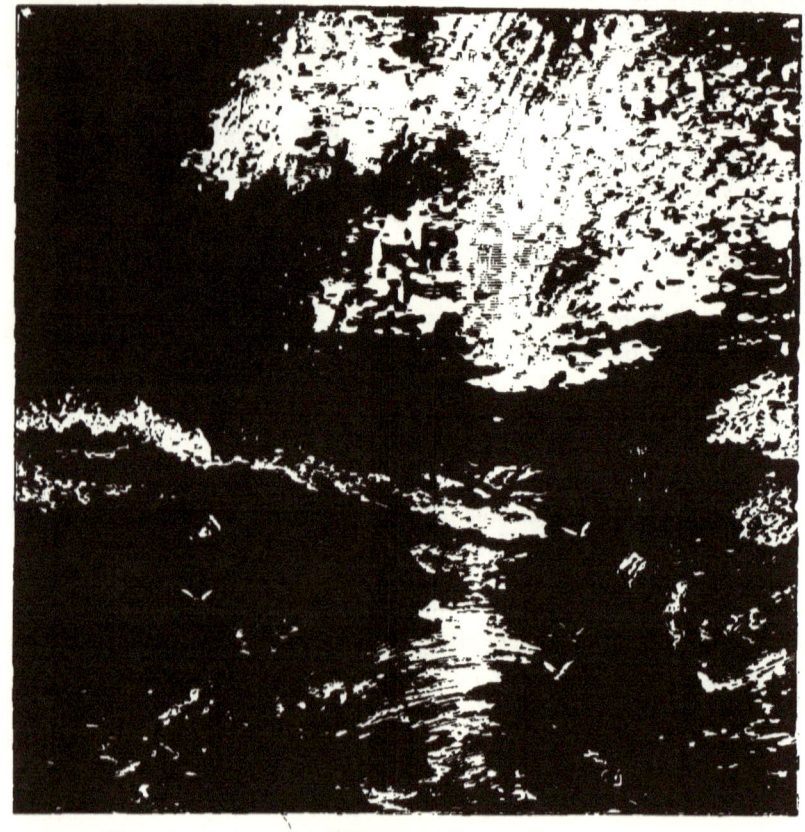

THE SLAVE-SHIP.

They believed that they were God's elect servants. The ships were becalmed in mid-ocean, and their water was running low; but Hawkins trusted in God to bring him and his cargo safe to Cuba. He wrote this

"TO BE SOLD AS SLAVES."

in his journal: "For the space of eighteen days we were becalmed, which put us in such fear that many of our men despaired of reaching the Indies, but the Almighty God, who never suffers his elect to perish, sent us, on the 16th of February, the ordinary breeze, which never left us until we came to the Islands of Cannibals, called Dominica."

In 1619 a Dutch vessel sailed up the James River with negroes stolen from Africa. They were sold to the settlers of Virginia, who were gathering rich harvests of tobacco. Little did the captain of that ship think what would be the outcome of that cargo of slaves—the misery, suffering, anguish, woe, and horrors; the death of myriads of human beings in the terrible passage across the sea, crowded into hot and stifling holds, panting for breath, dying of fever, thirst, hunger, confinement, homesickness; and when the terrific typhoons came on, to lighten the ship, the living and dead cast overboard to a multitude of ravenous sharks, ever following in the wake of the vessel, looking upward with hungry eyes for their expected prey!

The great artist, Turner, has pictured the horrible scene:

> "Aloft, all hands! Strike the top-masts and belay!
> Yon angry setting sun and fierce-edged clouds
> Declare the Typhoon's coming.
> Before it sweeps your decks, throw overboard
> The dead and dying. Ne'er heed their chains.
> Hope! hope! fallacious hope!
> Where is thy market now?"

Little did Sir John Hawkins, or anybody else have any conception of what would one day be written upon the historic page of our country —the desolation of a great civil war, death upon the battle-field and in prison of half a million of men! We, even, do not comprehend what is to be the ultimate result of that sale of sixteen slaves. What part are the four millions of the African race to take in the future of our country? What will they yet do for Africa? Who knows but that they will be the means of carrying a Christian civilization and Republican institutions to the continent where they had their origin?

In the "Story of Liberty" is an account of Ignatius Loyola, who founded the society of the Jesuits. He inspired others with his own lofty zeal. The members of the society went forth to convert the world, to thread the jungles of India, traverse the deserts of Africa and the steppes of Asia; uphold the Cross on the banks of the Amazon, and plant it upon the peaks of the Andes; to rear churches amidst the fertile vales of Mexico; make their home in a palace or the hut of a savage; brave every danger, suffer every hardship; endure every privation; to die of hunger, thirst, cold or heat, disease or violence; to labor without reward, except that which the Virgin Mary would extend to them, through their sacrifices to save souls from the clutches of the devil. They were to persuade men where persuasion was available; employ force where force was possible. It was their province to spy out the actions of men—meddle in all their affairs; fathom the secrets of human hearts; interfere in households, in cabinets, in halls of justice and legislation; set father against son, and son against father; stir up strife between husband and wife, mother and daughter. All earthly relations, all human considerations, all the ties which men deem sacred, were subordinated to the idea that baptism into the Church was of more value than anything else; that they were commanded by the Virgin to rescue men from perdition.

To bring about that end any means were justifiable. Each member

THE TOMAHAWK AND SCALPING-KNIFE DOING BLOODY WORK.

was to watch every other member; report their faithfulness or unfaithfulness. They had one watchword—"Obedience." With a zeal such as the world had never before witnessed, the Jesuits went forth upon their missions. Their history is interwoven with that of every nation—a record of self-denial, hardship, suffering, martyrdom; of burning zeal, fiery energy, tireless activity, unquenchable ardor; of religious devotions, worldly wisdom, benevolence, and charity; deceit, falsehood, hypocrisy, cruelty, and despotism. If they have been charitable and kind, they have also blackened history by the darkest of crimes. If they have lifted men to higher and nobler lives, they have also sent myriads to prison, and burnt hundreds of thousands at the stake. Time has not quenched their zeal; and though three hundred and fifty years have passed since their organization, they are still making their power felt in every country, controlling the consciences and actions of men.

The tomahawk and scalping-knife, at the bidding of the Jesuits, will do bloody work from the Penobscot to the Ohio, and the lurid light of burning dwellings will illumine the midnight sky. Men, women, and children will pass through the gloomy wilderness, from their ruined homes on the banks of the Merrimac and Connecticut to Quebec and Montreal, to be sold into slavery. The old and young, the strong and weak, will redden the snows of winter with their blood. It was the disappointment of Ignatius Loyola in love, and the firing of a cannon at Pampeluna that started this crimson stream.

In the "Story of Liberty" is a chapter about the man who split the Church in twain—Henry VIII.—who, through his love for Anne Boleyn, defied the Pope, and set up a church of his own, himself the head: it was in 1539. His daughter, Mary Tudor, did what she could to restore things as they had been before Henry established the Church of England; she burnt so many men and women who refused to accept the Pope as head of the Church, that she was called "Bloody Mary." Her half-sister, Elizabeth, when she came to the throne, re-established the Church which her father had founded, making herself the head. James I., who succeeded Elizabeth, endeavored to make everybody conform to the ritual which the bishop had written out. Those who refused to do this were called Non-conformists. In the "Story of Liberty" is an account of the persecutions endured by the people of Scrooby and Austerfield, because they held meetings of their own on Sunday in an old manor-house, listening to the preaching of John Robinson; how they fled to Holland, and finally sailed to America in the *Mayflower*.

Some of the ministers of the Church of England did not like to make the sign of the cross when they baptized a child, and there were other things distasteful to them in the ritual which the bishop had established. They desired a *purer* form of worship, and so were called Puritans by those who ridiculed them. They were not Separatists, like those plain farmers of Scrooby and Austerfield, but remained in the Church. When James came to the throne, several hundred Puritans requested a change in the ritual. He answered them rudely:

"I will have," he said, "one doctrine, one discipline, one religion; I alone will decide; I will make you conform, or I will harry you out of the land, or else do worse—hang you."

Convictions of what is right and true are forces for good which oppression and tyranny never can suppress. Obedience to such convictions led the men and women of Scrooby to flee from their pleasant homes to Holland, and from thence to America, to find peace and quiet in the solitude of the wilderness. Conviction of what was right and true also led the Puritans—some of whom lived in fine houses, with spacious halls,

DINING-ROOM IN A PURITAN MANOR-HOUSE.

where they entertained their friends in princely style—to turn their backs upon all the comforts and refinements of life to which they had been accustomed, and make their humble homes in the wilderness, laying the foundations of a State which, though small in area, has wielded a wonderful influence on the history of our country.

In obedience to this conviction, George Fox preached in the fields, the streets, entered churches unbidden, wearing his hat, and dressed in sheepskin clothes. He preached that men should always be guided by the "inner light" which God would reveal to every honest heart. The justices sent him to prison as a fanatic and disturber of the peace; but as soon as he was out he resumed his preaching, making many converts to his ideas.

On other pages of this volume we shall read of the persecutions, sufferings, and obloquy endured by the Quakers; of their fanaticism and mistakes, and also the founding of the State of Pennsylvania by the follower of George Fox.

How strange that the firing of a gun on the shore of Lake Champlain should set in motion a train of events which have had a mighty influence upon the destiny of our country! In another chapter we shall accompany a hardy pioneer from France (Samuel Champlain) along the shore of the lake that bears his name. He will fire a gun whose echoes have not yet ceased to reverberate through the wilderness. Insignificant the event; but it will set the Mohawks, Onondagas, Senecas, Canandaiguas, and Cayugas—the five tribes composing the Iroquois Nation—forever against the French. They will make their power felt in the great struggle between France and England for supremacy in America.

Such are some of the forces that gave direction to the early history of our country. It is a history not designed by man; for the men of one generation cannot lay a plan for the generation that succeeds it. Every person exercises his own individual will; and it is only a Divine hand that out of the greed, selfishness, avarice, ambition, and passions of the multitude—out of their blunders, mistakes, and crimes—out of all the turmoils and conflicts of centuries—can mould a great Republic in which law, order, liberty, and an exalted sense of justice and right shall be supreme.

CHAPTER III.

FIRST SETTLEMENTS.

THE century of discovery closed, and the period of settlement began. Elizabeth was Queen of England, Henry IV. King of France, and Philip II. of Spain. A great fleet of vessels crossed the ocean every year from England and Brittany to the Banks of Newfoundland to obtain fish. The hardy sailors moored their little craft upon the banks, rode out fear-

RIDING OUT A GALE ON THE BANKS.

ful gales, or, when the storms came on, hoisted sail and ran to the harbor of Newfoundland for shelter. Some of the fishermen passed through the Straits of Canso into the Gulf of St. Lawrence. Others coasted along Nova Scotia, and dropped anchor in the harbor of Maine—the sailors opening trade with the Indians, purchasing a large pile of beaver skins with a

FIRST SETTLEMENTS.

few knives, fish-hooks, or bits of tin; carrying the furs to France, and selling them to the hatters, making quite as much money on their furs as on their fish.

A gentleman of Brittany, the Marquis de la Roche, resolved to capture and keep to himself a goose that would lay no end of golden eggs, by obtaining from the king the exclusive privilege of trading with the Indians. The King of France had no claim to America, except through the discoveries made by John Verrazani and Jacques Cartier; but he granted De la Roche's request, and made him Governor of Canada, Newfoundland, and

RUNNING FOR SHELTER.

Labrador—a vast undefined territory—with power to raise troops, declare war, build cities and forts; to give away the land to whomsoever he pleased. The marquis tried to induce the people of Brittany to emigrate to Canada, but they preferred to remain at home and enjoy the comforts of life in their native villages. Not being able to get any settlers, De la Roche obtained leave to ship criminals from the prisons, and set sail with forty thieves and murderers. It was not a promising beginning, for the villains pummelled and pounded one another fearfully on the voyage.

One morning they beheld the long yellow beaches of Sable Island, off the shore of Maine. As De la Roche had not decided where to make a settlement, he landed the criminals, and sailed away to explore the coast; but a storm came on, and the north-west winds blew so furiously that he

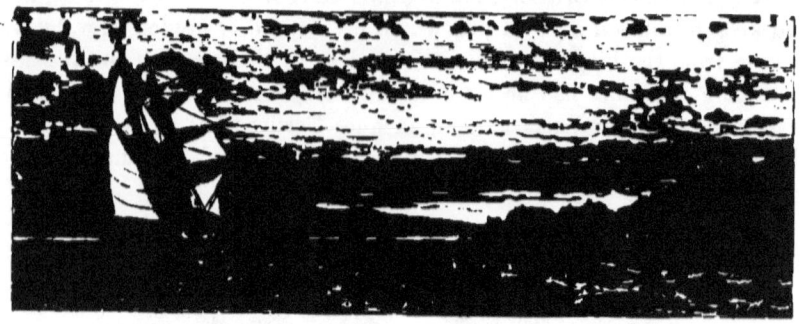

STRAIT OF CANSO.

was swept nearly across the Atlantic, and found himself so near home that he returned to St. Malo.

Forty thieves, with no one to govern them, no law—no authority—what will they do? what will become of them?

A vessel had been wrecked on the island years before, and the hulk lay half buried on the beach; from its planks they built some huts. Herds of wild horses cropped the stunted grass in the meadows, and the sea was alive with fish, so that they would not lack food. There were troublesome times in France, and De la Roche could not visit them. Five years went by, when a vessel approached the island and sent a boat on shore. Twelve men, wearing clothes made from the skins of foxes, were all that remained: the others had been killed, or had died from exposure or homesickness. The weak had gone down before the strong; might had made right. So ended the first attempt of the French to make a settlement in America.

The merchants of Bristol, England, began to turn their eyes to the New World, and sent Bartholomew Gosnold on a voyage of discovery. He sailed in 1602, in the ship *Concord*, descrying first the white granite ledges of Cape Ann. Turning southward, he discovered a sandy promontory, which he named Cape Cod. He dropped anchor in the harbor of Provincetown, caught many fish, sailed south once more around the cape to the islands of Nantucket and Martha's Vineyard, entered Buzzard's Bay, and landed on an island which the Indians called Cuttyhunk. He was charmed with the country, the tall forest-trees, the grapevines which grew along the shore; built a fort, intending to leave six

FIRST SETTLEMENTS.

men, but was so short of provisions that he was obliged to abandon the project. He loaded his ship with sassafras, which was greatly esteemed in London, the doctors using it as a medicine, and hastened away, having only a single biscuit left when he reached England.

The next year the Bristol merchants sent Martin Pring to see what he could discover. He sailed along the coast of Maine, entered Casco Bay, Kennebunk Harbor, the Saco, and Piscataqua. It was midsummer, and the fields on the west shore of the Piscataqua were so red with strawberries that he named it Strawberry Bank. The quaint old town of Portsmouth now covers the ground where the sailors feasted themselves upon red, ripe berries.

Captain Pring was so enthusiastic over what he had seen, upon his return to England, that Richard Hakluyt, one of the ministers of Bristol,

CAPE ANN.

became greatly interested, and wrote letters to influential friends — Sir George Somers, Edward Wingfield, and others in London — telling them that it was the duty of Englishmen to do something to checkmate Spain, who had already obtained possession of Mexico, South America, and Florida, and who was in a fair way to control the whole Western World.

While Richard Hakluyt was thus endeavoring to awaken an interest among his friends, there was a gentleman in France, Pierre de Guast, who saw that it was time for France to be getting a foothold in America. Henry IV. bestowed the title of Sieur de Monts upon De Guast, and gave

PORTSMOUTH, NEW HAMPSHIRE.

him the territory now comprised in New Brunswick and Nova Scotia, to which was given the name of Acadia. He gave to De Monts, Baron Pontrincourt, and Samuel Champlain, as he had once given to De la Roche, the sole privilege of trading with the Indians. They were to build up the empire of New France in the New World.

It was a strange company that sailed from Havre de Grace, April 7th, 1604. There were De Monts, Pontrincourt, Pontgravé, Champlain, several Jesuit priests and Huguenot ministers, and a crowd of thieves and vagabonds which De Monts had taken from the prisons. The Jesuits and Huguenots were almost at swords' points; and when they could not convince one another by argument, fell to with their fists, while the thieves blackened each other's eyes in their frequent quarrels. They sailed into the Bay of Fundy, laid out a town on the sandy island of St. Croix, built a great house for the noblemen, and smaller houses for the others; and then the vessels returned to France, leaving De Monts, Champlain, and seventy men.

What a dreary winter it was! The snows whirled around the houses,

FIRST SETTLEMENTS.

and the nights were so cold that the wine which De Monts had brought from France was frozen in the casks. Disease thinned their ranks. Before spring one-half died.

In the spring a vessel came from France with forty men, whom De Monts had hired. He saw that the soil of the island was poor, and sailed in search of a better place—visiting the Kennebec, Saco, and Piscataqua rivers and the Isles of Shoals, discovering the Merrimac River, which he named for himself, La Rivière de Guast. He called Cape Ann Cape St. Louis, and Cape Cod Cape Blanco. He landed at Nausett; and while the sailors were obtaining fresh water an Indian darted from behind a tree and seized a kettle.

A crowd of Indians were upon them, letting fly their arrows; but Champlain fired a gun, which so frightened them that they fled.

De Monts returned to his settlement, sailed eastward, and selected a beautiful site on the eastern shore of the Bay of Fundy, and laid out a town which he named Port Royal, putting up a spacious house, containing a great hall with a wide-mouthed fireplace, a row of smaller buildings, and a church. So France obtained her first foothold in the Western World.

DE MONTS.

Gold! gold! The ships of Spain were bringing it by the cart-load from Mexico and South America. For more than a century rich cargoes had been gathered in by the rapacious gold-hunters of Castile, Arragon, and Andalusia. The people of England began to have the gold hunger, and fondly imagined that gold could be found almost anywhere in America. Poets pictured the attractions of the New World in glowing lan-

CAPE COD.

guage. In one of the plays, Captain Seagull narrated to a fellow named Spendthrift wonderful accounts of the country beyond the sea:

Spendthrift. "Is there such treasure there as I have heard?"

Seagull. "I tell thee, gold is more plentiful there than copper is with us. For as much copper as I can carry, I'll have thrice weight in gold. Why, man, all their pots and pans are of purest gold; all their prisoners are fettered in gold; and as for rubies and diamonds, they go forth and gather them by the sea-shore to hang on their children's coats and stick in their children's caps."

FIRST SETTLEMENTS.

Spendthrift. "Is it a pleasant country?"

Seagull. "As ever the sun shone on: temperate, and full of all sorts of excellent viands. Wild-boar is as common there as bacon is here, and venison as mutton. You may be an alderman there, and not a laborer; an officer, and not a slave."

Night after night crowds flocked to the theatres to see the play, and have their imaginations fired by the exhibition of pieces of gold supposed to have been brought from America.

Queen Elizabeth was dead, and James was on the throne, and the merchants of London and Plymouth petitioned him for a grant of land in America: he complied with their request, and gave the London merchants the country between Long Island and Cape Fear; and to the Plymouth merchants the country between Long Island and Nova Scotia.

The Plymouth men sent out Captain Weymouth to explore the coast. He reached Cape Cod on May 13th, 1605, then sailed north and landed on the island of Monhegan. He entered a harbor on the coast of Maine on

MONHEGAN.

Pentecost Sunday, and named it Pentecost. He landed the next day, and the sailors dug up a patch of ground and sowed some garden-seeds— the first sown by the hands of Englishmen in the Western World.

Captain Weymouth sailed up the Kennebec River, entered Booth Bay, and landed at Pemmaquid. The Indians flocked around his ship in their bark canoes. He enticed them on board, treacherously seized five, and sailed away to England.

What an excitement there was in the old town of Plymouth when the ship *Archangel*, with five Indians on board, dropped anchor in the harbor! All the town came to see Squanto and his red-skinned fellow-savages. Sir Fernando Gorges, the governor, became greatly interested

PEMMAQUID.

in them. Wherever they went great crowds flocked to see them, which set everybody to talking and thinking about America.

Sieur de Monts, the while, was spending his money freely in buying provisions and supplies for his colony on the Bay of Fundy, treating the Indians kindly, feasting their old chief, Membertu, at his own table, and tossing strips of bear-meat to the dusky warriors who squatted on the floor of the great hall. The savages grunted their satisfaction, and looked up with longing eyes for more; it was better than tramping through the forest all day in pursuit of game—they would always be friends of the French.

A vessel sailed into the harbor, bringing a letter for Sieur de Monts: "Your enemies have persuaded the king to deprive you of the sole privilege of trading with the Indians," was the message.

CAPTAIN JOHN SMITH.

Everything was abandoned—houses, furniture, all—and with a sad heart Sieur de Monts sailed away; so the second attempt of France to get a foothold in Canada ended in failure.

The vessel which carried the disappointed Frenchmen back to France almost came in contact, in mid-ocean, with three ships from London, which were bearing to Virginia the men who were to make the first permanent English settlement in America at Jamestown.

FIRST SETTLEMENTS.

In April, 1607, Captain Newport, Bartholomew Gosnold, Captain John Smith, and a party of colonists sailed into the peaceful waters of Chesapeake Bay, dropping anchor off a point of land where everything around was so pleasant: after tossing so many weeks on ship-board, they named it Point Comfort. The vessels sailed up a noble river, which Captain Newport named the James, in honor of the king. He made a settlement on an island, to which he gave the name of Jamestown.

The expedition had been fitted out by the London Company of mer-

ARRIVAL AT JAMESTOWN.

chants. The colonists consisted of four carpenters, a few laborers, and forty-eight "gentlemen," sons of noblemen, who had wasted their fortunes, and who expected to find gold lying in heaps. They had vague ideas of a life of exciting adventure in the wilderness. How different the reality! They found no gold; the sun blazed in the heavens like a fiery ball, and they wilted beneath the heat; fever set in; death began to pick them off; provisions failed; and had not Captain Smith obtained corn from the Indians, all would have perished. Instead of gold and adventures, sickness, death, and disappointment!

While this was transpiring in Virginia, William Brewster, William Bradford, and the farmers of Scrooby and Austerfield, in obedience to their convictions of duty and obligation, were fleeing from England to Holland—the country which the sturdy, patient, plodding Dutchmen had banked in from the sea, pumped dry with their windmills, and converted it into farms and gardens—the only country on the face of the earth where they would be wholly free to think for themselves.

"What land is this, that seems to be
A mingling of the land and sea?

HOLLAND.

This land of sluices, dikes, and dunes?
This water-net that tessellates
The landscape? this unending maze
Of gardens, through whose latticed gates
The imprisoned pinks and tulips gaze;
Where in long summer afternoons
The sunshine, softened by the haze,
Comes streaming down as through a screen;
Where over fields and pastures green
The painted ships float high in air,
And over all and everywhere
The sails of windmills sink and soar
Like wings of sea-gulls on the shore?"

Sir Fernando Gorges, Governor of Plymouth, who took so much interest in the Indians which Captain Weymouth carried to England, enlisted his friend, Chief-justice Lord John Popham, in American affairs. Lord John had been wild in his youth, but having an ambition to get on in the world, became sober-minded, and worked his way into Parliament, and had been appointed chief-justice of the realm. He was harsh and cruel, and sent so many men to the gallows, that people called him "Hangman Popham." He joined Sir Fernando Gorges in fitting out an expedition to make a settlement in Maine, but made a fatal mistake. Thinking that anybody would count one, he emptied the jails, and sent a pack of criminals to establish a colony.

To build a State we must have *men*, not the riffraff of society.

The spot selected for a settlement was at the mouth of the Sagadahock, or Kennebec, River, in Maine. Trees were cut down, and houses, church, and a log fort erected.

Though the Indians had not forgotten the treachery of Captain Weymouth, they held friendly intercourse with the new-comers, who, in return, loaded a cannon to the muzzle with bullets, and induced the Indians to take hold of the drag-ropes and help them draw it. When all were in a line, one of Sir John's villains touched a live coal to the priming; there was a flash, a cloud, a roar, and the ground was strewn with corpses. The Indians, indignant at such treachery, fell upon the villains with their tomahawks. The cowards fled to their ships, and the Indians rushed into the fort. Suddenly there was an explosion, and the fort and the Indians went up into the air. The savages had touched off the magazine, and blown up the fort and themselves. Those who had been sent out by Sir John to manage affairs, saw that after such an affair it would be impossible to establish the colony. They returned to England, and Sir John, who had hoped to add to his wealth, found himself out of pocket.

Although the King of France had taken the monopoly of the fur-trade away from Sieur de Monts, that gentleman was ready for new enterprises, and fitted out two vessels, appointing Samuel Champlain and a

SAMUEL CHAMPLAIN.

merchant of St. Malo—Pontgravé—commanders. The cargoes were trinkets, knives, blankets, and other knickknacks for the Indians.

On the 5th of April, 1608, Pontgravé, Champlain, and the sailors attended mass in the old church of St. Malo, bade good-bye to their friends, and sailed out upon the ocean. Pontgravé entered the Gulf of St. Lawrence, reached Tadousac, on the northern shore, where he found a party of Spaniards trading with the Indians.

TADOUSAC.

"This is French territory; you have no right here," said Pontgravé, running out his cannon and opening fire upon the Spanish vessel; but the Spaniards were strongest, and the French were getting the worst of it, when Champlain fortunately arrived and conquered the Spaniards, allowing them to go home to Spain, but holding on to their furs.

Up the river St. Lawrence sailed Champlain to the spot where, in 1535, stood the Indian town of Stadacone; but the wigwams were no longer there—all had disappeared.

"It is a good place for a town," said Champlain, and set the men to work erecting houses, surrounding them with a palisade, planting his cannon, clearing a bit of ground for a garden, and giving the name of Quebec to the settlement.

It was the first permanent planting of the civilization, language, and literature of France in America.

The English are in Virginia, the French in Canada. Feeble both the plantings. Which will have the most vigorous growth? What are the forces lying behind to give them strength? One is of the Magna Charta—

the *right* of the many; the other of the Feudal ages—the *privilege* of the few, and the *right* of none. In England the *people* are questioning the privileges of the king; in France the king is absolute, and no one asks any questions. England rejects the supreme authority of the Pope;

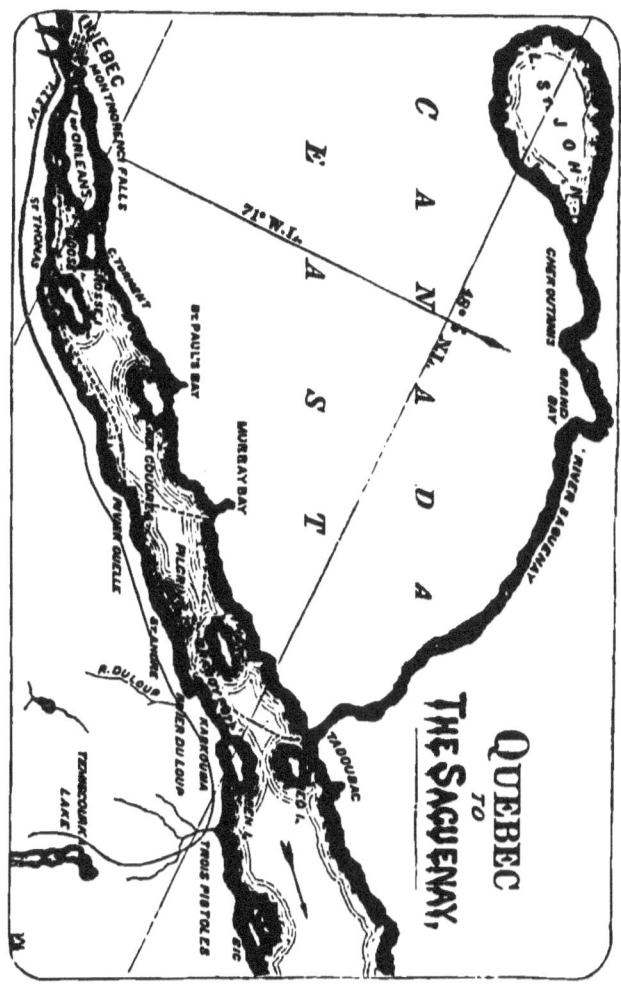

France accepts it. In the great struggle between these two diverse civilizations, which will most likely go down? which, for the well-being, happiness and advancement of the human race, ought to go down?

Samuel Champlain, of Brittany, is ever looking into the future of this

Western World. He is dreaming of the time when there shall be a new empire, under the dominion of France and the sway of the Pope. He will make the Indians his allies; will conquer them by kindly acts, attach them forever to France by making them his friends, and use them to obtain territory and power. With the aid of the Jesuits he will convert them to Christianity, and so extend the dominion of the Church. During the winter he feeds them, and the simple-hearted red men are ready to lay down their lives for such a benefactor.

Spring opens. The Indians of Canada are at war with the Iroquois, and Champlain resolves to take part in the struggle. They as-

THE BEGINNING OF TRADE ON THE HUDSON.

"THEY SEE A LIGHTNING FLASH, AND HEAR A ROAR."

cend the St. Lawrence, enter the Richelieu, carry their canoes past the falls, launch them once more, and glide along the peaceful waters of Lake Champlain. On the western shore, as the sun is setting, July 29th, 1609, the Algonquins discover a war party of their enemies. Morning comes, Champlain loads his gun, puts on his breastplate of glittering steel, and in his cap a plume.

The Iroquois have won many victories over the Algonquins, and expect an easy triumph. The warwhoop resounds through the forest; the arrows fly. The Iroquois behold what they never before have seen—a strange being with the sunlight glistening on his breast. They see a lightning-flash, and hear a roar. A chief and a warrior are weltering in their blood. Another flash, more warriors going down. The warwhoop changes to a despairing cry on the one side, and victory on the other. In an instant the Iroquois are gone, and the victory is with the Algonquins. Champlain is their great chief. They rend the air with shouts. Now they will ever be victorious. Champlain rejoices with them. He has bound them to himself forever. Ah! if he could but lift the veil that hides the future, he would see that in the flash of his gun there was more than the securing of the friendship of the Algonquins; that there was, in addition, the undying hatred of the Iroquois toward the French; that for a century and a half the Iroquois would never forget that defeat.

How strangely things come about! Champlain was laying foundation of empire in Canada; but if he had gone southward from that battle-field two days' journey, he would have beheld a vessel from Holland—the *Half-Moon*—commanded by Henry Hudson, through whom the Dutch were to gain a foothold in America. He would have seen the Indians flocking around the *Half-Moon* in their canoes, the chiefs feasting Hudson on baked dog, pigeons, pumpkins, and grapes, filling the vessel with fur in exchange for trinkets—the opening of trade on a river along whose peaceful waters the commerce of an empire is now borne to the sea. It was the beginning of Dutch influence in America, hostile to France and the Pope, antagonistic to the designs of Champlain and the Jesuits, the subsequent enlisting of the Iroquois as their allies, re-enforced by the power of undying hatred of the French.

CHAPTER IV.

THE WISE FOOL OF ENGLAND AND HIS TIMES.

HOW quickly we can learn to hate! If anybody wrongs us, we do not soon forget it. How little do we understand that what we sow that we shall also reap! We know that if we sow thistles we shall have a crop of thistles; but it has taken the human race many hundred years to comprehend that if they sow Bigotry they will reap a harvest of the same.

When "Bloody Mary," as she was called, burnt hundreds of men and women at the stake because they were Protestants, she did not stop to think of what might come of it; that it would set in motion a train of events that would sweep the Roman Catholic Church out of England; that the people would come to regard the Pope as the embodiment of all wickedness.

Queen Mary was daughter of the King of Spain, and that country was the great champion of the Church of Rome. The Spaniards were hard-hearted, treacherous, vindictive. The Jesuits had the consciences of the Spaniards in keeping, teaching them to do any evil that good might come. When Elizabeth was queen, they planned to have her assassinated; and the assassin, Somerville, who was to commit the bloody deed, received the host at their hands before starting for London. They bargained with one of Elizabeth's servants to poison her. When the plots were discovered, the people were so enraged that the Jesuits were banished from England. They conspired with Anthony Babington, and other Catholics who were in Elizabeth's household, to kill her; when she was out of the way, they hoped to put Mary of Scotland on the throne. The people shuddered with horror when the plot was discovered, and London blazed with bonfires when the conspirators were condemned to death. Spain and the Jesuits were hated more than ever. When Spain fitted out the great armada to invade England, the spirit of all the people was aroused. Spain conquer England? Never! Catholics were as loyal as the Protestants. They were all Englishmen. They were so loyal that Elizabeth appointed Lord Howard, a Catholic, as one of her admirals.

The Armada sailed up the Channel—one hundred and thirty vessels—carrying 2500 cannon, 8000 sailors, and 20,000 soldiers. The English had only eighty ships; but Sir Francis Drake, Sir John Hawkins, and Martin Frobisher, who had sailed amidst the icebergs of the Northern seas, were

THE ROCKY CLIFFS.

commanders of Elizabeth's squadrons. They sailed boldly out, cutting off ship after ship from the Armada. "We picked their feathers one by one," said the seamen. Then came a great battle. Lord Howard sent ships adrift piled with hemp, smeared with tar, and all ablaze, to burn the ships of the Armada at anchor on the coast of France. A fair wind wafted them upon the Spaniards. What a panic in the Armada—the galleons cutting their cables, hoisting sails, steering anywhere to get away! Drake, Hawkins, and Frobisher close in upon them, with the wind in their favor—running out their cannon, pouring in broadsides. Masts and spars go down with a crash. The vessels of the Spaniards are slaughter-pens. Three great galleons, with gaping holes in their sides, where the shot had ripped out the timbers, go to the bottom: others are driven ashore, and the waves complete the work of destruction. "We are lost!" cries the faint-hearted, incapable Medina Sidonia, commander of the Armada.

He calls his officers together. "What shall we do?"

"The wind is south, but we can sail around England and Scotland, and so get back to Spain," said the Spaniard.

Only fifty vessels ever reached Spain. One by one they went to the bottom, or were dashed upon the ledges of the Orkneys, or lay their bones upon the rocky cliffs of Ireland. Eight thousand Spaniards perished between the Giant's Causeway and the south of Ireland. More than twenty thousand perished in battle and by shipwreck. In every town and city of England bonfires blazed. The bell-ringers rung out their most joyful peals. Again the Spaniards and Jesuits had been foiled in their plans.

On March 24th, 1603, Elizabeth died, and James, son of Mary of Scotland, whom Elizabeth had beheaded, came to the throne. England, Scotland, and Sweden were the only Protestant countries of Europe; all others were Catholic; for Spain had Holland by the throat, and Henry IV. of France had abjured the Protestant faith.

LEDGE OF THE ORKNEYS.

The Jesuits had not given up the hope of bringing England once more under the authority of the Pope. James was a bigot. He would have no religion except that of the Church of England, and was so hard upon the Catholics that he drove six thousand out of the country. The Jesuits resolved to strike back, and laid a plan which they fondly believed would make England a Roman Catholic nation once more.

Parliament was to meet November 5th, 1605. If James, the bishops, lords, and commons could all be got rid of at a stroke, it would be easy for Spain to take possession of the realm, and then Protestantism would be crushed forever.

Robert Catesby conceived the plan. The Jesuits fomented it. Priests

THE BELL-RINGERS HUNG OUT THEIR JOYFUL PEALS.

in disguise visited the Catholic lords, let them into the secret, and obtained their promises to aid. They were to be ready to strike. Arms were sent over from the Netherlands. The Roman Catholic gentlemen were to meet the first week in November; word was to be given out that they were going to have a grand deer-hunt. When Parliament assembled, Guy Fawkes and four other villains were to touch off barrels of powder, which they would secrete in the cellar of the building, and there would be an ex-

STREET LEADING TO PARLIAMENT-HOUSE.

plosion that would shake every house in London. King, ministers, lords, and commons would go sky-high. Before the people could inquire what had happened, the conspirators would seize the king's two sons and hurry them across the Channel. A Spanish army would land, and the Protestants would be under the heels of the Pope and Jesuits.

Conscience is ever a good angel, warning us whenever we set ourselves to do wrong. The conscience of one of the conspirators troubled him; for one of the members of Parliament, Lord Monteagle, was his friend. It is only the vilest wretch that can deliberately murder a friend.

The thought of what he was about to do so troubled the conspirator's conscience that he wrote a letter to Lord Monteagle, warning him not to attend Parliament at its opening. It was afternoon, November 4th, that Lord Monteagle received the letter. It contained a sentence that puzzled him: "Though there be no appearance of any stir, yet I say this Parliament shall receive a terrible blow, and yet they shall not see who hurts them."

What was the meaning of it? Lord Monteagle hastened to the king's ministers. "Let us search the cellar of the Parliament-house," they said; and the sheriff and his men, with drawn swords, went down into the cellar, groped through dark passages with lanterns, and discovered Guy Fawkes and four other villains placing the barrels of powder and laying the train. The sheriff's men ran their swords through two of the conspirators, and seized the others.

All England held its breath over the astounding revelation. Is it a wonder that the people hated the Pope, the Jesuits, and Spaniards more than ever? "Down with the Jesuits! Hang them! No popery in England!" they cried.

Some of the leaders were hung; some fled to other countries; many were imprisoned. So intense was the hatred that a Roman Catholic was not safe on the streets. If one appeared, the mob pelted him with stones. They could hold no worship, and could only cherish their belief in silence.

The bishops of the Church of England, the ministers in all the parishes, preached bitter sermons against the Papists and Jesuits. The ballad-writers wrote songs against them, which were sung by minstrels at all the county fairs, arousing the hatred of the people. Ever as November 5th came round, the boys in London, and in every town and village, made a mock pope, stuffing old clothes with straw, putting a mitre on the head of the image, dragging it through the streets, and pelting it with stones. He who could hit it in the eye was the best fellow. When evening came they tied it to a stake, piled fagots around it, and danced in savage glee while it was burning. "Pope's Day" was the jolliest of the year. It was a day on which all England drank the health of the king and shouted "No popery!"

The Jesuits had sowed Bigotry, and they were reaping the legitimate fruit. If they were having a hard time in England, the Protestants were having a harder time in France, Holland, and Germany. Bigotry and Intolerance alike were regarded as virtues by the Church of Rome and the Church of England. The world was very far from understanding

TOBACCO-SHOP.—(FROM AN OLD PRINT.)

the meaning of Christian charity. We need not wonder if, farther along, we see Intolerance taking root in the New World.

James was so wise in some things, and foolish in others, that he was called a "wise fool." He believed that men and women, by making a league with the devil, could bewitch people, and wrote a book about witchcraft; also a book against the smoking of tobacco. He tried to suppress the habit, but smoking increased; tobacco-shops were opened all over London.

James believed that he was especially and divinely appointed of God to be king—to rule as he pleased—and that subjects had only to obey. The bishops agreed with him, and said that he was inspired by the Holy Ghost.

When the king travelled, he was accompanied by a great number of earls, lords, and bishops. Noblemen spent their fortunes in entertaining him. One Sunday he dined with Sir Arthur Lake at Houghton Hall, and this was the bill of fare:

First Course.		Second Course.	
Pullets.	Hot pasty of Venison.	Hot Pheasant.	Rabbits.
Boiled Capon.	Roast Turkey.	Quails.	Ducks.
Boiled Mutton.	Burred Veal.	Partridges.	Burred Chicken.
Boiled Chicken.	Roast Swan.	Poults.	Pea Tarts.
Boiled Duck.	Hot Chicken-pie.	Roast Pigeon.	Plovers.
Roast Mutton.	Cold Rabbits.	A made Dish.	Red Deer-pie.
Roast Veal.	Jiggets of boiled Mutton.	Turkey-pie.	Burred Pig.
Pallets.	Snipe-pie.	Hogs Cheeks, dried.	Hot Roast Heron.
Cold Roast Heron.	Boiled Breast of Veal.	Cold Turkey.	Roast Lamb.
Custards.	Roast Capon.	Artichoke-pie.	Gammon of Bacon.
Roast Venison.	Cold Tongue-pie.	Chicken.	Pullets and Greens.
Burred Capon.	Boiled Sprod.	Roast Curlew.	Dried Tongue.
	Roast Pig.	Buttered Pease.	Pheasant Tarts.

A great deal of meat, and not much besides.

After dinner the servants presented a petition to the king, requesting permission to engage in sports and games on Sunday afternoon. The king gave them liberty to wrestle, run races, play ball, pitch quoits, throw iron bars; but they were not to set cocks to fighting, or worry bulls with dogs on Sundays. On week-days they might attend cock-fights, or engage in any other brutal sport. He had a cockpit of his own near the palace, and took great delight in seeing the cocks peck one another to pieces.

James took great pleasure in attending the theatres, although many of the plays were very indecent. The theatres were foul places. The king, the ladies and gentlemen of the court, the noblemen, occupied the boxes, but down in the pit there was a dirty crowd, sitting on benches that had no backs. Between the acts they guzzled beer, which was drawn from a barrel in the centre of the pit. The language of the plays was vile, and interlarded with oaths and ribaldry. There were indecent scenes; but the king, queen, lords, and ladies witnessed them without blushing.

THE DINNER.

Writers record the thoughts of the age in which they live, and the spirit of any period will ever be seen in the literature of the time. Ben Jonson tells us how vile the drama was in the time of James.

GLOBE THEATRE.

"In dramatic or stage poetry," he says, "nothing but ribaldry, profanation, blasphemies, all license of offence toward God and man is pictured. Nothing but filth of mire is uttered."

The actors ridiculed the Bible, called Moses a juggler, and maintained that religion was a farce. Many ladies and gentlemen thought it an accomplishment to use profane language; and if a person did not interlard his conversation with oaths, he was set down as being a Puritan, and subjected to all manner of ridicule.

"Every stage and every table," wrote Lucy Hutchinson, "belched forth profane scoffs upon the Puritans. The drunkards made the songs, and all fiddlers and musicians learned to abuse them."

Shakspeare never ridiculed the honest convictions of men. He wrote nothing against the Puritans, perhaps because his daughter Judith, as is supposed, was a Puritan; perhaps because he never forgot the Sundays of

THE WISE FOOL OF ENGLAND AND HIS TIMES.

his boyhood, when he walked beneath the stately trees in the church-yard at Stratford, on the green banks of the Avon, and listened to the sermons preached in the old stone church. Either from the sermons or from the Bible, he obtained such a comprehension of duty, obligation, conscience, and retribution, that when, in after years, he sat down to write, he produced plays which portray vice in its hatefulness and virtue in all its loveliness.

James had married Anne of Denmark, and when her father, the King of Denmark, came to make a visit, Ben Jonson, the poet-laureate, wrote a dramatic poem which represented the visit of the Queen of Sheba to Solomon.

James gave a grand entertainment in his palace to all the ladies and gentlemen of the court, some of whom were selected to perform Jonson's play. Unfortunately, the noble lady who personated the Queen of

HOUSE IN WHICH SHAKSPEARE WAS BORN.

Sheba had drunk so much wine, that when she kneeled before the King of Denmark, who personated Solomon, to present a tray containing a goblet of wine, a dish of custard, a pitcher of cream, and a plate of cakes, she

HOLY TRINITY CHURCH, STRATFORD.

lost her balance and spilt them in his lap. The King of Denmark was in a sorry plight, but the servants came with napkins and wiped him off. He attempted to dance, but was so tipsy that he lost his footing and tumbled upon the floor. Three ladies, representing Faith, Hope, and Charity, had drunk so much wine that they could not speak their parts. Ben Jonson had prepared a part for Victory, but the wine had gone to her head, and she became crazy for the time being, slapped the lords and ladies in the face with her olive-branch of peace, and made so much disturbance that the servants were obliged to put her out of the hall.

The people loved games, and on market-days, in the country towns, there was cock-fighting, worrying of bulls by dogs, and games in which women and girls took part—running for prizes, or seeing which could make the broadest grin or loudest yawn; noblemen, courtiers, and many ministers spent much of their time in gambling with cards and dice in the tobacco-shop, for the people were learning to smoke.

The Puritans believed that life was not a holiday, but that men were

STRATFORD PORTRAIT OF SHAKSPEARE.

in this world for a grand purpose; that they were accountable to God for every act; that it was the duty of everybody to live soberly and righteously. They brought the power of the world to come to bear upon every thought and act. No person had a right to be idle. A frivolous life was a wasted life.

Such ideas were distasteful to the crowd of courtiers, who ridiculed the sober-minded men and women who were ever talking of duty and obligation. Thus it came about that society was divided into two classes: the king, nobility, courtiers; bishops, the ministers who had fat livings and who loved their ease, the rich tradesmen, the play-actors, those who loved sports on Sunday, on one side; on the other were many farmers

BEAR-GARDEN.

and peasants, some tradesmen and mechanics, some ministers, not many of the nobility, and very few of the courtiers. Only a small portion of the people were Puritans while James was king, but their numbers increased as the years rolled on; not altogether because people became more religious, but because of the arbitrary acts of James and his son Charles. Political questions made men Puritans.

James wanted more money than Parliament was willing to grant, and obtained it by selling titles. If a man wished to be a viscount, he must pay one hundred thousand dollars; if an earl, one hundred and fifty thousand.

"Why not create a new title and raise more money?" suggested Sir Thomas Shirley. James acted upon the hint, and created the title of baronet, and reaped a harvest of a million dollars.

Parliament had granted the king duties on all goods brought into or sent from England, at a fixed rate; but James discovered a way to put money in his pockets by increasing the rates. Vessels, for instance, which came from Greece brought cargoes of dried currants, which paid two shillings sixpence on every hundred pounds; James raised it to seven shillings sixpence without consulting Parliament; and so with everything else—putting all into his own pocket.

The judges of the Star-chamber and the bishops of the court of High Commission did as he desired. The laws said that no man who was accused of a crime should be compelled to testify against himself, but the judges and bishops disregarded it. Two men were brought before the bishops for not conforming to the ritual, and to answer other charges.

"We will not take an oath to testify against ourselves," they said.

The bishops sent them to prison; but they appealed to the judges of another court for a writ of *habeas corpus*, which means "to have the body;" that is, the judges of the other court had power to order the sheriff to take the two men from prison, and bring them before their court for examination; and they could order their release if they pleased, or send them to prison again. Mr. Fuller argued the case before the judges of the King's Bench.

"They ought to be released," he said, "because the High Commission has not been empowered by law to fine or imprison, neither to administer oaths."

That was a blow at the authority of the bishops, who summoned Fuller to appear before them; and, when he refused to take the oath, they threw him into prison, and compelled him to pay a fine of one thousand dollars. The judges of the King's Bench did not interfere, and the Starchamber and High Commission went on with their oppression. Men were put into prison, whipped, branded on the cheek, or had their noses and ears cut off for not conforming to the ritual, or for denying the authority of the bishops.

For light offences men were subjected to cruel punishments. In every village there was a whipping-post, pillory, and stocks. If a woman scolded her husband or neighbors, she was put in the pillory, or whipped, or tied to the ducking-stool and soused in a pond. If a man spoke disrespectfully of the bishops or king, he was flogged. For stealing or breaking into houses, men were hung.

It was a ghastly spectacle that the passengers across London Bridge beheld—skeletons hanging in chains and swinging in the wind. Those who passed beneath the Temple gate saw rows of skulls grinning upon them from the parapet.

It was believed that unless bodily pain was inflicted; unless offenders were whipped, or had their noses cut off; unless they were imprisoned or hung, there would not be a proper administration of justice, and society would not be secure. The laws were brutal, because the people were brutal. What we call the spirit of the age, is only our own spirit. When criminals were hung, thousands flocked to behold the hanging, and made sport when the sheriff swung them off. The multitude experienced a savage pleasure in seeing Jack Ketch cut off a man's head.

The judges had a great deal to say about the majesty of the law. Bishops claimed the right to compel everybody to believe as they believed and worship as they worshipped, and had power to punish by fines, flogging, and imprisonment all who would not obey their commands.

Will the people who cross the Atlantic to settle America, who have been subject to persecution, at once become charitable? Change of place cannot change the spirit of an age. Time alone can do it.

MEDAL OF JAMES I.

CHAPTER V.

THE BEGINNING OF TWO CIVILIZATIONS.

A COACH blazing with gold, with white lilies on its panels—the arms of France—rumbled through a narrow street in Paris on the afternoon of July 14th, 1610. In the coach was a gray-haired man, with a hooked nose, sharp chin, wrinkled face, and stiff gray mustache. Fifty-

BIRTHPLACE OF HENRY IV.

seven years had passed since his birth in an old stone castle at Pau, in the Pyrenees, where his fond grandfather poured wine and garlic down his throat to make him strong (see "Story of Liberty"); twenty years had gone by since his white plume, waving in the thickest of the fight at

Ivry, had won a great victory for the Huguenots—toleration for them and peace to France—through the Edict of Nantes, that alike protected

THE INDIANS AT HOME.

Catholic and Huguenots. Henry IV., beloved by the people, hated by the Jesuits, was riding alone through the narrow street, where the quaint old houses, jutting story over story, shut out the sunlight. Two carts blocked the way, and the coach came to a stand-still. A stout man with red whiskers, deep-set, wolfish eyes, the Jesuit Ravaillac, wearing a cloak, stepped up to the window. A dagger gleamed in the air, and then was buried to the handle in the heart of the king. A gasp, a gurgling in the throat, a sinking of the body upon the cushions, and all is over. He is gone; gone also the peace of Europe, the tranquillity of France, the hope of the Huguenots; but there is rejoicing in convents and nunneries, for no more will the Jesuits be thwarted in their plans by Henry IV.

Marie de Medicis, pliant, unprincipled, wicked—regent for her little son till he shall become king—will be a supple tool in their hands; whatever they ask she will grant, and they will train the son to follow in the footsteps of the mother.

What glorious news! The red men of America all becoming Christians! Young Biencourt, son of Baron Poutrincourt, brings the intelligence.

Four years had passed since the abandonment of Port Royal by Sieur de Monts, who, having lost much money, sold all his rights in Acadia to Baron Poutrincourt, who hastened across the sea to take possession of his purchase. There was rejoicing in the wigwams of the Indians when his vessel dropped anchor in Port Royal. The houses and the furniture remained just as Sieur de Monts had left them. Membertu, the Indian chief, who was very old, welcomed his friends the French once more.

"I have served the devil all my life, and now I want to be good," he said.

Possibly he remembered the dinners he had eaten in the great hall with Sieur de Monts, and would like to partake of other feasts.

"I would like to accept the white man's God, and my squaws and children will also accept him."

On the day of St. John the Baptist there was an imposing scene at Port Royal. Baron Poutrincourt and the other gentlemen of the expedition, wearing glittering breastplates and plumed hats, guarded by soldiers, keeping step to the drum-beat, marching in procession, escorted the Jesuit priests from the little log church to the sea-shore. The sailors and colonists gathered in groups around, greatly interested in all that was going on; also the dusky warriors who had come to see their old chief and his wives become Christians. Membertu and his family kneeled upon the pebbled beach, the priest sprinkled them with holy-water, a *Te Deum* was sung, the cannon thundered on ship and shore.

"Henceforth you will be called Henri," said the priest to Membertu, naming him for the King of France.

"I give you the name of Marie," said the priest to wife No. 1, bestowing upon her the name of Marie de Medicis.

Another thundering of cannon, and the old chief and all his family were Christians.

Indians far away heard that Membertu had accepted the Frenchman's religion, and hastened to Port Royal to be baptized.

"Will they have such good dinners in the next world as you give here?" they asked.

Captain John Smith the while was exploring Chesapeake Bay, travelling in an open boat three thousand miles up the eastern and down the western shore, and up the Potomac, till stopped by the falls above Washington. We may believe that the thought never came to him that upon the northern bank would one day stand the capitol of a great republic.

Several hundred new colonists arrived at Jamestown, sent out by the London Company. An historian of Virginia has given this description of the new-comers:

"They were gentlemen reduced to poverty by gaming and extravagance, too proud to beg, too lazy to dig; broken tradesmen with some stigma of fraud yet clinging to their names; fortune-hunters who had expended in their mother country the last shred of honest reputation they had ever held; rakes consumed by desires, and shattered by the service of impurity; libertines whose end of sin was yet to run; and unruly sparks packed off by their friends to escape worse destinies at home."

"Do men gather grapes of thorns, or figs of thistles?"

The greatest of all teachers put this question eighteen hundred years ago, and history has always confirmed his answer. States are not built of such material.

The merchants of London had not grasped the idea that Industry, Thrift, Economy, Virtue, Intelligence, Integrity, and Character are needed to make a prosperous community; that what does not help, hinders; that the idlers and vagabonds could pull down faster than they could build up. They repeated Sir John Popham's mistake.

All was confusion at Jamestown. The new-comers ate up the provisions of the colonists. They were lazy.

"We did not come here to work," they said.

"Then you shall not eat," said Captain John Smith, and ruled them with a determination that soon brought order out of confusion. But when he sailed for England the vagabonds had things their own way; they robbed the Indians, and the Indians, in revenge, split open the skulls of the robbers. Famine came. Thirty of the scapegraces seized one of the vessels in the river and turned pirates. The Indians became more bold—cutting off all stragglers. In six months after Captain Smith's departure the settlers dwindled from four hundred and ninety to sixty; and they were eating their last provisions when Sir Thomas Gates arrived from the West Indies. What a scene was that which he beheld! A few haggard, starving wretches on the verge of despair!

Sir Thomas had suffered shipwreck at the Bermudas, but had built two small vessels there, and had reached Jamestown with very little food to give to the starving colonists.

"We must abandon the settlement, make our way to Newfoundland, and join the fishermen," said Sir Thomas.

"We will burn the cursed place," shouted the colonists, ready to set the houses on fire; but Sir Thomas prevented them from carrying out their plan.

They sailed down the James; but their hearts were made glad at meeting Lord Delaware in a ship bringing supplies and emigrants. With fresh courage they went back to begin once more the foundations of an empire. Lord Delaware was appointed governor. He ruled mildly but firmly. The new colonists were more industrious. Early in the morning they all gathered in the little church while prayers were read, and made their devotions more pleasant by keeping the building adorned with flowers. After prayers they had breakfast, and then worked from six till ten. They rested while the sun was hottest, but labored from two till four in the afternoon. "He that tilleth the land shall be satisfied with bread." Solomon said it three thousand years ago, and the colonists quickly proved its truth. The harvest was bountiful, and there were abundant supplies.

Lord Delaware returned to England, and Sir Thomas Dale succeeded him as governor. A code of laws printed in England was sent out. The governor had all power, and could inflict severe punishment. If a colonist used an oath against the king, he was to be put to death.

The poets, who a few years before had written plays picturing the richness and attractiveness of Virginia, now held the country and settlers up to ridicule, which so grieved Rev. Mr. Crashaw that he wrote this prayer for the use of the settlers, and which was printed with the laws:

"Whereas, we have, by undertaking this plantation, undergone the reproof of a base world, insomuch as many of our own brethren laugh us to scorn, O Lord we pray thee fortify us against this temptation. Let Sanballat and Tobias, Papists and players, and such other Amorites and Horonites, the scum and dregs of the earth—let them mock such as help to build up the walls of Jerusalem. They that be filthy, let them be filthy still."

In 1611 three hundred men and one hundred cattle were sent to Virginia. Part of the emigrants settled at Hampton, and part up the river beyond Jamestown. The laws were made more severe. If a man stayed away from church on Sunday, he was to suffer the loss of a week's provision; for a second offence he was to be whipped; and for staying away three times, was to be put to death. If he refused to tell the minister what he believed in regard to religion, he was to be whipped till he complied. If a washer-woman stole a piece of linen, she was to be tied to the whipping-post and flogged. If the baker did not put a given amount of flour into his loaves, he was to have his ears cut off.

The company held everything in their own hands, and there was no incentive to labor, no hope of reward. A new policy was inaugurated by the governor—the giving of a few acres of land to each settler for an orchard and garden. The land was taken from the Indians, no regard being paid to their rights, nor anything given in return, and the settlers helped themselves to corn which the Indians had raised.

The company in London wanted money; and as no revenue had been received from the colony, the king gave a new charter, with the privilege of their setting up a lottery. They advertised great prizes, but, when the drawing took place, the people who had purchased tickets found that there were sixty thousand blanks to one prize!

It was a dreary winter, that of 1612, to the Jesuit fathers, and the few Frenchmen in the little settlement on the eastern shore of the Bay of Fundy. They had little to eat, and could give no such feasts to the Indians as De Monts had spread for them seven years before. Father Biard was studying the Indian language, giving them bits of bread to induce them to talk. The Indians made game of him.

"What are the Indian words for Faith, Hope, Charity, Sacrament, Baptism?" asked the priest.

The unsuspecting father wrote down, in all soberness, the low, scurrilous, and indecent words which they gave. He made a catechism, but was greatly perplexed at the laughter of the savages when he came to use it.

In midwinter, when their provisions were running low, a vessel from France arrived, bringing information that Baron Pontrincourt had lost much money, and was obliged to sell his rights in Acadia to Madame de Guercheville, a rich and noble lady, deeply religious, who was ready to employ her wealth in converting the Indians to the Catholic faith. The Jesuits told her of the glory and honor that would await her in the next world if she should be the means of saving the souls of the Indians. Her zeal was fired for the Church.

In grand old cathedrals, amidst the pomp and gorgeous ceremony of the Church, women weary of the world were bidding good-bye to its frivolity, taking the veil, consecrating themselves to lives of penance and self-denial, that they might win heaven. Madame de Guercheville planned

THE BEGINNING OF TWO CIVILIZATIONS. 95

to send a company of nuns and Jesuit fathers to carry on the work already begun. She infused a little of her own spirit into the indolent,

NUN TAKING THE VEIL.

frivolous, voluptuous crowd that swarmed around the boy-king, Louis XIII., so that they opened their purses and contributed liberally to her enterprise.

The Jesuits laid far-reaching plans, persuading Madame de Guercheville to ask Louis to give her all the country between the St. Lawrence and Florida. What was a wilderness on the other side of the sea to a boy? What did he know or care about it? Nothing. He granted all that Madame de Guercheville asked, giving her the whole of America north of the territory claimed by Spain, including Virginia. The Jesuits

MOUNT DESERT.

were delighted; the continent was theirs! Not quite. There were other forces at work, and other wills and plans besides theirs. Time would reveal them.

Along the towering cliffs of Mount Desert, into the peaceful waters of Somes Sound, sailed a ship from Honfleur. It was the month of May, and the forest was robed in green, and the air fragrant with the odors of spring. The vessel was owned by Madame de Guercheville, and commanded by an officer of the Court of Louis XII., De Saussaye. The vessel had touched at Port Royal, and taken on board Father Biard and other Jesuits. Madame de Guercheville had sent out a company of colonists, who, with the priests, were to establish missions to convert the Indians.

A signal fire was blazing on the beach, kindled by the Indians, and Father Biard hastened to the shore. The Indians knew him; for they had been to Port Royal and eaten good dinners at the hall.

"Our chief is sick, and will die, and live in hell forever if he is not baptized!" they said.

The priest hastened to see the chief, and found that he had only a bad cold, and was in no danger of dying. But he saw what a beautiful place it was—a green and grassy slope descending to the sea—a delightful harbor protected from the ocean's waves.

THE BEGINNING OF TWO CIVILIZATIONS.

The colonists went on shore. The priest set up the cross, and mass was said. The four white tents which Madame de Guercheville had sent were pitched on the verdant slope, and the boxes, bales, and chests of goods unloaded.

What vessel was that sailing into the harbor, with a red flag and the cross of St. George at the mast-head, and sixteen cannon protruding from the port-holes, and sixty men on her deck?

It was a ship commanded by Samuel Argall, who was roving the sea, trading to the West Indies, and fishing near Virginia. He had been to Jamestown; had coasted northward to the Isles of Shoals; from thence had sailed into Penobscot Bay. Indians came out in their canoes, and climbed on board.

"Normans," they said, pointing eastward.

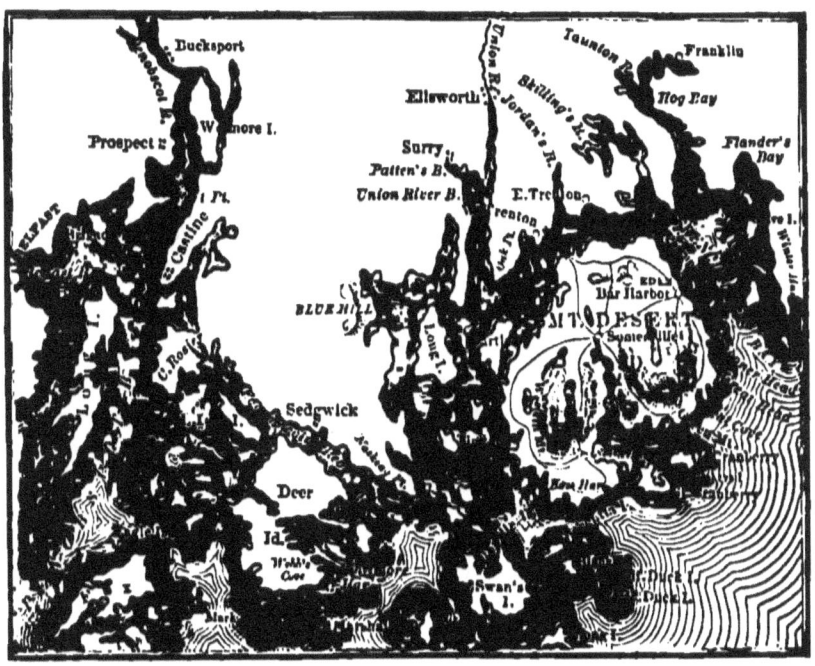

PENOBSCOT BAY.

Captain Argall understood by their signs and words that the French were in that direction, and sailed for Mount Desert. Frenchmen making a settlement on English territory! He would see about that. He descried the vessel sent out by Madame de Guercheville at anchor, and the white tents on the beach. Saussaye was on shore, but Lieutenant La Motte and the Jesuit priest De Thet were on shipboard.

"Who are you? What do you want?" shouted De la Motte.

A roar from all his cannon was Argall's answer.

"Fire! fire!" shouted De Thet. He touched off a cannon, and the next moment was lying wounded on the deck, knocked down by a ball. Over the railing climbed the English, capturing the vessel. Saussaye and those on shore fled to the woods, while Argall landed and searched the chests and boxes, putting into his pocket the commission which the king had given Saussaye.

To remain in the woods was to die of starvation, and the Frenchmen gave themselves up as prisoners.

"King James owns this country," said Argall.

"I have authority from the King of France to make a settlement here."

"I would like to see it, if you please."

Saussaye searched his trunk, but could not find it.

"You are a robber, and deserve to be hung. I shall take possession of your property," said Argall. He set some of the captives adrift in a boat to find their way to the French fishermen at Newfoundland, and took the remainder to Virginia.

"I will hang the rascals," said Sir Thomas Dale; but as France and England were at peace, he did not quite dare to; but he made short work of the colony at Port Royal by sending Argall to stamp it out.

A few days later, charred brands and heaps of ashes alone marked the site of the great hall; and Biencourt, the governor, and the colonists were wanderers in the wilderness, living through the winter in wigwams, on roots, and the bark and buds of trees, and clams from the sea-shore, and such morsels as they could get from the Indians.

So a rover of the sea, acting on his own responsibility, upset all the plans of the Jesuits. They must begin again. It was the first conflict in the great struggle on the American continent between the two systems of civilization.

CHAPTER VI.

HOW BEAVER-SKINS AND TOBACCO HELPED ON CIVILIZATION.

ON April 14th, 1614, two vessels, one commanded by Captain John Smith and the other by Captain Hunt, dropped anchor off the Island of Monhegan, on the coast of Maine. They had been sent out by the London Company to explore the coast. Captain Smith set some of the men to work building a boat; and while they were sawing out the planks he sailed with eight men eastward to the Bay of Penobscot, exploring the islands and harbor; then steering west, he sailed past Whale's Back Island, and entered the beautiful Piscataqua, and saw the bank from which Martin Pring had picked strawberries. Seven miles off the shore he saw a group of islands—mostly barren ledges and high cliffs, with rocky reefs, on which the waves were breaking, and named them the Isles of Shoals.

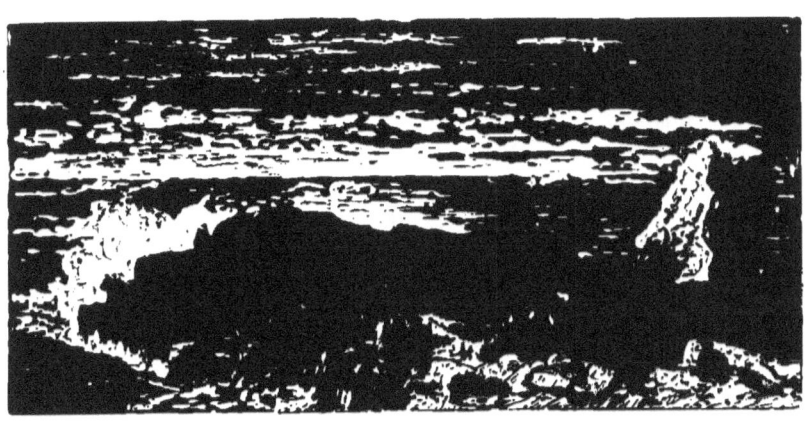

SMUTTY-NOSE.

One of the group bears the name of Smutty-nose; another, Star Island, on which a monument has been erected in honor of the intrepid man who did so much to make the country known to people in England, and who did more than all others to build up the settlement at Jamestown.

From the Isles of Shoals Captain Smith steered south to Cape Ann, and into Massachusetts Bay; cruising among the islands, he entered a

CAPTAIN JOHN SMITH'S MONUMENT, ISLES OF SHOALS.

river, which he named Charles, in honor of King James's second son. He found two vessels from France at anchor in the bay, the crews trading with the Indians.

We are to remember that France claimed all the country, through Cartier's and Verrazani's discoveries, and that the boy-king of France has given it to Madame de Guercheville.

Leaving the French ships, Captain Smith and Captain Hunt sailed along the coast, past the ledges of Cohasset to Cape Cod, where they parted company—Smith returning to Monhegan, and from there to England, where he made a map of the coast, which he presented to Prince Charles. Captain Hunt enticed some of the Indians on board his ship, and carried them to England to sell into slavery.

If Captain Smith, instead of returning to England, had kept on around Cape Cod to the Hudson River, he would have found Adriaen Block, of Holland, hard at work building a little vessel on the island of Manhattan. He had been trading with the Indians, buying furs for the hat-makers of Amsterdam, and had nearly filled his ship with beaver-skins, when it took fire and was burnt. Captain Block was not a man to sit down and wring his hands over his loss, but built a log-house for his crew, and set them to work, with such tools as they had, to construct another vessel, and soon had it ready for sea. It was only sixteen tons burden. He called it the *Onrust*, or Restless. Although so small, the Dutchman set sail, hoping to fall in with some larger vessel in which he could make his way to Holland. The tide swept the little bark through the surging waters of Hell Gate, and a south wind wafted it to Connecti-

CAPTAIN BLOCK BUILDING THE "ONRUST."

cut River — the first white sail ever seen by the Pequot Indians, who gazed upon it from the hills along the shore.

Captain Block steered for the island that bears his name, and from thence eastward, past Nantucket and Martha's Vineyard, around Cape Cod to Nahant.

A sail! How the hearts of the men on board the *Onrust* were gladdened at the sight of that white speck upon the horizon off Cape Ann! How joyful to meet Hendrick Christiansen! He was from Amsterdam, on his way to the Hudson to buy furs. They exchanged vessels—Christiansen going westward, and Block striking boldly across the Atlantic.

In the city of Hague, or the *hedge*, in Holland, is the grand old Bin-

VIEW AT THE HAGUE.

nenhof, the building in which the government of Holland in old times held its meetings. In one of the rooms, on October 11th, 1614, sat John of Barneveld, the founder of the Dutch Republic. He was sixty-eight years old. His hair and beard were white. He had large features, high cheek-bones, a sharp nose, broad forehead, firmly-set lips, and mild blue eyes. He wore a velvet robe trimmed with sable, and a starched white ruff. Around him were the members of the Council of State, in velvet robes and white ruff—men of influence—wealthy burghers of the Republie. A door opened, and Adriaen Block, with the merchants from Amsterdam, entered.

"I have a map of a part of the New World that I have visited to present to you," said Captain Block; and he spread upon the table a map showing Hudson River, Long Island, the Connecticut River, Block Island, Narragansett Bay, and all the shore along which he had sailed. Barneveld and those with him followed his finger as he pointed out the location, and spoke of the trade that might be opened in America with the Indians.

"By-and-by that region may be of great political importance to the Dutch Republic," said Barneveld; and the men around him assented.

"We are here to obtain a special license to open trade in those regions," said the merchants.

JOHN OF BARNEVELD.

The Council granted their request, and drew up a paper in which the country, nameless before, was called New Netherlands. The merchants were to have the sole privilege of trade with the Indians between Newfoundland and Virginia.

Hendrick Christiansen sailed up the Hudson River, and on an island just below Albany built a log-house, surrounding it with a palisade, digging a moat, mounting two cannon and eleven small guns on swivels, and naming it Fort Nassau. He made friends of the Indians, and filled his vessel with beaver-skins.

Hendrick Christiansen did not know, while he was building the fort, that out in the forest, toward the setting sun, a battle was raging, which in its results would be far more effective than his cannon in preserving peace with the Indians. Before seeing the battle, we must go back a little.

About two hundred years before John and Sebastian Cabot discovered America, a young man in the town of Assisi, in France, became wild on the subject of religion. He had strange dreams, and heard supernatural voices. He took a vow to be a beggar all his life; thinking, with all other monks and friars, that to be dirty, wear rags, and go barefoot, was a sign of humility. To show that he renounced the world, he stripped off all his clothes, wearing only a mantle around his loins. The people flocked in crowds to his preaching. He was so much of a fanatic that he went out into the fields and preached to the ducks and geese, doves and sparrows. He took the name of St. Francis; and though he called himself a saint, he robbed his father to obtain money to build a church, declaring that, as the object was good, the action was right. Other men went wild with religion, and to show their humility became dirty and wore rags, and, instead of working, begged their living. They went on missions, and spread themselves over all the world.

In May, 1615, Samuel Champlain, with four priests of the Order of St. Francis—Denis Jamet, Jean Dolbean, Joseph le Caron, and Pacific du Plessis—landed at Quebec. The settlers came out and kneeled as they stepped on shore, while the cannon of the ship and fort thundered a salute. They had come to convert the Indians. Jean Dolbean went down the north shore of the St. Lawrence to tell the Indians of that region about Christianity. He slept in their wigwams, which were so full of smoke that he came near losing his sight, and returned to Quebec. Joseph le Caron was to go to the Hurons around the upper lakes.

Samuel Champlain had a great plan; he wanted the Indians converted, but he desired also to build up a great empire in America. He was a statesman, and saw that if he could establish his influence over the various tribes, the vast region could be brought under the dominion of

HOW BEAVER-SKINS AND TOBACCO HELPED ON CIVILIZATION. 103

France. Spain had already acquired Mexico, Florida, and South America; and if he could make his influence supreme, he could, in time, drive out the few English at Virginia, and save by far the largest portion of North America for France. Grand and magnificent the ideal.

There was a great gathering of tribes at Montreal to fight the Iroquois. The gun fired by Champlain at Ticonderoga had not ceased to reverberate. The defeat of the Iroquois in that battle had stirred them

GOING TO FIGHT THE IROQUOIS.

to fresh endeavors, and every year they had carried home many scalps from Canada. The Indians welcomed Champlain.

"We go to fight our enemies. If our father will go with us, we will beat them," they said.

There were twenty-five hundred warriors. It was a great opportunity; by going with them and fighting their battles, Champlain would make his influence supreme. He accepted their invitation, and joined them with

AGREEMENT BETWEEN THE DUTCH AND IROQUOIS.

twelve soldiers. The route was up the Ottawa River to Lake Huron, then south through a chain of small lakes to Lake Ontario. They secreted their canoes on the southern shore of the lake, and then marched south to Lake Oneida, capturing seven Iroquois men and four women. The Hurons held a great dance, and then put their prisoners to death.

It was on October 10th when the Hurons reached one of their Iroquois towns on the shore of the lake not far from Syracuse. The Iroquois had built a palisade thirty feet high around it. They came out to

A HURON WAR-DANCE.

fight, but were greatly astonished when they heard the sound of guns, and when the bullets struck them down. They fled inside the palisade. Champlain set the Indians at work building a tower, and in a short time they had one so high that from the top of it he and his companions could pick off the Iroquois, who fought bravely, and wounded Champlain with an arrow. "Set the palisade on fire!" he shouted.

The Hurons built a fire, but the Iroquois dashed water upon the flames. All the while both sides kept up a terrible warwhoop. Champlain tried to direct the Hurons, but they would not hear him, and were finally compelled to retreat, with several killed and wounded.

While this was going on, Hendrick Christiausen was trading with the Mohawk Indians. The other Iroquois heard of it, and hastened to make friends with the Dutch, that they might obtain weapons that would spit fire and kill their enemies. They met the Dutch beneath a great tree. The Iroquois chief held one end of the belt of peace, and the Dutch the other, and so they agreed to be friends. They buried a hatchet, and the Dutch said they would build a church upon the spot, that it might never be dug up.

This agreement never was broken, and the Iroquois became the allies of the settlers of New York, in all the conflicts with the French and Indians, till the English became masters of Canada, one hundred and forty-three years later.

Captain Argall became governor of Virginia in 1618, and issued hard laws. He had one price for goods. The settlers might sell tobacco for three shillings a pound; but if they charged more or took less, they were to be sold into slavery for three years. No man could hunt a deer without permission from the governor. Any person staying away from church on Sunday, or on holy days, was to be tied neck and heels overnight, and be a slave for a week; for the second offence he was to be enslaved for a month; the third, a year.

Many of the settlers were little better than slaves. Men who were in debt in England were sold by their creditors. Although so many of the settlers were scrapegraces and vagabonds, King James thought there was room for more, and sent over one hundred thieves and robbers. He appointed Sir George Yeardly governor, who found things in a sorry condition upon his arrival. The houses in Jamestown were tumbling to the ground. In Richmond there were only three dwellings, and a church that was little better than a hovel. There were only three ministers in the colony, and only one of them had authority from the bishop to preach. The settlers were ground down by the cruel laws. Men were flogged and had their ears cut off for very slight offences.

Sir George Yeardly was humane, and informed the people that they should be governed by the laws of England. The company of planters had all power, and the people none. He proclaimed that the people should have a voice in government; that there should be a general assembly of delegates or burgesses from each borough, who were to be elected by the inhabitants, and the burgesses were to make all needful laws. They assembled at James City; John Pory was chosen speaker. A prayer was read, and the first Legislature that ever assembled in the New World was ready to proceed to business. The burgesses accepted the

CULTIVATION OF TOBACCO.

privileges which Governor Yeardly had given them as their great charter. The Church of England was established as the Church of the colony, and the ministers were to receive the value of two hundred pounds a year, to be paid in tobacco. Laws were passed against idleness, drunkenness and gambling. If people wore costly clothes they were to be taxed for them; everybody was required to attend church twice every Sunday; and everybody who owned a gun was to carry it, to be ready to fight if attacked by the Indians. The price of first quality tobacco was fixed at three shillings per pound; second quality, half-price.

It was the beginning of a new state of affairs. The settlers took heart, and built good houses. Virginia was their home. There were only about six hundred inhabitants; but now that the cruel laws were repealed, and the rights of the people recognized, there were thousands in England ready to emigrate. In twelve months twelve hundred and sixty-one persons crossed the Atlantic to find new homes on the banks of the James.

Sir Edwin Sandys and the Earl of Southampton were members of the London Company. They were large-hearted men, and through their influence the company granted a written constitution to the settlers. The company were to appoint the governor and his council, while the people were to elect the burgesses.

There had been so many wars, and so many men had been killed in battles, that there were far more women than men in England. There were very few women in Virginia; and in order to supply the settlers with wives, the company sent out a ship-load of girls, who were ready to emigrate for the sake of getting husbands. There were ninety of them. The company paid the cost of their going; but each settler must pay one hundred and twenty pounds of tobacco for the girl whom he might select. The tobacco was reckoned at three shillings a pound; so they must pay three hundred and sixty shillings for a wife, which they were ready to do, and in a very short time every girl was provided with a husband. Wives were in such demand that sixty more girls were sent out, and the price raised to one hundred and fifty pounds of tobacco.

While the settlers were purchasing their wives, a Dutch ship sailed up the James with sixteen negroes on board, which were purchased as slaves by the tobacco-raisers of Jamestown. It was the beginning of African slavery in America.

As things are constituted in this world, the innocent suffer for the guilty. In Virginia some of the settlers were hard-working, industrious, and thrifty, doing what

FIRST SETTLEMENTS ON THE CHESAPEAKE AND DELAWARE.

they could to build up the colony; but many others were indolent, shiftless, and vicious. Instead of working for a livelihood, they stole the corn which the Indians had raised. No one likes to be plundered. In civilized society robbers are put into prison; but the Indian knows nothing of courts of law or jails; the tomahawk is his administrator of justice.

The Indians laid a plan to fall upon the settlements along the James, and at a blow finish the white men who were taking their land, stealing their corn, and driving the game out of the country.

What a scene the sun rose upon on the 22d of March, 1622! Three hundred and forty-seven massacred, and the colonists fleeing to Jamestown pursued by the blood-thirsty savages. The Indians were brave to strike blows, but fled like cowards when the bullets began to whistle about their ears.

The total number of emigrants had been nearly four thousand; some had gone back to England; but there were still twenty-five hundred people.

A ship carried the news to England. There was great consternation. The city of London and gentlemen of fortune contributed money to purchase arms to send to the colonists.

"You must roast out the savages!" was their message.

There were brave men in Virginia, who had no thought of sitting down and wringing their hands. George Sandys, Governor Yeardly, and Captain Madigan enlisted men, and marched into the Indian country, burning their wigwams, driving them from their hunting-grounds, and giving them little rest. Notwithstanding this, the colony languished. The shares of the company were worthless. The members were at loggerheads with each other and with the king. They had fierce discussions in their meetings. James had made concessions in the charter, for he saw that it gave the colonists some rights which he wished to recover. He wanted to be an absolute monarch, and ordered the judges of the court to take measures to revoke the charter. Under such a state of affairs, the colony came to a stand-still.

CHAPTER VII.

THE PILGRIMS.

IN England, Holland, France, and Germany there was a great difference of opinion in matters of religion. Men everywhere were thinking for themselves, instead of accepting the opinion of pope, bishop, or priest. In England the people were nearly all Protestants; in France the majority were Catholics; in Holland they were nearly equally divided. In England the Protestants would not tolerate anybody who did not accept the Church which Henry VIII. had set up; in France the Catholics were ever ready to persecute the Protestants; in Holland men could be Catholic or Protestant as they pleased. So it came about that the men and women of Scrooby, when persecuted for separating themselves from the Church of England, and meeting in William Brewster's house on Sunday for worship, fled to Holland, as the place where they could think and act for themselves. They settled at Leyden, working hard to keep the wolf from the door. They were industrious, and so honest, minding their own business, that the Dutch treated them with great respect. Instead of frequenting the beer-houses, and taking part in the Dutch revelries, they remained quietly at home when their days' work was done; and instead of carousing on Sundays, they met in the house of John Robinson for worship. They used no prayer-book, nor had they any particular form of worship. They organized themselves into a Church with Christ as their head. All were equal. They elected their deacons, who were to be their servants. It was a Church in which the rights of every person was respected. They believed that Christ and the apostles organized just such churches; that a bishop, instead of having any authority to rule them, should only be their minister or servant; that they had authority from Christ to rule themselves. *Ruling themselves!* Let us not forget it. When men rule themselves there will be the largest freedom; they will respect the rights of their fellow-men, for only by so doing can they have their own rights.

Through all the centuries, presbyters, priests, bishops, and popes had

ruled in religious matters; but these men of Scrooby rejected all such authority, and made their declaration to the world—
The people alone have the right to rule!

Ten years passed. No one molested them in their religious opinions; none disturbed their worship; but Holland was divided into two great political parties—Prince Maurice being at the head of one, and John of Barneveld, before whom Captain Block laid his map of Hudson River,

DUTCH REVEL.—(FROM AN OLD PICTURE.)

and of the coast along which he sailed in the *Onrust*, was at the head of the other.

James of England, Louis of France, and Philip of Spain, all were interfering in the affairs of Holland. Civil war broke out, armies were on the march, and the whole country was disturbed.

It was a terrible scene which the people at the Hague beheld at sunrise on May 13th, 1619—John of Barneveld, seventy-two years old, kneel-

EXECUTION OF BARNEVELD. [FROM MOTLEY'S "LIFE AND DEATH OF JOHN OF BARNEVELD."]

ing on a wooden scaffold in front of the Binnenhof. All the morning the drums had been beating, the trumpets sounding, and soldiers marching. A great crowd had gathered. The old man drew the black cap over his white locks, and kneeled with his face toward his own house, a little distance away. One blow, and the head of the true-hearted patriot rolled upon the planks, and the crowd, scrambling upon the scaffold, dipped their handkerchiefs in his blood, to keep as souvenirs of his death. So Holland's great statesman died, at the hands of those who hated him, because he was so great. He had done grand things for his country, but intrigue, political faction, and jealousy could not be content till he was in his grave.

The men who had fled from Scrooby to find a home in Holland loved peace. They stood aloof from wrangling. Their true-hearted pastor, John Robinson, taught them to love all men. They could find no comfort amidst such scenes. What should they do? The question confronted them. They could not go back to England without conforming to the ritual of the Church; that they would not do. Why not emigrate to America? But how could they get there? They were poor. William Brewster was trying to earn a living by working in a printing-office; one laid bricks, another was a carpenter; one was a blacksmith, another a tailor.

They learned that there were men in England ready to help them. The Plymouth Company of merchants, who had obtained the grant of land between Long Island and Nova Scotia, wanted the country settled. They were anxious to obtain furs, and, as they were ready to venture their money, were called "adventurers." One of the number was Thomas Weston, of London, who heard that the Pilgrims were ready to go to America, and went to Holland to see them.

"I will help you. I will lend you money and obtain ships," he said, thinking the while how good a bargain he might make.

A plan was agreed upon. The "adventurers" were ready to supply money and ships; the Pilgrims were to go as planters. The Pilgrims formed themselves into a company, fixing the shares of stock at fifty dollars. Every settler sixteen years old was to be equal to one share. Every man who furnished an outfit worth fifty dollars was to have an additional share, and children between ten and sixteen years of age were to be counted as half a share. All the settlers bound themselves to work together for seven years, their labor to go into a common fund, and all to be supported from it. At the end of that period the property was to be divided according to the shares. For seven years they were to put all their hardships, dangers, and work on an equality with the money advanced by the merchants, who would thus be enabled to speculate on their toil. The conditions were hard, yet, for the sake of bringing up their children in the principles that were dearer than all things else, they would accept them.

On the 22d of July, 1620, the Pilgrims met for the last time at the house of John Robinson in Leyden, to spend the morning in prayer, and to hear the parting words of their beloved pastor. After the sermon they ate together and sung a psalm. Their ship, the *Speedwell*, was lying at Delftshaven, fourteen miles from Leyden, whither they went, accompanied by their pastor and friends, and where they spent the night. Morning came, the wind was fair, and the captain in haste to be gone. They kneeled upon the deck, the minister offering a parting prayer. The farewells were spoken, the vessel swung from her moorings, the sails caught the breeze, and swept them out upon the ocean and across the Channel to Southampton, where the *Mayflower* was waiting.

> "They passed the frowning towers of Breil,
> The 'Hook' of Holland's shelf of sand,
> And grated soon with lifting keel
> The sullen shore of Father-land."

How hard it is to tear things up by the roots—to leave home, friends, things we love, around which our affections are entwined! It was not a hard thing for the scapegraces of London to cross the Atlantic in search of adventure in Virginia. They pulled nothing up by the roots; they had no roots. Gamblers, spendthrifts, vagabonds, who do nothing for the world, who give nothing to society, never can have any roots.

The Pilgrims were exiles. England was no longer their home; but their friends were still living in the dear old land. While they were in Holland, they could hear from them often; but now they were going far away, to make their homes in the wilderness. Never more would they gaze upon the green fields, or meet face to face those most dear; but, in obedience to their convictions of what was true, just, and right—of what they owed to God rather than man—calmly and unflinchingly they could pull all up, and make their homes in the wilderness.

Thomas Weston was at Southampton. He was a grasping, avaricious man, and wanted to change the agreement, making it still harder for the Pilgrims. But they would not change, whereupon he refused to pay one hundred pounds, which, according to agreement, he ought to pay.

"I'll let you stand on your own legs!" he said, and left them.

THE PILGRIMS.

The Pilgrims would not leave England with a debt hanging over them, and to pay it sold eighty firkins of butter, resolving to do without butter on their bread rather than to be beholden to Weston, or in debt to any man.

They were men who loved order. They knew it was necessary to have some one in authority on shipboard. They cast their votes for a governor, electing John Carver. Let us not forget that they *elected him.* He was not appointed by the king, but chosen. *It was the beginning of a new order of things.*

The ship sailed from Southampton; but almost before they were out of the harbor the *Speedwell* was found to be leaking, and they put into Dartmouth for repairs. Two weeks passed, and they sailed again; but the captain of the *Speedwell* declared that the vessel was not sea-worthy, and they put into Plymouth. Some of the Pilgrims were discouraged, but

DARTMOUTH.

others were not. They had no money to obtain another vessel, and all who were anxious to go crowded into the *Mayflower*—one hundred in all.

Again, on the 16th of September, they bade farewell to friends—to the land that gave them birth, from which they had been exiled.

OLD TIMES IN THE COLONIES.

> "No home for them! too well they knew
> The mitred king behind the throne;
> The sails were set, the pennon flew,
> And westward ho! for worlds unknown."

On the 21st of November, 1620, the *Mayflower* dropped anchor in the calm waters of Provincetown harbor, Cape Cod. While on the voyage, Mrs. White gave birth to a babe, whom they named Peregrine.

PROVINCETOWN.

Among the men sent out by the merchants was John Billington; he was not one of the Pilgrims, but a servant, who gave out word that he should do as he pleased when he reached land; that no one should have any authority over him, for John Carver had no commission, nor had the Pilgrims any charter from the king.

The Pilgrims had ruled themselves as a church, but had been subject to the laws of Holland; they saw that they must organize themselves into a State, make their own laws, and execute them. They met in the cabin of the *Mayflower*, signed their names to a paper, organizing as a body politic, agreeing to obey the laws which they might make, and the governor whom they might elect.

The world never before had seen such a paper. *It was a constitution formed by the people—the beginning of popular government.*

It was Saturday, and the women went on shore, kindled fires, and washed their clothes. At night they returned on shipboard, and on Sunday prayed and sung as they had done through the voyage.

During the following week, Captain Miles Standish and sixteen men marched along the shores, and came upon some Indians, who quickly fled.

They found some corn, which they took, intending to pay the Indians if they ever saw them.

On the 16th of December, Captain Standish and a party, with Thomas Clark, the mate of the vessel, started in a boat to find a suitable place to make a settlement, camping at night on shore. While they were cooking their breakfast the next morning, they heard a strange cry, and arrows fell around them; but a volley from the muskets of the Pilgrims put the Indians to flight. They came near losing their lives in a cold storm, but landed, kindled a fire, and saved themselves from freezing. In the morning they discovered that they were on an island, which they named Clark's Island, for the mate. The next day was Sunday, but they regarded it as holy, and remained where they were. On Monday they pulled to the main-land, climbed a high hill, and beheld a charming prospect. Under the brow of the hill was a brook and a spring of fresh water. It was so delightful that they decided to recommend it to those on the ship

PLYMOUTH.

as the place for the building of their town. They returned to the vessel, and on Sunday, William Brewster, whom they had chosen to be their minister, preached his last sermon on shipboard. The next morning the

Mayflower sailed across the bay and came to anchor. The men went on shore and examined the place once more, and, after praying God to direct them wisely, took a vote as to where they should build their houses. *It was the first town meeting ever held in America.* The majority decided affairs, and the new State, the new order of things—self-government—had begun.

On the morning of the 22d the long-boat of the ship, filled with men, women, and children, glided over the still waters to a rock that made a convenient landing. They stepped from the boat upon the rock, and the new State was in possession of its future home.

There were no idlers in the party. All hands knew how to work, and labor was a duty which they owed to one another and to God. They cut down the trees, split them into planks, and built a house for the storing of their goods, making the roof flat, and mounting their cannon upon it. They laid out a street at the foot of the hill and built their houses, covering them with thatch, for they had not learned to peel the bark from the oak-trees or split the pines into shingles. Death came. Degory Priest was the first to be laid beneath the earth, January 1st, 1621. On Sunday, January 14th, the thatch on their common house, in which was stored all their goods, caught fire, and they had hard work to put it out; if that had been consumed, quite likely they would have been compelled to return to England, or else would have perished. On the 29th of January a great grief came to Captain Standish. His beautiful young wife, Rose, had been fading day by day; the hardships were too great for her. Possibly she pined for the green fields and pleasant home far away. She had never been in Holland, but joined the Pilgrims at Southampton. But heaven was nearer than her old home. With tearful eyes and swelling hearts they carried her to the burying-place upon the hill, and made this entry in their journal, mournful in its briefness: "Jan. 29, *Died, Rose, wife of Captain Standish.*"

The Pilgrims were greatly surprised, one day, at seeing an Indian march boldly into their settlement and hear him say, "Welcome, Englishmen!" His name was Samoset. He had been to Pemmaquid, to Sir Fernando Gorges's colony. The Pilgrims treated him kindly, and he soon brought another Indian, Squanto, who had been kidnapped by the villain Hunt. He had been in London, and could speak English. Samoset informed them that four years before a terrible disease had destroyed nearly all the Indians in that region. Massasoit, the chief of the Indians, came with sixty warriors. Governor Carver sent Edward Winslow to meet him, and assure him of the friendship of the Pilgrims. Captain Stand-

WHERE THEY WERE BURIED.

ish, with six men carrying their guns, escorted the chief into one of the houses, and spread out a yellow rug and cushion for a seat. The governor came in state, the drummer beating his drum, the trumpeter blowing a trumpet, attended by all the soldiers with their muskets. The governor and chief kissed each other's hands, then they ate and drank together, and agreed to be friends forever. Massasoit never broke his pledge, neither did the Pilgrims violate theirs; but so long as he lived they were true friends.

Spring came, with its smiling sun; but of the one hundred and one who had landed in December, forty-six were at rest beneath the ground on Burial Hill, with the earth smoothed over them, that the Indians might not count the graves and discover how many had died. They had drooped, one by one, through the hardships of the long passage and want of food.

The Pilgrims caught fish and lobsters, and, when the tide was out, gathered clams along the sandy beach. From the mud-flats they obtain-

PLYMOUTH ROCK.

ed eels. Now and then they killed a deer. They had so little to eat that they staggered, through faintness. When spring came, they planted corn upon the graves of the dead, that the Indians might not discover where they had been buried.

Through these months the *Mayflower* had been swinging at anchor in the harbor, but the time had come for the departure of the vessel.

Though everything wore so gloomy a prospect, though they were so few in number, and death was thinning their ranks, they had no thought of returning to England. Many months would pass before the ship would come back, and none but God knew what might happen the while. The vessel might go down in mid-ocean, and then their friends in England never would hear from them.

With tearful eyes they stood upon the hill above the graves of their loved ones, and saw the white sails fade away. When the ship disappeared, they went calmly about their work. Their destiny was fixed. It is well for the world that such heroic souls have no fear of the future. They might die, but Truth and Liberty were eternal!

The next day after the departure of the *Mayflower* their beloved governor was suddenly taken ill, his sickness ending in death. But the State did not die. The people elected William Bradford as his successor. A new truth dawned upon the world—that so long as there are people to rule themselves, there will be a State.

"WITH TEARFUL EYES THEY SAW THE WHITE SAILS FADE AWAY."

CHAPTER VIII.

FIRST YEARS AT PLYMOUTH.

"THERE can be no lawful marriage without a priest to perform the ceremony: marriage is a sacrament," said the Churches of Rome and England. But the men and women who had established themselves in the wilderness at Cape Cod rejected all ecclesiastical authority. Edward Winslow had laid his beloved wife, Elizabeth, down to sleep on Burial Hill, and Susanna White, with two children—the youngest born while the *Mayflower* was at Cape Cod—had no one to care for her: why should not he be her helper and husband? "You cannot be married without a minister," said the laws of England. "We will be married, as were Boaz and Ruth, in the presence of the people," said the Pilgrims.

So Edward Winslow and widow White joined hands before the newly-elected governor, William Bradford, and were married.

What audacious things that little company were doing! forming a constitution to guide them, electing their own officers, ordaining their own minister, marrying themselves without the aid of minister or priest. What a cutting loose from the customs, traditions, and usurpations of the ages!

They had no laws except of their own making, based on their sense of Justice and Right. No edict from King James could have added anything to the validity of their laws; nor could any high constable make them more effective. They recognized their governor as head of the State, and entitled to honor and respect. On Sunday, Captain Standish, with the trumpeter, drummers, and the settlers carrying their guns, escorted the governor to meeting; not because he was William Bradford, but because he represented what they reverenced—law and order.

When gathered in their little meeting-house, they listened with great respect to William Brewster's preaching, because they had elected him to expound to them the truths of the Bible. William Brewster had no authority except what they had delegated to him: he was their minister, nothing more.

9

Not all of the settlers were Pilgrims. Stephen Hopkins had two servants, who were bound to him for a term of years, and who were foolish enough to attempt to settle a quarrel by fighting a duel with swords,

GOVERNOR BRADFORD'S HOUSE.

which Governor Bradford looked upon as a crime against the peace and dignity of the State. He made the whole community a court, and it was voted that the two be tied neck and heels together for twenty-four hours, with nothing to eat or drink. The Pilgrims could tolerate no duels. If they were quick to punish, they were also tender-hearted; for, when the offenders had endured the punishment one hour, and promised to behave themselves, Governor Bradford ordered their release. In every prison in England and throughout Europe were terrible instruments of torture designed to inflict pain; but reformation, instead of pain, was the Pilgrim's idea of punishment. Governor Bradford was no milksop, but as courageous as he was tender-hearted.

Canonicus, one of the Narragansett Indians, regarded the English as intruders, and tied the skin of a rattle-snake around a bundle of arrows, and sent it to Governor Bradford as a declaration of his hostility. Governor Bradford filled the skin with powder and bullets and sent it back, which so frightened Canonicus that he would not touch it, and it was brought back to the settlement.

Of the one hundred and one who landed from the *Mayflower*, only fifty remained when spring opened. The Indians knew how weak they were, for nearly every day some of the Indians came to see them, and were always kindly treated.

"We never have paid the Indians for the corn which we took on

EDWARD WINSLOW.

Cape Cod," said Governor Bradford; and to make amends, and cement the friendship that had sprung up, he sent Edward Winslow and Stephen Hopkins to make Massasoit a present.

132   OLD TIMES IN THE COLONIES.

With Squanto to guide them, they travelled through the wilderness forty miles. Massasoit was delighted to see them. Winslow and Hopkins saluted him by firing their guns, gave him a red coat trimmed with

PLYMOUTH WILDERNESS.

lace, and put a copper chain around his neck. Massasoit gave them some corn to plant, renewed his agreement to always be their friend, and confirmed it by smoking the pipe of peace. Massasoit had very little to eat.

His wigwam was swarming with fleas, and Winslow and Hopkins were glad enough to get back to the settlement.

Squanto taught the Pilgrims how to plant corn, dropping the kernels in a hill and putting in a herring to fertilize it. The brooks and rivers were alive with fish, and through the summer they had sufficient food, such as it was. Their corn and barley ripened; they dried the fish which they caught; ducks and geese reared their young along the marshes; in the woods were deer and wild turkeys.

Massasoit came one morning with ninety men to visit the Pilgrims. The Indians went into the woods and killed five deer; the Pilgrims contributed fish and corn, and for three days they held a feast, giving thanks to God for all his goodness—the first Thanksgiving in the Western World.

An Indian came to the settlement with the startling news that there was a vessel across the bay, in the harbor at the end of the Cape. And now from the hill the governor could see the white sail; the ship was steering toward them. Was it a French ship? If so, it was an enemy. The settlers were out in the fields and woods.

"Fire a cannon to call them home," was the order of the governor.

The roar of the gun echoed along the shores, and the men and boys seized their guns, ready to fight if need be. Nearer came the ship, with the banner of England floating at the mast-head. It was the *Fortune*, sent out by the London merchants. Robert Cushman and some of their fellow-pilgrims from Holland were on board; also some wild fellows who had come as adventurers. Instead of bringing supplies, of which the settlers were in great need, there was not food enough on the ship to last the crew on their return voyage, and the settlers had to supply them.

Thomas Weston, who thought of nothing but getting great interest on his money, sent a letter complaining that the settlers had not sent him any beaver-skins in the *Mayflower*.

WAMPUM.

The selfish man could not see that the Pilgrims had all they could do to keep soul and body together during the first dreary winter, instead of hunting beaver and catching fish. They had been very industrious, however, so that they were able to load the *Fortune* with lumber and furs to the value of five hundred pounds.

They gave the Indians knives, beads, trinkets, fish-hooks, and blankets in exchange for furs. The Indians used sea-shells strung upon a string for money; they called it "wampum:" its value depended upon the length of the string. It was easy to obtain such money, and its value soon declined.

Christmas came. We think of it as the most delightful day of the year, but the Pilgrims associated it with the Church of Rome, the Jesuits, the Church of England, and with all the persecutions they had endured. They had suffered a great deal at the hands of the Bishop of England, who made Christmas a holy day. The Pilgrims did not so recognize it, and went on with their work. The wild fellows that came in the *Fortune* refused to work.

"It is against our conscience," they said.

"If it is a question of conscience, I will excuse you," said the governor.

The Pilgrims went out into the woods, attending to their labor, but when the governor came home at noon the new-comers were playing ball, and seeing which could throw an iron bar farthest. He took the bar and ball away from them, and ordered them into the house.

"If it is against your conscience to work to-day, it is against my conscience to allow you to play while others work." There could be no fooling with such a governor.

Those plain men and women from Scrooby had become exiles for conscience' sake, and they had discovered a great truth, that no man has a right to control another's convictions of duty and obligations toward God. Popes, bishops, kings, usurped authority over men's convictions; but they recognized the right of every man to think for himself in matters of religion, with due regard in their actions to the rights of others. Governor Bradford respected the scruples of the dissolute fellows who came in the *Fortune*, so long as they regarded Christmas as a holy day; but when they made it a holiday, and began a carouse, it was an offence against the convictions and rights of the community who had elected him their governor, and it was his duty to put a stop to it. It was the rule of the majority. The new State, with no authority from king, bishop, or pope, but from the people, deriving their ideas from the Bible, recognizing what was just and right between man and man, and obligation to God, emancipating itself from the Past, inaugurated its mighty Future.

Thomas Weston, thinking that there was a chance to make money by fishing, and trading with the Indians, sent out forty men at his own expense to make a settlement at Weymouth, twenty miles north of Plymouth; but instead of attending to business they idled their time away. When their provisions failed, they stole the Indians' corn.

To the honest, hard-working men at Plymouth that was not only an

FIRST YEARS AT PLYMOUTH.

offence but a crime. What should they do? Weymouth was outside of their grant, and they had no jurisdiction over the territory; but if the reckless fellows were allowed to go on, would not the Indians rise in their anger, and destroy them all?

If they had no authority from the king to interfere, they had the authority which God gives to every man—that of preserving his own life.

One of the Indians, Witnamit, had already killed two white men, and was planning to massacre all at Plymouth and Weymouth. Governor Bradford ordered Captain Standish to settle matters. He was a small man. He had fought the Spaniards in Holland, and was not afraid of

KITCHEN OF STANDISH HOUSE.

Indians or anybody else. He selected eight men. It is said that he made a bowl of smoking-hot punch before starting.

> "'Twas on a dreary winter's eve, the night was closing dim,
> When old Miles Standish took the bowl and filled it to the brim;
> The little captain stood and stirred the posset with his sword,
> And all his sturdy men-at-arms were ranged about the board."

Captain Standish and his men sailed out of Plymouth harbor, steered north past the rocky shore of Cohasset, entered Massachusetts Bay, and

CAPTAIN STANDISH STIRRING THE PUNCH.

found the *Sparrow*—Mr. Weston's vessel—at anchor, with no one on board. The half-starved men were wandering along the beach searching for clams, or in the woods digging ground-nuts. They were very much frightened when informed of the plans of the Indians to kill them all. The Indians sent a challenge to Captain Standish through Hobbamoc, a friendly Indian who lived with the Pilgrims.

"Tell the captain that we are not afraid of him!" they said, ready for a fight.

Captain Standish gave them all the fighting they wanted. He ran his sword through Teoksnat and Witnamit. His men killed another, and hung a fourth. In all, seven Indians were killed, and their conspiracy was nipped in the bud. It was the sword against the tomahawk. The victory struck the Indians with terror.

FIRST YEARS AT PLYMOUTH.

The Pilgrims supplied Weston's men with food, and sent them back to England.

Captain Wollaston made a settlement not far from Mr. Weston's. One of the colonists was Thomas Morton, a lawyer from London, who came to America to enjoy unrestrained license where no justice of the peace could reach him. The forty men who accompanied him were as reckless as himself. They sold the Indians rum, guns, and ammunition. They set up a pole eighty feet high, with deer-horns on the top, hanging garlands around it on the first day of May, holding a grand revelry, drinking rum, firing their guns, and dancing with the half-naked Indian women. They called the place Merry Mount.

Such revelry was an offence to the staid and sober people at Plymouth. Governor Bradford sent a remonstrance to Morton; but what cared the London lawyer for that? He was beyond the reach of courts of justice, and would carouse as he pleased. He was outside of Governor Bradford's territory and jurisdiction; besides, who was Governor Bradford? He had no commission from the king or anybody else; he was only elected by the people. The people! they had no authority! Ah! a new order of things was beginning in human government, as Thomas Morton soon discovered. Captain Standish and a little handful of reso-

STANDISH'S SWORD, AND THE BARREL OF THE GUN WITH WHICH PHILIP WAS KILLED.

lute men from Plymouth made their appearance at Wollaston. Morton's men were in a log-house. It was strong as a fort; they had plenty of powder, and three hundred bullets. They took a drink of rum, and stood ready to pick off the little captain and his men whenever they should make their appearance. The man who had fought the Spaniards, who had cut off Witnamit's head and carried it in triumph to Plymouth, was not at all afraid of the swaggering lawyer and his drunken crew.

"Surrender, or I will burn the house down over your heads!" he said.

Why did not Thomas Morton bring his gun to his shoulder and put a bullet through Miles Standish? Why did not the drunken crew riddle him in an instant? Because they were cowards, and because they were confronted by law and order. Through all ages people had called the king "*His* Majesty," but now the people themselves were Majesty, exercising authority, and able to deal summarily with Thomas Morton or anybody else.

Did Thomas Morton fire? Oh no; he opened the door, became as meek as a lamb, was marched down to Plymouth, and packed off to England.

Captain Standish had laid his beautiful young wife, Rose, down to sleep on Burial Hill, but why should he live alone? Why not make that sweet girl, Priscilla Mullens, Mrs. Standish? There were wrinkles on his brow; the crows'-feet were gathering in the corners of his eyes; he had seen hard service, been in many a battle; his hair was turning gray. Priscilla was young and fair; perhaps she might say "No." He thought that it would be better to get bashful John Alden, who was about Priscilla's age, to open the matter to her.

"Why don't you speak for yourself, John?" said Priscilla.

So it came about that Priscilla, instead of going over to the hill on the other side of the bay, to be mistress of Captain Standish's house, became Mrs. John Alden. William Bradford—governor, not a minister but a magistrate—bade them join hands, pronounced them husband and wife; and we may believe that they could not have been any happier if a bishop had conducted the ceremony.

The settlers of Plymouth had been knocked about so much that few of them had had any time to acquire knowledge. All could read. All who signed the agreement in the cabin of the *Mayflower* wrote their names in full. William Bradford, William Brewster, and Edward Winslow could speak several languages.

"We have no common school for want of a fit person, or means to maintain one, though we desire now to begin," wrote William Bradford in 1624.

They were poor; were bound by a hard bargain to the London merchants. Half their number had died. They had their houses to build, their corn to plant; everything to do, with none to lend a helping hand. Instead of being helped, twice they had to supply Mr. Weston's ship and his starving men with provisions, and to take care of the sick left on their hands. How could they support a school? The mothers taught the children what they could; but children worked. There were no drones in the hive.

As the years went on, some of the settlers crossed the bay and settled Duxbury. Miles Standish built his house there. Edward Winslow went farther north. The settlements together were known as the "Old Colony." They were kind to the Indians, treating them fairly when buying their beaver-skins, and the Indians treated them kindly in return.

William Bradford
Tho: Prence.
Edw: Winslow
Nathaniell Morton
Willm Brewster
Thomas Cushman
Myles Standish
John Winslow
Isaac Allerton
Constant Southworth
John Bradford
Tho: Southworth

AUTOGRAPHS OF SOME OF THE PILGRIMS.

These were the rules which the Pilgrims hung up in their houses to guide them in the affairs of life:

"Profane no Divine ordinance. Touch no State matters. Urge no healths. Pick no quarrels. Encourage no vice. Repeat no grievances. Reveal no secrets. Maintain no ill opinions. Make no comparisons. Keep no bad company. Make no long meals. Lay no wagers."

In what other age has there been such seed sowing? What will come of it? What sort of institutions—what civilization—what good to the world will spring up from such seed-corn? Time will show.

THE PILGRIM MONUMENT, PLYMOUTH.

CHAPTER IX.

SETTLEMENT OF NEW HAMPSHIRE, NEW YORK, AND CANADA.

CAPTAIN John Mason and Sir Fernando Gorges obtained a grant of land extending from the Kennebec River to the Merrimac, which they called Laconia. Captain Mason took the section between the Pis-

MOUTH OF THE PISCATAQUA—WHALE'S-BACK LIGHT.

cataqua and the Merrimac, extending sixty miles inland, and named it New Hampshire. David Thompson, and Edward and William Hilton, came to make settlements and carry on the fishing business. Mr. Thompson built a house not far from the Piscataqua, and called the place Little Harbor. He laid off a tract of a thousand acres for Captain Mason, who intended to build a great manor-house, and live there like an English lord.

Edward and William Hilton went up the Piscataqua ten miles, and built their houses at Dover: they set their nets in the stream, caught shad and salmon, sailed down the river to a ledge of rocks called the Whale's Back, made trips to the Isle of Shoals, or coasted along the sandy beaches to the Merrimac. They reared their houses in 1623, and were the first settlers in New Hampshire.

While the Hiltons were building their houses on the Piscataqua, a lumbering Dutch vessel was sailing from Amsterdam with a company of men, women, and children, who were looking for the last time upon a city that had given them refuge during days of bitter persecution. Who were they? Years before, when the Jesuits were burning thousands of heretics in the country along the Rhine, the fathers of these men and women left their homes, abandoned their vineyards along the Rhine and Moselle, and fled to Holland for refuge. They called themselves Walloons.

The merchants of Amsterdam, who were with Captain Block when he exhibited his map to John Barneveld, and who had been sending their ships to America, were incorporated as "the West India Company." Their capital was $2,500,000. Their charter gave them all the land they could obtain in America, with power to build war-ships, appoint governors, raise armies, and take any steps they pleased to help on their trade. They were made a great and powerful corporation. Spain and Holland were at war, and the company sent out its armed ships to plunder the Spanish towns in the West Indies and South America. They captured so many ships laden with gold and silver, that in a short time their $2,500,000 became $6,000,000.

The company did not wish, however, to carry on war, but to purchase furs of the Indians. The beads, bits of looking-glass and tin, the bright-colored blankets and knives which the Indians wanted, cost but little, while the furs obtained for them were of great value.

The ship *New Netherlands*, commanded by Cornelius May, was fitted out, and thirty families of Walloons bade farewell to Holland. The ship entered Hudson River; eight families landed on Manhattan. Some of them went up the river, and built a new fort at Albany, which they named Fort Orange.

SETTLEMENT OF NEW HAMPSHIRE, NEW YORK, AND CANADA. 143

Peter Minuet was appointed Governor of New Netherlands. On a bright May morning he met the Indians for a trade. He wanted the island of Manhattan; while they wanted the buttons, beads, and trinkets which he displayed before their longing eyes. The bargain was made, and for twenty-four dollars he obtained the island of Manhattan.

Having purchased the island, he set Krym Frederick to building a battery, upon which were planted several cannon pointing down the harbor, with a palisade protecting the rear, naming it Fort Amsterdam. He built a stone house, thatched it with grass and rushes, in which the

LANDING OF THE WALLOONS.

goods were stored. More vessels came with Walloons, and by midsummer Manhattan contained thirty houses.

It was an Old World and an old time idea that men must be governed by force—by the fear of punishment. The idea had not dawned upon rulers that men would obey laws because laws were good. The trouble was that the laws were not always good; that they were often made not for the people but in the interest of the rulers, who looked upon people as their subjects. Instead of ruling by just and equitable laws, rulers, endeavored to force men to obedience. To this end Governor Minuet erected stocks and pillory in the square at Manhattan.

OLD TIMES IN THE COLONIES.

MANHATTAN.

The grain which the Walloons sowed on the cleared patches of ground grew luxuriantly, and they reaped a grand harvest of wheat, rye, oats, barley, and beans.

The Walloons appointed two of their number as "comforters to the sick," and who read the Bible and led their prayers on Sunday.

Peter Minuet lived in state, with three negro slaves to wait upon him. One day the negroes met an Indian in the woods with a lot of beaver-skins. A thought came to them: why not seize his skins? They had been stolen from Africa by the white men, and were in slavery. Might they not plunder the heathen Indian? They fell upon him, and in the melée the Indian was killed; but his nephew, a little boy, saw the clubs smash his uncle's skull.

"I shall have my revenge!" he said to himself, as he fled through the woods.

The West India Company voted that any member who would send fifty adults to New Netherlands should have sixteen miles of land along

ON THE DELAWARE.

the Hudson River, extending back into the country without limit, and they were to have the title of *Patroon*, or Feudal chief. They were to pay no taxes for ten years; the settlers were to be serfs; the *Patroons* were to have the exclusive right of trade, except in furs. The wives of the serfs were not to spin any yarn, weave any cloth, or manufacture any hats; but the company and the *Patroons* were to have all the profits on the sale of goods upon which they could fix their own prices.

Samuel Godyn and Samuel Bloomaert having turned over the scheme before its adoption, sent a trusty agent to prospect the country, who selected a beautiful region on the south side of Delaware Bay, near Cape Henlopen. A company sent out by the two burghers began a settlement—the

ESPLANADE HILL, QUEBEC.

first in the State of Delaware. Gillis Hosset was governor. He nailed a glittering piece of tin upon a tree, representing the sovereignty of Holland. It shone so brightly, that one of the Indians tore it down and cut it into strips for jewellery. Gillis Hosset, not reflecting that the Indians were like children, that they knew nothing of its meaning, regarded it as an insult and outrage, and put the Indian to death.

The Dutchmen had a great bull-dog, of which the Indians were very much afraid, as the dog always showed his teeth and growled at them. One day, when all the colonists except two were in the field at work, a company of Indians came with beaver-skins as if to open trade, but, watching their opportunity, buried their hatchets in the heads of two men at the trading-house, shot twenty-five arrows into the dog, set the buildings on fire, went into the fields and killed all the others; thus wiping out the settlement.

It was in 1615 that Samuel Champlain set himself to work to build up the empire of New France; years had passed, and instead of an empire there was only a settlement.

At Quebec there was the house which he had built in 1615, and close by were the stores which the traders had built, and around which Indians were ever loitering, looking with longing eyes upon the blankets and trinkets, knives, little mirrors, and tinkling bells, which they could only obtain with skins of the beaver, marten, sable, fox, and other animals.

There was one other building, the chapel of the friars, with its sweet-toned bell tolling for mass or vespers. Within, on the walls, were pictures portraying in bright colors the torments of hell and the bliss of heaven. Overlooking all, upon the cliff, was the fort, and around it fields and gardens.

The whole French population was only about fifty; they were all fur-traders or friars. Some of the fur-traders were Catholics, some Huguenots. The king had forbidden the Huguenots from holding meetings in New France; but the king was far away, and the Huguenots sung and prayed, which gave great offence to the friars.

The company had forbidden all trade with the Indians, except by their permission; but there were sailors on shipboard, and citizens who traded on the sly, to the great vexation of the regular traders. There was constant irritation—everybody picking at everybody.

The Duke de Montmorenci paid eleven thousand crowns for the privilege of being Viceroy of Canada. The river, which pours over a high precipice just below Quebec, and down which the people of the city glide on sleds and sledges in winter, enjoying royal sport, bears his name. He appointed Champlain governor. There was so much trouble between the fur-traders of St. Malo and Rouen, that Montmorenci withdrew their privileges and appointed two Huguenots—William and Emery de Caen—to manage the fur-trade, which was only jumping from the frying-pan into the fire. The old fur-traders refused to give up the privileges by which they were growing rich. They quarrelled with the new-comers. The friars joined with them. Huguenots control the trade with the Indians? Never! One of the friars hastened to France. The Jesuits there were powerful. They besieged the king, who, to make peace, allowed both parties to trade.

The young Duke de Montmorenci, weary of being vice-king of a country which contained only one little miserable village, sold out his

FALLS OF MONTMORENCI.

title to the Duke de Ventadour, his neighbor, who was so religious that he had turned his back on the gay court at Fontainebleau, bade farewell to all the vanities of the world, became a Jesuit priest, and set himself to make New France a country in which the Jesuits should have full control.

Charles Lalemant, M. and Jean de Brebeuf, obeying the order of their superior, sailed for Canada. A little later, Fathers Noirot and De la Noue landed at Quebec.

The two Huguenot traders were singing and praying in public, and the sailors, and some of the laborers which the Jesuits had taken over, flocked to hear them.

"There shall be no more psalm-singing by Huguenots," was the order sent over by the Jesuit viceroy. Champlain could stop their singing, but not their praying.

A great man was wielding affairs in France—Cardinal Richelieu—who saw that, to build up an empire in the New World to checkmate England, vigorous measures must be adopted. He founded the company of "New France," composed of one hundred of the dukes, marquises, and noblemen of France, with merchants and ministers. He placed himself at the head. The king gave them the whole of America, from the Gulf of Mexico to the Arctic Sea—from Newfoundland to the Pacific Ocean. They were to have the monopoly of the fur-trade forever. Already the Indians were crossing from the waters of the Far West, bringing twenty-five thousand beaver-skins per annum to Quebec. The company was to have control of all traffic for fifteen years. The king gave the company two ships of war, armed and equipped. The company made this stipulation, that every person settling in New France was to be a Catholic. None of the hated Huguenots were to be allowed to enter.

Perfect the plan for building up an empire in which there should be no heresy, but where everybody would owe allegiance to the Pope, and where the Jesuits would have complete control of the consciences of men. We think our plans perfect, and so they may be, so far as we are concerned; but there are other plans than ours. No one plan can be independent of all others; but on the contrary our plans are constantly interfered with. Richelieu and the Jesuits had their plans. Charles I. of England and the Duke of Buckingham had theirs. Richelieu undertook to put down the Huguenots; the Duke of Buckingham tried to sustain them. War broke out between the two countries. A Scotchman—William Alexander—had tried to establish a colony in Newfoundland, and he put it into the head of the Duke of Buckingham to send a fleet up the St. Lawrence to seize Quebec. David Kirk, a Huguenot, who had been driven from France, was appointed commander of a fleet which sailed up the river and appeared before Quebec. Champlain could make no resistance,

COURT OF THE WHITE HORSE, FONTAINEBLEAU.

and was compelled to see the flag of France give place to that of England on the fort at Quebec.

For the moment all the plans of Richelieu and the Jesuits were upset; but when peace was brought about, the King of England gave up, and the Jesuits and French began once more to build up an empire in America.

CHAPTER X.

THE PURITAN BEGINNING.

ON March 25th, 1625, James died, and Charles I. became King of England. He thought that he could strengthen himself by marrying the sister of the King of France, Henrietta Maria, a young girl who had played in the garden of the old palace of Fontainebleau, but who knew very little about England or the English people. She was only fifteen, while Charles was old enough to be her father. Charles met her at Dover. She was at breakfast when he arrived, but came down-stairs, kneeled at his feet, intending to say, "Sir, I have come to be commanded by you," but was so frightened she could not recall a word, and was so mortified that she covered her face with her hands and burst into tears; but the king raised her to her feet and kissed them away.

Henrietta was a Catholic, and brought with her a bishop, thirty priests, and a great company of French cooks, servants, chamber-maids, and hangers-on—in all, about four hundred persons. She established the mass in her own chapel, which gave great offence to the people, who had not forgotten the efforts of Bloody Mary to establish popery. The hatred of the Puritans to the Pope was so intense that they would not observe Christmas; the custom, so beautiful and delightful to us, of adorning our homes with evergreens whenever the day comes round, they denounced as idolatrous.

When a man deliberately sets himself to do as he pleases, without any regard for the rights of other men, he is pretty sure to find trouble. Charles attempted such a course of action, and found trouble enough. That determination of his started a train of events which have been of far-reaching influence upon the history of our country. We can only follow a few of them.

There was no written constitution, nor is there now a written constitution in England; but from time to time laws were passed in accordance with customs which former kings had respected, so that by usage it was understood that the king could not collect taxes without the consent

CHRISTMAS.

of Parliament; neither could he put a subject in prison without due process of law. This being so, it followed that the Commons were able to control the king's actions. Charles determined not to submit to any such control; he would do as he pleased.

When James came to the throne, he persecuted the Puritans, compelling William Bradford, and the men and women of Scrooby, and thousands more, to leave the country; but as the years went on there began to be discussions about the Prayer-book, especially about the ritual for bowing and kneeling, adopted in the time of Elizabeth, which made the service much like that of the Church of Rome. Two parties arose —the Ritualists, who accepted the Prayer-book; and the Calvinists, as

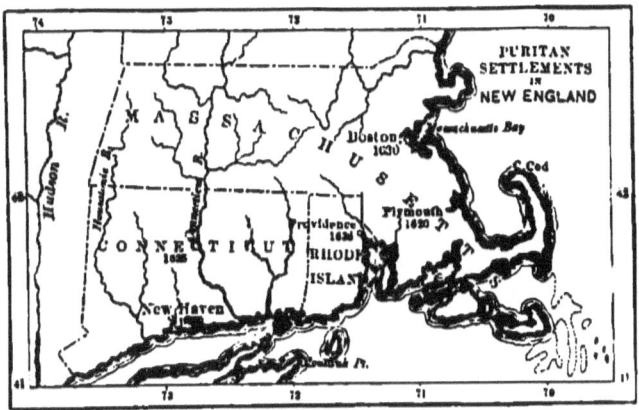

they were called, who adopted the idea of John Calvin, of Geneva. The Calvinists were nearly all Puritans, who wanted the ritual made more simple. Charles sided with the Ritualists, and appointed William Laud to be Archbishop of Canterbury. The bishops whom Laud appointed urged Charles to put down all such doctrines as those taught by the Calvinists.

"Kings receive their authority from God, and not from their subjects; subjects must obey the king's orders, even though they are contrary to acts of Parliament," was the doctrine laid down by the bishops.

"The king needs no act of Parliament for taxation. To oppose the king is to insure eternal damnation!" said Bishop Mainwaring.

Such preaching was pleasing to Charles, who, thus supported, was more determined than ever to have his own way.

Through the years the fishermen of England were catching codfish along the shores of New England; but so much time was lost coming and going, that the merchants of Dorchester, who were fitting out vessels, resolved to build houses on Cape Ann for the fishermen to live in while

GLOUCESTER, MASSACHUSETTS.

the ships were crossing the ocean to and fro. They selected Gloucester harbor as a good place, and built huts along the shore, sending over Roger Conant to manage affairs.

Rev. John White, a Puritan minister in Dorchester, knew that the fishermen must have a lonely time, and became greatly interested in them. Through his influence Rev. John Lyford sailed to Cape Ann, to look after the moral welfare of the fishermen. But the merchants soon discovered that the enterprise did not pay expenses, and the men whom they had employed went back to England—all except Roger Conant, Rev. Mr. Lyford, and one other. Conant was pleased with the country, especially with the region a little south of Gloucester, which the Indians called Naumkeag.

The Dorchester merchants were Puritans. They had lost money; but, if they were to go themselves with their families and cultivate the ground, they thought they might make it profitable. A company was formed, and the members petitioned Charles for a grant of land. Quite likely the king was glad to have them go; but, be that as it may, he complied with the request, and gave them a grant extending from three miles north of Merrimac River to three miles south of the Charles, and westward to the "South Sea." Where the "South Sea" was, no one knew, only that it was far away.

John Endicott, of Dorchester, a member of the company, a stern Puritan—brave, honest, clear-headed, with decided opinions of his own—was elected governor of the colony which they proposed to establish.

In June, 1628, the ship *Abigail*, with John Endicott, his wife, and one hundred colonists, set sail for the beautiful harbor where Roger Conant

JOHN ENDICOTT.

had built his log-cabin. They reached it in safety, and it was so peaceful a place that they named it Salem.

Endicott brought cattle, and garden-seeds, and fruit-trees. One of the pear-trees set out by him is still living; the white-weed which he sowed in his garden, to be used for medicine, has spread pretty much over the country.

While John Endicott was sailing to America, the king, the bishops, and Archbishop Laud were carrying things with a high hand in England. Charles published a declaration, which still stands in the Prayer-book of the English Church in front of the Articles, that no man was to preach or

ENTRANCE TO SALEM HARBOR.

write on doctrines about which men did not agree. Who was to judge? The bishops. What was that but putting manacles upon the intellect and conscience of every man, woman, and child in England? But there were men who would not be thus manacled. Puritan ministers went on preaching their own convictions of what was right and true, and Archbishop Laud and the bishops went to work to silence them. They had a powerful engine for that purpose, called "the Court of High Commission," established by Elizabeth. This court had no power originally to send men to prison; but Archbishop Laud was determined to crush out the Puritans, and the court therefore usurped the power to imprison men. If a minister preached what the bishop did not like; if any one sold a book or pamphlet which contained anything they did not relish, the court condemned them to prison, the whipping-post, the pillory, or to have their ears cropped off and noses slit.

The bishop's officers were soon hunting out offenders, and there was so little comfort for the Puritans that they turned their eyes toward America as a place of refuge.

Charles levied illegal taxes, which greatly offended the people. John

Eliot, a member of Parliament, thinking it time to put a stop to the usurpations of the king, introduced a bill into the House of Commons declaring that whoever should introduce popery, or whoever should levy taxes not granted by Parliament, or whoever should voluntarily pay any such taxes, was to be regarded as an enemy of the country.

"I will not read the paper," said the Speaker of the House, who sided with the king.

"Neither will I," said the clerk.

"I will read it myself, and I demand that it may be put to vote," said John Eliot.

"The king has commanded me not to put it to vote," said the Speaker, and sprung out of the chair; for if any one were to put it to vote while he was in the chair it might be regarded as a legal act. But there were resolute men in the Commons, and the Speaker found himself back in his seat, and held down by two strong men, while Denzil Hollis put the vote.

Charles was very angry, and sent the sheriff, who arrested John Eliot, Denzil Hollis, and the other two members, and put them in the Tower. The king soon had them up before his court, called the Privy Council.

"We will not answer to the Privy Council. We are answerable only to Parliament," they said; and the Commons sustained them.

ENDICOTT'S PEAR-TREE.

"Go home, you vipers! There shall be no more of your meetings while I am king!" said Charles, dissolving Parliament.

Having sent Parliament home, Charles set himself to levying more taxes, selling exclusive privileges to those who would pay him most. He issued an order forbidding everybody from making soap, except the London Soap Makers' Company, who paid him ten thousand pounds for the

CHARLES I.

exclusive privilege, and who agreed to pay him eight pounds for every ton they might manufacture. Everybody was obliged by law to buy that company's soap. The poor washer-women complained bitterly, and went through the streets of London with their wash-tubs, denouncing the soap-makers, and the miserable stuff manufactured by them.

"It rots the clothes!" said one. "It is nothing but lime and tallow!" said another. "It eats our flesh to the bone!" shouted a third.

In order to show what mean stuff it was, and to enlist the sympathy of the people, the women held public washings, trampling the clothes in

OLD-FASHIONED WASHING-MACHINES.

their tubs with their bare feet, or scrubbing them with their hands. The people took their part, and made an outcry which the soap company were obliged to heed.

Charles made every trade and occupation a monopoly, and kept a great company of officers travelling through the country as spies, or to collect revenue; thus providing for an army of place-hunters, who obtained their living by fleecing the people. He issued an order forbidding the building of any more houses in London.

"The city is large enough," he said.

Mr. Moore, not heeding the order, built a house; the Star-chamber ordered him to tear it down before Easter, and because he did not, was condemned to pay two thousand pounds. The sheriff pulled down forty-two houses that had been built near St. Martin's Church. They also destroyed a great many in the country.

The tavern-keepers had to pay roundly for the privilege of keeping a hotel. Some paid six thousand pounds.

Charles wanted money to build ships, and assessed taxes upon land. John Hampden was a plain farmer, and his tax was only twenty shillings, which he could have paid many times over, but it was illegal, and he made up his mind that, come what might, he would not submit to the imposition.

When a man has right on his side he can afford to make a brave fight. Riches, ease, comfort, position in society, the favor of the king, are nothing in comparison with right. Money is of little account, if we did but know it. Fire burns it, thieves steal it. Ease and comfort are delightful, but they are of the present moment, while Right is forever, and by-and-by it is going to conquer Wrong.

John Hampden would not pay his tax, and the case went into the courts, and before the courts were through with it all England was aflame with John Hampden's spirit.

The Puritans had obtained a grant of land from Charles; but they wanted something more—a charter under which they would have authority to govern their colony. Sir Dudley Carleton, who bore the name of Lord Dorchester, was Secretary of State, and the Puritans had no difficulty in obtaining a charter, which, considering that the king had determined to rule England without a Parliament, was a remarkable document. The merchants were incorporated under the name of the "Governor and Company of Massachusetts Bay." They were to choose their own governor, a deputy-governor, and eighteen assistants. The members of the company were called freemen, and four times a year they were to meet in a general court to make such laws as they pleased, that were not in opposition to the laws of England. Here are some of the provisions:

Permission to make their own laws. Choose their own officers. Power to punish all offenders. To pardon. To rule. To require everybody in the colony to take an oath of allegiance to them. Power to expel or punish any one annoying them.

"The king has given us the land, but if the Indians claim it you are to pay them. Let no wrong be shown them," were the instructions of the company to John Endicott. They desired that the Indians should become civilized and Christianized, and for a seal they adopted the figure of an Indian standing erect with an arrow in his hand, and underneath the words, "Come over and help us."

The Puritans were members of the Church of England; they had not, like the Pilgrims, separated from it. It was dear to them, and it cost them a pang to think of turning away from all that they had loved and cherished. When Rev. Francis Higginson, of Leicester, the first Puritan

COSY THE HOMES THEY LEFT BEHIND THEM.

minister who came to America, stood upon the deck of the vessel and saw the old land fading away, he wrote these words:

"We will not say, as the Separatists are wont to say, 'Farewell, Babylon! farewell, Rome!' but we will say, 'Farewell, dear England! Farewell, the Church of God in England, and all the Christian friends there.' We do not go as Separatists from the Church of England, though we cannot but separate from the corruptions of it."

Cosy the homes they left behind them; but, with confidence in themselves and God, they looked forward to the time when they would have equal comforts far from priestly rule.

Little did he know the sorrow that awaited him. Two days later his daughter Mary was down with the small-pox, and when the ship was tossing in mid-ocean the sailors sewed her lifeless body in a shroud and consigned it to the deep.

Before the ship sailed there was a sifting of those on board, and some servants, who were idle, were sent ashore.

"We will have no drones," said the emigrants. There were to be no idle hands in their new homes.

So long as there are human beings there will be differences of opinion, and it is well for the world that it is so; for only by looking at Truth from every side will men attain the highest happiness. What we need to learn is to permit everybody else to exercise the same freedom that we claim for ourselves. When the Puritans began their settlement on Cape Ann, men had only just begun to emancipate themselves from the thraldom of the ages. They were beginning to obtain a glimpse of the principles which underlie Liberty, and made many grievous mistakes. They expected, perhaps, to live in perfect peace, and to have no such trouble as had made life unbearable in England, but forgot that it is impossible for all men to think alike.

Two of the Salem men, John and Samuel Brown, had great reverence for the Prayer-book; and, instead of attending meeting, set up a meeting of their own, and conducted the service. There was a discussion and conflict of opinions and actions. What should be done? John and Samuel Brown were good men, but the Prayer-book was hateful, because the archbishops and bishops were tyrants who had imprisoned Puritans, and cropped off their ears and noses. If the Prayer-book was tolerated, in a very short time there would be a bishop among them, and then good-bye to freedom, peace, happiness, and everything else. A majority decided that the Prayer-book should not be used, and that the Browns were stirring up strife. If the majority were not to rule, there was an end to the colony. Under the charter they had all authority to regulate their own affairs; and as John and Samuel were disturbers of the peace and welfare of the community, Governor Endicott sent them back to England.

The persecutions of the bishops made life so bitter to the Puritans in England that many rich and influential men were desirous of emigrating to America, while others, who were not quite ready to bid farewell to the old home, were willing to help those who needed a helping hand. Mat-

THE PURITAN BEGINNING. 165

thew Cradock, a rich London merchant, gave liberally to fit out ships and otherwise help the emigrants.

One of the men well to do in worldly affairs was John Winthrop, of Groton, a little village in Suffolk County. There his father and grandfather had lived; they had attended service in the old stone church. It was a delightful place; but John Winthrop, though of a calm and even temper, was not the man to sit quietly down and lead an easy do-nothing life in the village of his ancestors, surrendering all his convictions of right, in subservience to the king and bishop. There were hardships, sufferings, and self-denial beyond the sea; but he was ready to accept anything that might come to him, rather than surrender his liberty. In the New World, under the charter which Charles had given, he would do what he could to establish a State in which God should be recognized as sovereign, and the Bible as the rule of man's conduct; in which there should be no worrying of bulls with dogs, or sports on Sunday, but where every man should respect the day, and where all should do what was just and right toward their fellow-men. He was elected governor, to succeed John Endicott.

JOHN WINTHROP.

Eleven vessels were fitted out to transport seven hundred men, women, and children across the Atlantic.

Among the ships purchased was the *Eagle;* but the name was changed to *Arbella,* in honor of Lady Arbella Johnson, sister of the Earl of Lincoln, who, after her marriage to Isaac Johnson, had lived in the town of Boston. Her minister was Rev. John Cotton, who preached in St. Botolph's Church—a grand old edifice, with a stone tower two hundred and eighty feet high, upon the top of which a lantern was displayed at night to light vessels out on the German Ocean into the harbor. It was from the town of Boston that the men of Scrooby attempted to escape to Holland in 1607, and were arrested and thrust into the filthy jail under the shadow of St. Botolph's. So rapidly had some of the ideas of the men of Scrooby advanced, that Rev. John Cotton and thousands of the citizens of Lincolnshire were now ready to follow them to America.

A very important meeting of the Massachusetts Company was held in London, at John Goffe's house, August 28th, 1629.

Matthew Cradock put this question to vote: "Shall the government of the colony be in New England or here? All in favor of transferring it to New England will hold up their hands." The hands were raised.

"It is a vote."

Was it simply the transfer of the management of a company across the ocean of men engaged in buying furs, catching fish, building houses, and opening farms? It was rather the transfer of a commonwealth. It was the beginning of a State. All the authority, all the power that they

GROTON CHURCH.

had desired from the king to make laws and execute them, was transplanted to America by this vote.

Isaac Johnson, Lady Arbella, and John Winthrop were passengers on the *Arbella*.

On the 10th of April they saw the land fade away, and on June 6th they sighted Cape Sable, and then coasted along the shores of Maine.

"NORMAN'S WOE."

The governor made this entry in his journal:

"We had warm, fair weather, and so pleasant and sweet airs as did refresh us, and there came a smell off the shore like the smell of a garden."

Southward they saw the Isles of Shoals, where there was a ship at anchor, the *Lyon*, Captain Pierce, who had been many times on the coast. Beyond the islands they beheld Cape Ann, its white ledges gleaming in the sunlight.

Out from the shore they beheld the waves breaking over "Norman's Woe," where many vessels since then have been wrecked. It was on those ragged ledges that the *Hesperus*, as described by the poet Longfellow, was torn to splinters by the angry sea:

> "Fast through the midnight, dark and drear,
> Through the whistling sleet and snow,
> Like a sheeted ghost the vessel swept
> Toward the reef of Norman's Woe."

The *Arbella* rounded the cape, and sailed proudly into Gloucester harbor. Her anchor was dropped, and the women and children hastened on shore to tread once more the green earth, to pick wild strawberries, and to sit beneath the stately trees. John Endicott arrived in his boat, and Governor Winthrop, Mr. Johnson, and Lady Arbella went with him to Salem, where they sat down to a supper of venison, pastry, and small-beer.

Governor Winthrop and John Endicott sailed down the coast past the cliffs of Marblehead, to find a place where they might build a town. They visited Noddles Island, where Samuel Maverick was living. At Mishawan they found Mr. Walford, who had been living there several years. William Blackstone, an Episcopal minister, who was not a Puritan, but who had left England because he loved solitude, had built a house on a peninsula on the opposite side of Charles River, south of Mishawan. The Indians called the place Shawmut, but the colonists renamed

THE CLIFFS.

it Trimountain, from three hills which dotted the peninsula. Mr. Blackstone had set out an orchard and planted a garden. A sweet spring supplied him with water. He had a library of several hundred books, and for seven or eight years had been enjoying himself far from the turmoil going on in England. Mr. Blackstone wanted them to settle at Trimountain, which was a peninsula with a narrow neck, and which could be easily fortified against the Indians. The Puritans accepted the invitation, and changed the name to Boston. One of the first buildings erected was a meeting-house.

BLACKSTONE'S HOUSE.

Many of the Puritans had lived in affluence in England, and it was a great change to pass from their former spacious mansions to the huts which they reared in the wilderness. Never in Old England had they seen such snows as drifted around them when winter came. Their provisions failed. Meal was so scarce, that one of the colonists wrote this to his friends in England:

"The crumbs of my father's table would be sweet to me. Once I had a peck of corn or thereabouts for a little puppy dog."

He obtained the meal of the Indians, who were very friendly. Sometimes the hunters killed a deer, and that gave them a bit of meat. They caught fish, and when the tide was out, the women and children used to wander along the beach and gather clams; but it was poor fare after what they had been accustomed to, and many sickened and died.

FIRST MEETING-HOUSE IN BOSTON.

Governor Winthrop knew that provisions would be wanted, and engaged the ship *Lyon*, which was at the Isles of Shoals, to hasten to England for supplies.

Months passed. Day after day the famishing people looked seaward to discern, if possible, the returning ship. February 5th, 1631, was a joyful day, for the people saw the *Lyon* sailing into the harbor. Their provisions were almost gone. Governor Winthrop had appointed a day of fasting, but it was changed into one of thanksgiving.

On the *Lyon* was a young minister, Roger Williams—a man of ardent spirit, conscientious, a great lover of liberty—who could not be turned a hair-breadth from doing what he thought was right.

The hardships and sufferings had been so great that, when the flowers bloomed again in spring, more than two hundred of the emigrants were at rest forever in their graves. Among the number were Isaac Johnson and Lady Arbella.

People in distress, with no one but God on whom they can call for help, do not need a prayer-book to make known their wants. Those who saw their loved ones fading away felt how unsatisfying were the prayers which the bishop had written to express their desires. The Pilgrims at Plymouth were getting along without prayer-books. Doctor Fuller, who hastened from Plymouth to help care for the sick, needed no prayer-book to read from as he visited the dying; so by various influences it came about that the colonists discontinued the use of written prayers, and became wholly independent of the Church of England, and, like the Pilgrims, managed their own affairs, calling their ministers; dismissing them when they pleased; electing their governor and his assistants in town-meeting, and conferring upon them authority to make their laws.

STATUE OF GOVERNOR WINTHROP.

CHAPTER XI.

THE PURITANS TAKE POSSESSION OF NEW ENGLAND.

THE Indians who lived on the banks of the Connecticut called it Long River. They heard that there were white men at Boston and Plymouth, and one of them made a visit to Governor Winthrop.

"I will give the white men eighty beaver-skins every year if they will settle on the Long River," he said.

He wanted the fish-hooks, hatchets, blankets, and trinkets which the white men had for sale. Governor Winthrop treated him kindly, but told him that the Boston men could not go so far away.

NANTUCKET.

The Indian visited Plymouth, and Governor Winslow was so impressed with what he had to say about the country that he sailed in the Pilgrim's little vessel around Cape Cod, past the Shoals, past Nantucket—which very few if any white men had visited—past Martha's Vineyard and Block Island, and along the Narragansett shore to the beautiful stream, beholding fertile meadows, rounded hills, stately forest-trees, and hanging vines. There were myriads of fish in the river, and the beaver were abundant along the smaller streams. He returned to Plymouth, resolving to take possession of the valley.

He had but just turned the prow of his vessel eastward when a sail appeared in the west—a Dutch ship from Manhattan, with John Van Corlear and six men on board, sent by Wouter van Twiller to occupy the country. The lumbering craft made its way up the stream as far as Hartford, where Van Corlear built a little fort, which he called Good Hope.

The summer passed, October came, and once more the Plymouth vessel was sailing up the Connecticut, with William Holmes and a company of resolute Pilgrims on board. Van Corlear was amazed when he saw the little vessel gliding defiantly up stream, all sails set to catch the favoring wind.

"Stop!" he shouted.

"I have a commission from Governor Winslow to go up the river," was the answer of Captain Holmes.

"Haul down your colors, or I will fire!" cried Van Corlear.

"I am ordered to go up the river, and am going!" Holmes replied; and before the Dutchmen could get over their astonishment at such audacity, Captain Holmes was out of sight. He landed at Windsor, put up a house, built a palisade around it, with loop-holes in the walls, and opened trade with the Indians.

Wouter van Twiller was astounded when he heard of it. Plymouth men buying beaver-skins under his nose, as it were! He would put a stop to it. He sent seventy men to Van Corlear, with orders to drive them out of the valley. With drums beating and banners flying, the Dutch marched from Fort Good Hope to Windsor.

"You must leave here!" shouted Van Corlear to Captain Holmes.

"I am ordered to stay here, and intend to obey orders!" said Holmes.

"I shall open fire upon you, and tear down your house," said Van Corlear.

"I shall return your fire!" said Holmes.

No doubt John Van Coriear was a brave man, but his men did not like the looks of those muskets peeping through the loop-holes, and refused to begin the fight. Van Corlear thought the matter over, and concluded that it would be better to let Wouter van Twiller settle the matter peacefully, rather than shed his blood for a few beaver-skins, and marched his men back to Good Hope. So it came about that the English and Dutch both obtained a foothold in the Connecticut valley in 1633.

Three years before this little flurry the Plymouth Company in Eng-

THE PURITANS TAKE POSSESSION OF NEW ENGLAND.

land had given the land, from Narragansett Bay northward to the Massachusetts line, and westward to the Pacific Ocean, to the Earl of Warwick. The gift took no notice of the Dutch on the Hudson. The Earl of Warwick, in turn, transferred it to Lord Say-and-Seal and Lord Brooke.

The Dutch claimed to have purchased it of the Pequod Indians. They did not care anything about cultivating the land; they only wanted to buy beaver-skins.

Who should have it—the Dutch or English? The people of Massachusetts settled the question. Emigrants were leaving England by the thousand, and settling along the coast of Massachusetts. A colony from Newbury, in England, had selected a beautiful site on the south bank of the Merrimac, and named it for their old home. Another colony from Salisbury had looked for the last time on the lofty spire of their grand old cathedral, and had settled a new Salisbury on the north bank of the Merrimac.

South of Newbury the settlers from Ipswich had started a new Ips-

COHASSET HARBOR.

wich. South of Boston the settlers from Dorchester had begun a new Dorchester. There were emigrants at Cohasset, at Hingham, up the Charles River, at Newton, Watertown, and Brookline.

The settlers in Boston wanted more pasturage for their cattle. They heard of the fertility of the Connecticut Valley, and in October, 1635, nearly sixty of them, with their wives, children, and cattle, started on

OLD MEETING-HOUSE, HINGHAM.

their journey to begin a settlement. No Englishman had ever threaded the pathless wilds. It was a wearisome journey. There were hills to climb, and streams to cross. The bright-colored leaves were falling; the chill winds of autumn swept through the forest; the rains were cold. There were many obstacles—rocks and fallen trees. Winter had set in before they reached the Connecticut, and they must construct rafts before they could cross. In December they reared their log-cabins on the western bank, and called the place Hartford. The snow fell, whirled by the wind into blinding drifts. Their cattle had nothing to eat, and began to die. Provisions failed. A vessel which was to have reached them did not come. The river froze. Death stared them in the face. They ate the bark of trees, scraped the snow from the ground beneath the oak-trees in search of acorns. The Indians were kind, and sold them a little corn; but they saw that if they attempted to remain, all would die of starvation. Some of them started through the forest; others went down the river and found a small vessel frozen in the ice, but it was two days before they could cut a channel with their axes to clear water; but they reached it, and, with almost the last morsel of food gone, reached their old homes.

The men of Massachusetts who had suffered such hardships in their journey gave glowing reports of the valley—of its wide meadows and fertile soil—and when spring opened a second party started to occupy the fertile acres. Their minister, Rev. Thomas Hooker, went with them. He had been an eloquent preacher in England. Earls and nobles often travelled many miles to hear him. He was as good as he was eloquent, but, because he could not conscientiously use the form of service which the bishop had prescribed, had been driven out of England. He had been at Cambridge, Mass., two years, and was greatly beloved. The flowers were in bloom, and the forest clothed in its richest verdure in June, when Rev. Mr. Hooker and his company, with their wives and children— one hundred in all—and cattle and sheep, struck out into the wilderness, travelling, as the compass guided them, through swamps, over hills, and across rivers. The men carried heavy packs on their backs. Some of the women walked, carrying infants in their arms. Mrs. Hooker was weak,

EMIGRANTS AT NIGHT.

and rode in a litter. The boys and girls drove the cattle and sheep, while their fathers cleared the way with their axes. Feather-beds were strapped upon the backs of the cattle and horses, together with pots and kettles. At night great fires were kindled beneath the trees. Morning and evening they had prayers. Two weeks passed before they reached the beautiful stream and began to rear their homes. It was midsummer. There were myriads of salmon and shad in the river; the woods were full of turkeys, pigeons, and herds of deer; the meadows green with grass. Amidst such riches of nature, and with such a company, began the settlement of Connecticut.

LADY FENWICK'S TOMB.

Charles I. was carrying things with so high a hand in England that John Hampden and his cousin, Oliver Cromwell, resolved to emigrate to Connecticut. They sent out young John Winthrop, son of the Governor of Massachusetts, to make a beginning. He built a fort on the west bank of the Connecticut at its mouth, and named it Saybrook. A little colony was started, and John Winthrop, Jr., was elected governor.

Hampden and Cromwell were ready to leave England. The vessels were in the Thames, at London, with their goods on board, when the king, exercising his arbitrary authority, stopped them. Far better for him if he had permitted their departure. One of the gentlemen who came with John Winthrop was Colonel Fenwick, who was accompanied by his beautiful young wife, Lady Alice. What a change it was for her, to leave the old country home, with all its luxury and refinement, and make her home in a log-cabin inside the fort at Saybrook! But she was always light-hearted. She knew how to fire a gun, and could ride horseback at a breakneck speed. She tamed the rabbits: the squirrels were her friends. She was the life of the little company while she lived. She died in 1648. Matthew Griswold erected a memorial stone above her grave. Her husband went back to England, and was one of the judges that condemned Charles I. to death.

The Pequod Indians lived along the sea-shore, east of Connecticut River. They occupied a fine country. In the woods were deer, turkeys, and pigeons; in the rivers salmon, shad, and alewives. In calm weather they paddled their canoes along shore, and caught cod and mackerel.

The bravest and proudest of the Pequods was Sassacus, lord of twenty-six sachems. He built two forts for the safety of the tribe; one was on a hill near Mystic River, the other near Connecticut River.

Sassacus was a statesman, and saw that sooner or later the English would be in possession of their hunting-grounds. The English were at Saybrook, at Weathersfield, Hartford, Windsor, and Springfield; they were in Rhode Island, and all along the shore to Plymouth, Boston, and Piscataqua. How long would it be before there would be no more deer in the woods, and no more flocks of turkeys? Quite likely, if we had been in Sassacus's place, seeing people from a foreign country taking possession of all the beautiful lands, we might have resolved, as he resolved, to make war upon them. He knew very little of natural rights, or that the only right which men can have in land is in its cultivation. Sassacus knew nothing of physical or moral laws. He was in possession of the lands of his fathers; they were his. Why should he not drive out the English? Relying upon the power and bravery of his warriors, he resolved to make war upon the English. He began by inciting his followers to murder Captain Stone, and the crew of a vessel, ten in all, who had come from Virginia to Connecticut to trade. The Governor of Massachusetts demanded the surrender and punishment of the murderer, but Sassacus put him off with fair speeches, and the murderers were not surrendered.

On a midsummer's day, 1636, John Gallup, with another man and two boys, were sailing past Block Island, when they discovered a vessel moving about strangely, as if those on board did not know how to manage the craft. Getting nearer, they saw that the deck was crowded with Indians. They knew that John Oldham, of Watertown, Massachusetts, was on a trading-cruise to Connecticut, and that this was his vessel. What should they do? There were fourteen Indians on

WILD TURKEYS.

INDIAN ROCK, NARRAGANSETT.

board, armed with bows, arrows, spears, and guns. John Gallup was brave. He had two guns, two pistols, and some shot, but no balls. They were four against fourteen; but they ran along-side, and so peppered the Indians with shot that they all crept beneath the hatches.

"Run them down!" shouted Gallup to the boy at the helm of his vessel. The wind filled the main-sail, and the prow came against the hulk of the other with a thump, which so frightened the Indians that six of them leaped into the sea. There came a second thump, and four Indians sprung overboard. Gallup leaped on board the vessel, and two of the Indians gave themselves up as prisoners. The other two would not come out from the hold, and he shut the hatches upon them. He found Oldham's body on board, still warm, the head split open, and feet and hands chopped off!

The Governor of Massachusetts sent John Endicott and Captain John Underhill to chastise the Indians. They burnt the wigwams of those on Block Island, and then sailed over to the main-land, burning more wigwams, and had a skirmish with the Indians, killing and wounding nearly forty.

Sassacus had been at war with the Narragansetts, but had made peace with them, and tried to enlist them on his side; but Governor Winthrop sent for Miantonoma and some of the other chiefs, who visited Boston and were kindly entertained, and who made a treaty of peace and friendship with the English. The Pequods began war on the English along the Connecticut River. They killed a man close to Saybrook fort. A few days after, in October, they captured two men in a boat, cutting off their feet and hands, gashing their flesh with knives, and filling the gashes with hot ashes! They killed the settlers' cattle, and burnt their hay-stacks. In February, 1737, ten men at work were waylaid and three of them killed: two were captured—their bodies split open and hung upon the trees. A man from Wethersfield was roasted alive! The Indians attacked that town, killed seven men, a woman, a child, and carried away two girls. The girls were not harmed, however, for the wife of the chief Mononotto became their friend and protected them.

The magistrates of Wethersfield, Hartford, and Windsor met in council. What should they do? Thirty English had been killed. War was upon them. They were two hundred and fifty fighting men against one thousand Pequods. A messenger was sent to Boston and Plymouth asking for aid. Massachusetts voted to send one hundred and sixty men, and Plymouth forty. Connecticut determined to act with vigor. Ninety men marched at once. Captain John Mason, who had fought against the Spaniards in Holland, commanded them. Seventy Mohegans joined them. Once they had paid tribute to the Pequods, but their chief, Uncas, had rebelled, and had placed himself under the protection of the English.

The grass was springing fresh and green on the 10th of May, when they dropped down the Connecticut from Wethersfield in their little vessels. The Pequods were on the hills, and shouted defiantly as they floated past. They reached Fort Saybrook, and were glad to find that Captain John Underhill had arrived with twenty men from Massachusetts. They were fearful that the Indians would fall upon their settlement in their absence and murder their wives and children, so twenty were sent back to protect them. Captain Underhill joined the expedition.

"You are to land at Pequod Harbor," was the order which Captain Mason had received from the magistrate. Should he obey it? The Pequods were there, ready for him. Why land where they wanted him to? "Never go where your enemy wishes you to go," was the maxim of Napoleon. Captain Mason thought it out one hundred and fifty years before Napoleon was born. The other officers thought they must obey the order of the magistrate. They believed in obedience; it was a duty. "We will ask Rev. Mr. Stone to pray over it," said Captain Mason. Rev. Mr. Stone was a man of sense as well as of prayer, and the next morning he declared Captain Mason's plan was the one to follow.

The little fleet sailed out upon Long Island Sound eastward. The Pequods behold the white sails disappearing in the distance. They shout, leap, and brandish their tomahawks. The English are afraid. They are on their way to Boston. They do not dare to fight.

Eastward all day Saturday sailed the vessels, dropping anchor at last in a harbor a short distance west of Point Judith. No one thought of marching Sunday; it was the Lord's-day. Monday was stormy, and the waves so high that they could not approach the shore. Tuesday evening they landed on a pebbled beach. Canonicus came with two hundred Narragansetts, and an Indian who had run all the way from Providence to inform Captain Mason that Captain Patrick with men from Massachusetts were on their way, but Captain Mason would not wait; he intended to surprise the Pequods. He had executed a flank movement, and would take them in the rear. They expected him to attack from the west; they thought that he had fled; but he would fall upon them from the east. It was forty miles to the fort that overlooked the beautiful

WHERE THEY LANDED.

harbor of Mystic. There were rivers to cross; there were rocks and fallen trees in the way, but onward moved the determined band, the Narragansetts and Mohegans in front, boasting of what they would do.

"Indians brave, white men afraid!" they said. Fifteen miles brought them to a fort of the Narragansetts, who would not permit the English to enter it. Captain Mason had his eyes open. If the Indians would not permit him to go into it, no Indian should come out of it during the night, to steal away and inform the Pequods that he was on the march. He surrounded it with sentinels.

The next night brought them within five miles of the Pequod fort. At sunset they came to a halt, threw themselves upon the ground, and ate their supper in silence. The Mohegans and Narragansetts who had been so boastful, who led off so bravely, dropped behind, saying nothing now as to what daring deeds they would do.

Once more the little band moved on in silence and in single file, till they could hear the Indian drums beating in the fort, and the shouts of the warriors, who were dancing in savage glee over the cowardice of the English. They are thinking of the scalps and plunder they will take when they fall upon the defenceless settlers.

"Halt!" The whisper runs down the line, and the men under Captain Mason drop upon the ground, sentinels keeping watch while the others sleep.

It is two o'clock, May 24th, and Captain Mason awakes the sleepers. The full-moon is riding in the heavens, and daylight will soon be streaming up the eastern sky. The soldiers uncover their heads while the chaplain prays, and then in silence they move on. The sounds of revelry have died away. There are no Indian sentinels keeping watch in the fort that crowns the summit of the hill. There are two entrances, one on the eastern and the other on the western side, with two rows of wigwams within. The Indians are sleeping soundly; their dogs have quicker ears than they; one barks. An Indian hears a commotion; the truth flashes upon him.

"*Owanux! Owanux!*"—"English! English!" he shouts.

Captain Mason and sixteen men are inside the palisade, and Captain Underhill and his men are coming in on the opposite side. The warriors rush out of their wigwams. The muskets flash, arrows fly. Mason drives them against Underhill, and Underhill drives them back again.

"Burn them!" Mason shouts, and springs into a wigwam and takes up a firebrand. A warrior draws his bow to send an arrow through his heart, but a soldier swings his sword and cuts the bowstring. The captain holds the brand against the wigwam, and in an instant it is ablaze. The wind sweeps the fire down the line of wigwams. There are six hundred Indians in the fort—warriors, squaws, and papooses. Humanity has no place in this fight. Old and young alike go down—some shot, others cut down by the sword, others roasted in the flames. The Mohegans and Narragansetts who have been outside the fort come in and finish the work. Seven escape, and seven only are taken prisoners. When the sun rises, its beams fall upon nearly six hundred ghastly corpses blackened by the flames. Two of the English have been killed, twenty wounded, out of the seventy-seven composing the party. It was a narrow escape, that of Lieutenant Bull's—the piece of hard cheese he had in his pocket stopping the arrow. John Dyer and Thomas Stiles each had arrows shot through their neck-cloths.

It was only a few miles to the other fort, but Captain Mason could not go over to attack it. His provisions were gone, his men exhausted. One-third were wounded or broken down. He must carry them to the vessels, which were miles away. He knew that the warriors of the other fort would soon be upon him, and wisely began his return. The

NEW HAVEN.

Indians of the other fort made their appearance. The forest echoed their howlings; but Captain Mason, hiring the Narragansetts to carry the wounded, kept them at bay, and reached the sea-shore. The vessels came and took them on board, bearing them safely to their homes.

A great blow had been struck. The Pequods lost all heart. Sassacus fled, and was killed by the Mohawks. In a few weeks the once powerful tribe was widely dispersed. Some of the captives were taken to the West Indies and sold into slavery by the Massachusetts people. No one questioned the rightfulness of such an act. If it was right to enslave negroes, why was it not right to sell Indians taken in war?

The blow struck terror to the heart of every Indian in New England; and for a long period the settlers lived in peace and security in the Connecticut Valley, and everywhere else east of the Hudson River.

The next year Theophilus Eaton and Rev. John Davenport, of London, with a party of colonists, settled New Haven. They were rich, and purchased the land of the Indians. They agreed that only members of the church should have any voice in public affairs. They chose Eaton for their governor.

Thus it came about that there were three distinct colonies in Connecticut—Saybrook, New Haven, and Hartford. Windsor and Wethersfield joined Hartford in establishing a government, and, in contrast to the New Haven Colony, agreed that everybody who had a good character should be allowed to vote. It was a government of all the people—the first in America. So, after ages of bondage, the human race arrived at the consummation of the grand idea that all men should have a voice in government.

CHAPTER XII.

RHODE ISLAND AND NEW HAMPSHIRE.

CHARLES I. and Archbishop Laud made life so bitter to the Puritans of England, that many thousands crossed the ocean and settled in New England. The king and archbishop were determined that everybody should accept the Prayer-book. They sent a minister to Edinburgh to force it upon the people of Scotland. When he undertook to read prayers in the cathedral, Jennie Geddis let fly a three-legged stool at his head. "What! ye villain! Will you say mass here!" she shouted.

HARVARD COLLEGE, 1720.

"Stone him! stone him!" cried the people, and the minister had to run for his life.

In a short time all Scotland was in an uproar, and a little later all England, and John Hampden, John Pym, and Oliver Cromwell had a hand in public affairs. Between 1629 and 1639 more than twenty thousand Puritans left England, and settled in Massachusetts and Connecticut.

"We must have a school, that our children may not grow up in ignorance," said the people around Boston. The general court voted to es-

GENERAL VIEW OF THE UNIVERSITY BUILDINGS, CAMBRIDGE.

tablish one, which was opened in Cambridge, 1638—the first in America. John Harvard, the minister of Charlestown, seeing the needs of the people, and taking a long look ahead, gave half of his property—about eight hundred pounds—and his library to the school; and the people, reverencing his memory, named it Harvard College.

Joseph Glover started from England with a printing-press and type, but died before reaching America, and Stephen Daye took charge of the press. The oath which men took when they became voters was the first printing in America. The first pamphlet was an Almanac for 1639. The next year, 1640, John Eliot and Thomas Welde translated the Psalms in metre, and Thomas Daye printed them, making a volume of three hundred pages—the first book printed in America north of Mexico.

Among the people who arrived in Massachusetts was a young minister, Roger Williams, and his wife. He had been educated at Cambridge. He was exceedingly conscientious, and so staunch a Puritan that the officers of Archbishop Laud compelled him to flee from England. He went to Plymouth, preached awhile, and visited the Narragansett Indians. He was kind-hearted, and they welcomed him as a friend. From the wigwams of the Indians he went to Salem to preach. He had an intense hatred of the Pope and all the superstitions of the Church of Rome; and he so stirred up John Endicott, who was captain of the militia, that one day, when the soldiers were drilling, Endicott run his sword through the flag and cut out the cross, because it was an emblem of superstition.

Mr. Williams maintained that the settlers had no right to occupy their lands. "King James," he said, "never owned the land in America. He never purchased it; never paid the Indians anything for it. Though he had given it to the colonists, he had no right to do so; and the colonists had no title."

This was calling in question not only their title to land, but everything else. Such an opinion sounded very much like treason. He was called to account by the governor, and promised to burn a pamphlet which he had written, thus making amends.

During Queen Elizabeth's reign a law had been passed that compelled everybody to attend church. James I. re-enacted the law. The men of Scrooby who would not obey it had been driven out of England to Holland, and from thence to Plymouth. The Puritans of England were just as strenuous as the king and the archbishop that everybody must go to meeting on Sunday. The Puritans who settled in Massachusetts and Connecticut re-enacted the law, but Mr. Williams disputed their right to do so.

"It is contrary to the liberty of conscience," he said. "Under it no man can be truly free. No man should be forced to attend worship or maintain worship against his own free consent."

He was right; and Elizabeth, James, and his fellow-Puritans were wrong. Through all past ages everybody had been wrong.

"Is not the laborer worthy of his hire?" asked the magistrates.

"Yes, from those who hire him," said Mr. Williams.

The justices of peace and the officers of government were selected from the members of the church.

"Do you employ a doctor because he is a member of the church, or because he is a good physician? Do you trust your ship to the pilot because he is a member of the church, or because he knows where the rocks are, and how to avoid them?"

"It is the duty of the officers to guard the people from error and heresy," said his opponents.

"The officers are the people's agents. Conscience belongs to the individual: it is not public property. The civil officer has nothing to do with conscience," Mr. Williams replied.

Never before had such an idea been advanced. The Puritans loved liberty, and their ideas of what constituted liberty were far in advance of those held by the bishop and nobility of England; but Mr. Williams could see what his fellow-Puritans could not discern—that neither the governor nor the justice of the peace had anything to do with the religious beliefs of men. Mr. Williams had promulgated a great truth which they could not understand; but he was not always right in his thinking or wise in his actions. The governor under the charter had authority to require every settler to take the oath of allegiance. Mr. Williams disputed that right, and said it was also a violation of the liberty of conscience.

Instead of continuing to preach to the people of Salem, he sent them a letter informing them that he would not preach in the meeting-house any more, nor should he have anything to do with the churches; for they were defiled by hypocrisy and worldliness, and they were false worshippers. The ministers were false teachers, and their doctrine corrupt. Unless the Salem people were ready to leave their church and follow him, he should preach to them no longer. He preached in his own house, but not in the meeting-house.

What should the governor, the magistrates, and his fellow-ministers do? Mr. Williams was defying authority, and stirring up trouble. If permitted to go on, the community would be divided into factions. If authority were overthrown, there would be anarchy. He was a good man, conscientious, self-denying, tenacious of his views, thinking that he was right and everybody else wrong. The ministers, the governor, and his assistants were equally conscientious. For the peace and harmony of the colony, it would be best to send him to England, as they had a right to do under the charter; but while they were deliberating Mr. Williams disappeared from Salem.

It was midwinter; but rather than be sent back to England he went out into the wilderness, wandering through deep snows, sleeping at night in hollow trees, finding shelter and food in the wigwams of the Indians.

Governor Bradford at Plymouth learned that he was with the Indians, and sent him a kind letter. Five friends joined him. He began to build a house at Seekonk; but Governor Bradford informed him that the location which he had chosen was within the boundary of Massachusetts, and advised him to go beyond it. Mr. Williams thought it wise to do so. He and his friends paddled their canoes down the Pawtucket River to the country of the Narragansetts.

"Welcome! wel-

WHERE ROGER WILLIAMS LANDED.

come!" said his old friends, the Indians. He landed upon a lovely spot, where a spring of pure water bubbled from the ground.

"Here we will make our home," said Mr. Williams, naming the place Providence, in acknowledgment of God's providential care.

Canonicus, chief of the Narragansetts, gave Mr. Williams a tract of land; but he was so large-hearted that he gave farms to all who wanted to build a home.

"I desire that it may be a shelter for persons distressed for conscience," he said.

People who had suffered persecution in England, and who did not like the rule of the Puritans in Massachusetts, flocked to Mr. Williams's

RESIDENCE OF GOVERNOR CODDINGTON, NEWPORT, 1641.

settlement, where they could do pretty much as they pleased. Mr. Williams persuaded Miantonoma, one of the Narragansett chiefs, to give the island of Aquidneck to William Coddington.

No matter what opinions a man held, he was welcome in Mr. Williams's settlement, and also in the town laid out in 1639 by William Coddington, which he called Newport.

The settlers knew that law and order were necessary for the prosperity of every community, and held a meeting in which everybody voted, declaring that all should have liberty of conscience forever; that they would obey the laws which the men whom they selected for that purpose might make. They were aware that they needed something more to give themselves a standing in the world—a charter.

The other colonies would not recognize them as a colony. To obtain a charter they sent Roger Williams to England, who, through the influence of Sir Henry Vane, obtained one from Parliament, which was fighting King Charles.

What a joyful day it was when Mr. Williams returned with it! When he reached Seekonk he found the river full of canoes. The whole settlement came to welcome him, and escorted him to his home.

Many people who were discontented otherwheres—in England, Massachusetts, and Connecticut—emigrated to Rhode Island, but not always to find peace. Some people have discontented natures, and are restless wherever they may be. They are not happy unless they are making it hot for themselves or somebody else. There were such people in Rhode Island, who were ever having a war of words with their neighbors. They had fierce discussions at town-meetings; but they had no tithes or taxes to pay, to support a minister who might preach what they did not believe. Whatever was given for religious worship was a voluntary contribution.

What a step it was! Nearly two hundred and fifty years have passed away, and England, the birthplace of every one of those settlers of Rhode Island, has not yet attained the grand ideal which put forth its first blossoms along the peaceful waters of Narragansett Bay!

The good minister, John Cotton, who preached in St. Botolph's Church, Boston, England, to whom Isaac Johnson and Lady Arbella had listened to for so many years, could preach there no longer. Archbishop

OLD-TIME HOUSES, NEWPORT.

Laud was hunting him down, because he would not conform to the ritual. He was hiding here and there, fleeing by night from place to place, making his way to London, and from there to Boston, in Massachusetts.

One of his parishioners, Mrs. Ann Hutchinson, so loved to hear him preach that she followed him to America with her husband. Mrs. Hutchinson was good and kind-hearted. Her old neighbors missed her, for when anybody was sick and needed help she was ever ready to assist them.

Mrs. Hutchinson had opinions of her own. She believed that the Holy Spirit told her just what to do every day in all the affairs of life. She maintained that there were two classes of Christians—the sound and the unsound; the sound were those who accepted her belief. She was living by grace, while those who did not believe with her were living by works. She was very charitable toward the poor and sick, and quick to

NEWPORT, FROM FORT ADAMS.

relieve their wants, but she used hard words toward those who differed from her opinion. Mrs. Hutchinson did not like the ministers of Boston and Charlestown, who preached against her doctrine, and called them "Unchristian vipers," and invited the neighbors in to discuss their sermons. In a very short time many were of her way of thinking, including Rev. Mr. Cotton and Sir Henry Vane, the handsome young governor just arrived from England.

Rev. John Wheelright, who, when a boy, attended school with Oliver Cromwell, and played foot-ball with him and became his fast friend, was minister at Dorchester. He was Mrs. Hutchinson's brother, and accepted her teachings. Mrs. Hutchinson, like Roger Williams, took great pleasure in holding an argument with somebody. Rev. Mr. Cotton liked to argue, and in a short time everybody in Boston and the surrounding settlements was discussing "grace and works." The community divided into two parties. Mr. Wheelright preached a sermon in which he used expressions which his fellow-ministers thought were calculated to create a disturbance. The magistrates held a court, and declared him guilty of sedition. Governor Vane protested; but the magistrates rejected his protest, whereupon he resigned and went to England. Election came on, and one great question before the people was of "Works against Grace." The ministers preached, and the people talked. Everybody discussed theology. They had been educated under bigotry and intolerance. The tyranny of the bishops had driven them out of England; and it was not possible for either Mrs. Hutchinson, Rev. Mr. Wheelright, John Endicott, John Cotton, John Winthrop, or anybody else to discuss the question calmly, or to exercise charity. The ministers used hard words in the pulpits. The people repeated them as they argued the questions by the blazing fires during the long winter evenings. Bitterness and hate sprung up between old friends as the controversy went on. The election was held, and Mrs. Hutchinson and her friends were defeated. The magistrates would put up with her no longer, or Rev. Mr. Wheelright, and ordered them to leave the colony. Mr. Wheelright was not a man to stay and make trouble, after the people had turned against him. He had his convictions of what was right. He would not go to Rhode Island, where there were so many discontented spirits; but, with Mrs. Hutchin-

son, went north to New Hampshire, sailed up the Piscataqua, purchased land of the Indians and made a settlement, naming it Exeter. Mr. Wheelright's friends joined him. They chose one of their number governor, appointed men to assist him, and all took an oath to obey whatever laws might be passed.

The people of Dover did the same, also those of Portsmouth. They were so few in number that they thought best to unite with Massachusetts, each town having the privilege of sending two representatives to the General Court; and so for thirty-eight years New Hampshire was under the jurisdiction of Massachusetts.

There were troublesome times in England between the king and the people. The great struggle for liberty was beginning. Governor Winthrop and the far-sighted men in Massachusetts were wondering what might come of it.

What if the Spaniards or French were to take advantage of England's disorder, and pounce upon the American settlements? He saw that the colonies might be united. Plymouth, New Hampshire, and Connecticut joined in the plan; commissioners from each, meeting in May, 1643, agreeing to stand by each other to defend themselves, and to make war if need be, each to pay its proportion of expense. They were to meet annually. They took the name of the "*United Colonies of New England.*" It was the beginning of the American Union, and of the first Congress in the Western hemisphere.

CHAPTER XIII.

AFFAIRS AT MANHATTAN.

THE *Zouterberg*, one of the West India Company's ships, with Wouter van Twiller, the new governor of New Netherlands, on board, dropped anchor in the harbor of Manhattan in April, 1633. The cannon on the battery and on the ship thundered a salute, the trumpeter blew a blast, the drums beat, the soldiers presented arms, as the short, dumpy governor, five burghers, who were to be his councillors, Rev. Mr. Bogardus, the dominie, and the school-master, Adam Roelandsen, stepped on

MANHATTAN.

shore. Casks of wine were tapped, and everybody in Manhattan drank the health of Wouter van Twiller.

Another vessel arrived, commanded by Captain De Vries, who reported to Governor Van Twiller that the Indians of the Delaware, who had killed Giles Hosset and the men with him, had been pacified, and that the traders would not be molested. So the new governor began his administration of affairs under favorable auspices.

WOUTER VAN TWILLER SWEARING GREAT DUTCH OATHS.

Still another vessel arrived, an English ship commanded by Captain Jacob Eelkins, who had founded the Dutch settlement at Albany, but who had been dismissed from the service of the West India Company. His ship, the *William*, dropped anchor, and Captain Eelkins invited Governor Van Twiller and the burghers on board to a sumptuous dinner. Captain Eelkins brought out his best wines, but kept his own counsel. The dinner over, the governor went on shore, and was greatly astonished, soon after landing, to see the English ship hoisting her sails and moving up the river, bound for Albany. Captain Eelkins was intending to trade with the Indians without leave or license.

"Get the cannon ready!" shouted the governor, and the soldiers wheeled the cannon into position and loaded it.

"Run up the flag!" cried Van Twiller.

Bang! went the gun. The governor expected to see the English ship haul down her sails and come to anchor, but Captain Eelkins ran up his flag instead, and fired a gun as if returning a salute.

Wouter van Twiller was dumfounded.

"Bring out a cask of wine," he cried, and the soldiers rolled out a cask and tapped it. The governor took a big drink, smacked his lips, wiped his forehead, and swung his broad-brimmed hat, and shouted,

"All you who love the Prince of Orange, and who care for me, do as I do, and help me stop the Englishmen."

The people of Manhattan were glad to do as he was doing—drink great bumpers of wine. They filled their glasses and winked at each other.

"The English are our good friends; and, as for drinking, we will empty six casks instead of one," they said to themselves, and laughed at the astonished governor, who was walking up and down the fort, gazing at the *William* sailing far away.

"Why didn't you fire shot? and why don't you send the *Zouterberg* after her?" De Vries asked. Van Twiller drank more wine, and went to bed to think about it, and finally concluded to send the *Zouterberg*.

Up the Hudson sped the *William*. Eelkins landed at Albany, pitched a tent, and traded his trinkets for furs.

A week passed, and the Dutch vessel, her deck covered with green boughs, sailed up the river. Just before reaching Albany, the captain gave the crew a drink of rum; and the trumpeter, standing on deck, took a long breath, puffed out his cheeks, and blew a great blast that echoed far up and down the Hudson. Jacob Eelkins had no intention of fighting, so he folded his tent and went down the river.

"Don't you men come here again to trade with the Indians!" shouted Van Twiller to Eelkins; and, "Don't anybody write anything to Holland about it," was his order to the people of Manhattan.

Governor Van Twiller built a house for himself with bricks brought from Holland. He also erected three windmills. The people were glad to see the great arms go round in the wind as they had seen them in Holland. He built a church with a steeple north-east of the fort, and close by a cottage for Dominie Bogardus, with a great brass knocker on the front door. He erected a guard-house, a gibbet and whipping-post, and a house for the officers of the Company.

The Dutch in New Netherlands were not getting on as well as the people of Massachusetts. On the Hudson the West India Company and

PAYING TRIBUTE.

the planters controlled everything, and the governor was absolute in authority; while in Massachusetts the people had a voice in public affairs, owned their farms, and could trade without restriction.

The West India Company sent over William Kieft as governor. It was not a wise selection, for he had once failed in business, and his portrait had been nailed on the pillory as a sign of his disgrace. He had been sent by the Dutch Government to Turkey, to redeem some sailors that were held in slavery: he did not redeem them, and no one but himself ever knew what became of the money. He was a fussy, bustling, self-conceited little man, with a sharp nose and deep-set, restless gray eyes.

"You may have as many councillors as you please," said the Company. William Kieft knew what he was about, and concluded that he would have as few as he pleased, and chose only one—Doctor John La Montagne.

"You may have one vote, and I will have two," said Kieft to the doctor. Under Wouter van Twiller the inhabitants had had their own way in many things, but William Kieft determined that they should bow to his will. These were his regulations:

No smuggling of furs. No smuggling of tobacco. No selling of guns to Indians under pain of death. No sailors on shore after dark. Nobody to leave Manhattan without a passport. Everybody must go to bed when the nine o'clock bell rung in the evening, and be up when it rung in the morning. "You must pay tribute of furs or corn," said the governor to the Indians.

The Indians came with bundles of furs, threw them down at the governor's feet, and went away with scowls on their faces. They could not understand it! Why should they pay tribute?

Gustavus Adolphus was King of Sweden—a large-hearted man—the great champion of Protestantism. He had seen towns and cities plundered and burnt, and he sickened at the sight. He fought only because he could see no other way to defend the right; but he thought that in a new country men might live together in brotherly love. To carry out that idea, he empowered a company to emigrate to America and begin such a settlement. There was to be no slavery or oppression. It was a beautiful plan; but before emigrants could be gathered, a great war, which lasted thirty years, broke out in Europe, and Gustavus had other things to attend to. He died, but the project was not altogether forgotten.

Ten years passed. In the spring of 1638 two vessels from Guttenberg, in Sweden, sailed into Delaware Bay, bringing emigrants to establish a colony.

GUSTAVUS ADOLPHUS.

The flowers were in bloom, the trees clothed with greenest verdure. The country was so delightful that they called Cape Henlopen Paradise Point. They sailed up the river, landed on the western shore, near a little creek, erected a fort, which they named Christina, for the child-queen of Sweden, built a church, and reared their log-houses. It was the beginning of settlements in Pennsylvania.

Peter Minuet, of New Netherlands, who had been dismissed by the West India Company, but who had sold his services to the Swedes, was

THE FIRST CHURCH IN PHILADELPHIA.

their leader. They built their huts along the western bank of Delaware River, cleared patches of ground, and erected a little building of logs, which was a church below and block-house above.

Other settlers came. They were industrious and hard-working, honest and frugal, and in 1642 built a brick church, which is still standing. All the settlers gave their time to erect it, the minister carrying the brick and mortar. Their friends in Sweden aided them, sending for ornaments the figures of two cherubs holding an open Bible, with this inscription:

"THE PEOPLE WHO SAT IN DARKNESS HAVE SEEN A GREAT LIGHT."

William Kieft, governor of New Netherlands, sent a message to Peter Minuet, commanding him and the Swedes to leave the country, as it was owned by the Dutch; but the Swedes paid no attention to the order, and went on with their work.

More Swedes arrived, and made settlements along the Delaware. Their governor, John Printz, planted his cannon to sweep the river, and compelled all the vessels of the Dutch that went past it to pay toll, which aroused the wrath of the traders of Manhattan. The Swedes had purchased the land of the Indians, but the Dutch claimed it because Henry Hudson had first sailed into the Hudson; therefore they vowed that the whole country belonged to them. To hold it, they built Fort Casimir,

AFFAIRS AT MANHATTAN. 201

near Philadelphia, only five miles from Fort Christina. The Swedes could not put up with such an insult, and tore it down.

The Indian boy who had seen the club, in the hands of Peter Minuet's negroes, crush the head of his uncle, had been biding his time. He was now a man, and had nursed his revenge through the years, and gratified it by killing a poor inoffensive old man who made cart-wheels.

"I will wage war upon the savages," said Governor Kieft.

"You have outraged the people, and they will not sustain you," said some of his friends.

The governor did not dare to go to war without consulting the people. William Kieft, quite likely, did not see what would ultimately come

OLD SWEDES' CHURCH, PHILADELPHIA.

from this calling of the first meeting of the people of Manhattan—that it would be the beginning of representative government.

Twelve men were chosen to consult with the governor, and they voted that peace ought to be preserved. Kieft was in a rage. He dismissed the burghers; then called them together again. He had ruled as he pleased, with absolute power; but the burghers informed him that thenceforth they were to have a voice in governing. He was more angry than ever, but conceded what they asked. They went to their homes, but, as soon as they were gone, he posted up a paper, forbidding the people to

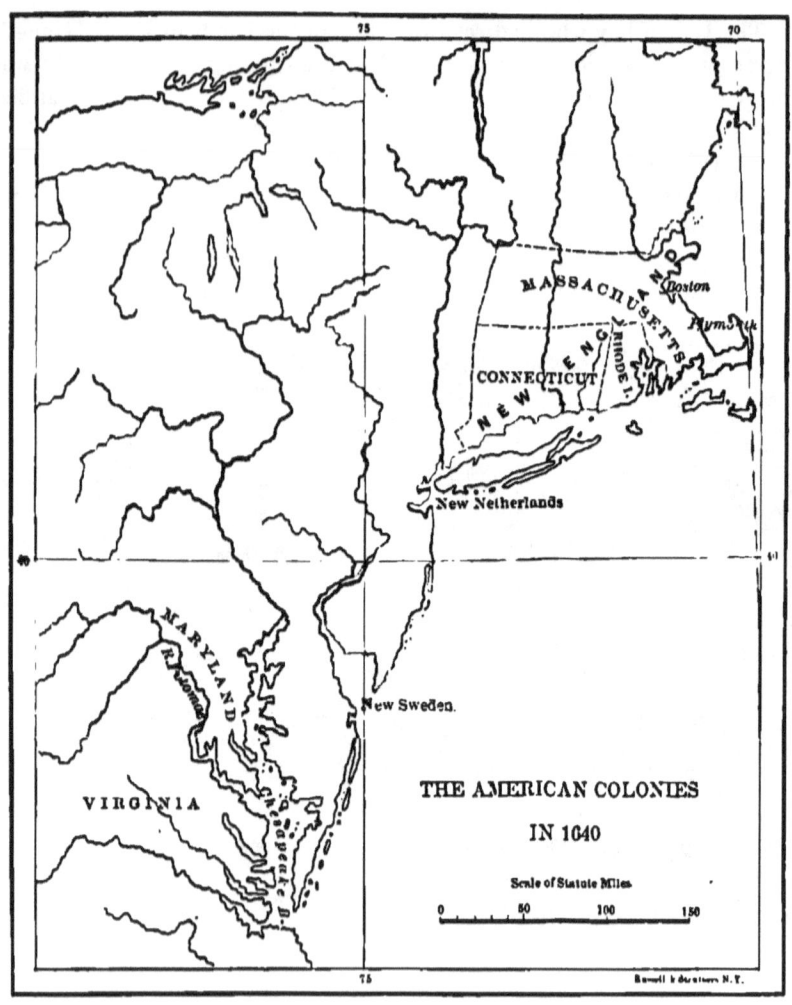

meet in any assembly without his permission, and taking back all he had agreed to.

The Indians loved rum, and the Dutch were ever ready to give a glass of liquor in exchange for a beaver-skin. Myndert van der Horst had a settlement at Newark, in New Jersey. One day one of the settlers sold rum to a Hackensack Indian, and when he was drunk stole his beaver-skin coat. The Indian, who was a chief's son, in his anger, not caring who he killed, shot James van Vorst as he was thatching his house. Governor Kieft was in a rage. "Deliver up the murderer!" he demanded of the Indians.

"You ought not to have sold him liquor! It was the rum, and not he that did it—he was crazy," said the Indians.

"I must have the head of the murderer!" the governor replied.

Jan Dam, one of the burghers, invited the governor and his secretary —Van Tienhoven—to a dinner-party. It was the 24th of February. Jan Dam treated the company to his best liquors. The more the governor drank, the greater his rage. The secretary drew up a petition, urging him, in the name of the twelve men, to make war; and Maryn Adriansen and two others signed it.

"I pray you, don't do it!" pleaded Dominie Bogardus.

"Wait till the next ship comes in," said Doctor La Montagne.

"Only three of the twelve have signed it; the others are opposed to it," said Captain De Vries.

What cared William Kieft for the twelve burghers? He was governor, and would do as he pleased.

"Go!" was the order to Sergeant Rodolf.

The soldiers stepped into the boats at the Battery and rowed to the Jersey shore. It was midnight, and the Indians—men, women, and children—were asleep in their wigwams. No suspicion of treachery on the part of the Dutch had ever come to them. Silently the soldiers landed, and surrounded the wigwams. The work of death began. Captain De Vries, friend of the Indians, stood on the Battery and saw the flash of guns. A wail of agony floated over the waters—the death-cry of eighty men and women at Pavonia, and thirty at Corlaer's Hook.

Men and women were shot down without mercy; infants in their mother's arms were hacked to pieces. The wounded were pinned to the earth with stakes, or tossed into the river to be swept away by the tide. What a sight was that which Captain De Vries beheld in the dim gray of the midwinter's morning! Indian women kneeling at his feet, with their hands chopped off, a foot gone, great gashes in their sides, begging his protection.

"The Mohawks have done this," they said, never dreaming that the Dutch had butchered them! Oh, how hard it was for the kind-hearted man to tell them that they whom they had treated so kindly, whom they believed to be their firm friends, had done it!

The soldiers returned to the fort, each man bringing the head of an

Indian. What a ghastly spectacle — a pile of bleeding heads! The people came to see them — some sickening at the sight, others rejoicing. The secretary's mother-in-law, in her glee, kicked the heads as if they were foot-balls. Is it a wonder that the Indians vowed vengeance? that the warwhoop rung through the forest? that the midnight skies were red-

THE MASSACRE OF THE INDIANS.

dened with the glare of burning buildings? that men, women, and children went down before the tomahawk and scalping-knife? Revenge was sweet! A few days later, and the settlers came flocking to New Amsterdam, while the Indians shot their cattle, horses, sheep, and pigs, and rioted upon the plunder of the houses. The wrath of the settlers rose against the governor.

"Give us back our murdered children!" cried the weeping mothers.

"You did it!" said the settlers.

"You must blame the freemen," the cowardly governor replied.

"You forbade the freemen to meet!"

"Maryn Adriansen and two others signed the petition, they are responsible."

"What lies are these you tell about me?" shouted Adriansen, drawing his sword and aiming his pistol at the governor.

"Put the assassin in prison!" cried Kieft; and he was marched off to jail.

There was a commotion in Manhattan—the people demanding Adriansen's release, and not a soul in the community offering to stand by the governor, who was compelled to permit twelve men, whom the people chose, to have a voice in public affairs.

There was one man in whom the Indians trusted—Captain De Vries —for he was always their friend; and through his good offices a treaty of peace was signed, and the settlers went out to their farms.

But there were some Indians who would not be bound by the treaty; they had their revenge to gratify, and the war broke out anew.

Among those massacred was Ann Hutchinson, who had been compelled to leave Boston on account of her religious opinions, and who had made her way to New Netherlands.

Captain John Underhill, who was in the attack upon the Pequod Indians, arrived, and was placed in command of the troops of Manhattan. With one hundred and eighty men, he sailed through Hell-gate, landed at Greenwich, and surrounded an Indian village, in which there were five hundred men, women, and children. The Dutch had guns, the Indians only bows and arrows. It was a fearful slaughter, and when it was over there was a heap of mangled corpses—the entire five hundred, except five who managed to escape. The Indians never recovered from the blow; it was the going down of the weak before the strong.

The West India Company had had enough of William Kieft. He had spent a great deal of money, and was so inefficient that he was ordered to return to Amsterdam, and the people rejoiced when he was gone.

CHAPTER XIV.

THE STRUGGLE FOR LIBERTY IN ENGLAND, AND HOW IT AFFECTED AMERICA.

THROUGH these years the lawyers of England were discussing the right of the king to levy a tax of twenty shillings upon John Hampden for ship-money when Parliament had not ordered it. The judges, wearing their big flowing wigs, met day after day; no end of documents and old musty parchments were examined; points of law were discussed, long arguments made, much Latin quoted, but the five judges appointed by Charles I. were ever ready to carry out his will, regardless of Right, and they decided that the king had power to levy the tax without consulting Parliament.

It was easy for the judges to make such a decision, but it was quite another thing to make the people believe it was righteous judgment. This people beheld bloody scenes. William Prynne, a lawyer, wrote a book against theatres, calling them the devil's chapels, and the players Satan's ministers. He denounced the setting up of May-poles, also dancing, wearing false hair, and the use of Christmas evergreens. He had the bad taste to denounce the queen for attending the theatre, and was put in prison; but while in jail he wrote a pamphlet denouncing the bishops, calling them wolves.

One of his fellow-prisoners was John Bastwick, who wrote a book denouncing the bishops. "Hell has broke loose, and the devils in surplices, hoods, and capes, are among us!" he said.

Mr. Burton wrote a book in which he said the bishops were robbers of souls.

What a scene was that in Palace-yard, January 30th, 1637! The three prisoners were brought out from their cells and put in the pillory; the court also condemning them to pay five thousand pounds each. A great crowd gathered to see the sheriff carry out the rest of the sentence. They saw him heat an iron red-hot and stamp it on their foreheads, then slit their nostrils, and crop off their ears! It was very affecting when Rev. Mr. Bastwick's wife stood upon a stool, and kissed him as he was in the pillory, and tenderly laid the pieces of his ears upon her handkerchief.

The sheriff marched the prisoners away with the blood streaming down their cheeks, taking them to distant prisons, a great crowd following, and the people showing their sympathy by putting Mrs. Bastwick in a carriage and almost smothering her with flowers, for her faithfulness and devotion to her husband.

Archbishop Laud wreaked his revenge upon Rev. Mr. Leighton, who, for saying that the bishops were men of blood, and the queen a daughter of Heth, was placed in the pillory, lost his ears, and was sent to prison for life! Peter Sanart, for saying "I hate those that love superstitious ceremonies and vanities," was condemned to spend eleven years in prison.

It was in 1629 that Charles said he never would have another Parliament, and he got along without one for eleven years; but he could go no longer, for, notwithstanding he had sold monopolies and levied illegal taxes, he could not get all the money he wanted; so it came about that he was obliged to call another meeting of the representatives of the people, who came together April 13th, 1640. John Hampden's twenty shillings taxes for ship-money confronted the king, for all the members had been compelled to pay ship-money, and they were angry. The spirit of liberty was rising. Charles asked for £840,000.

"If you will grant it, I will give up collecting any more ship-money," he said.

"We have been illegally taxed. We demand that the judges shall be punished before we vote any supplies," said the Commons.

The king, in a great rage, again dissolved Parliament, but before the year was out called the Commons together again. The members came with a spirit and determination such as never before had been seen in England. They had their arms filled with petitions from men who had lost their noses, who had been branded on the forehead, asking for release from prison and redress of their wrongs.

Oliver Cromwell presented the petition of John Lilburn, a printer's apprentice, who had been whipped and imprisoned for having sold one of Prynne's books.

"Let us have the prisoners before us," said the Commons, and commanded the jailers to bring them.

What a sight was that for Charles I. to look upon!—four thousand men on horseback, two hundred coaches, and a great crowd of people with bouquets of flowers in their hands, escorting, Prynne, Burton, Bastwick, and

Lilburn into London! The spirit of the people was rising like a flood against oppression.

"There are some cobwebs that must be swept away, and there are some things that we must pull up by the roots," said John Pym to George Hyde.

One of the cobwebs that John Pym had in mind was the Earl of Strafford, who had urged the king on to do illegal acts.

"I ask that everybody not a member be excluded from the hall, and the doors locked," said Pym.

The doors were locked, and Pym began the work of pulling things up by the roots.

"There is one man," he said, "who has become the greatest enemy to

STRAFFORD ON HIS WAY TO EXECUTION.

the liberties of his country, and the greatest fountain of tyranny that any age has produced—the Earl of Strafford."

It was late in the night, but the Peers were in their chamber, wondering what the Commons were doing with the doors locked, so that no one could come out. The door suddenly opened, and Pym, with three hundred men following, marched across the hall to the chamber of the Peers.

"In the name of the House, and of all the Commons of England, we impeach Thomas Wentworth, Earl of Strafford, of high-treason, and ask his arrest."

It was a tap-root which the Commons had taken hold of, and an hour later the earl found himself a prisoner in the Tower. A few days later, Archbishop Laud and the two judges who had given the unjust decision against John Hampden found themselves in the Tower. The Earl of Strafford was found guilty of high-treason—that is, conspiring against the State—and was condemned to death. He was a brave old man. When the sheriff marched him out to be executed he walked with a firm step. When they reached the window of Laud's cell, the earl kneeled upon the stone pavement to receive the archbishop's blessing. All London came to witness the execution. A stroke, and it was over.

"His head is off! His head is off!" shouted the multitude.

Bells rung and bonfires blazed. So the people manifested their joy at the death of Thomas Wentworth, who had conspired to overthrow their liberties.

The Commons passed laws which the king did not like, and Charles determined to have his revenge. He started from Whitehall with four hundred soldiers to seize John Pym and four other members. The soldiers stood guard at the door while the king went into the hall.

"The birds are flown, I see, but I will have them yet," he said.

"Our privileges! Our privileges!" shouted the members, as the king went out. What right had the King of England to enter the hall with an armed force? None. He had trampled on the privileges of the people. All London was in an uproar. Military companies were forming. Not much longer would they submit to such outrages. The people were marching with pikes, spears, and guns.

The Commons passed a bill regulating the militia.

"Will it not be best to grant what they desire?" asked one of Charles's friends.

"I will not yield!" the king replied, swearing a great oath, determined to let the Commons and everybody else know that he was master.

The nobles, the gentlemen, the bishops, the aristocracy sided with Charles, while the merchants, shopkeepers, boot and shoe makers, mechanics, apprentices, and men of all trades, the Puritans, and many of the farmers, were in favor of Parliament.

The Marquis of Newcastle, at York, set himself to raise an army for the king, and Charles, turning away from London, made haste to Nottingham. In a few days he had an army of twelve thousand men. High-spirited gentlemen on high-spirited horses, accustomed to the chase, joined him.

Charles made a mistake at the outset by appointing his nephew, Prince Rupert, only twenty-three years old—headstrong, imperious, self-willed—

to command his cavalry. He was brave, but not wise. The king was confronted by the army of Parliament, numbering twenty-five thousand, commanded by the Earl of Essex. One of the captains of the Parliament cavalry was Oliver Cromwell, forty-three years old—a rough, ungainly farmer, who had been elected to Parliament. John Hampden was his cousin.

"Who is that sloven?" asked Lord Digby, one day in Parliament, when Oliver was making a speech.

"That sloven, if we should come to a breach with the king, will be the greatest man in the kingdom," John Hampden replied.

Oliver Cromwell raised two companies of cavalry, and gave five hundred pounds toward supplying the soldiers with an outfit.

On Sunday, October 23d, 1642, the two armies met at Edge Hill. It was two o'clock before the battle began. The drums beat, the cannon thundered.

Sir Faithful Fortesene, commanding a regiment of cavalry in the Parliament army, proved himself unfaithful, turned traitor, led his men across the field, and joined the king. What joy on the part of Prince Rupert and the Royalists! They would win an easy victory.

"Forward!" Prince Rupert gives the word; the gentlemen draw their swords, eager to trample down the farmers and clodhoppers, mounted on their cart-horses. And they do it. They sweep over the field, leaping hedge-rows and fences, and fall upon the Parliament cavalry. Some of the clodhoppers are trampled upon, their skulls split open; the others flee, pursued by Prince Rupert, two miles along the roads and fields, till stopped by John Hampden, who is hastening to the battle with infantry and cavalry. Prince Rupert thinks the day is won, but is greatly mistaken. The infantry in the ranks of the Parliament army have stood like a wall of adamant; and when the king's troops charge upon them, they are rolled back as the waves of the sea are tossed back by the granite ledges. When Prince Rupert reaches the battle-field he finds that the Earl of Lindsay has been mortally wounded, and taken prisoner, and that the king's colors have been taken.

Night shuts down upon the field. The king has lost one-third of his army; the Parliament one-third of theirs. Neither party has won. Neither is ready to fight the next day.

Oliver Cromwell and John Hampden talk about the battle. Oliver bitterly recalls the discomfiture of the Parliament's cavalry.

"No wonder we were swept away," he says, "with such a miserable set of animals—old broken-down cart-horses—and the men only tapsters,

THE STRUGGLE FOR LIBERTY IN ENGLAND. 211

good-for-nothing fellows, and people of that sort, while the king's men are sons of gentlemen, accustomed to the chase, and their horses the best in the kingdom. Do you think that such vagabonds as we have will make a stand against gentlemen full of resolution?"

"You are right, Oliver, but how can it be helped?"

"I will show you. I will have men who will fear God—men of conscience—and I promise you that they shall not be beaten."

THE BATTLE FIELDS.

Oliver Cromwell was looking for a long war, and a terrible struggle. He was also looking into the nature of things. The Cavaliers, as the gentlemen were called, had resolution, and a high sense of honor and loyalty to the king; but he believed that men who feared God, who put conscience into everything, would be animated by a higher loyalty; that they would be brave in battle, and esteem death better than life if they fell in defence of their convictions.

He chose for his soldiers young Puritan farmers who were rich enough to own good horses, who could ride as well as the gentlemen; men who had listened to the preaching of ministers, who would not conform to the ritual, and who were fired by lofty ideas of duty and obligation; who used no oaths; who prayed night and morning, and before going into battle.

The war went on. The people in the eastern counties of England mainly sided with Parliament, while those in the western counties were more in favor of the king. The line on the map given above shows how the country divided. Many battles were fought.

On Marston Moor, a wide plain six miles from York, June, 1644, a terrible battle was fought—sixty thousand men taking part in it. It began at sunset, and lasted until ten o'clock; cannon thundering, muskets flashing, pike-men stabbing each other to the heart, beating out each others' brains; five thousand cavalry, on the high-spirited, mettled horses, dashing against the young Puritan farmers, who, just before the battle began, held a prayer-meeting.

What a shock it was! Ten thousand men on horseback; two great armies meeting in the middle of the plain! Loyalty to the king on one side; loyalty to God on the other. The highest and noblest motives by which men are actuated—to give courage, resolution, strength; to be regardless of death; thinking of nothing but duty and obligation. Cannon-shot ploughed through them, volleys of musketry swept them down. Horses and men struggled in the fight. Five thousand killed; many thousands wounded; the cavalry of Prince Rupert broken, routed, scattered to the winds; fifteen hundred prisoners, twenty-five cannon, ten thousand muskets taken, the fruits of victory to the army of Parliament. When it was over, the iron-sided men sung a psalm and gave God the glory.

A year later, June 12th, 1645, the two armies meet on the field of Naseby.

"Queen Mary!" shout the Cavaliers, as they prepare to dash across the green fields and fall upon the Puritans. Honors, loyalty to the king and queen, to their ideal of divine right to rule, is the thought that animates the Cavaliers.

"*God with us!*" shout the iron-sided men. When the battle closes the king is fleeing westward. All is over.

"This is the head of a traitor," said the executioner, as he held up the bloody head of the king before a great crowd of people

THE WASHINGTON HOUSE, LITTLE BRINGTON.

in London, June 30th, 1649. The people, for the first time in human history, trampled beneath their feet the doctrines preached by Pope and Bishop—the divine right of kings to rule.

The Puritans had cut off the king's head, but they had not obtained a correct conception of what constitutes true liberty. They could not at once throw off, as the caterpillar casts its shroud, the ideas of the past; they could not rule themselves, for they were divided in opinions, and

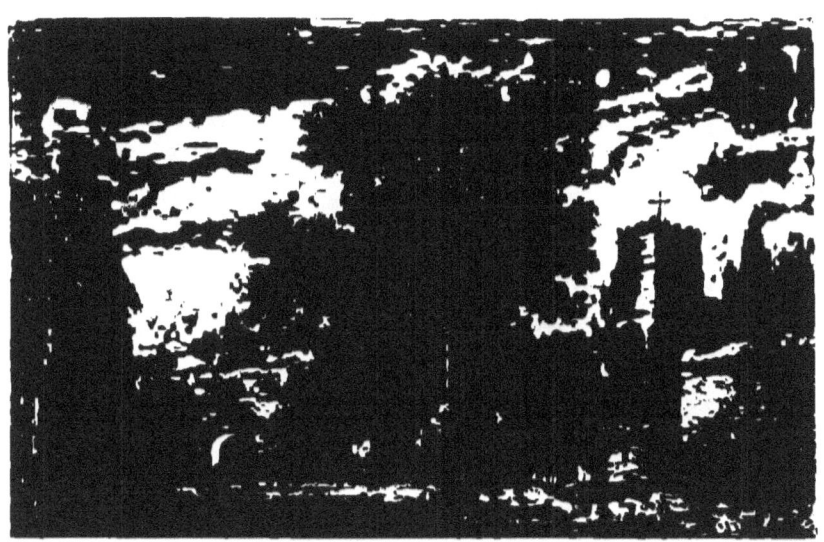

IRINGTON CHURCH.

the "sloven," the man whose iron-sided soldiers had never been defeated, Oliver Cromwell, became Protector of England—a king all but in name. He made the power of England felt as never before among the nations.

But what has this to do with the history of our country? A great deal.

When James began his persecutions the Pilgrims fled to Holland, and from thence crossed the sea. When Charles came to the throne, and began his persecutions of the Puritans, they emigrated to America; and when the Royalists saw their last hope die out at Naseby, when the king lost his head, and Oliver Cromwell controlled affairs, they too looked to America as a place of refuge, for fear of what might happen to them. They selected Virginia as their future home, for of the American colonies it alone had remained loyal. In Virginia they could attend the king's church, and many gentlemen who had followed Charles through the great struggle sold their estates, and crossed the Atlantic to begin life

CHURCH IN WHICH SIR JOHN WASHINGTON WORSHIPPED.

anew along the James and Potomac. They were not persecuted, but emigrated of their own free will, carrying to Virginia the ideas of Church and State, the prejudices, hates, manners, customs, and refinements of the Royalists. They were men who never had been accustomed to work with their own hands, but who were rich enough to employ servants. They regarded classes in society as the natural and divine order of things. Men who labored belonged to one class; they to another, higher, better, with nobler blood in their veins.

Virginia had been settled nearly half a century, but had made little progress. It was weak and feeble. Some of the planters were getting rich by raising tobacco and slaves, but a great majority of the colonists were poor, and others shiftless and lazy, with no ambition to better their condition.

Like produces like. It is one of Nature's laws. We reap what we sow. The first settlers of Virginia were either gentlemen, spendthrifts, or vagabonds. James made it a penal colony, and sent several ship-loads of criminals to form a part of the community. How could their children be much better than they?

The men who had stood by Charles in the great struggle were not vagabonds; they had been animated by lofty ideas. They were refined and intelligent, as refinement and intelligence then were rated, and their advent in Virginia was the beginning of a higher civilization.

One of the emigrants was Sir John Washington, whom James had knighted in 1622. He had followed Charles in all his misfortunes; but when the king lost his head, when the outlook for the future, as he saw it, was only dark and gloomy, he sold his old home, bade farewell to all that was dear—the lands which he had owned, the old church, the graves of his fathers—crossed the Atlantic, and made him a home on the banks of the Potomac.

CHAPTER XV.

THE QUAKERS.

IT was Thursday, June 11th, 1656, but no one was at work in Massachusetts. The oxen, instead of being yoked to the plough, were chewing their cuds in the pastures; the blacksmith's hammer was resting on the anvil; the joiners had laid aside their planes, the shoemakers their lapstones. No one ate any dinner; it was a day of fasting and prayer, proclaimed by the governor, that the Lord would save England from the Ranters and Quakers.

And who were they? They were followers of George Fox, a shoemaker, who, before he was twenty-one years old, left his business and wandered by himself in the fields and woods, wearing a broad-brimmed hat and sheepskin coat and pantaloons, sleeping at night in hollow trees or under hay-stacks. He fancied that the Lord told him everything he ought or ought not to do; that it would be wrong for him to take off his hat as a mark of respect; that he must not say "good-morning" or "good-evening;" that he ought to say "thee" and "thou" when speaking to people; that it was wrong to fight, or to take an oath, even when commanded by a judge. He called the churches "steeple-houses." The ringing of the sweet-toned church-bells offended him; also the preaching of the ministers, whom he called "hireling priests," because they were paid. It

GEORGE FOX.

was revealed to him that he must "testify" to what the Lord had made known to him.

All this was a matter of conscience. George Fox was sincere in his beliefs, and he conceived great truths which the people of that time could not comprehend; but he was not always wise in his actions. He entered a church one Sunday and began to talk without taking off his hat; the constable hustled him to jail, from whence he was taken before a justice.

"I bid thee tremble before the Word of the Lord!" Fox said to the magistrate.

"I bid thee quake before the law!" the justice replied; and from that time he and his followers were called Quakers.

Fox was put in prison many times, but was so steadfast in his belief, and persistent in preaching, that he made many friends. His followers called themselves "Friends," and in a short time there were hundreds of men and women travelling through England, preaching in the fields or entering churches, disturbing the congregations, or getting themselves into prison. They believed that their imaginations were revelations from God. Some of them were very religious, and were actuated by pure motives, while others did many foolish things. William Simpson felt that he was was "moved of the Lord" to take off all his clothing and go into the streets and churches to preach. Robert Huntington wrapped himself in a white sheet and went into Carlisle Church "to testify." Richard Sale astonished the people of Westchester by coming to church at midday with a lighted candle in a tin lantern. James Naylor rode into Bristol, a woman leading his horse, other women spreading their shawls and cloaks in the streets, and shouting "Hosanna! blessed is he that cometh in the name of the Lord." The people said it was blasphemy; and Parliament condemned him to be whipped, his tongue bored through, and to be branded on the forehead and imprisoned two years.

Sarah Goldsmith laid aside all her clothing, and, with dust on her head, walked through the streets of Bristol, saying that the Lord had told her thus to testify against the wickedness of the people. The mayor thought it was indecent behavior, and sent her to jail. Many of the best men and women of England believed that the Quakers were deluded by the devil; and one minister was so sure of it, that he wrote a book entitled "Hell let Loose!" They increased so rapidly, that four years after George Fox began to preach they numbered eighty thousand.

Every vessel arriving in Boston brought intelligence of the unaccountable behavior of men and women who seemed to have lost all sense of shame. Need we wonder that the people of Massachusetts, when they heard of it, were sincere in their belief that Satan was indeed let loose, and that it was their duty to fast, and pray that the Lord would circumvent the wicked one?

The Quakers were moved by a fervent zeal, and went out as missionaries to other lands. Mary Fisher was whipped and imprisoned for preaching; but it only made her more zealous to proclaim what to her was the truth. She went to Barbadoes with Anne Austin, and from thence sailed for Boston in the ship *Swallow*, commanded by Simon Kempthorn.

Governor Endicott was not at home; but Lieutenant-governor Richard Bellingham and the Council determined that no such emissaries of Satan should have a chance to preach in Massachusetts, and ordered the sheriff to put them in jail and have them examined, to see if there were any warts or other witch-marks on their persons. Everybody in those days believed in witches—even George Fox; but the women who examined them found none of the devil's marks. For five weeks they were kept in jail, and not allowed to communicate with any one. Their backs were burnt with hot irons. When the *Swallow* was ready to sail the women were placed on board, and Captain Kempthorn was ordered to take them back to Barbadoes, or pay a fine of one hundred pounds. Though not permitted to preach in New England, Mary Fisher's zeal was not in the least quenched. She made her way to Turkey, and preached to the sultan, Mohammed IV.

A few days after the *Swallow* departed another vessel arrived from England with eight Quaker preachers on board, who were put in jail while the vessel was in port, and then sent back to England. Governor Endicott and his Council were determined that there should be no Quaker preaching in the country, and a law was passed for the whipping and imprisonment of any who should attempt it.

By the terms of the charter they had a right to pass such a law. We are to keep in mind the fact that the governor and Council, and nearly everybody else, sincerely believed that the Quakers were deluded by the devil, and that they would be answerable to God if they did not do all in their power to preserve the colony from the wiles of the adversary. The other colonies, with the exception of Rhode Island, passed similar laws.

The people thought that severe punishments would deter the Quakers from coming to America. They had little knowledge of human nature. They did not see that the determination to adhere to their religious convictions—the same desire which had impelled themselves to leave England—would stimulate the Quakers to brave everything for what they believed was the truth; that duty would be to them the pillar of fire by night and cloud by day, to lead them on to obey what they believed were God's commands. The Puritans had no conception of the peace of mind experienced by such women as Mary Fisher and Anne Austin.

In passing rigorous laws, they believed that they were doing God service. The Quakers, on the contrary, believed that they were serving God by violating such laws, and were ready to take the consequences.

It is a noble faculty in our nature that inspires us to brave suffering and death in doing what we believe to be right; but what, in our ignorance and short-sightedness, we think is right, we sometimes find, to our sorrow, is all wrong. If the Quakers did what they believed to be their duty, equally sincere were they who opposed them; both were mistaken, both wrong. Time alone could open men's eyes to what was really true.

William and Mary Dyer lived in Rhode Island. They had a beautiful family of children, and, strange as it may seem, Mary felt that it was her duty to bid good-bye to those she loved, cross the Atlantic, and "testify" to the people of England. Quite likely her neighbors thought it was her duty to remain at home and care for her children; but the conviction to "testify" had taken possession of her, and was above every other consideration. She went to England, and, after preaching awhile, sailed with Anne Burden to Boston. The governor, instead of permitting them to preach, put them in jail. Mary's husband came and took her home, while Anne was sent back to England. Their books were burnt, and they were compelled to pay their jail fees. Very soon after, six of those who had been sent to England by Governor Endicott the year before returned. Two, John Copeland and Christopher Holder, went into Salem meeting-house on Sunday wearing their hats, and disturbed the meeting. Christopher attempted to speak, but the constable held him down upon the seat, and stuffed a glove into his mouth. They were whipped and sent to jail. Samuel Shattuck, and Lawrence and Cassandra Southwick, sympathized with them, and they in turn were whipped and put in jail, also several others. The governor and Council, believing that the emissaries of the devil, in spite of the law, were getting a foothold in the colony, determined to make it still more severe: that whoever entertained a Quaker should pay a fine of forty shillings for every hour of entertainment, and be imprisoned till the fine was paid; that every Quaker entering the colony should have his right ear cut off, and if he came back after being sent away, must lose his other ear. Women were

to be whipped, put in the House of Correction, and if they came into the colony a third time, have their tongues bored through. The law was not passed in malice, but with a conviction that it was for the protection and well-being of the community. Very cruel it seems to us, but the laws were cruel all over the world.

QUAKERS DOING THEIR DUTY.

In England many had lost their ears; thousands had been imprisoned; hundreds had been hung or burnt for denying that the bread became Christ's body when blessed by a priest. Thousands also had been imprisoned, and others hung, for not accepting the ritual of the bishops; and had not thousands been forced to leave their homes to escape persecution?

In Germany, Holland, France, and Spain, hundreds of thousands of men and women had suffered death because they would not accept the Pope as the head of the Church.

Under the charter the people of Massachusetts had the right to make such laws as they pleased for the preservation of the colony. Would not God hold them responsible in the last great day, if they did not do all in their power to protect the community from the wiles of Satan? We must put ourselves in their place, must see things just as they saw them, to understand the motives actuating the governor and Council in passing a law imposing the penalty of death upon every Quaker who, after being sent out of the colony, should return. Did the laws deter any one from becoming a Quaker? Not in the least. They went on instead doing foolish things; the men wearing their hats, and the women taking their spinning-wheels to meeting, and persisting in spinning while the minister was preaching. Some of them, carried away by a strange fanaticism, acted indecently. Lydia Wardell, laying aside all her clothing, went into the Newbury meeting-house, saying that the Lord had directed her to do so. The constable quickly had her in jail; but her imprisonment did not

OLD TOWN CHURCH, NEWBURY.

deter Deborah Wilson from walking naked through the streets of Salem. Patience Scott, only eleven years old, travelled from Providence to Boston to "testify;" and Mary Wright, thirteen years old, travelled from Long Island to Boston for a like purpose.

Thomas Newhouse went into a meeting-house in Boston with two glass bottles which he smashed, shouting to the people, "So shall ye be broken in pieces."

Margaret Brewster clothed herself in sackcloth, sprinkled ashes in her hair, and went into the Rev. Mr. Thatcher's meeting. John Demen, Mrs. Marshfield, and Mary Ross stripped off their clothing, and danced together.

One Quaker attempted to offer his son in sacrifice, in imitation of Abraham, but was prevented by his neighbors.

William Robinson, Marmaduke Stevens, and Mary Dyer, who had been sent out of Massachusetts, returned in defiance to the law. Mary could have no peace in her soul till she had "testified" in Boston.

"Why do you come to Boston?" asked Governor Endicott.

"In obedience to a divine call," she replied.

What should the governor and Council do? Ought they to execute the law? Were not the children of Israel commanded to put blasphemous Sabbath-breakers and witches to death?

"Joyfully shall I go to my death," said Mary, when sentenced to die. Death had no terror for her. She was doing her duty; and when, with faltering voice, Governor Endicott pronounced her doom, he felt that he was doing his duty.

It is August 27th. The pathway over the narrow strip of land, the only road leading into Boston from Roxbury, is crowded with men, women, and children. Boats ply to and fro between Charlestown, Cambridge, and Boston, filled with people hastening to the hanging. The drums beat, and William Robinson, Marmaduke Stevens, and Mary Dyer, guarded by soldiers and followed by the crowd, march from the jail to the Common, where the gibbet has been erected. The prisoners walk cheerfully to their death. There is no blanching of their cheeks. If it is sweet to die for one's country, it is far sweeter to die in defence of the truth.

"We suffer not as evil-doers, but as those who have testified to the truth!" Robinson exclaimed.

Robinson and Stevens are hung. Mary Dyer sees their bodies swinging in the air. The rope is put upon her neck. "This to me is the hour of greatest joy I ever had in the world. No ear can hear, no tongue can utter, no heart can understand the sweet income and the refreshings of the spirit of the Lord I now feel," are her words. But a messenger comes with a reprieve; she is taken back to jail and sent to her home. She is restless there. Once more she leaves her husband and children, and makes her way to Boston. She has shown her fidelity to her faith by going calmly and joyfully to the gallows; can she do more? Yes, she must die for the truth.

What shall the governor do? She will not stay away, but has outraged clemency by returning. Can the government submit to a defiance of laws? Is she not, indeed, led on by Satan?

Once more the drum-beat is heard, and the sheriff marches her to the gallows.

"Do not be deluded longer by the devil. Repent and live!" is the exhortation of Rev. Mr. Wilson.

"I come here not to repent; I have been in paradise already several days."

No more may she be reprieved; and Mary Dyer, in obedience to what she believes to be a divine call, swings upon the gallows.

William Ledden, who had been banished, returned, and was executed. Four in all were hung, and forty-seven sent out of the colony. Quakers were imprisoned, whipped, or otherwise punished in all the colonies, except Plymouth and Rhode Island.

In another chapter we shall see how they were treated by the Dutch in New Netherlands. They were persecuted and hung in Virginia. In all the colonies, between one and two hundred were arrested. In England, though none were hung, more than thirteen thousand were put in prison; many had their tongues bored through or their noses slit, and their ears cropped off.

The truth had not come to the world that convictions of right and duty can never be extinguished by force. Paul, afterward apostle, attempted it, and failed. He was sincere in his conviction that Christians ought to be put to death that Truth might be preserved. Those who persecuted the Quakers, without doubt, were equally sincere, but terribly mistaken.

On the other hand, William Robinson, Marmaduke Stevens, and Mary Dyer, while holding important truths, which most men now accept, never once suspected that they were not doing right in all respects. Time has cleared away the haze, and we can see that the Governor and Council of Massachusetts on the one side, and Mary Dyer and her companions on the other, were grievously mistaken in their conceptions of Right and Duty.

CHAPTER XVI.

THE END OF DUTCH RULE IN AMERICA.

PETER STUYVESANT was appointed governor of New Amsterdam. He had lost a leg in a battle with the Spaniards, and stumped round upon a wooden one. He was so resolute and determined in every-

PETER STUYVESANT, THE LAST GOVERNOR OF NEW AMSTERDAM.

thing that the Dutch called him "Hard koppig Piet," or Headstrong Peter. Some of them called him "Old Silver Leg;" but he soon brought order out of confusion.

The Swedes at Christina, on the Delaware, demolished Fort Casimir,

THE END OF DUTCH RULE IN AMERICA.

which the Dutch had erected near by. Hard koppig Piet was not the man to submit to such an outrage. He settled the matter by sailing with seven war ships and several hundred men, capturing Fort Christina, and putting an end to Swedish rule in America.

Governor Stuyvesant could not settle matters in Connecticut quite so summarily. On the contrary, the Connecticut people were crowding him out of Long Island. They were getting possession of all the good land,

ANNA MERICA BAYARD, WIFE OF PETER STUYVESANT.

altering the names of the towns, and electing delegates to represent them at Hartford in making laws.

Hard koppig Piet would have no heresy in New Netherlands, but everybody must attend the Reformed Church. There were a few Lutherans who wished to worship God in their own way.

"I shall fine every one of you twenty-five pounds for every offence," said the governor, and sent their minister out of the country.

"You must have your children baptized in the Reformed Church," he said to the Lutherans, and when they refused the sheriff marched them to prison. The Baptists held a meeting; but the governor put a stop to that sort of thing by fining their minister one thousand pounds, and banishing him from the country.

There was strict law in Manhattan. De Sille, who acted as deputy-governor, accused a man of stealing, and the Court sentenced the culprit to be whipped and banished. Jan Adamzen slandered his neighbors, and was condemned to have a red-hot iron run through his tongue, and be banished from the country. Wolfert Weber removed a pile of stones that belonged to Nicholas Verbuth. Wolfert, when brought before the Court, offered to replace them with other stones. "I want the same stones," said Nicholas; and the Court ordered Wolfert to carry back the same stones within eight days, or suffer the consequences.

Robert Hodgson and other Quakers came to New Netherlands. The governor heard of their arrival, and, to nip their heresy in the bud, imposed a fine of fifty pounds upon any one who might give shelter to a Quaker for a night: if any ship's captain brought one into New Netherlands, his vessel and cargo were to be confiscated. John Chatterton and Henry Townsend broke the law: they were fined five hundred guilders, and sent to prison.

Tobias Feek and Edward Hart were selectmen of Flushing, and, because they would not carry out the governor's order against the Quakers, were thrown into prison.

Robert Hodgson was arrested, and also two women, one with a babe in her arms. The sheriff put the women into a cart, tied Robert to its tail, and took them to New Amsterdam, and thrust them into filthy dungeons. Robert was brought before the judge and tried. His sentence was in Dutch, of which he did not understand a word, but was told that he must pay six hundred guilders, or work two years, with a negro, chained to a wheelbarrow.

Feeling that he had not done any wrong, he refused to work; whereupon the sheriff ordered a negro to give him one hundred blows. All day long he was chained to the barrow. At night he was put into a dungeon, and in the morning chained to the barrow, but he would not work. The next morning a rope was tied around his waist, a log of wood to his feet, and he was drawn up to a ring-bolt overhead till he could not touch the floor with his toes, and whipped again—the rope cutting great gashes in his back, and the blood streaming upon the floor. After two days he was tied up again, and whipped till he fainted away. Through all the cruel scourging he had sweet peace in his soul. He was suffering for the truth, as he believed. The governor's sister was a kind-hearted woman, and through her intercession he was set at liberty.

THE END OF DUTCH RULE IN AMERICA. 227

A Quaker visited Long Island, and held a meeting in Henry Townsend's house, whereupon Governor Stuyvesant sent a company of soldiers, and arrested Mr. Townsend, and set a guard to prevent any more meetings.

John Brown, of Flushing, suspected of being a Quaker, was fined and banished to Holland; and John Tilton and his wife were ordered to leave the country.

"There shall be no religious meetings except those of the Reformed Church!" was the governor's proclamation.

On a day in April, 1662, John Winthrop, governor of Connecticut, was

ushered into the king's presence, at Whitehall, London. He had crossed the ocean to obtain a charter for Connecticut. He had written it out in a clear hand, and had no difficulty in obtaining an audience with

Charles; for Lord Say-and-Seal, keeper of the king's privy seal, and the Earl of Manchester, the king's chamberlain, were his friends.

Though John Winthrop's home in Connecticut was a plain edifice,

THE DUTCHMAN AT HOME.

though he lived in the wilderness, he was accustomed to good society, for he had been educated at Cambridge, in England. He had pleasing ways. He wore a ring of curious workmanship upon one of his fingers, which he gave to the king.

"Your majesty's grandmother, Anne of Denmark, gave it to me. Shall I have the pleasure of presenting it to your majesty?"

Charles was greatly pleased. What could he do for Governor Winthrop in return? Governor Winthrop wanted nothing for himself; but the people of Connecticut had no charter, and if his majesty would but grant one it would be a generous act, certainly. His name was written upon the paper, and Connecticut had a charter as a separate and distinct colony, with jurisdiction over the country, bounded north by Massachusetts, east by Narragansett Bay, south by Long Island Sound, and west by the *Pacific Ocean!* It lapped Connecticut right across New Netherlands. The English were crowding the Dutch in every direction; they were taking possession of Long Island; were pushing westward from the Connecticut to the Hudson. The Dutch were good, easy, slow-going people, who loved to smoke their pipes, thinking of nothing in particular, while the English were quick, active, hard-working. The English who had settled in the territory of the Dutch gave no attention to Governor Stuyvesant's commands. They paid taxes to Connecticut. Governor Stuyvesant sent Burgomaster Van Cortlandt and two others to Hartford to settle matters. Governor Winthrop showed them their charter. The Dutch opened their eyes wide: they were astonished.

"If your province extends to the Pacific Ocean, where is New Netherlands?" they asked.

"Really we do not know," said the Connecticut men, chuckling in their sleeves.

"We made a treaty with you in 1650 about boundaries. How are we to regard that?"

"Of no force whatever—the charter has abolished it," said the Connecticut men.

It was a little matter for Charles II. to sign his name to the charter which Governor Winthrop had obtained, and it was just as easy for him

THE VAN CORTLANDT MANOR-HOUSE.

to sign a second paper, giving his brother James, the Duke of York, all the country from Connecticut River to the Delaware. James wanted it, and Charles gave it to him. Very little did Charles care for the Dutch, or their claim to the country. Sebastian Cabot discovered and sailed along the shores a hundred years before the *Half Moon* dropped anchor in the Hudson. Were not the Dutch interlopers on English soil? Their gift to the Duke of York included more than half of the territory which Charles had just given to the people of Connecticut; but what of that? Could not a king take back to-day what he granted yesterday? England and Holland were at peace, but there was a quarrel going on between the African Company of England and the West India Company of Holland. The African Company was composed of London merchants, lords, and dukes. James had an interest in it, and they were trying to crowd the Dutch out of the West India and African trade. The London merchants wanted to control the trade in rum and slaves, which gave rise to many fights between the Dutch and English sailors on the coast of Africa. James and the London merchants conceived the plan of taking possession of New Netherlands. Charles furnished ships and soldiers to carry it out.

Little did the West India Company, or any one else in Holland, mistrust what was in the wind when four war-vessels, with four hundred and fifty soldiers on board, steered west for a voyage across the Atlantic.

"The English are going to take New Netherlands!" was the message which Richard Lord, of Lyme, in Connecticut, sent to Thomas Willet in New Amsterdam, who hastened to inform Governor Stuyvesant.

There was a sudden assemblage of the burgomasters in the Stadt House. The treasury was empty, but Jeremias Van Rensselaer was ready to let the governor have all the money he wanted. They would defend New Amsterdam to the last.

"The King of England has sent out some frigates to compel the people of New England to become Episcopalians!" was the word brought to New Amsterdam by a vessel arriving from Holland.

The burgomasters went home, and Governor Stuyvesant sailed up the Hudson to look after matters at Fort Orange.

"The English squadron is on its way from Boston to seize the city!" was the word which came to Stuyvesant, and he hastened back, set his slaves to thrashing wheat and carting it to the fort. He was in dismay when he discovered that he had only six hundred pounds of powder! besides, the reflection came to him that all the English in the province would be against him. He could muster only four hundred soldiers, and they were poorly armed; but men were set to work repairing the fort— he would defend it to the last.

The ships of the Duke of York sailed into the harbor. Richard Nichols, commanding the troops, sent a messenger, demanding the surrender of New Amsterdam. Governor Winthrop was on board the fleet, and sent a letter promising freedom, security of property, and all their old privileges, if the fort was surrendered.

There was a great crowd around the Stadt House.

"Read the letter to the people," said the burgomasters, who did not want to fight.

"I will not!" the governor replied.

"All that concerns the public welfare should be made public," said Van Cortlandt.

At that the governor, in his rage, tore the letter in pieces. The burgomasters, with lowering brows, turned their backs upon Hard koppig Piet, and marched out of the chamber. The men at work in the fort, hearing what the governor had done, threw down their shovels, rushed to the Stadt House, and shook their fists in his face.

"Give us the letter — the letter!" they shouted. Nicholas Bayard picked up the pieces of paper, laid them together, and read the letter to the people.

Stuyvesant wrote a letter to Nichols: "Let us discuss the question," he said.

"I shall come with my ships and soldiers to discuss it," Nichols replied, and the ships sailed in nearer the fort.

"It is not soldiership to attempt to hold the fort," said Vice-governor De Sille.

"I am governor. I am here to defend this place, and I will!" said the governor.

The soldiers stood ready to open fire on the English ships.

"It is madness," said Dominie Megapolensis, laying his hand on the governor's shoulder. "What will our twenty guns do against the sixty-two cannon of the ships? There is no help for you. Pray do not be the first to shed blood!"

"There is a paper signed by seventy-three of the principal men, beseeching you not to doom the city to ashes"—a burgomaster handed the governor a paper.

His lips were white; there was no one to stand by him.

"I had rather be carried to my grave!" He gulped down his grief. The struggle of a brave heart was over.

"Hoist the white flag!" he said.

A little later the flag of Holland gave place to the cross of St. George, and New Netherlands took the name of New York.

Very low down, indeed, is that man who will not resent an insult

So thought the people of Holland. The seizure of New Netherlands was not by a lawless company, but it was the perfidious action of the English nation.

James was Lord High Admiral—the commander of all the fleets of England. Charles had supplied him with ships, sailors, and soldiers.

HIS LIPS WERE WHITE.

The people of Holland had once cut the dikes, letting the sea in upon their towns to drive out the Spaniards, and they had not lost their high sense of honor. They declared war against England, which raged for three years. The people who lived along the southern coast of England saw the fleets of the two countries sail up and down the Channel, their sides aflame, cannon-balls ripping through their timbers, masts tottering, and the sea strewn with wrecks and mangled corpses.

Admirals Van Tromp and De Ruyter commanded the Dutch fleets, and James, Prince Rupert, and the Duke of Albemarle the English fleets. One of the English commanders, Admiral Penn, had a son who, instead of fighting, was attending Quaker meetings, to the grief of the admiral. We shall make the acquaintance of the son a little further on.

Terrible the conflicts! Hundreds of ships were battered to pieces, set on fire, blown up, or sunk with all on board. It is said that in one battle Admiral Van Tromp, having fired away all his shot, kept up the fight by using round Dutch cheeses for cannon-balls!

The English landed on the coast of Holland, and set the towns along the shore on fire. John De Witt, who was at the head of the Dutch government, determined that England should smart for it. There came a day when the people of London stood aghast, for they could hear the roaring of cannon down the Thames, and see columns of black smoke rising heavenward. The Dutch fleet was there making sad havoc with the English vessels, setting the shipping on fire, capturing four frigates, one of them the *Royal Charles*, which had brought Charles across the Channel in 1660.

While the people were listening, with white lips, to the roar of thunder, Charles was at Greenwich, with a heartless crew of courtiers around him, playing with his dogs, and saying soft things to the frivolous and voluptuous women who kept him company.

"Things would not be as they are if Oliver Cromwell were living," said the people, who remembered the days when England was a power in the world. They were beginning to be sick of Charles and the fops around him.

Those were terrible days in London; seventy thousand people had just died of the plague, and now the Dutch were destroying the shipping and paralyzing trade. The nation was paying a round price for dancing to the tune which Charles and his brother James were playing. A few days later came a terrible fire—thirteen thousand houses, eighty-six churches licked up by the flames, and two hundred thousand homeless people wandering in the fields, and starving beneath hay-stacks and hedges.

"Now that the rebellious city is in ruins, the king can have his own way," said one of the scapegrace courtiers, as he beheld the heaps of ashes, the crumbled chimneys and walls.

The city had opposed Charles I. in his efforts to trample out the people's liberties, and the merchants and tradesmen were opposing Charles II.; so the heartless courtiers, who were spending their time in idleness, living upon the people's bounty to the king, gloated over the ruins.

The Dutch sent a fleet across the Atlantic, and once more the flag of Holland floated over New Amsterdam for a short time; but when peace came, the Dutch gave up New Netherlands to the English, who thenceforth held undisturbed sway from Maine to Florida.

CHAPTER XVII.

THE TIMES OF CHARLES II.

THE Commonwealth in England was at an end. John Pym, John Hampden, John Milton, and Oliver Cromwell, the far-sighted, strong-hearted, liberty-loving men who had overthrown Charles I., were dead. The people of England were not far enough advanced in their idea of liberty to govern themselves. Charles II. was invited to come to England and be king. He had been long in exile in France. Just before crossing the Channel, he issued a proclamation promising pardon for everybody, so far as he was concerned, for all that had been done against his father. If Parliament should decide not to pardon everybody, that was another matter. Parliament was to be free, and there were to be no more persecutions on account of religion.

The vessel which brought him to Dover was the *Naseby*, named from the battle-field where his father had suffered defeat. He renamed it the *Royal Charles*. He ate a hearty breakfast of pork and pease, stepped into a boat, and was rowed to the shore, all the cannon thundering. When he landed, the Mayor of Dover knelt at his feet and presented a Bible.

"I love it better than anything else in the world," said Charles; yet he cared very little for the Bible. He was tall and swarthy, gay, careless, and kind-hearted. He had few sober thoughts. He loved ease and pleasure. His tastes were low; his life impure. He was a scapegrace, and yet all London turned out to welcome him; bells rung; bonfires blazed. It was a grand holiday; people drank wine and beer till they could drink no more, and were wild with delight to think that they had once more a king.

Charles had promised pardon to offenders; but Parliament had something to say. Charles's father had been condemned to death by judges appointed by Parliament; but twenty-five of them were dead. Of the living, nineteen fled to other countries. Two, John Goff and Edward Whalley, secreted themselves on a ship and crossed the Atlantic.

Twenty-nine were arrested by Charles's sheriffs. A few days later, as

John Evelyn was taking a walk in London, he saw a sight that made him shudder—baskets filled with the mangled bodies of some of the judges, whom the executioners had hacked to pieces at Charing Cross. King Charles was seated in a pavilion and gloated over the scene.

Cromwell was dead, and so was his son-in-law, Mr. Ireton, and Judge Bradshaw, who read Charles's condemnation. They had been buried in Westminster Abbey; but the king had the bodies torn from the coffins and hung up at Tyburn, from nine in the morning till sunset, and then taken down and thrown into a pit.

Admiral Blake had defeated the enemies of England in many hard-fought battles on the sea, but Charles had his body taken out of its coffin and burnt in St. Margaret's church-yard.

There had been no May-poles, no wrestling-matches, no worrying of bulls with dogs, during Cromwell's time; but now the May-poles were set up, and bulls were worried on market-days. For twenty years there had been little gambling; but gambling-houses sprung up all over London. Charles set the example. Every Sunday evening there was a carousal at Whitehall Palace—Charles, the dukes, earls, lords, and ladies of the court playing cards, winning or losing great heaps of gold.

During the Civil War, and through Cromwell's time, men and women dressed plainly; but the Cavaliers took great pleasure in adorning themselves with laces, ruffles, and ribbons. They wore their hair long, to spite the "Roundheads," as they called the Puritans, who cut theirs short. The Cavaliers adorned their hats with plumes.

The ladies of Charles's court adopted the fashion of covering their faces with patches. It is said that one lady used court-plaster to cover up a pimple, that it at the same time added to her beauty; that from such a beginning the fashion went on, till the cheeks and forehead were covered with sun, moon, stars, and fanciful designs.

A CAVALIER, TIME OF CHARLES II.

The court of the king was gay, frivolous, and wicked. Charles married Catharine of Portugal—a plain, simple-hearted girl; but he cared far more for Lady Castlemaine, for the actress Nell Gwynne, and a vain, false-hearted woman sent out by Louis XIV. of France to exercise her fascinations upon the foolish king. He was so completely under her thumb that he made her Duchess of Portsmouth, and lavished one hundred and thirty thousand pounds upon her in a single year. Never was there such drinking, swearing, and indecency in the palace of the king. Duchesses, countesses, ladies of the bed-chamber —all could swear great oaths, sing indecent songs, and never a blush come upon their cheeks. The Puritans were laughed at, scoffed, ridiculed, despised, and contemptuously treated. Although the king said he loved the Bible better than anything else in the world, he cared very little for religion. He was determined, however, that everybody should use the Prayer-book; and because the Puritan ministers would not use it, more than two thousand of them were thrust out of the pulpits on St. Bartholomew's Day, 1662. Parliament passed a law declaring that all meetings held on Sunday by those who would not use the Prayer-book were seditious, or in conspiracy against the government. If more than four persons were present in such an assembly, it was sedition. If there were more than four persons in a family, there could be no blessing asked at table.

PATCHES, IN THE TIME OF CHARLES II.

In a very short time the prisons were filled with Quakers and Puritans. One was a poor tinker, who used to travel through the country mending pots and pans. He was very profane and wicked, but became a good man, and went to preaching to his associates that they ought to lead purer lives. If he had spent his time in gambling, worrying bulls, or dancing, the bishops would not have thought of putting him in prison; but Charles and the bishops would not permit any praying without a Prayer-book, and so one morning John Bunyan found himself in Bedford jail, where he was kept, half-starved, for twelve years. The bishops thought that, by so doing, they would stop his preaching; but two and a quarter centuries have rolled away, and John Bunyan has been preaching through all the years, and will preach on to the end of time; for the "Pilgrim's Progress," written in the old stone prison of Bedford, deals with things invisible and eternal. Charles and the bishops are dead, but John Bunyan lives. For him there is no death.

John Goff and Edward Whalley reached Boston. Whalley had been a lieutenant-general, and Goff a major-general in Cromwell's army. They were learned and agreeable gentlemen. They stayed in Cambridge until February, 1661; but the king's officers were on their tracks, and they went to New Haven, in Connecticut, and stopped with Rev. Mr. Danforth. Thomas Kirke, who, a few years later, put scores of men and wom-

NELL GWYNNE.—(FROM A PAINTING BY SIR PETER LELY.)

en to death in Scotland, was following Goff and Whalley, with Thomas Kelland, another officer appointed by Charles.

They called upon Governor Winthrop at Hartford, who treated them courteously, not because he wanted to aid them, but because they were officers of the king.

"General Goff and General Whalley are not here," said the governor,

NEW HAVEN.

and the officers pushed on to Milford, and called upon Deputy-governor Leet.

"We would like to confer with you in private. We are on the track of the rascals; we are sure that they are here. We must have men to help us," they said.

"The gentlemen whom you seek have been here, but I have not seen them for several weeks. I do not believe they are in New Haven. Have you authority to arrest them?"

"Here are our papers."

Governor Leet began to read them aloud.

"Please do not read aloud; somebody may overhear, and get wind of our business."

But the governor went on reading aloud.

"I must consult with the Council; for this is a grave matter. It is late to-night. We will ride to New Haven in the morning, and call the Council together," said the governor.

The officers went to bed; but while they were asleep an Indian stole out in the darkness, and ran through the woods to New Haven. The governor and the officers rode there in the morning, and the Council met and consulted all day.

"This is a very important matter. We dare not act without calling the Assembly," they said.

"The king will resent any concealment of such archtraitors," said the officers.

"We are always ready to honor the king, but we have tender consciences, and we must let the Assembly decide."

The commissioners were in a rage. They would search for themselves, and ransacked Mr. Danforth's house, and treated him rudely because he had befriended the refugees. Mrs. Eayers had given them shelter, and the officers knocked at her door. Mrs. Eayers was very polite.

Oh yes! she knew General Whalley and General Goff: they were very courteous gentlemen. They had been to her house, and she hoped to have the pleasure of meeting them again. These may not be her ex-

UNDER THIS BRIDGE THE JUDGES WERE CONCEALED.

act words; but Mrs. Eayers was so much of a lady that the officers could not think of searching her closets to see if the refugees were there.

240   OLD TIMES IN THE COLONIES.

The officers took their departure, little suspecting that the two men were up-stairs the while. But they could stay there no longer; they fled and secreted themselves under a bridge, and not long after heard the hoofs of the officers' horses upon the planks above them. William Jones concealed them; but the officers were still on their track, and they found refuge in a cave on the side of a hill, which they named "Providence Hill." The pursuit was getting hot, and again they disappeared; which way the officers could not discover. They were completely baffled, and returned to England denouncing the people of Connecticut as enemies of the king.

THE JUDGES' CAVE.

CHAPTER XVIII.

KING PHILIP'S WAR.

PHILIP, son of Massasoit, was chief of the Wampanoag Indians. He lived at Mount Hope, near Bristol, Rhode Island. From the summit of the rounded hill he could look out upon the country occupied by his tribe. Northward and eastward were their hunting-grounds; southward were the calm waters of Narragansett Bay, swarming with fish and dotted with green islands; westward, beyond the bay, was the country of the Narragansetts.

Philip had been selling his land, piece by piece, to the English. From his wigwam he could see the blue smoke curling up from their hearthstones in every direction.

The English in New England never took the lands of the Indians without paying for them. It was not much that they paid; but to the Indians the glass beads, little tinkling bells, the knives and red blankets of the white men, were of more value than the woods and meadows. They were only children in their ideas of property, and when the trinkets were lost, and the blankets worn to rags—when they saw that the lands remained, that there were gardens, flowers, fields of waving grain, where a few months before there was only the forest, they came to the conclusion that the white men had cheated them. They could no longer live by hunting, for cattle were feeding in the former haunts of the deer. They ate the corn which the squaws had planted.

"Build a fence around your corn," said the white men.

"Indian no build fence," was the reply.

Labor was degrading. Squaws might work, but braves never.

"You give us rum, and when we are drunk you cheat us."

The white men laughed in their sleeves, for they knew that the Indian would part with everything for rum. They called it "Killdevil."

Philip's warriors were restless. All through the years, from 1620 to 1675, they had not been to war save with the Narragansetts. There was excitement in war, bravery and daring to waylay their foes, fall upon them in ambush, burn their dwellings, split their skulls with the tomahawk, take their scalps, humble them in the dust—that was worth living for! The English were extending their laws over them. If one Indian killed another, the Boston men hung the murderer, cut off his head, and placed it on the gibbet, where the birds could pick out the dead man's eyes. What right had the white man to interfere in the affairs of the Indian?

From 1670 to 1675 there were reports that Philip was meditating a war. Many things occurred to lead him on. Quite likely Philip saw that he had made foolish trades, and was angry with himself. The white men had hung one of his men for murder: they had demanded that the Indians should give up all their guns. His warriors were urging him to

MOUNT HOPE.

fight; if he did not, would they not call him a coward, and depose him from being chief?

All the Indian tribes from Narragansett Bay to Merrimac River had recognized his father as their great chief; would they not look with contempt upon him if he remained at home in his wigwam, and allowed the white men to overrun the country? Is it any wonder that he sent messengers to the Nipmuck, Narragansett, Nashua, and other tribes to see what they thought about matters? It is not quite certain that Philip wanted to go to war. He is represented as having been wily and bloodthirsty, but that does not appear to have been his character. He was proud and haughty. He had influence over other tribes, and exercised it; but it is not clear that he delighted in brutality.

"I am sorry," he said, when he heard that the war had begun; and this was the way it began:

John Sassamon, who had been taught to read and write by John Eliot at Natick, and who sometimes wrote letters for Philip, informed the white men that the Indians were planning war. For giving this information three of Philip's men killed him, and put his body under the ice in Middleborough pond, whereupon they were arrested by the Boston men and one of them hung, which greatly angered Philip's men, who killed the cattle of the Swanzey people. They did not fire upon the settlers; they waited for the white men to shed the first blood, believing what their medicine men told them, that the party that drew the first blood would be beaten.

It was on June 19th, 1675, that a Swanzey man fired upon an Indian for shooting his oxen, and wounded him. This was the signal. Blood had been shed by the white man, who would be vanquished in the struggle.

Thursday, June 24th, was fast-day. The settlers of Swanzey were going home from meeting in the afternoon, when there was a sudden rattle of guns from an unseen foe. One fell dead, and several were wounded. Two men who went for the doctor to dress the wounds were killed. When night closed, six had been killed and many wounded.

Messengers rode in haste over the country. The next afternoon drums were beating in Boston, and the beacon was blazing on the hill. In a few hours men from Boston, Plymouth, and other towns were on the march. The war which they had feared had come at last; instead of peace and security, there were alarm and terror.

KING PHILIP.

It was on the afternoon of Saturday that the Dedham men started for Swanzey. That night there was an eclipse of the moon. The soldiers knew very little about eclipses. The moon was of the color of blood, and there was one dark spot which looked like a scalp. As the eclipse came on the shape of the moon was like a bow when the arrow is about to fly. Such the superstition and imagination as they marched through the gloomy forest.

Philip was not at Swanzey when his men began the war, but at Mount Hope. Captain Thomas Savage, with sixty men on horses and sixty on foot, marched directly to Mount Hope, and came so suddenly upon Philip, who was at dinner in his wigwam, that he barely escaped capture. Captain Savage killed fifteen Indians, took all of Philip's cattle and hogs, and destroyed his cornfield. In front of his wigwam were the heads of eight white men on poles; but in Boston, on the cross-beams of the gibbet, were the skulls of Indians and murderers bleaching in the summer sun. Philip was no more brutal in that respect than the people in Boston, London, and Paris. It was the custom of the time.

Captain Moseley, of Boston, with one hundred and ten men, had a fight near Swanzey, in which several Indians were killed.

Lieutenant Oaks, in command of a party, killed three Indians, whose scalps were sent to Boston. Captain Church went to Pocasset, now Tiverton, Rhode Island, across the narrow arm of Narragansett Bay, east of Mount Hope. He had thirty-six men, and found himself suddenly attacked by three hundred Indians. He retreated to the water-side, piled flat stones one upon another, and built a barricade, and fought till Captain Golding came to his relief in a sloop. The sloop could not come to the shore, and the canoe that plied between the shore and the vessel could only carry two at a time. Church was the last to go. A bullet grazed his hair; another struck a stake in front of him; two passed through the canoe; they riddled the sail of the sloop, but not a man was killed.

Philip, having been driven from Mount Hope, began the war in earnest. On the 14th of July he fell upon Mendon, killed five white men, and burnt the houses.

There was one tribe that he could not prevail upon to join him— the Mohegans. Uncas was still alive. He was Philip's rival. He had seen Sassacus and the Pequods destroyed; and now in his old age he would renew his alliance with the white men, who would soon vanquish the Wampanoags.

He sent his two sons with a party of warriors to Boston, offering to fight against Philip. They were of great service in piloting the white men through the forests.

The Indians attacked Brookfield, Massachusetts. Eighty settlers fled to the garrison-house, which was built of logs, and loop-holed. The Indians set the other houses on fire, and then attacked the garrison, sheltering themselves behind trees and fences. They crept through the grass on their bellies; but there were sudden flashes at the loop-holes, and Indian after Indian was killed. There were six or seven hundred of them, who howled like wolves hungry for their prey. Not to be thwarted, they obtained a cart, piled bundles of flax upon it, sheltered themselves behind it, set the flax on fire, and wheeled the cart toward the house. There were flashes at the loop-holes; one by one the Indians fell. The building was on fire; but one of the brave settlers ran out and extinguished it, the balls rattling round him like hail. Soon after the hearts of the settlers were gladdened by the arrival of Major Willard and a party of soldiers, who came to their relief. They found eighty dead Indians.

FIGHT AT TIVERTON.

The Narragansetts had joined Philip. They built a strong fort in a swamp, which had only one entrance over a log across a brook. In the fort were their wives and children, their stores of corn and acorns, which the women had gathered while the warriors were on the war-path. There were five hundred wigwams within the enclosure, and nearly three thousand Indians.

The colonies united to strike a blow which the Indians would feel. Massachusetts sent five hundred and twenty-seven men; Plymouth one hundred and fifty-eight; Connecticut three hundred and fifteen. Volunteers from Rhode Island joined, which, with one hundred and fifty

ONLY ONE ENTRANCE ACROSS A LOG.

Mohegan Indians, made the largest army ever assembled in America at that time—numbering more than eleven hundred.

It is Sabbath morning, December 19th. The troops have slept on the snow, making their beds of hemlock boughs. They eat breakfast before daylight, and are on the march before the sun rises. Governor Winslow is commander; by his side is Captain Church. The fort is fifteen miles distant, but they reach it by one o'clock. An Indian who has been in the fort pilots them, and tells them that it is very strong; that it encloses several acres; that there is a high palisade, and that trees and brush have been laid against the walls; that there is only the one entrance across the log, which will be swept by the fire of the Indians.

The army forms. The men who are to lead the attack know that death is certain; but there is no flinching. They remember the desolate homes; the murdered men, women, and children all along the frontier. They have come to be avenged; to fight, to die, if need be. They rush toward the log. The walls of the fort blaze, and the men upon the log go down. Others take their places; they too fall, men and officers together—six captains, one after another. But the white men are so determined, there are so many of them, that the Indians cannot load their guns quick enough to keep them back. They run across the log, gather upon the opposite bank, and rush to the fort, and swarm inside the enclosure, pouring their fire upon the astonished Indians. Now comes the hand-to-hand fight—the white men using their swords and hatchets, the Indians their tomahawks. It is the fight of civilization against barbarism; power against weakness; the Future against the Past. The Past goes down in the terrific struggle. The Indian warriors flee to the other side of the fort, leap over the wall, and disappear in the forest, leaving their wives and children in the wigwams. Nearly four hundred of the white men have been killed or wounded. The infuriated soldiers will have their revenge: they set the wigwams on fire. Captain Church protests against it. "We can live on their corn, and make our wounded comfortable," he says.

But the blood of the soldiers is up, and they will not listen to reason; and as the sun goes down the flames of the burning wigwams illumine the wintry sky, and night closes in upon the ghastly scene of three hundred blackened corpses roasting in the flames, and upon the dying and the dead slain in battle.

The troops bearing their wounded take up their line of march. A storm has risen. Snow is falling, and the chill wind sweeps through the forest. Many of the wounded die, and the snow is their winding-sheet. They reach their rendezvous in the morning. Their victory has been dearly bought; but they have accomplished their object—the wiping out of the Narragansett nation.

Out in the forest are the Indians. It is a terrible night to them; their stronghold lost; their wives and children massacred or burnt to death; their provisions gone. Nothing left but eternal hate. The white man shall suffer—the Indian will have his revenge.

The war goes on; Canonicus, chief of the Narragansetts, is captured.

"We will spare your life if you will procure a treaty of peace," said his captors.

"The Indians never will cease fighting," he replied.

"You are condemned to death."

"I like it. I shall die before I speak anything unworthy of myself," is the heroic reply.

Lancaster, Medfield, Weymouth, Groton, and Marlborough, in Massachusetts, were burnt by the Indians. In Rhode Island, Providence and Warwick. From the east Philip went west to attack the towns on the Connecticut—Springfield, Hadley, Hatfield, Deerfield, and Northampton.

It is fast-day in Hadley, and the people are attending meeting. They hear the war-whoop of the Indians; behold their houses in flames, and their wives and children fleeing along the street, and rally to their defence.

Suddenly an old man with long white beard appears among them, directing them. He is brave, cool, collected. He speaks with authority. The Indians are driven off, and the white-haired man disappears. Who is he? None know. They think of him as God's angel sent for their deliverance. Years go by before they learn that it was one of the men who sat in judgment upon King Charles—William Goff, who has been secreted, with Edward Whalley, in the house of the minister, Rev. Mr. Russell.

All through the summer of 1676 the war goes on. Philip sees that his men are being killed, that his power is waning. He tries to enlist

DEATH OF PHILIP.

the Mohawks, but they will not listen to his proposal. He can only obtain powder from the French in Canada or Acadia. He will not hear of peace, and kills one of his followers who makes the suggestion.

Revenge! How sweet to gratify it! How many great plans have been upset by it!

The Indian struck down by Philip in his anger had a brother, who, when he saw the tomahawk crash through the skull of the murdered man, determined to have his revenge. No longer would he recognize Philip as chief, no longer be a friend, but a bitter, unrelenting enemy. In the darkness of the night he stole away to give himself up to the English—to lead them on the track of Philip.

Captain Church captures Philip's wife and child; this is a sad blow.

"My heart breaks! I am ready to die," said the chief. His warriors were disheartened; there were only a few left. He had carried desolation to the whites: he had fought bravely, but the struggle was over. Never again could he rally his followers. An archangel's trumpet only could summon them from their graves. Those who remained were plotting against him. He was disheartened. The white men had sold his wife and child into slavery in Bermuda. Broken in spirit, he returns once more to his old home, Mount Hope. The avenger is on his track. On Saturday morning, August 12th, Captain Church and Captain Golding, with their men, surround a swamp in which Philip has concealed himself. He is awakened by the footsteps of the soldiers, springs to his feet, and dashes through the forest.

Caleb Cook and the avenger stand side by side; Cook's gun misses fire, but the Indian sends a bullet through Philip's heart, and then with his hatchet chops off his head and bears it in triumph to Plymouth, where it is set upon the top of the gallows. The Indian is avenged upon his dead brother; and so perishes the son of Massasoit—the last chief of the Wampanoags.

The once powerful tribe was extinct; those who escaped joined other tribes—quite a number casting in their lot with the Indians in New Hampshire and Maine, who had been committing depredations upon the English, killing settlers at Dover, Exeter, and Berwick.

The Governor of Massachusetts sent one hundred and thirty men to Dover to arrest the murderers, and make a new treaty of peace. Major Waldron sent word to all the well-disposed Indians to come to the garrison. He was well known to the savages, who put faith in him. The dusky warriors assembled, and with them the Pequods. How shall they be seized? Major Waldron proposes to the Indians to have a sham fight.

"You shall fire first blank cartridges," he says.

The parties divide; the Indians fire; their guns are empty. In an instant the troop closes around them, and they are prisoners. Two hundred of them are sent to Boston, and from thence to the West Indies, to be sold as slaves. It is a perfidious, cruel act. Will the Indian forget it? He will bide his time!

One Indian escaped, and ran into the house of Elizabeth Heard, who secreted him till the soldiers were gone. It is an act of kindness which the Indian will never forget.

It has been a costly war to the English; thirteen towns have been burnt. More than six hundred men have been killed in battles; many have been maimed for life; and the colonies are burdened with a debt of more than half a million of dollars. There is grief in every household, and distress everywhere. Starvation stares them in the face. Connecticut has not felt the desolation; and the people of that colony generously contribute one thousand bushels of corn, which is sent to Massachusetts to be distributed among the needy.

CHAPTER XIX.

LOUIS FRONTENAC IN CANADA.

ON a summer day in 1672 Louis Frontenac, fifty-two years of age, just arrived from France, stepped on shore at Quebec—the first governor-general of Canada. Sixty years had rolled away since Champlain erected the first house in Canada, and so slow had been the emigration that there

COLBERT.

were not more than three or four thousand Frenchmen in the New World.

There had been civil war in France, but peace had come. Louis XIV. was king. Colbert was his prime-minister. He saw that the English were settling along the Atlantic coast, that the Dutch were driving a

A TRAPPER GOING HIS ROUNDS.

profitable trade on the Hudson with the Indians; that Spain had colonized the West Indies and Mexico, were masters of South America, and had a foothold in Florida; while France had done very little toward developing the vast empire, extending from the Gulf of St. Lawrence to Mexico, and westward to the Pacific Ocean.

The energetic prime-minister selected Count Frontenac to manage matters in New France. We may think of Frontenac as turning over in

LOUIS FRONTENAC IN CANADA.   253

his mind the work before him, the helps and hinderances. As he spreads
out the map which the geographers have made, he sees the St. Lawrence
and the lakes, the Ohio, Illinois, and Mississippi rivers, and their tribu-

LOUIS XIV.

taries, forming natural highways, by which the *coureurs de bois*—the
rangers of the woods, as they are called, half Indian and half French—
reach every section of the vast domain.

He sees that the English have no such great natural routes for travel, that all the rivers emptying into the Atlantic have their sources in the great mountain range, extending from the White Mountains, in New Hampshire, to Alabama. The mountain range is a barrier which nature has established between the Atlantic slope and the Mississippi Valley. In the valley of that river, on the banks of the Ohio, and upon the broad prairies of Illinois, the peasants of New France could rear their homes.

The king—who came to the throne when he was but four years old—Louis XIV., whose armies had won great victories, would give men and money. The Church of Rome would aid. The priests of St. Francis and the Jesuits had been among the Indians of the Great West, enlisting them on the side of France, and against the Dutch and English. The Dutch traders had never been beyond Niagara, while the French every year were chaffering with the Indians at Mackinac and on the Mississippi.

All the Indians had been won to the side of France except the Iroquois, who had never forgotten that their fathers had been driven from the St. Lawrence, nor that Champlain fought against them many moons before. Jean de Lamberville, a Jesuit missionary, was living with the Onondagas, trying to convert them to Christianity, and to call Louis XIV. their great father; but the warriors, who had carried their victorious arms to Tennessee, who had compelled the Illinois to pay them tribute, would call him brother only; never father.

Years before they had buried a hatchet with the Dutch beneath a great tree at Albany; the Dutch had treated them kindly, and would pay them twice as much for beaver-skins as the Canadian traders. Count Frontenac might give them presents, speak honeyed words, make large promises of friendship, but he could not make them his allies; the old grudge would always be kept in remembrance, but never would they resign their independence.

On what foundations shall the empire of France in the Western World be constructed—on the natural rights of man? No; for neither the king, the Romish Church, nor the Jesuits have any conception of natural rights.

"I am the State," shouts Louis XIV., striking his hand upon his breast. Neither in France nor in Canada can the people have a voice in public affairs. Pope, bishop, and priest alone have the right to say what men shall believe, or how they shall worship. There shall be no schools, unless taught by priests and nuns.

The government which Count Frontenac established consisted of himself, the Intendant, the man who had charge of the trade, the bishop, the attorney-general, and five councillors. These nine men made the laws. They divided the land into great estates, called seigniories. The owners, who called themselves seigniors, or noblemen, rented it to the farmers, who had nothing to do with government except to pay the taxes.

Count Frontenac does not see that such a system of government will

THE RIVAL COMPANIES SOLICITING TRADE.

end in failure; but he will learn by-and-by that in the New World the instinctive love of freedom which exists in every human heart will make itself manifest; that the woods, the vast reaches of country, the influences of nature, will awaken new thoughts and aspirations in the minds of men. The king will be far away. Count Frontenac will have no army to enforce the laws which he and the other eight men may make; his subordinate officers will grasp all the money they can as it passes through their hands; there will be quarrels between the governor and the intendant, between the governor and the bishop. The Jesuits will attempt to control affairs. These are some of the obstacles to the building up of the new empire which he will encounter.

For ten years Count Frontenac labored. Ship-load after ship-load of emigrants arrived from France, but the intendant thwarted his plans. The bishop quarrelled with him. The Iroquois would not be cajoled; and in 1682 he went back to France. Governor De la Barre succeeded him, but, after serving three years, was succeeded by Denonville.

The Iroquois had been at war with other Indians. They had conquered tribes in Virginia, compelling them to become Iroquois. They paddled along the southern shore of Lake Erie, through lakes Huron and Michigan, to the terror of the Hurons; invaded Illinois, wiped out the war-parties of their enemies; returned with hundreds of prisoners, and boats filled with beaver-skins, which the fur-traders of Canada had purchased, and which they had captured. They were ruining the fur-trade of Canada. "Capture the Iroquois, and send them as slaves to France," was the word which Louis XIV. sent to Denonville. The new governor, who read his prayer-book a great deal, but who knew very little about the Iroquois, determined to punish the haughty tribes who were carrying things with so high a hand.

Near the outlet of Lake Ontario were some Indians related to the Iroquois. Governor Denonville invited them to come to Fort Frontenac and have a feast. They accepted the invitation; but when they were inside the fort, he seized them all—thirty men, ninety women and children— and sent out a party, who returned with eighteen more warriors, and sixty women and children. He had them baptized, and the men sent as slaves to France. He summoned the tribes from the West—from lakes Huron, Michigan, and Illinois—to come and be revenged upon their enemies. A few weeks later a great fleet of canoes came down from the upper lakes filled with dusky warriors.

On a bright sunny day, July, 1687, the warriors from the St. Lawrence, from the shores of Michigan and the banks of the Mississippi, drew their canoes on shore in Irondequoit Bay, Lake Ontario, north-east of Rochester, New York. Never before had there been such an army in the service of Louis XIV.—soldiers in the uniforms of the king; officers, who had danced at Versailles; Jesuit priests, who had threaded the Far Western wilds, educated in the seminaries of the Old World, yet becoming savage in their modes of life, that they may win the heathens to the

Church; Indians in war-paint and feathers, wearing skins of the buffalo, the horns branching from their foreheads, the tails trailing upon the earth, wielding their tomahawks, brandishing their scalping-knives around the camp-fires at night, as they rehearse the deeds of daring they will undertake to destroy their haughty enemies.

The chief town of the Senecas is only fifteen miles away, and a broad path leads to it. Governor Denonville resolves that it shall be a heap of ashes; that the waving fields of corn shall be cut down; that the haughty tribes shall be brought into subjection. The army of two thousand French and Indians marches southward. The day is hot and sultry. The French officers pant beneath the terrible heat. Scouts, who have been reconnoitring around the village, report that no warriors are to be seen—only a few squaws. The invaders pass through a defile, but no Iroquois are in ambush; they pass a second defile, but no war-whoop resounds through the forest. Their enemies must have fled in terror. They reach the third, pass through it in haste, pressing on to surprise the town. Suddenly a yell, fiercer than the howl of a thousand wolves, breaks the stillness. Guns flash in their faces and upon their flanks. The Iroquois spring from the ground, confronting them with defiant shouts. Some of the French officers fall flat upon the earth, terror-stricken by the sudden apparition. The air is thick with flying arrows. Governor Denonville is brave; he encourages his men, orders the drums to beat, and stops the soldiers who start to run. The Canadian Indians leap from tree to tree, and exchange shots with their old enemies. For a few minutes the battle rages, and then the Senecas, who are only three hundred, disappear, carrying their wounded and some of their dead. Six French were killed, and thirty wounded. The Senecas had thirty or more killed, and sixty wounded. In the morning the army marched on to destroy the town, but found only a heap of ashes; the Senecas themselves burnt it several days before, and had retired southward, with their wives and children. Governor Denonville could only destroy their corn. Having done that, he went back to the lake, dismissed his allies from the Far West, and returned to Montreal, after building a fort near Niagara Falls. In a few days the Senecas were back again building new wigwams.

"If you overturn a wasp's nest, you must kill the wasp, or you will get stung!" said an Indian to Governor Denonville, on his way back to the lake. Denonville discovered after awhile that the wasp had stings.

Dongan was Governor of New York. He invited the Iroquois to meet him in council, and the chiefs came to Albany.

"You are subjects of King James," he said; "you must not make treaties with the French without my consent. You ought to drive the French out of the West, so that you can get all the beaver-skins from that section. You ought not to let the Jesuits live among you."

"We will fight the French as long as we have a warrior left," replied the Iroquois.

They went back to their homes with presents, with the promise of the governor that the King of England would stand by them in their struggle against the French.

Fifteen hundred of them stole along Lake Champlain, paddling their canoes by night, secreting themselves in the forest during the day. On the morning of August 5th, 1689, they crawled on their hands and knees into the village of Lachine, six miles from Montreal. Just as the robins and swallows were singing their songs in the early summer morning, the terrible war-whoop rung through the settlement, and the butchery began. There were three forts near by, from which the soldiers looked out and saw the inhabitants fall before the tomahawk. All the morning the bloody work went on, the street running with blood, the tall column of smoke ascending to heaven; the Iroquois hanging men, women, and children on stakes, and drinking themselves drunk on brandy.

Colonel Subercose started with four hundred men, and arrived at the burning village in the afternoon.

"The Indians are only a mile and a half away, dead drunk," said a Frenchman who had escaped.

Colonel Subercose started to attack them, when an officer came in hot haste from Montreal.

"The governor orders that you stand on the defensive, and run no risks."

Subercose was brave. He believed that the Indians, in their drunken stupor, could be routed; but at the command of the frightened governor he had to turn about; and the next day, the wasps, having recovered from their drunk, attacked a party of eighty soldiers, and defeated them.

For more than two months the Iroquois roamed the country around Montreal, killing, scalping, torturing their prisoners, paralyzing all Canada, wreaking terrible vengeance.

CHAPTER XX.

GOVERNOR BERKELEY AND THE VIRGINIANS.

"I THANK God there are no free schools in Virginia, and I hope we shall not have them these hundred years." So said Sir William Berkeley, whom Charles II. had appointed governor of Virginia.

Sir William lived in a stately house on the banks of the James. He rode in a lumbering old coach, and kept a retinue of servants. His table was spread with silver; he ruled pretty much as he pleased, and was king in a small way. He hated schools and printing-presses, for he knew that

BERKELEY, NEAR HARRISON'S LANDING.

knowledge is power, and that if the people were educated he would not be able to keep them so completely under his thumb. He cared so little for their prosperity that no roads were built. The highway was only a path. All travel was by boats on the river. Berkeley was arbitrary, avaricious, and cared more for feathering his own nest than for the interests of the people. There was not a bridge in Virginia. He allowed public interests to take care of themselves. He had a monopoly of trade with the Indians, and he alone possessed the right to sell them gunpowder.

"ALL TRAVEL WAS BY BOATS ON THE RIVER."

The Cavaliers, who had emigrated from England because they could not bear the Puritans' rule, favored aristocracy. They regarded the men who worked for a living with haughty contempt. They little knew how, without schools, the common people of the colony were being educated— how the freedom of the woods, the necessity of caring for themselves, was making them self-reliant; and how, when the time came, they would take matters into their own hands. The time came in 1675. The Indians on the Upper Potomac killed three settlers, and then, growing bolder, came down the James River, and killed thirty-six. Governor Berkeley ordered Sir Henry Chicoley to pursue them with troops; but when the troops were all ready, Berkeley ordered them to disband. If he chastised the Indians, of course he would have no more profits from trade. The Indians went on plundering and murdering, and laying the country in waste. Before the year was out they killed more than three hundred settlers.

"We are ready to wipe out the savages," said the settlers to the governor.

"No troops shall march without my orders," was the reply. Self-preservation is a greater law than any edict which Governor Berkeley could issue; and with Nathaniel Bacon at their head, three hundred settlers took matters into their own hands, and wiped out the Indians at a blow.

Bacon was only thirty-three years old; he had been in Virginia only two years, but had seen a great deal of the world. He hated tyranny. The people elected him to the Assembly; and through his influence a law was passed, which deprived Governor Berkeley of some of the fat fees which he had ingulfed. Bacon had marched against the Indians without orders; he held no commission. Berkeley would not overlook such conduct.

"You are a traitor and a rebel," said the governor; but, notwithstanding his hate, he was obliged to yield to the demands of the people and

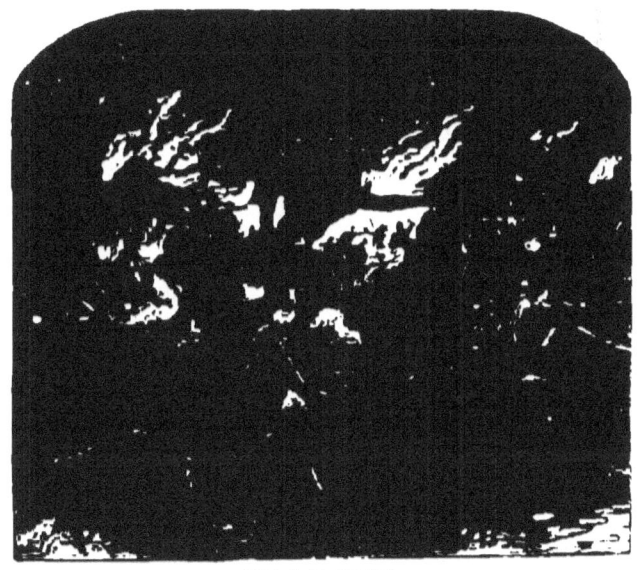

INDIAN MASSACRE.

give Bacon a commission, who started once more to drive the Indians out of the colony. When all were ready, Berkeley forbade them going, and denounced Bacon and his men once more as rebels and traitors.

"We are ready to lay down our lives for our wives and children, and for the colony; we will go and see why he calls us traitors," said Bacon. "Amen!" shouted the troops.

The drums beat, and they took up their march to confront the governor. Berkeley fled across Chesapeake Bay, and Bacon halted at Williamsburg.

"The flight of the governor is to be regarded as abdicating the governorship. The people must take matters into their own hands," said Bacon, and the Assembly came together at his call. He disbanded nearly all of his soldiers.

The men who adhered to Berkeley rallied around him, and he went up to Jamestown. Bacon hastened thither with his handful of men. There was a fight, but Bacon won the victory, and his soldiers, in the exultation over the governor, set the town on fire. The flames licked up every house, leaving nothing but chimneys and the crumbling walls of the church. It was an unhealthy locality; so malarious the climate, that Bacon sickened and died a few days later.

The people were without a leader. Berkeley set Robert Beverly to hunting down those who had taken part in the rebellion. Thomas Hansford was the first to suffer, "You die as a rebel!" said the governor.

"I die a loyal subject, and a lover of my country!" said Hansford, as he gazed unflinchingly upon the gibbet.

Mr. Cheeseman was condemned to be hung. "Let me die instead of my husband," said Mrs. Cheeseman. "He joined the revolt because I wanted him to."

She fell upon her knees before Berkeley. "Away!" shouted the hard-hearted governor.

"You shall be hanged in half an hour!" he said, smilingly, to William Drummond, whose wife and children were turned out upon the world to beg their living. The implacable man was not satisfied till thirty-two had been hung. "The old fool!" said Charles II., when he heard of it; "he has taken away more lives in that miserable country than I for the murder of my father."

"Had we let him alone he would have hanged half the country," said a member of Parliament. Charles sent over an order to the lieutenant-governor to assume the government.

"He is under me, and I will not yield," said Berkeley, and told the hangman to drive the commissioners who brought the letter out of the country. Charles II. would not submit to such an insult, and the next ship summoned Berkeley to England.

Governor Culpepper arrived in Virginia in 1680. He was cunning and avaricious. Before leaving England, he induced the king to have his salary raised one thousand pounds, and the perquisites increased, so that it would be equal to two thousand pounds income additional per annum, which the colonists had to pay. Tobacco was the only thing they cultivated, and the price of the plant was all the time falling.

Governor Culpepper thought out a plan to make towns grow. The vessels which went up the river and gathered the hogsheads from the plantations were ordered to call only at certain places. The governor thought that a town would spring up at each landing, but no towns appeared. There were no industries in the colony to make towns grow. The planter, who had been shipping his tobacco from his own plantation, under the order was obliged to drive it many miles to the landing, thus adding to the cost. The price of tobacco was falling. Was it because people were leaving off smoking? On the contrary, it was in greater demand than ever.

"The price is low because we raise too much," said some of the ignorant people, who could not see that the taxes and the restrictions ate up the profits.

"Let us cut up the plants," shouted a mob, which went into their neighbors' fields and destroyed many acres. To destroy tobacco was to diminish the governor's salary, and Governor Culpepper let them know that he was master by hanging several of the ringleaders.

"Five shillings shall be reckoned as six shillings in all trades between yourselves; but in the payment of my salary five shillings shall be only five," said the governor.

The Assembly protested against such an unrighteous act; but he was master, and drove them out of the chamber.

Culpepper stayed four years, and then was succeeded by Governor Effingham, who taxed the people still worse. If they remonstrated, he became more exacting. While he was in office, ship-loads of poor creatures, seized by the king's officers for having been concerned in a rebellion, arrived in Virginia, and were sold into servitude for ten or twenty years.

When William and Mary came to the throne, Sir Francis Nicholson was appointed lieutenant-governor while Effingham was in England. He saw that the people needed roads, and built one through the most thickly settled section. He encouraged the people to dress skins of cattle and sheep, and to cultivate flax. He tried to stop the terrible profanity which the people indulged in by putting them in the stocks.

While he was governor, Rev. James Blair, who was the commissary of the Bishop of London, and at the head of the Episcopal Church in Virginia, obtained a grant from the king and queen for a college. It was named William and Mary, and was liberally endowed by them.

"What is the use of having a college in Virginia?" asked Seymour, the attorney-general of the crown, when Mr. Blair called upon him to see about the charter.

"The people of Virginia, as well as people in other parts of the world, have souls to be saved."

"Curse your souls! Raise tobacco!" Seymour replied.

Nevertheless, the king and queen having ordered it, he was obliged to make out the charter, which he did in 1692—the second in America.

There were none but Episcopal churches in Virginia. The law would not allow the existence of other denominations. Mr. Blair, who had obtained the charter for the college, was a good man; but most of the other ministers were graceless scamps who read prayers for a living, and the planters were obliged to give them many pounds of tobacco per annum. The ministers were illiterate. They spent their time in hunting, fishing, or in getting drunk. On Sundays they read prayers, and preached what they called a sermon—a few commonplace words strung together, with quotations from the Bible; and, when service was through, drank their grog, and were ready for another week of idleness and carousal.

Governor Nicholson went to England in 1705, and for five years the people ruled themselves; and they did it so peaceably and sensibly that they were the five happiest and most prosperous years the colony had ever seen.

In 1710 Governor Spotswood came, bringing the privilege of the writ of *habeas corpus*. He ruled twelve years. During that period and through the following years the colony took on new strength.

In 1732 Joiste Hite went into the Valley of the Shenandoah with a colony from Pennsylvania, and began a settlement at Winchester. John Lewis settled Staunton.

Between 1730 and 1740, many Germans, Scotch Presbyterians, and Quakers crossed the Upper Potomac, and settled that region. They were industrious, hard-working, thrifty, religious, and intense lovers of liberty. They rejected the Established Church, chose their own ministers, and supported them. So it came about that there were two distinct settlements in Virginia—that east of the Blue Ridge, and that in the Valley of the Shenandoah.

CHAPTER XXI.

HOW THE KING TOOK AWAY THE CHARTERS OF THE COLONIES.

THERE was too much liberty in America to suit the King of England. The people of Massachusetts, under the charter given them by the grandfather of Charles II., were making their own laws and governing themselves, and Charles II. determined to take it from them. The King's Court issued a writ of *quo warranto*—that is, commanding the people of Massachusetts to appear before the Court and show by what authority they held the charter. If they were to say, "It was granted by King James," the Court could reply, "If the king had power to grant it, the king has power to take it away." The people of Massachusetts employed a lawyer to defend them; but the judges were ready to do the king's bidding, and the charter was revoked October 23d, 1684.

For fifty years the people had elected their own officers, but now the king was to appoint the governor, make laws, and levy taxes. There were to be no more general courts. It was to be absolute power on one side, and abject humility and serfdom on the other.

Charles II. laid his plans, or his ministers laid them for him, but Death stepped suddenly in, putting an end to a worthless life. His brother, the Duke of York, became King James II. On May 14th, 1686, a war-ship arrived at Boston, bringing Edmund Randolph, whom James had sent out to establish a new government. James appointed Joseph Dudley president, giving him authority to seize one of the meeting-houses in Boston. The Bishop of London sent Rev. Robert Ratcliffe to read prayers.

"The prayers in the book are nothing but trash; they are like leeks and garlic," said the people, hating the Prayer-book more than ever.

"I want you to have the bell tolled every Wednesday and Friday at nine in the morning, for the people to come to prayers," said the new governor to the owner of one of the meeting-houses.

"It is against our conscience; besides, we own the meeting-house. We will not do it!"

Sir Edmund Andros arrived, bringing his commission as governor of all New England. James had determined to carry out his brother's plan. He would see if he could not have prayers in church.

"The governor demands the keys of the meeting-house," said Edmund Randolph, whom Andros sent to obtain them.

"The land and the house belong to us, and we will not let him have them," said the pew-owners; but the sexton, being terribly frightened,

DISCUSSING THE CHARTER.

gave them up, and Rev. Mr. Ratcliffe read prayers on Good-Friday. It was the beginning of absolute government in Massachusetts. Governor Andros appointed Joseph Dudley, William Stoughton, John Usher, and Edmund Randolph justices of the court to settle all questions of law. He appointed Edmund Randolph to collect the taxes. A few men had nice positions in government, charging what fees they pleased. The people had bought and sold land under the charter, but Governor Andros said the titles were worthless, because the charter had been revoked, and that they must take out new titles, for which they were to pay roundly.

Andros ordered each town to choose a man to act with the selectmen in levying taxes. Rev. John Wise and John Appleton, of Ipswich, advised the people to pay no attention to the order, but to do as they always had done. But Governor Andros soon let them know that he would not permit such talk. He had them up before the Court.

"You have no privileges; you ought to be sold as slaves," said Dudley, who was ready to deprive them of every right.

"We send you to prison for twenty-one days, and you are to pay a fine besides," was the sentence of the judges, and the sheriffs marched them to prison.

"We cannot levy any taxes which the Assembly have not voted," said Shadrack Wilbur, town-clerk of Taunton, whereupon the judges sent him to jail for three months for his impudence. Andros ruled as he pleased, giving to his friends not only fat offices, but the farms which people had bought and paid for.

Having established his authority in Massachusetts, he went to Connecticut, to take away the charter which Governor Winslow had obtained

THE CHARTER OAK.

from Charles II. He rode in state, accompanied by sixty gentlemen, with a company of soldiers as his body-guard. The people of Connecticut received him respectfully, a troop of horsemen escorting him from Wethersfield to Hartford.

The governor and council called a meeting in the evening of the last day of October, 1687, to compel a surrender of the charter. There was a crowd in the chamber. The box containing the charter was placed upon the table. Two or three tallow-candles threw their dim light upon the document under which they had elected their own officers and made their own laws. Somebody lifted a finger, or made a sign; and in an instant the candles went out. There were no matches in those days. They must strike a light with a flint and steel, or get a coal from somewhere. We can only imagine what Governor Andros and everybody else was thinking about, sitting there in the darkness while somebody was going to the nearest house for a light; but when the candles were lighted, the charter was nowhere to be seen. No one knew what had become of it; no one but Captain James Wadsworth, who was wise enough to keep his knowledge to himself. It was not in his house or any other building, but secreted in a hollow oak-tree out on the Common.

Although Governor Andros had not got possession of the charter, he set up his own government, and his secretary wrote this in the records:

"His Excellency Sir Edmund Andros, Knight, Captain, General, and Governor of his Majesty's Territory and Dominion in New England, by order from his Majesty James the Second, King of England, Scotland, and Ireland, the 31st of October, 1687, took into his hands the government of the colony of Connecticut, it being by his Majesty annexed to Massachusetts and other colonies under his excellency's government. FINIS."

The word was written; but nothing is final in this world that is not based on Right, as Governor Andros discovered after a while. New England for the time being was under his heel.

The governor returned to Boston, fitted out an expedition, sailed eastward to the Penobscot, and plundered the French at Castine, in Maine. He kept six hundred soldiers in arms, compelling the people to pay the taxes. Edmund Randolph, the tax-collector, sold out his privilege to John West, who seized the goods of those who did not pay.

It was on the 4th of April, 1689, that a vessel entered Boston harbor from Nevis, with a sailor named John Winslow on board, which sailed from that island in February. Just before he left there, a vessel sailed in bringing copies of the Prince of Orange's proclamation.

The word ran through the streets.

"You are wanted at the governor's house," said a messenger.

"Why didn't you come here at once?" asked Andros.

"It is not customary for a passenger to go to the governor when the master of the ship has the news."

"Where is the Declaration of the Prince of Orange that you brought? I want it."

"I will not give it to you, because you are not willing the people shall know what has taken place."

"You are a saucy fellow. Sheriff, take him to the justice of the peace; let him deal with him."

"Give us the Declaration of the Prince of Orange," said the justice.

"I will not; you keep the news from the people. I bought it with my own money."

"Away with him to prison!" and the sheriff marched him off. The people of Boston did not know what was going on in England, only that William had landed. But their blood was rising. Governor Andros saw it, and moved into the fort on Fort Hill. Out in the harbor was the frigate *Rose*, swinging at anchor.

It was election-day, April 18th, and people came in from Cambridge, Roxbury, and Dorchester to hear the minister of the First Church preach. They were early; some of them discovered Captain George on shore, and put him under guard. Somebody beat a drum at nine o'clock. A man climbed up the staff on Beacon Hill and hung out a flag. All Boston saw it, and the people out in Cambridge. Captain Hill's company suddenly made its appearance in King Street, marched to the State-house, escorting Simon Bradstreet, Thomas Danforth, and several of the old magistrates who had sympathized with the people. In a very short time Edmund Randolph, who had done so much to help Andros, Justice Foxcraft, John Sherlock — the sheriff who had marched John Winslow to jail — and many others who had held offices under Andros, found themselves in jail. The jailer himself, who had turned the key on so many good men, found himself in a cell, and Mr. Scates, a bricklayer, turning the key upon him. There were twenty companies under arms in Boston; drums were beating; men were running with their muskets. There was a great crowd on the shore at Charlestown — four hundred men, with guns, ready to help. Parties were coming down Charles River from Newton — down the Mystic from Medford.

Never before had there been such a crowd in King Street. Somebody read a paper from the balcony of the State-house, setting forth the oppression they had suffered, and resolving to have justice.

The *Rose* was opening her port-holes, running out her guns. The lieutenant was issuing his order, swearing great oaths at the insults to the captain. He sent a boat and soldiers to bring them on board; but the people seized the guns of the sailors, and marched them to the Town-house. John Nelson commanded the troops. He marched to the fort, and planted his cannon.

"Surrender the fort!" was the order to Andros. He gave it up, and Captain Fairweather turned the gun upon the frigate. Captain George promised that the frigate should not fire, and ordered the sails to be brought on shore.

Great crowds poured into town all the afternoon, ready to take their revenge upon Andros, who was marched off to the fort. He tried to escape by putting on woman's clothes. He passed two sentinels, but the third discovered his thick-soled shoes, and marched him back. The people elected Simon Bradstreet governor, and absolute rule was at an end in Massachusetts.

On the 29th of May a vessel sailed into the harbor, bringing joyful news. William, Prince of Orange, was King of England, and there was an end forever of absolute rule in England. In commemoration of the event the people of Boston sat down to a grand dinner in the Town-house, providing an abundance of wine, everybody eating and drinking till the sexton rung the bell at nine o'clock in the evening, when they made their way home, rejoicing over the downfall of King James, Andros, and all their minions.

CHAPTER XXII.

KING WILLIAM'S WAR.

AT three o'clock Tuesday morning, December 11th, 1688, James II., King of England, rose noiselessly from his bed, passed with stealthy step from his palace, entered a carriage in waiting, was driven rapidly to the bank of the Thames, where he stepped into a boat and was rowed swiftly down the stream. As the boat shot past the old palace of Lambeth, he flung into the river the Great Seal of England, used in stamping all the royal documents to give them validity.

He was fleeing from his palace, his throne, his kingdom, from a people whom he had outraged in his attempts to set up a personal and absolute government by his tyrannical acts. The people had risen against him. They had invited his son-in-law, William of Orange, to aid them in overthrowing the government. He had landed at Torquay, had been welcomed by the nation, and James was a fugitive, seeking refuge in France with Louis XIV., whose adopted daughter, Mary of Modena, was James's wife.

On the last day of December, James entered the old palace of St. Germain, on the bank of the Seine, near Paris, which Louis XIV. had placed at his disposal.

The Queen of England, with her infant child, arrived two days before. Louis went out to meet her with a great retinue of courtiers.

"St. Germain shall be your home," he said. He gave her a key to a casket which contained twenty thousand dollars in gold.

"You are still King of England, and I will aid you to recover your kingdom," he said to James, and prepared for war against England.

It was not simply a generous act on the part of Louis to a fellow-sovereign who was in trouble, but there were ideas behind it. Louis XIV. and James II. believed in the absolute right of kings to rule as they pleased; that the people should have no voice in the government; that kings were appointed of God to govern, and that the people must do their bidding. They had the right to levy taxes, to wage war, and compel the people to fight at their pleasure. "*I am the State!*" said Louis, and that comprehended all. Not another being in France was of any account.

William, on the other hand, believed that the people had a right to make their own laws through a Parliament of their own choosing; that

WHERE WILLIAM LANDED.

the Parliament should be free to act, and that it was the duty of the king to execute the laws.

James and Louis were Roman Catholics. James had done what he could to crush out the Protestant and establish the Roman religion in England. Louis hated Protestants, and drove them from his kingdom. He took pride in calling himself "the most Catholic King." He regarded himself as the great defender of the Roman Church.

William was a Protestant; his wife Mary, daughter of James, was a Protestant, and he was regarded by the Protestants of all Europe as the defender of their religion.

So the war was not waged merely that James might regain his crown; but it was to be a great struggle between the absolute right of kings and the freedom of the people.

On the banks of the Rhine, the Danube, the Po, in the meadows of Holland, on the plains of Germany, amidst the vineyards of Italy, in the wilderness of North America, upon the Penobscot, the Piscataqua, Merrimac, and Mohawk, the struggle is to go on—not whether James shall be once more King of England, but whether the people shall have a voice in government, and think for themselves in matters pertaining to religion.

Quenchless the ardor of the Jesuits. Through all the years, from the landing of the missionaries sent out by Madame de Guercheville, the black-gowned fathers were making their influence felt among the Indians of the Penobscot and Kennebec.

Gabrielle Dreuillet, bidding farewell to France, obedient to the orders of his superior, crossed the Atlantic and established a mission on the Kennebec, raised a chapel, set up the cross and an image of the Virgin Mary, gave presents to the dusky warriors, and reaped a rich harvest of converts so far as baptism was concerned. When the Iroquois, from beyond the Hudson, stole through the wilderness and fell upon the tribes in Maine, Father Gabrielle visited Boston, to ask the Puritans to use their influence in constraining the implacable Iroquois. He was hospitably entertained, and the Governor of Massachusetts used his influence to restrain the Mohawks. Three Jesuits succeeded Father Gabrielle—Father Thury, and the two brothers Bigot. They stirred up the Indians to make war upon the English.

"My children," said Thury, "how long will you suffer your lands to be encroached upon by heretics? By the religion I have taught you, I exhort you to resist them. The hatchet must be cleaned of its rust. Night and day a continual prayer shall ascend to heaven for your success; an unceasing rosary shall be observed till your return, covered with the glory of triumph."

During these years the Indians had made themselves at home in Dover, New Hampshire, coming and going as they pleased. There were five houses in the town, strongly fortified, in which the settlers slept at night.

It was the evening of the 27th of June, 1688, when two squaws called at Major Waldron's garrison and asked if they might sleep there.

"Indians are coming to trade to-morrow," they said.

Major Waldron was pleased to hear it, for trade with the Indians always meant a good bargain to the white man.

"Supposing we should want to go out in the night, how shall we open the door?" asked the squaws.

They are shown how to undo the fastenings.

Major Waldron is eighty years of age, white-haired, wrinkled; but there is force yet left in his arm, and he is as courageous as ever. He has no fear of any Indian that walks the earth; and the vague rumors and whisperings are as idle as the wind to him. He lies down to sleep. The lights in all the houses are extinguished. No sentinel walks the street. In the darkness dusky forms glide noiselessly through the town. The doors of the houses open. The terrible war-whoop breaks the stillness of the summer night.

A half-dozen Indians enter the room where the brave old man is sleeping. He springs from the bed, seizes his sword, and single-handed drives them from the chamber into the large room. In the darkness one steals behind him, strikes a blow, and he falls. It is their hour of triumph. He has been a ruler and a judge. The Indians can be sarcastic. They seat him in his arm-chair, lift him upon the table. It is his throne.

"Get us supper!" is their command to the family.

They eat, and then turn to their bloody work. One by one they slash their knives across his breast.

"So I cross out my account," they say. They are settling an account that has been standing thirteen long years.

An Indian cuts off one hand.

"Where are the scales? Let us see if it weighs a pound."

Major Waldron bought beaver-skins, and was accustomed to put his hand as a weight upon the opposite scale when he weighed them. One cuts off his nose, another his ears. The old man's strength is gone, and, as he falls, one holds his sword, which pierces his body.

In one of the garrisons is a faithful dog, whose barking awakes the inmates. The Indians rush upon the door. Elder Wentworth throws himself upon the floor, holds his feet against it, braces himself with all his might. The bullets whistle over him, but do him no harm, and he holds it fast.

Elizabeth Heard, with her children, on this evening has come from Portsmouth in a boat. They are belated, and the Indians are at their bloody work when she reaches Major Waldron's house. Her children flee, while she sinks in terror upon the ground. An Indian with a pistol stands over her, but does not fire.

"No harm shall come to you," he says. It is the Indian whom she befriended thirteen years ago.

When the morning dawns it is upon the smouldering ruins of burning dwellings, upon the mangled bodies of twenty-three men and women, and upon twenty-nine women and children going into captivity—a long

MAJOR WALDRON'S TERRIBLE FIGHT.

and weary march through the woods to Canada, to be sold as slaves to the French or kept in servitude by the savages.

Louis XIV. saw that France could build up a new empire in America; but to accomplish such a result a man with a strong hand must be sent out to direct affairs, and Count Louis Frontenac was selected as the one most suitable for the work, with which he was already familiar. He reached Quebec, and laid his plans to strike three blows at the same time upon the English — one in the Valley of the Mohawk, one in New Hampshire, and one in Maine.

In was in mid-winter that the three picked parties of French and Indians started—one from Montreal, the second from Three Rivers, the third from Quebec. Let us follow them, and see how the French and Jesuits carried on this war of ideas in the wilderness of the Western World.

In the middle of January, 1690, one hundred and sixty French and ninety Indians, who had been baptized by the Jesuits, started from Montreal on snow-shoes, carrying heavy packs, and dragging their provisions on sleds.

They toiled day after day through the snow to Lake Champlain, along its entire length on the ice, and then through the woods to the Valley of the Mohawk. On a Saturday night they halted two miles from Schenectady. The sun went down in a haze, and the night was bitter cold.

At eleven o'clock they reached the town. Schenectady is so far from Canada, the snow is so deep, the cold so severe, that no enemy would undertake a hostile raid. So thought the easy-going Dutch settlers, who at nine o'clock raked up their fires, laid aside their pipes, and went to bed, little dreaming of the blow that was about to fall upon them. The party was commanded by D'Aillebout de Mantet and Le Moyne de Sainte-Hélène, who had with him his two brothers, Le Moyne d'Iberville and Le Moyne de Bienville, whom we shall see again.

The night was cold; the wind howled through the forest; snow was falling. The men stamped their feet to warm them. They were impatient of delay. French and Indians alike longed for the moment when the bloody work was to begin. The officers post their men. Then comes the war-whoop, the breaking in of doors. The settlers leap from their beds to fall before the tomahawk; women seize their children and run into the streets, to be shot down alike by French and Indians. Turn which way they will, there is nothing but death. The snow is crimsoned with their blood. The streets are strewn with the dead and dying. The flames of forty dwellings illumine the wintry sky, and in the lurid light the Indians, with strings of bleeding scalps of white-haired men and helpless women and fair-faced girls hanging at their sides, dance in frantic joy. The haze that settled down at night upon the horizon was the precursor of an approaching storm. The wind howls through the forests, sweeping the snow in blinding drifts. Yet out in the storm, barefooted, clad only in their night-dresses, men and women are fleeing with infants in their arms, freezing where they fall.

Ah, what a scene is that which Captain Mantet and Lieutenant Sainte-Hélène beheld on Sunday morning! the peaceful village in ruins—smoul-

SCHENECTADY.

dering ashes instead of houses—every house except two burnt; sixty ghastly corpses in the snow; infants with their brains dashed out; men and women and maidens ruthlessly butchered. So those soldiers reared in France have massacred the inhabitants of this village, so far away in the wilds of the American Continent. At sunrise they are on their way with twenty-seven prisoners, and all the horses, making a swift retreat to Canada.

Count Frontenac was greatly pleased with the result of the expedition, and wrote these words to Louis XIV.: "You cannot believe the joy that this slight success has caused, and how much it contributes to raise the people of Canada from their dejection."

The second party sent out by Frontenac consisted of twenty-four French and twenty-five Indians, commanded by Francis Hertel de Rouville, whom we shall see again.

On the 28th of January the fifty-one men started from Three Rivers southward through the wilderness, up the valley of the St. Francis to the highlands between the Atlantic and the St. Lawrence, to the head-waters of the Connecticut, across Northern New Hampshire to the Saco; and from the Saco to the Piscataqua they made their way through ice and snow, animated by the thought that they would strike terror to every Englishman on the continent.

On the 27th of March they reached the English settlement at Salmon Falls, on the Piscataqua, ten miles only from the sea. Seventy years had passed since Edward and William Hilton had reared their fish-houses at Dover, only five miles distant; and this settlement of Salmon Falls was the frontier town in New Hampshire—so slow had been the advance of civilization.

While Hertel and his men were preparing for their bloody work, the scouts crept in the darkness up to the residences of the settlers. They discovered a saw-mill, where men had been at work through the day, a fortified house, and two stockades, and scattered farm-houses. No sentinel challenged them. No one was astir. The water was falling over the dam; no other sound broke the stillness of the night.

In the darkness Hertel posted his men, and the work began: thirty persons tomahawked and shot, fifty-four women and children captured. Morning dawned upon the scene of desolation—mangled corpses and burning dwellings, with Hertel and his prisoners moving away. A few hours later a party of settlers came up with him. He saw them approach, and posted his men on the bank of a river. It was nearly night when the fight began. The English lost two killed and seven wounded. Hertel lost several; but he prevented the English from crossing the stream, and hurried his captives away, giving some of them to the Indians—Christian Indians, who had been baptized by the Jesuits, who tied them to trees, and put them to death with horrible tortures.

The third party sent by Frontenac started from Quebec, consisting of fifty French and sixty Christian Indians, commanded by a Canadian officer, Captain Portneuf, and Lieutenant Courtmanche. They reached the Kennebec River in May. They travelled slowly, catching fish, and killing moose and deer. Upon the Kennebec lived the Abenakis Indians, who joined the expedition. The Jesuit priests had been among them, and had used their influence to stir them up to wage war upon the English. From the Penobscot came St. Castine, with some French and Indians.

Hertel, in his return to Canada, had taken the route of the Kennebec, and joined Portneuf. Altogether there were nearly five hundred men.

On the shore of Casco Bay, at Portland, was Fort Loyal, and a little village with four block-houses. On the morning of the 20th of May the people saw their cattle in the pastures running and tossing their heads in fright. The news of what had taken place at Salmon Falls had reached Portland, and the settlers had flocked into the village. There were one hundred of them in the fort, commanded by Captain Davis. The men in the garrison heard a gun fired, and then the yells of Indians. Portneuf's Christian Indians had killed a man, and could no longer restrain themselves. Their shooting alarmed the garrison, and every man seized his gun. Captain Davis resolved to keep his men in the garrison; but Lieutenant Clark was for going out to find the enemy. There was little discipline, and he went out with thirty men, when suddenly there came a volley from an unseen enemy which killed or wounded every man, and only four succeeded in reaching the fort, into which all the settlers, with their families, fled.

The French commander had no cannon; but collecting the shovels of the settlers, he began to dig a trench to undermine the fort. While some of his men were at work, others were lying in secure places, ready to pick off any soldier that attempted to fire. For three days and nights the French worked in the trench till it was close to the fort.

"Surrender!" shouted the French commander.

"Will you give me good quarter, with liberty to march to the nearest English town, and have a guard for our defence and safety?" Captain Davis asked.

"You shall be protected; I swear it!" said Portneuf, lifting his hand and taking a solemn oath that everything that was asked for should be granted.

The gates were opened, the garrison laid down their arms, and then the work of death began. The tomahawk crashed through the skulls of men and women alike. The scalping-knife encircled their brows; infants were dashed against the stones; and all that were spared were taken into captivity.

"You have violated your solemn pledge," protested Captain Davis.

"You are rebels against your lawful king, James II.," replied Portneuf, who, setting the town on fire, retreated to Canada, having wiped the settlement from the face of the earth.

Captain Davis and four other men were spared. Upon reaching Quebec, he was brought before Frontenac.

"We were promised good quarter. I thought I had to do with Christians that would have been careful of their engagements, and not violate their oaths," said Davis, fearlessly.

"You are rebels against your rightful king," said Frontenac; but he treated Captain Davis courteously, and liked him for his outspoken opinions.

About twelve miles from the sea, on the Merrimac River, in Massachusetts, is the beautiful town of Haverhill. It was a small settlement in 1690, but it was easy for the Indians to descend the river in their canoes and attack it.

In the month of August, 1692, John Keezar went into his meadow with his scythe to cut grass. He took his gun with him, and leaned it against a tree. While mowing, an Indian crept through the woods, reached the tree, and seized the gun.

"Me kill you now," he said, bringing his gun to his shoulder.

John Keezar was brave, and he was quick to act. He was not the man to flee; that would be certain death. He could yell louder than any Indian. With a screech he rushed upon the savage with his scythe, who dropped the gun and took to his heels; but Keezar overtook him, and gave a stroke which cut a fearful gash across the half-naked body of the savage, who fell dead at his feet.

Two boys, Isaac Bradley, fifteen years old, and Joseph Whittaker, eleven, were at work one day in Mr. Bradley's field, when a party of Indians sprung out of the woods and seized them. Isaac was small, but was bright and brave; Joseph, though four years younger, was as large as Isaac, but he had less heart and strength. The Indians did not stop to kill any of the settlers, but hastened away, travelling through the woods to the beautiful Lake Winnipissaukie, where they had established their camp for the winter. In a very short time Isaac picked up enough of their language to know what they were saying.

"We shall go to Canada in the spring," was what he heard them say.

April came; the snow was gone, the flowers were beginning to appear. In a few days the Indians would be on their march to sell them to the French. But Isaac had no intention of going to Canada. Day after day he thought over the matter. He knew that the English settlements were far away to the south, but there was no path. He had no compass. How could he ever reach them? He would be guided by the sun by day and the stars by night. He would make the attempt. He might perish, but death was better than captivity.

"I am going to try it to-morrow night. I am afraid you won't wake," he said to Joseph, who always slept soundly, and snored in his sleep.

"Oh yes, I will!" Joseph replied.

The Indians had killed a moose, and Isaac managed to secrete a large piece of the meat in the bushes near the camp. He filled his pockets with bread. Night came; all were asleep except Isaac, who was so stirred by the thought of escaping that his eyes would not close. Every sense was quickened. He arose softly and touched Joseph, who was sound asleep. He did not stir, and Isaac shook him harder.

"What do you want?" Joseph asked.

In an instant Isaac was stretched out by his side, and snoring. The Indians did not wake; and after a little while the boys arose softly, and crept out of the wigwam, Isaac with an Indian gun and ammunition. They made their way to the meat, took it in their arms, and started upon the run, guiding their way by the stars. On through the wilderness, amidst the tall trees, over fallen trunks, over stones, through thickets and tangled brushwood, they travelled till morning, and then crept into a hollow log.

Great the consternation in the camp of the Indians. Their captives gone! A gun lost! At daybreak the Indians, with the dogs, were on their track, and in swift pursuit. The boys heard the barking of the dogs, which soon came sniffing round the log. What shall the boys do now? Isaac is quick-witted.

"Good fellow, Bose! Good fellow! Here is some breakfast for you;" and he tosses the moose-meat to them. The dogs know his voice, devour the meat, and are as happy as dogs can be. The boys are their friends; they cease barking, and trot around with no further concern. The Indians come upon the run. The boys hear their voices as they hasten, followed by the dogs!

Through the day they lie secreted in the log, and when night comes strike out once more in a different direction from that taken by the Indians. All night long they travelled, nibbling the bread in their pockets. Morning came, and again they concealed themselves. Once more at night they are on the march. On the third day Isaac shoots a pigeon, but does not dare to kindle a fire, and they eat it raw. They find a turtle, smash its shell, and eat the meat. On, day after day, they toil,

"HE STAGGERS WITH HIM THROUGH THE WOODS."

eating roots, and the buds of the trees just ready to burst into leaf. The sixth day came, and they suddenly find themselves close to an Indian camp. They peep through the underbrush, and see the warriors sitting round their camp-fire smoking their pipes. They steal softly away, and then run as fast as their legs can carry them. The morning of the eighth day comes. Joseph's strength is failing; his courage is gone. He cries bitterly. They are in the wilderness, they know not where, with nothing to eat, their clothes in rags, their feet bleeding.

"Cheer up, Joseph! Here are some ground-nuts. Here, drink some water!" says Isaac.

No brave words, no act of kindness can quicken the courage of the fainting boy. What shall Isaac do? Stay, and die with him, or try and find his way out? Sad the parting—the younger lying down to die upon a mossy bank, the older turning away, alone, lost in the wilderness.

With faltering steps Isaac pushes on, and discovers a house! No inhabitants are there; but he knows that there must be white men not far away. With quickened pulse he turns back to the dying boy, awakens him from sleep, rubs his legs and bathes his temples.

"Come, Joseph, we are saved! Help is near."

He leads him a few steps, then takes him on his back, staggers with him through the woods, and strikes a beaten path.

Glorious Isaac Bradley! The world's history has many a story of heroic action, but none nobler or braver than this act of yours. Before night they reach a fort upon the Saco River, and astonish the soldiers with the story of their adventures.

In March, 1697, Thomas Dustin, of Haverhill, was at work in his field, when he heard the terrible whoop of Indians, and ran toward his house. He had eight children—the youngest only a week old. The mother was in bed with her infant, tended by her nurse, Mary Neff.

"Run for the garrison!" he shouted to his other children. They fled, the oldest carrying the youngest, while Mr. Dustin rushed into the stable for his horse. The Indians were close upon him. He could not save his wife; but would try and save some of the children. He came up with them. Which should he take? All were equally dear to him, and he would try and save all. The Indians reach the house, and seize Mrs. Dustin and Mary Neff. They dash the infant against a rock, and the mother beholds its bleeding corpse. They rush after the fleeing family. "Run for your lives!" shouts Mr. Dustin to his children, then leaps from his horse, shelters himself behind the animal, rests his gun across the horse's back, taking deliberate aim upon the foremost Indian. He fires, springs into the saddle, and is away, with the bullets flying around him. He loads his gun while on the gallop, reaches his children, dismounts, and is ready for the pursuers; so, keeping them at bay, he reaches the garrison, saving all the children.

In a few moments, twenty-seven men, women, and children in the settlement are massacred, their houses set on fire, and the Indians are fleeing toward Canada.

It was the middle of March. In the woods there was still much snow. The streams were swollen with its melting, and yet, with but one shoe, Mrs. Dustin began her march through the wilderness, driven by her captors. Her feet were torn and chilled. Every step was marked by her blood. Some of her fellow-captives grew faint and fell, and then the tomahawk despatched them. All except Mrs. Dustin and Mary Neff were killed.

Three days brought them to the Indian rendezvous, a little island at the junction of the Merrimac and Contoocook Rivers, in Boscawen, New Hampshire. It was a place where the Indians could catch fish, and where Mrs. Dustin found a little boy, Samuel Leonardson, who had been a captive for more than a year, and who had learned the Indian language.

In a few days, all except twelve of the Indians started upon another marauding expedition. Upon their return, the captives would be taken to Canada. The woman who has seen her infant dashed against a stone has an heroic spirit. Death will be preferable to captivity. They who would be free must strike the blow that will give them freedom. She lays her plan.

"Ask the Indians where they strike with the tomahawk when they want to kill a person quick," she says to Samuel.

"Strike 'em here," the Indian replies to Samuel's question, placing his finger on Samuel's temples.

Little does the savage think that his own hatchet will be buried in his brains by the keen-eyed woman who watches his every movement. The Indian shows Samuel how to take off a scalp, all of which Mrs. Dustin observes.

Night comes, and she informs Mary Neff and Samuel of her plan, and stimulates them by her heroic courage.

There are twelve Indians in all who lie down to sleep, feeling that their captives cannot escape. No one keeps watch. The wigwam fires burn low. No sound breaks the stillness of the night except the waters of the Contoocook sweeping over its rocky bed. Mrs. Dustin rises, seizes a tomahawk, gives one to Mary Neff, another to Samuel. Each selects a victim. A signal, and the hatchets descend, crushing through the skulls of the Indians, blow after blow in quick succession. It is the work of a

WOMEN STANDING GUARD.

minute, but in that brief time ten of the twelve have been killed; the two escape in the darkness!

The prisoners, prisoners no longer, gather up the provisions, take the guns of the Indians, scuttle all the canoes but one, and take their depart-are down the Merrimac. A thought comes to the woman: will their friends believe the story they will have to tell. They will have indisputable evidence.

A few strokes of the paddle bring them back to the island. Mrs. Dustin runs the scalping-knife around the brows of the dead Indians, takes their scalps, and starts once more, guiding the canoe with her paddle, landing, and carrying it past dangerous rapids, reaching Haverhill, sixty miles distant, with her bloody trophies, to the astonishment of her friends, who thought her dead. The Government of Massachusetts made her a present of fifty pounds; and in these later years the people of the Merrimac Valley, to commemorate her heroism, have reared a monument upon the spot where she achieved her liberty.

All along the frontier, from the Penobscot to the Hudson, the Indians murdered, plundered, and carried the settlers into captivity. The people could have no security only as they huddled into forts. If they worked in the fields, some kept watch, while others ploughed, mowed, or reaped. On Sunday every man carried his gun to meeting, and the men always sat nearest the pew-door that they might spring out first in case of an attack. Scouts roamed the woods, and sentinels kept watch day and night. The colonies did very little in retaliation except to send an expedition under William Phipps to Acadia. He captured Port Royal (Annapolis), and went on to capture Quebec, but failed. Some of his ships were wrecked in a terrible storm, and the men drowned. Several hundred perished in the expedition.

The colonies had gathered four hundred troops at Albany to invade Canada; but there was a scarcity of provisions, the commanders disagreed, and the troops were disbanded.

Captain John Schuyler, of Albany, was indignant at the failure, and with twenty-nine white men and one hundred and twenty Mohawk Indians swept down Lake Champlain and the Richelieu to Chambly, and fell upon the French settlement at La Prairie, killing and capturing twenty-five persons, burning houses and killing cattle—giving the French just such warfare as they waged upon the English. Down in Maine Le Moyne d'Iberville took the fort at Pemaquid.

So for eight years, while great battles were being fought in Europe, the bloody, indecisive contest raged in America, over the ideas spoken of at the beginning of this chapter, till peace was declared at Ryswick in 1697—Louis XIV. consenting to recognize William and Mary King and Queen of England.

CHAPTER XXIII.

NEW JERSEY AND MARYLAND.

THE Dutch called the Delaware "South River," and the Hudson "North River." When Peter Minuet came to be governor of Manhattan, some of the settlers crossed the North River, and made a settlement on the western bank at Pavonia, as a good place to trade with the Indians. It was the first settlement in New Jersey. They also went up the South River, and built a trading-house at Burlington; but not till after the end of Dutch rule in America were there any more settlements.

MIDDLE COLONIES.

Charles II. gave New Jersey, as well as New York, to James, who sold the southern half to George Carteret and Lord Berkeley. Carteret took the east and Berkeley the west half. Carteret had been governor of the island of Jersey, and they agreed to call his half East Jersey, and Berkeley's West Jersey. Carteret laid out a town, and called it Elizabeth, in honor of his wife.

Robert Treat and some other people from Connecticut explored the country around Elizabeth, and Newark purchased it of the Indians, and made a settlement.

Other settlers came—a great many Quakers, Presbyterians from Scotland, Huguenots and Dutch from New York. One of the Dutchmen was Arent Schuyler, who bought a large farm, built a great house, and had many slaves. One of the field hands discovered a piece of stone, green and heavy. He showed it to Mr. Schuyler, who sent it to England. Word came back that it was very rich copper ore. Mr. Schuyler had a great deal of the ore on his farm, and shipped many loads to the brass founders of England, and became very rich.

FIRST CHURCH IN NEWARK.

"What shall I do for you?" he asked of the slave, Cæsar. "Name any three things you want, and you shall have them."

"Please, massa," said Cæsar, "I should like to live with you always; second, please let me have all the tobacco I want; and, third, I should like a dressing-gown like yours, massa."

"Oh, ask for something of value."

"Well, then, Massa, please give me a little more tobacco."

Mr. Schuyler had a son, Peter, a resolute, sturdy man, who had much to do with what was going on in public affairs. He had many weary marches through the forests around Lake Champlain, up the Mohawk, in the French and Indian wars.

Philip Carteret, son of George, was appointed Governor of East Jersey. He wanted things his own way, but found that the men from Connecticut, the Presbyterians from Scotland, and the Quakers had ideas of their own. They compelled him to grant them the right to have a voice in the making of laws.

THE OLD SCHUYLER MANSION.

Their charter said: "No person shall at any time, in any way, be called in question, or in the least punished or hurt, for opinion in religion."

In 1702, Carteret and Berkeley gave up their rights to Queen Anne, and the two colonies became one, the queen appointing the governor. From that time on there was little disturbance, and the people were so prosperous that travellers said there were no poor in the colony.

Before Charles I. became king, he went to Spain to see if he could bring about a marriage between himself and the King of Spain's daughter. George Calvert went with him to manage affairs; but the Spaniards wanted to drive such a hard bargain, politically, that Charles went back to England utterly disgusted.

PETER SCHUYLER.

Nevertheless, when he came to the throne, he rewarded George Calvert by making him Lord Baltimore, and giving him the island of Newfoundland. Lord Baltimore undertook to plant a colony there, calling it Avalon; but the fogs, rain, sleet, and snow were so disagreeable that he could not induce people to settle there, and Charles gave him a tract of country bounded on the south by the Potomac River, from its mouth to the Alleghanies, and on the north by the fortieth parallel of latitude.

William Claybourne, a surveyor from London, sent out by the London Company to Virginia, had already surveyed a portion of the country, and had purchased the island of Kent in the Chesapeake, and made a settlement there in 1631.

George Calvert died before he could carry out any plans for the settlement of his new colony; but his son Cecil

ARMS OF THE CALVERT FAMILY.

sent his brother Leonard, with three hundred emigrants, in two ships, the *Ark* and the *Dove*, to make a beginning.

Most of the settlers were Catholics; and the Jesuits, ever on the watch

FIRST MASS IN MARYLAND.

to get a foothold in America, sent Father White and two other priests of the order of Loyola.

On March 25th, 1634, the day of Annunciation, the priests set up a cross on the western shore of Chesapeake Bay, and celebrated mass. They laid out a town, and named it St. Mary's. Lord Baltimore gave the name of Maryland to the province.

The Indians flocked around, and were kindly treated. Lord Baltimore bought the land of them, and made them liberal presents. The Indians had cultivated large fields of corn, their wigwams were well made, and they gave two of the largest to the Jesuit priests.

There was trouble at the outset.

"You are under my authority," was the word sent by Lord Baltimore to William Claybourne and the men of Kent.

Claybourne was acting under the Governor of Virginia; besides, he had purchased the island of Kent.

"What shall I do?" was the question put by Claybourne to the Governor of Virginia.

"Stand by your rights."

Claybourne went on trading with the Indians for their furs; whereupon the St. Mary's people, watching their opportunity, seized a vessel loaded with furs owned by the Kent people. At that the Governor of Virginia sent a vessel to demand redress. There was a fight, and several were killed; but the St. Mary's people were victorious.

William Claybourne hastened to England, and the trouble was referred to the court. The judges discussed the question of authority. It took them a long while to do it; but in 1639 they informed Claybourne that Lord Baltimore had all authority.

The judges did not know that the people in Maryland the while were quietly taking things into their own hands. Lord Baltimore and his friends, to whom Charles had given the territory, sent out a code of laws; but the settlers, instead of accepting it, formed a code of their own, in which they said that everybody, slaves only excepted, should have equal rights.

"We will have a government of our own, elect our representatives, and make our own laws," they said.

The spirit of liberty was rising. It was having a great uplift in England, and all along the eastern shore of America, from the Piscataqua to the Potomac.

There were many petty troubles in Maryland during the conflict between the King and Parliament, and during Cromwell's time. William Claybourne never lost sight of his claim. In 1655 quite a battle was fought between Governor Stone and Claybourne and their followers. Stone was taken prisoner, and some of his officers were hung. There was anarchy for several years.

Things were more quiet after Charles II. came to the throne; but when James II. became king, he sent out Sir Lionel Copley as governor, who established the Church of England, and who would not permit the Catholics to have any voice in government.

There was so much disturbance, the laws of England in regard to commerce were so unjust, that no great towns sprung up. It was not till 1730 that Philip Jones went out with his compass and chain, and laid out the city of Baltimore.

The people had very little trouble from the Indians; and during all the years that the New England colonies were fighting the French and Indians the people of Maryland were living in peace and quiet.

LAYING OUT BALTIMORE.

CHAPTER XXIV.
SETTLEMENT OF PENNSYLVANIA.

ONE of the commanders of the English navy who fought the Dutch on that day when Charles II. and the frivolous Cavaliers were at Greenwich, and heard the roar of cannon down the Thames, was Admiral

WILLIAM PENN.

Penn. He was a brave man, and so loyal that he lent the king a large sum of money. His son William was a student at Oxford, who for attending a Quaker meeting was expelled from college.

"William has become a Quaker, or some melancholy thing," said his old associates, when they heard of his expulsion.

"A Quaker! William a Quaker!"

The admiral could not believe it; but when he found that William was thinking seriously about becoming a follower of George Fox, he became furious, and turned him out-of-doors.

The admiral died in 1670, leaving a great estate, which fell to William. Part of the property was the money which the king had borrowed—amounting to sixteen thousand pounds. Charles could spend thousands of pounds every week foolishly, but never had any for the payment of his debts. William Penn, probably understanding that it would not be easy to obtain the money, proposed to take it in land in America. A grand idea came to him. The Quakers could have little peace in England; he would start a colony in America, where they would be exempt from persecution. Charles was delighted at the proposition. Of what value to him was a wilderness three thousand miles away, inhabited by savages? To cancel the debt, he gave Penn all the territory now included in Pennsylvania.

On September 1st, 1682, the ship *William*, with Penn on board and one hundred Quakers, sailed from England for their new home. It was a sad voyage, for the small-pox broke out; and before the ship entered Delaware Bay, one-third had died.

It was a day of rejoicing when they reached Newcastle. The Swedes and the Quakers who had already settled near there welcomed him as their benefactor.

Other vessels came—thirty-three in all—bringing Quakers who were eager to turn their backs upon England, where they had suffered bitter persecution.

"There shall be freedom of thought and speech to all. You shall be governed by laws of your making. I shall not usurp the right of any, nor suppress any person," said Penn.

Three Swedes, sons of Swan Swanson, owned a strip of land between the Delaware and Schuylkill rivers; Penn picked it out as the site for the city of "Brotherly Love," which he proposed to build. He purchased the land, and set Thomas Holmes to surveying it, who laid the streets straight from river to river, and named one Chestnut, another Walnut, a third Mulberry.

The king had given Penn the land, but he made the Indians his friends by purchasing it of them. He invited the chiefs to meet him beneath the wide-spreading trees on the banks of the Delaware. "We are

SETTLEMENT OF PENNSYLVANIA.

one flesh and blood, brothers," said Penn. "We will live in love as long as the sun and moon shine," the Indians replied. Penn gave them blankets, knives, kettles, axes, beads, and trinkets, which cost him but little, but which were of great value in the eyes of the confiding Indians. It was a recognition of their right, and they were satisfied. They regarded every man who wore a broad-brimmed hat as their friend.

The Quakers were taught by George Fox that they ought not to follow the fashions of the world; and so their clothes were never out of fashion, for they were made after an unchanging pattern. Their meeting-

LANDING OF WILLIAM PENN AT PHILADELPHIA.

house was plain. Sunday they called First Day. No one preached unless moved by the Spirit, which they believed would tell them what to say or do at all times. Nevertheless, a whipping-post and stocks were set up

FIRST BRICK BUILDING ERECTED IN PHILADELPHIA—GIVEN BY MR. PENN TO HIS DAUGHTER.

for the punishment of offenders. They regarded theatres as demoralizing.

The Quakers lived in the city of "Brotherly Love," but they found that they could not get on without judges and courts. They claimed to be guided by the "inner light," but could not free themselves from superstition.

Margaret Mattson and Jeshro Hendrickson were accused of being witches, and brought before Penn for trial. The neighbors testified against them; but the judges said the testimony would not warrant hanging them, and they were set at liberty. The settlers were superstitious. They believed that the devil was prowling here and there, seeking whom he might devour. Rev. Mr. Hesselins—the Swedes' minister—cousin of Emanuel Swedenborg, wrote an account of the devil's doings; how a captain of a ship, who was very profane, was seized by the devil and thrown into the river in sight of the people. He also had a marvellous tale to tell how, for fifteen days, it rained upon a black oak-tree, while all the rest of the forest was dry!

Gabriel Thomas wrote to his friends about matters in Philadelphia during the first year of its settlement. There were thirty carts in the colony. William Penn rode in a coach or on horseback. Laboring men could get paid as much for their time as in England. Women could get very high wages—from five pounds to ten pounds per annum. No girl need be an old maid, for there were more men than women, and a girl could have her pick of the young men.

Gabriel and his fellow-citizens used to drink their grog at the Blue

SETTLEMENT OF PENNSYLVANIA.

Anchor Tavern. It was only when a ship came from England that they had any news to tell. They discussed the affairs of their neighbors, and told stories of pirates and robbers.

William Penn remained two years, and then returned to England, leaving his secretary, James Logan, to look after affairs.

After he was gone the great "Walking Purchase" of land took place. The settlers wanted more land, and made a bargain with the Indians to give them so many blankets, kettles, knives, and axes for what land a man could walk around in a day.

The Quakers laid out a path, removed the fallen trees, made a smooth way, picked out the fastest walker that they could find, and put him in training.

JAMES LOGAN, SECRETARY TO WILLIAM PENN.

The Indians came to see him walk, and were astounded when they saw him walking so fast that they had to run to keep up with him, going round a great tract.

"The land is ours now; you must build your wigwams somewhere else," said the Quakers.

"We have been cheated; we will not leave," said the Indians.

PENN'S HOUSE.

It was the beginning of no end of trouble; but the white men were the strongest, and the Indians had to leave.

In December, 1699, William Penn, after being fifteen years in England, revisited Pennsylvania once more.

"I am going to my American Desert," he wrote when he was about to leave England. But Pennsylvania was not a desert. The inhabitants numbered more than twenty thousand, and Philadelphia was a town. William Penn had a charming country residence on the Delaware above the city. An avenue of poplars extended from the house to the river, and the grounds were laid out in lawns and gardens. There were apples, peaches, plums, grapes, and strawberries, and flowers of every hue. If the governor wanted to enjoy himself on the river, he had but to step into his barge. There was a cook-house, a wash-house, a brewery where he could brew his own beer; and it took a great deal to supply the people who came to transact business, or to pay their respects to him.

In the great hall were long tables, where everybody, the poor as well as the rich, Indians, negroes, all could find something to eat, with servants to wait on them. Once when he gave an entertainment there were so many to eat that the tables were spread beneath the trees, and the people ate one hundred roast turkeys, besides other meats.

He brought furniture from England—covered chairs, oaken tables, ware manufactured in the potteries of England, damask curtains, and plush cushions.

He lived in the style of an English gentleman, but did not look upon himself as being any better than other men because he had money. One Sunday, when he was going to meeting on horseback, he overtook Rebecca Ward, who was trudging along without shoes or stockings.

THE PENN SEAL.

"Will thee ride, Rebecca?" he asked; and, seating her upon the pillion behind him, gave her a fine ride. William Penn purchased several slaves, but treated them kindly. He was always a true friend to the Indians; and in 1701 invited the chiefs of all the tribes to meet him, to make a treaty under which they should have the same rights before the law as the English.

In 1701 he was obliged to return to England, to look after his interests there. He never visited Pennsylvania again.

CHAPTER XXV.

WITCHES.

ALL the world believed in witches—that men and women, by making a bargain with the devil, had power to torment whomsoever they pleased. Everybody believed that the devil was very much like a man in form, only that he had wings like a bat, a tail, cloven feet, and horns; that he was able to confer great power on witches, enabling them by infernal arts to raise storms, sink ships, afflict children with fits, kill cattle, set chairs and tables to dancing; that they had power to make themselves invisible, creep through key-holes, ride on broomsticks through the air, and that it was a special delight to hold their orgies in thunder-storms. To doubt the existence of witches was to reject the teachings of the Bible. Were not the children of Israel commanded not to suffer a witch to live?

In 1488, four years before Columbus sailed in search of the New World, a storm swept over Constance, in Switzerland, which destroyed the corn and grapes; and the people accused Anne and Agnes Mindelen of having raised it. They confessed that the devil put them up to it, and were burnt to death. Two years before this, Pope Innocent VIII. issued a bull directing that witches should be burnt. When the wicked and cruel Alexander VI. was in the papal chair, he set the Inquisitors to work to rid the world of witches. They burnt six hundred poor old women in the bishopric of Bamberg, in Germany. By the shore of Lake Geneva, in 1515, during three months more than five hundred were burnt to death. What a scene! Innocent women, accused of horrible crimes by their neighbors and best friends, led out by the score, chained to stakes, fagots piled around them, their bodies smeared with pitch, that the fire might take surer hold upon the quivering flesh!

In 1549 the good Archbishop Cranmer gave these directions to the bishops: "You shall inquire whether any one makes use of charms, sorcery, enchantments, witchcraft, soothsayings, or any like craft invented by the devil."

The Countess of Lennox, who conspired against Queen Elizabeth, consulted witches.

In 1591 Archbishop Spotswood spent nearly all his time in examining witches. All through Spain, France, Germany, and Holland, during these years, thousands of men and women were burnt. In the village of Lindheim, in Germany, containing only six hundred inhabitants, thirty were

LAKE GENEVA.

put to death in one year. More than one hundred thousand were burnt in all.

In 1618 seventeen witches were condemned to death in Lancashire; sixteen in Yarmouth; fifteen at Chelmsford.

When a woman was accused of being a witch, her hands were tied to her feet, and she was thrown into a pond; if she did not sink, it was regarded as positive proof that she was a witch — that the devil alone enabled her to float. If, on the contrary, she went to the bottom, she was supposed to be innocent. Very few floated; nearly all the poor creatures were drowned while showing that they were innocent.

Matthew Hopkins was appointed witch-finder. He travelled through England, having his expenses paid, and a fat fee besides, arresting whomsoever he pleased, examining their bodies for witch marks. If a pimple, wart, or wen was discovered, it was a sure indication that the person was in league with bad spirits. They were the devil's marks. The accused were subjected to terrible torture to make them confess. In a short time more than one hundred persons were hung through Hopkins's zealous efforts. He was aided by some of the best men in England. One of those who suffered death at the hands of Hopkins was a good old minister, eighty years of age, who had preached for half a century. Hopkins threw him into a pond; but, as he did not sink, it was clear that he had sold himself to the devil. The good man died, declaring to the last that he was innocent.

Hopkins was greatly reverenced by the people, as endowed with superior wisdom; but after awhile he himself was accused, and had a taste of his own medicine. His thumbs were tied to his great toes, and he was tossed into a pond. He managed, however, to swim, and stoutly protested that he was not a witch, and so saved his neck from the halter.

Sir Matthew Hale, lord chief-justice, was a good man, an upright judge, and presided at the trials of many witches. Amy Duny and Rose Cuilender were accused by Margaret Arnold of bewitching her little girl, who was afflicted with fits.

"One day," said Margaret, "a bee flew into the face of my child, and a few minutes after she vomited up a two-penny nail. At another time my little girl caught an invisible mouse which she threw into the fire, and it instantly flashed like gunpowder."

Nearly all the testimony was as silly as this.

Sir Matthew called upon Sir Thomas Brown, a great and learned physician, to give his opinion.

"I am clearly of the opinion," said Sir Thomas, "that the fits are natural, but heightened by the devil co-operating with the malice of the witches at whose instance he did the villanies."

Sir Matthew was tender-hearted; but here was the testimony of the greatest physician in all England that the devil and two old women had a hand in making the child sick. The Bible commanded him to put them to death, and he ordered them to be executed. Sir Matthew wrote a book about witchcraft. Rev. Richard Baxter, a learned and godly minister, wrote another. Rev. Mr. Perkins published a third, all detailing the horrible crimes and incantations of the witches. The printers of London kept their presses going, printing pamphlets about witches. No one doubted the stories told by the accusers, especially when many of the accused confessed that they were in league with the devil.

Every vessel crossing the Atlantic brought accounts of the doings of witches in England, and books and pamphlets found their way into the settlers' homes all over New England and Virginia. Governors, judges,

STORIES WERE TOLD OF WHAT THE WITCHES WERE DOING.

ministers, and people alike read them, firmly believing what such good men as Chief-justice Hale and Richard Baxter had written. When anything strange happened that they could not account for, it was ascribed to witches. If the butter would not come in churning, the cream was bewitched; and the way to get the witch out was to heat a horseshoe red-hot and drop it into the churn, which would so scorch the hag that she would leave in a twinkling. A horseshoe nailed over a door would prevent witches from entering it.

Ministers preached about witches, warning their hearers that the Prince of the Power of the Air was round about them, going up and down the earth seeking whom he might devour. By the wide-mouthed fireplaces in the old kitchens stories were told of what the witches were doing. The eager listeners felt their flesh creep, and their hair stand on end as the stories were rehearsed. Timid people were afraid to go out-of-doors after dark, fearing that they might encounter a ghost or hobgoblin. Boys and girls, if sent down cellar after a mug of cider or for apples, felt their hearts leaping up their throats as they beheld fantastic shadows on the walls. When they crept up-stairs to bed, it was with quick and nervous step, for there was no knowing what might be behind the boxes and barrels in the garret. When the lightnings glared, and the rain beat against the windows, they thought of the witches that were careering through the air on broomsticks or holding a revel in the forest. The dim, pale light which they sometimes saw along the marshes was will-o'-the-wisp—the devil's wisp—ready to lure them into some snare. The devil was ever round about them, and the witches would do his bidding.

About the time that Matthew Hopkins was tossing women into ponds and hanging them, the people of Charlestown, Massachusetts, in 1648, accused Margaret Jones of being a witch. She doctored people with roots

THEIR HEARTS LEAPING UP THEIR THROATS.

and herbs. The idea was abroad that she had a "malignant touch;" that if she laid her hands upon persons in anger they would become blind, deaf, or in some way afflicted. She was put in prison, and the man who guarded her said that he saw a little child with her, which instantly vanished.

THE IDEA WAS ABROAD THAT SHE HAD A "MALIGNANT TOUCH."

Notwithstanding she declared her innocence, the deluded people protested that she was in league with the devil, and she was executed. John Winthrop, who kept a diary, says, "The day and hour she was executed there was a very great tempest in Connecticut, which blew down trees, and did much damage"— the superstitious and credulous people firmly believing that the devil was thus taking vengeance upon the country.

Margaret's husband, Thomas, had a sorry time of it after she was hung; people pointed their fingers at him, and made life so unpleasant that he went on board a ship bound for Barbadoes. It was a small vessel, and there were eighty horses on the deck, which made it top-heavy. While at anchor in the harbor the craft began to roll fearfully, and the superstitious sailors said that Thomas Jones was the cause of it, and hustled him on shore and into prison as a witch.

People were such firm believers in witchcraft, and so credulous, that it was easy to create a suspicion against a person, and many women were accused of being witches by their jealous and envious neighbors. One of the settlers of Springfield, Massachusetts, Hugh Parsons, sawed boards and planks for a living. He worked hard during the day and filed his saws at night, and made money faster than some of his neighbors, who through jealousy, perhaps, accused him of being a witch. He was arrested; and Hannah Lankton and her husband testified that one day they had a boiled pudding for dinner, and when they took it out of the bag it was cut open lengthwise, as if with a knife. They did not know what to make of it, and said it was bewitched. They threw a piece of it into the fire, and soon after Mr. Parsons came to the door, which convinced them that he had bewitched it. A neighbor could not get a tap out of a beer-barrel, but Mr. Parsons pulled it out without any difficulty, which was sure proof that he was a witch. Mrs. Parsons was sick and became insane, and the ignorant people said that she had sold herself to the devil. Her little child died, and they said that she and her husband had poisoned it. They were put in prison, and the neighbors testified against them. One man saw snakes in his room at night. A woman saw a light flickering around her petticoat; a cow would not give down her milk; a woman had a pain in her breast; a little girl said that she saw a dog, though no one else could see it. Others saw things that they could not account for, which made them think that their neighbor Parsons was a witch. Although he and his wife were cast into prison, the judges did not think they were witches, and they were not put to death. In nearly every town there were men and women who were suspected of being witches.

Hampton, New Hampshire, had a witch—General Moulton—who made money so fast that his superstitious neighbors said that the devil helped him. One day his house caught fire and was burnt, and they said that the Evil One had done it because the general fooled him. He bargained with Satan to fill one of his boots every night with gold. The devil came to fill it, and was amazed to find that it took several cart-loads. Wondering how so small a boot could hold so much, he made an examination, and discovered that the general had cut a hole in the sole and another in the floor, that the gold had run through it, and that he had filled the cellar; whereupon he blew a flame from his mouth and set the house on fire!

The saddest story in the history of our country is that of the witch craze at Salem, Massachusetts, brought about by a negro woman and company of girls. The negress, Tituba, was a slave, whom Rev. Samuel Parris, one of the ministers of Salem, had purchased in Barbadoes. We may think of Tituba as seated in the old kitchen of Mr. Parris's house during the long winter evenings, telling witch-stories to the minister's niece, Elizabeth, nine years old. She draws a circle in the ashes on the hearth, burns a lock of hair, and mutters gibberish. They are incantations to call up the devil and his imps. The girls of the village gather in the old kitchen to hear Tituba's stories, and to mutter words that have no meaning. The girls are Abigail Williams, who is eleven; Anne Putnam, twelve; Mary Walcot and Mary Lewis, seventeen; Elizabeth Hubbard, Elizabeth Booth, and Susannah Sheldon, eighteen; and two servant-girls, Mary Warren and Sarah Churchill. Tituba taught them to bark like dogs, mew like cats, grunt like hogs, to creep through chairs and under tables on their hands and feet, and to pretend to have spasms.

Mr. Parris had read the books and pamphlets published in England—how persons bewitched acted like animals, and went into spasms, and he came to the conclusion that they were bewitched. He sent for Doctor Griggs, who said that the girls were not sick, and without doubt were bewitched.

The town was on fire. People came to see the girls, who, delighted with the success of their play, crept about all the more like cats and dogs, barking, mewing, and uttering piercing screams.

Sunday came; and when the congregation had finished singing, Abigail Williams said to Mr. Parris, "Now stand up and name your text."

The minister and everybody else was amazed, but he read his text.

"It is a long one," said Abigail.

The minister went on with his preaching.

"There, we have had enough of that," shouted another girl.

"There is a yellow bird on the minister's hat," cried Anne Putnam.

The parents of the girls stood aghast, and Mr. Parris, believing that they were assaulted by the devil, invited the ministers of the other parishes to come and hold a day of fasting and prayer. The ministers assembled, saw the girls go into fits, rolling their eyes, holding their breath, muttering gibberish, peeping like frogs, barking like dogs, and devoutly believed that they were bewitched. They prayed solemnly and fervently, recalling the saying of Jesus Christ—"This kind goeth not out except by fasting and prayer."

The news spread, and the people came in crowds to see the girls.

"Who bewitches you?" they asked.

"Sarah Good, Sarah Osburn, and Tituba," said the girls.

Sarah Good was a poor old woman, who begged her bread from door to door. Sarah Osburn was old, wrinkled, and sickly.

What a scene was that around the meeting-house, March 1st, 1692! All Salem was there; for the women who were accused of being witches were to be examined by the justices.

> "A gathering on the village green—
> The cocked hats crowd to see;
> Their clothing ancient velveteen,
> With buckles on their knee.
>
> "A clustering round the tavern-door,
> Of square-toed village boys,
> Still wearing as their grandsires' wore—
> The Old-world corduroys."

Sheriff and constable escorted the justices, John Hathorne and Jonathan Corwin, from Thomas Beadle's tavern to the meeting-house, and gave them seats in front of the pulpit. Rev. Mr. Parris prayed that God

THOMAS BEADLE'S TAVERN, 1692.

would direct them. The girls were there, and Sarah Good was brought in by the sheriff.

"Have you made a contract with the devil?" asked Justice Hathorne.

"No."

"Children, is this the person who hurts you?"

"Yes; she is sticking pins into us!" and the girls screeched.

"Why do you torment the children?"

"I do not."

The girls went on with their screeching, and the justice and all the people were so deluded, and were such firm believers in witchcraft, that they accepted all that the girls said as truths, and the denials of the wrinkled old women as lies.

"Sarah Osburn, have you made a contract with the devil?" asked the justice.

"I never saw the devil."

"Why do you hurt the children?"

"I do not hurt them."

"She does! she does!" said the girls, and the people decided in their minds against her.

"Tituba, why do you hurt the children?"

"I do not."

"Who is it, then?"

"The devil, for aught I know."

"Did you ever see the devil?"

"Yes, he came to me and bid me serve him. Sarah Good and Sarah Osburn wanted me to hurt the children, but I would not."

"How does the devil appear when he comes to you?"

"Sometimes like a hog, and sometimes like a great black dog."

"What else have you seen?"

"Two cats; one red, and the other black. I saw them last night, and they said 'Serve me;' but I would not."

"What did they want you to do?"

"Hurt the children."

"Did you not pinch Elizabeth Hubbard?"

"Yes, they made me pinch her, and wanted me to kill her with a knife."

"How do you ride when you go to meet the devil?"

'On a stick. I ride in front, and Sarah Good and Sarah Osburn behind me. We go up over trees, and in a short time are in Boston or anywhere else."

Tituba had a great many other things to narrate—that the devil sometimes wore a tall black hat; that one of his imps was about three feet high, hairy all over, and had a long nose; that the imp came into Mr. Parris's house and stood by the fire.

The people believed her. Would she be likely to admit that she was a witch if she were not one? The girls accused her of pinching them, and she acknowledged that she did so; and the girls, therefore, were telling the truth, and Sarah Osburn and Sarah Good, in denying that they were witches, were telling a lie. So the justice and the people reasoned, and the sheriff took them to Ipswich jail, ten miles away, and the people went home to talk over the wonderful event.

The ministers of Salem, Boston, and the surrounding towns met to consult upon the matter. Among them was the learned Cotton Mather, who accepted as truthful the terrible accounts that reached him from England. Few if any doubted that the girls were bewitched; and they, finding it pleasant to have so much notice taken of them, went on with their creeping, barking, mewing, and falling into convulsions, and crying

REBECCA NURSE'S HOME.

that somebody was sticking pins into them. They accused Martha Corey and Rebecca Nurse, two women who were kind to the poor, and very religious; but so credulous were Rev. Mr. Parris and Rev. Mr. Noyes, and everybody else, that they were arrested. When they were examined before the justice, the girls all cried out that the women were tormenting them. "I am as innocent as a child unborn," said Mrs. Nurse; but the people, the ministers, the justices, all had lost their heads, and the women were committed to prison. Mrs. Good had a little girl, Dorcas, five years old, and the bewitched girls said that Dorcas helped her mother in tormenting them. "She bites me!" they cried, and showed the prints of teeth on their arms. The sheriff thereupon arrested Dorcas and put her in prison, where she was chained with her mother; for it was believed that unless the witches were chained they would fly out through the key-hole. Sarah Cloyse and Elizabeth Proctor were the next persons accused. The judges met sometimes at Thomas Beadle's tavern, sometimes in the meeting-house.

The news spread. No one doubted that the devil had come in great wrath to afflict the good people of Salem. Rev. Mr. Lawson, Rev. Mr. Parris, Rev. Mr. Noyes, and other ministers preached sermons against witchcraft, setting forth that these manifestations were without doubt produced by the devil. The whole colony was excited, and Lieutenant-governor Danforth and his councillors—six hundred men—went to Salem to sit in judgment at the trial of Sarah and Elizabeth. Abigail Williams brought a horrible accusation.

"I saw a company of witches at the Rev. Mr. Parris's house," she said; "there were forty of them. They had a sacrament, and Sarah Cloyse and Sarah Good were their deacons, and the witches drank blood."

When Sarah Cloyse fainted at the terrible accusation, the girls went into convulsions, and John, Mr. Parris's negro, rolled and tumbled upon the floor, and all cried that the witches were tormenting them. Governor Danforth and his councillors were amazed. The prisoners had no one to help them, for there were few lawyers in America in those days. The governor and the judges asked them questions, assuming at the outset that they were witches, and the poor women, friendless and alone, astounded, knew not what to say. They could only say, "We are innocent." Though they said it, the governor, judges, and everybody else believed the girls, and the poor women were thrust into prison.

Instead of there being fewer witches, there were more, and in a short time the jails were filled with men and women. Among those arrested was Rev. George Burroughs, who had once preached in Salem, but who was living in Maine. The sheriff made a long journey to arrest him.

Not only the girls and Tituba, but others accused those arrested of being witches. If a man had anything against his neighbor, it was easy for him to take revenge by accusing him of exercising witchcraft. Samuel Shattuck, who dyed clothes for a living, had trouble with Bridget Bishop. John the negro also had a grievance against her, and testified that she was a witch. "I saw her go through a hole no larger than my hand," said John; and the judges accepted his testimony. Samuel Shattuck's child had fits. "I believe it is the work of Bridget," he said. What should the judges do? What but condemn them to be hung. The Bible commanded that witches should not be suffered to live. For one hundred and fifty years the laws of England had been in force against witches. Thirty thousand had been executed in England. Parliament had appointed a witch-finder. King James had written a book against them. Archbishop Jewell had begged Queen Elizabeth to burn them. Rev. Richard Baxter, whose name was reverenced everywhere, had written against witches. In all lands they were regarded as the enemies of God and man, and here they were conspiring with the Evil One against the lives, the peace, and happiness of the community. The great and good Lord Chief-justice of England, Matthew Hale, had condemned those to death who were not near so diabolical as the accused, and had written a book showing from the Bible that witches were in league with the devil. Besides everybody in Salem, the friends and neighbors all believed that the accused were witches, and ought to be put to death. They were magistrates, appointed of God, as they believed, to administer the laws faithfully and impartially. They themselves had seen the girls go into convulsions, and heard them cry when the witches pinched them. With the rest of the world, the judges lost their heads, and condemned the poor creatures to death.

Through the streets of Salem rattled the cart that bore them to the place of execution, out to a hill overlooking the village, where a gallows was erected. They climbed the ladder with the halter around their necks, men and women, the minister, and those who had listened to his preaching. People gazed in horror upon their old friends and neigh-

SHATTUCK'S HOUSE.

bors, swinging in the air and struggling in the throes of death; and when life was extinct, the bodies were thrown into holes, and earth heaped above them. They trampled it down, and thought of them as suffering the torments of the devil. How horrible! yet, if we had been living then, we too should have lost our judgment, reason, and common-sense, as the people, the wisest and best men of 1692, lost their judgment, under the terrible delusion, wild foundation, and lamentable ignorance of that period.

THE HILL ON WHICH THEY WERE HUNG.

Sad to think that nineteen were hung; that Giles Corey, who would either say "Guilty" or "Not Guilty," had rocks piled upon him till he was crushed to death; that one hundred and fifty men and women were thrown into prison before people came to their senses!

The wife of Rev. Mr. Hale, of Beverly, was accused. There was not a woman in Massachusetts more beloved, honored, and respected. The people were amazed. They could not believe that so godly a woman could be in league with the devil. They began to see, what they had not before thought of, that the testimony of the girls had been only assertion that the witches were tormenting them. The judges had not questioned the girls, but the accused instead; and the denials of the accused had been regarded as lies, while the assertion of the girls had been accepted as the truth.

The spell was broken. People saw that they had been under a delusion. One of the judges, Samuel Sewall, made a humble confession on Sunday in the Old South Church in Boston, with tears rolling down his cheeks, and ever after, so long as he lived, kept a day of fasting and repentance once a year to manifest his sorrow to the world.

"Touching and sad a tale is told,
Like a penitent hymn of the Psalmist old,

> Of the fast which the good man life-long kept,
> With a haunting sorrow that never slept,
> As the circling years brought round the time
> Of an error that left the sting of crime."

The sheriff threw open the prison doors, and the girls, finding that no one believed their accusations, had no more stories to tell of being tormented. So the great wave of superstition, that had sent hundreds of thousands to an untimely grave in Europe, died out in the village of Salem.

Some of the girls made humble confession of their sin and folly, and endeavored by right living to atone for the past, but found little happiness in life, for ever before their eyes were the swinging forms of those who had died upon the gibbet. Nothing that they could do could ever recall the dead from their graves. What they had begun in sport ended in a terrible tragedy.

CHAPTER XXVI.

THE LEGACY OF BLOOD.

SPAIN was a great empire—including South America, Mexico, Florida, the West Indies, Italy, and Sicily. The King of Spain, Charles II., was dying. He was childless; who should succeed him? His oldest sister was Queen of France, wife of Louis XIV.; his youngest Empress of Germany, wife of Leopold of Austria. All Europe would be by the ears if a descendant of either of the sisters were to be king of the whole Spanish realm.

Louis XIV. for France, and William III. for England and Holland, set themselves up as administrators of the estate of the King of Spain in advance of his death. They agreed that the Archduke Charles of Austria should succeed him, and have the Netherlands, America, and the West Indies: that France should have the Spanish possessions in Italy. They never consulted the people of those countries as to what would be agreeable to them, but laid their plans regardless of the wishes of everybody.

While making this agreement with William, Louis XIV. was pulling secret wires, sending ambassadors to Rome to pull wires in the Vatican, and other ambassadors and agents to Madrid, to manage affairs there in the palace of the dying king; and when, on the 3d of November, 1700, Charles died, and all the grandees of Spain and the ambassadors of England and Austria assembled in the great hall of the palace to hear the reading of the king's will, they learned that Charles had bequeathed everything to the grandson of Louis XIV., Philip of Aragon. Leopold of Austria was not the man to sit down submissively after such a blow between the eyes; he made preparations for war.

It was midsummer, 1701, and James II. of England was dying in the palace of St. Germain. For thirteen years he had waited for some event that would restore him to the throne of England. Vain his waiting. He had thrown away his crown, and the people of England never again would recognize him or his descendants as their legitimate sovereign. Mary of Modena, a bigoted queen, but a loving and devoted wife, watched by his side through the waning hours, thinking of the future of her boy of thirteen. If Louis would but recognize him as rightful heir to the throne of England, perhaps in time he might be king. Madame de Maintenon was her friend, and Louis would do anything for madame.

Louis XIV. rode from Versailles to St. Germain to bid a last farewell to James.

"I am come to say that, whenever it shall please God to call your Majesty out of this world, I will take your family under my protection, and recognize your son as Prince of Wales, and as the heir of your three realms," said the King of France.

Louis had no thought as to what would grow out of that promise;

PALACE OF ST. GERMAIN.

possibly, even if he had foreseen the future, he would not have recalled it. What cared he for human woe! He did not see that it would be the beginning of a mighty struggle between France and England; that three-quarters of a century would roll away before it would end. In consequence of those words the scalping-knife and tomahawk were to gleam in the hands of blood-thirsty savages, from the Penobscot to the Hudson: men would be shot in cold blood; women would see their infants dashed upon the rocks, and they themselves would endure all the horrors of captivity in the wilderness. Burning dwellings would illumine the midnight sky, and there would be no end of woe.

Up to the utterance of that promise, England had taken no part in the contest over the question of who should be King of Spain; but Louis had violated the agreement made at Ryswick, and England joined in the mighty struggle.

On the bank of the St. Lawrence, ninety miles above Quebec, was the Indian town of St. Francis, established by the Jesuits. It was a cluster of wigwams, with a chapel and a parsonage for the priests. The Indians were the remnants of several tribes, which war had thinned out. Morning and evening they met in the chapel, counted their beads, kneeled before the image of the Virgin Mary, and said the prayers taught them by the Jesuits; but in everything else, in habits, in all Christian virtues and graces, they were savages still. They were called St. Francis Indians, and were ever ready to do the bidding of their priests.

Although war had been raging in Europe, and the armies of England and France had met in battle, all was peaceful in America. The settlers were clearing the forests, sowing and reaping. Why should they trouble themselves about conflicts three thousand miles away? Not so the Jesuit priests at St. Francis, Quebec, and Montreal; they were taking part in the struggle. England was Protestant, France Roman Catholic. Protestants were heretics—enemies of God—who ought to be exterminated. It was right to employ any means, to commit murder even, if the glory of God could be promoted. They urged the Indians to begin war against the English in Maine. Governor Dudley, of Massachusetts, heard of their doings, and invited all the chiefs, from the Merrimac to the Penobscot, to meet him for a friendly talk, and they assembled at Falmouth—now Portland—June 20th, 1703. Bomazeen, one of the chiefs, spoke for them all:

"The French friars have asked us to go to war, but their words have not moved us. As far as the sun is from the earth are our thoughts of taking the hatchet."

The Indians gave the governor a belt of wampum, and heaped a pile of stones, to let him know that they spoke the truth.

August came, the settlers were harvesting their grain, not knowing that through the summer months the priests had been urging the Indians to wipe out all the settlements at Berwick and Kittery, on the Piscataqua; at York, ten miles eastward; at Wells, Scarborough, and the hamlets on Casco Bay, at a single blow; that along the entire distance for fifty miles, five hundred Indians were ready to begin their bloody work at the same instant.

On the morning of August 10th the blow fell. At Berwick five were killed; but the other settlers, hearing the alarm, fled to the garrison, and Captain Neale and his men killed nine Indians, and wounded several others. The Indians, in their rage over their ill-success, tied Joseph Ring to a stake and burnt him to death. They went out in their canoes and captured a vessel, killing the crew, seven in number. At Spurwink, one of the settlements on Casco Bay, the Indians butchered twenty-two. At Purpoodnck they massacred twenty-five, and captured eight.

They appeared before the new fort at Falmouth, where Major March was in command, held up a white flag, and made signs that they had no arms. Major March and two men went out to talk with them, when suddenly each Indian (there were three of them) whipped out a tomahawk from beneath their blankets, and struck at the major and his companions. Crack! crack! went the guns of several Indians in ambush. One of the men with the major fell mortally wounded. The major was brave and strong. He knocked one of the tomahawks aside, wrenched another out of the hands of an Indian, and kept all at bay until Lieutenant Hook came to his rescue. They retreated to the fort, carrying the wounded man. The Indians spent a week around the fort, but could not capture it.

What a scene is that which the sun of August 10th reveals! one hundred and fifty-five mangled corpses—tall columns of smoke ascending

GARRISON HOUSE, YORK.

to heaven; all the way from the Piscataqua to Casco, a crowd of men, women, and children going into captivity!

The Indians tried to capture Stephen Harding, who lived in Wells. He was a great hunter, and knew all their tricks, and could follow a trail as well as they. Often he went into the wilderness as far as the White Mountains, while hunting. He loved the solitudes; but he had married, and his wife and young child were dear to him. He saw signs that the Indians were near.

"Take the baby and go through the cornfield to an oak-tree, and wait for me. I will see if the redskins are prowling around here," he said to his wife.

She went with the baby. He gave a whoop. Instantly a party of Indians ran toward the house, thinking one of their number had given the signal. All rushed to the door. While they were trying to burst it open he leaped through a window, joined his wife, but alas! she had fainted. He was strong, took her under one arm, and the baby and rifle under the other, and ran through the woods. The Indians did not dare to follow; they knew that he never fired without killing his game. Night came, and Stephen kept guard while his wife and baby slept. They had only blueberries for supper and breakfast; but they reached the fort, nine miles distant, in safety.

So, through the instigation of the Jesuits, the bloody work began. Winter came. The snow was deep, but not too deep to prevent François Hertel, who had massacred the inhabitants of Falmouth, from marching once more to plunder and destroy the English. He started from the village of St. Francis with three hundred and forty French and Indians. They loaded themselves down with heavy packs, piled their provisions on hand-sleds, and walked on snow-shoes. They toiled through the wilderness of Canada to the head-waters of the Connecticut, and down its valley to the little town of Deerfield, in Massachusetts. On the last day of February, Hertel stood on a bluff amidst the tall pines, two miles north of the settlement. There was a hard crust, and across the gleaming snow he could see the little settlement. Leaving their packs, the French and Indians moved stealthily toward the garrison. No sentinel was on the watch. The snow lay in a huge drift against the palisade; they walked over it and entered the village. De Ronville posted his men, two or more at each house. Then came the whoop, and the bursting in of doors. Mr. Williams is the minister. He springs from his bed, seizes a pistol, aims it at the heart of an Indian. It misses fire, and he is seized and tied. Two of his children are massacred before his eyes. Mrs. Williams has a young child, but she is pulled from her bed and driven out into the snow. All around the work of death goes on. What a scene is that which the sun shines upon in the morning! Forty or more mangled corpses; the snow crimsoned with blood; burning buildings. One hundred and eight men, women, and children driven—some of them barefooted and thinly-clad—through the snow, northward, toward Canada, to perish in the wilderness; to be starved, to fall before the tomahawk, to endure the hardships, toil, suffering, and woe of the terrible march. At sunrise

IN AMBUSH.

De Rouville is on his march. He has struck his blow, and is hastening away with his captives, knowing that the settlers of the valley will be upon him if he lingers. Day after day, in the snow or wading through streams, the captives drag their weary limbs, loaded down with the plunder of their own house, which their captors compel them to carry. Mrs. Williams's strength is failing. She talks with her husband sweetly and serenely of a house not made with hands, eternal in the heavens. She comes to a swollen river, whose rushing waters sweep her down; but with a struggle she reaches the shore. Her Indian captor, who calls himself a Christian Indian, steps behind her and buries his tomahawk in her skull. She sinks upon the snow, crimsoning it with her blood.

The promise of Louis XIV. to the dying James is bearing its fruit. One by one the sick and weak go down beneath the tomahawk, and the bodies are left in the wilderness.

Not all the houses in Deerfield were burnt. One was courageously defended by seven men, who fired from the windows upon the enemy; the brave women with them ran bullets and loaded their guns. Many times the French and Indians tried to set the house on fire, but without avail. Captain Stoddard, watching his chance, leaped from a window, and ran to Hatfield and gave the alarm. Quickly the people were on De Rouville's track, came up with him and had a battle, but were obliged to retreat. The French officer hastened up the valley of the Connecticut to White River, and then divided his party—a portion going to Lake Champlain, and a portion up the Connecticut to Montreal. He had destroyed a settlement, killed or captured nearly one hundred and fifty, losing about forty of his own men.

How should the war be waged? It was little use for the English to follow the Indians. Their bloody work was done in an hour, and in a few days they would be back in Canada. They were more savage than the wild beasts. Why not treat them as such? Massachusetts and New Hampshire offered a reward of twenty pounds for every Indian captured under ten years of age, and forty pounds for every scalp of an Indian over ten. If the Jesuits were to make it a war of extermination, so would they.

In 1704, Captain Benjamin Church, with five hundred and fifty men, ravaged all the French settlements east of the Penobscot—burning buildings, and capturing all he could lay his hands upon.

The price set upon the Indians' heads made them more afraid. But in 1705 they fell upon the settlers at Cape Neddick, in Maine, and killed seven. At Kittery they shot Mr. Shapleigh, and carried his son to Canada. An Indian cut off the boy's fingers, and then thrust the bleeding stumps into their hot tobacco-pipes and laughed at his agony. They attacked the settlements in New Hampshire at Dover and Durham.

One day Colonel Hilton went out with a scouting-party and killed four warriors, and captured a squaw. She begged for her life. "I will show you more Indians," she said, and led them to a camp where eighteen were asleep. It was just at daybreak. Colonel Hilton posted his men; each picked out an Indian. Crack went their guns; all were killed but one, who was captured.

At Winter harbor, not far from Saco, there were two fishing-boats at anchor, with eight men on board. Suddenly a great company of Indians appeared in their canoes. The men in one of the boats jumped into the other, cut the cable, and hoisted the sail. There are eight in all, who pour a volley into the canoes. Some of the Indians drop into the water, others leap on board the fishing-boat. They do not know how to manage it; but the Indians in the canoe take it in tow, ply their paddles, and hasten on. They are a fine mark for the sailors, who pick them off one by one. There are one hundred and fifty Indians against eight white men. The bullets fly thick and fast, boring holes through the sail, striking the keel, spattering into the water. One strikes Benjamin Daniels, who knows that he has but a few moments to live.

"Give me a gun, quick! that I may kill one more before I die," he cries, fires his last shot, and lies lifeless upon the deck.

Not till nine are killed and eighteen wounded do the Indians give up the battle. Daniels is the only one injured on the vessel.

Twice has François Hertel massacred the English, and he thirsts for more blood. A grand expedition is planned. Once more he starts, traversing the pathless wilderness to the White Mountains, and southward to the beautiful Winnipisseogee. He sets up his camp upon the shores of the lake, and waits for the Indians of Maine to join him. The Jesuits have been among them; but they have lost so many warriors, there is such a price upon their heads, that they are weary of war, and would be glad to bury the hatchet. Hertel has intended to wipe out Portsmouth, at the mouth of the Piscataqua; but, as the Indians do not come, he does not dare to make the attempt. He will fall upon Haverhill.

August 29th, 1708, is a calm and peaceful day. The settlers of the little village lie down to sleep, having no suspicion of the presence of the foe. The daylight streaks the east. Hertel arouses his Christian savages. They ask the Virgin to protect them, divide into parties, and give the war-whoop. They rush upon the minister's house — Rev. Mr. Rolfe's.

There are three soldiers on guard within, but are so frightened that they know not what to do. Mr. Rolfe springs out of bed to hold the door. The Indians fire through it and wound him in the elbow, burst it in, bury their hatchets in his skull, kill Mrs. Rolfe, dash out the brains of their infant child upon a stone, and hack the cowardly soldiers to pieces. They shoot Thomas Hartshorn and his two sons, smash the skull of the third, shoot John Johnston, massacre his wife by his side. Simon Wainwright is killed at the first fire. Mrs. Hartshorn, with all of her children except the baby, which is on a bed up-stairs, go down through a trap-door into the cellar. The Indians do not discover the door, but they go up-stairs and toss the baby out of the window, which, though it falls upon a pile of boards, is not killed—only stunned. The Indians and French attack Mr. Swan's house. Mrs. Swan is a plucky woman, and holds the door against them. One of the savages gets it partly open and runs his arm in to undo the fastening, but Mrs. Swan, seizing an iron skewer, drives it through his arm, to pin him to the door-post. Nathan Simons shoots two of the savages. Mr. Davis is an intrepid man. He runs out of his house and shouts, "Come on!" as if he had a company of men. The enemy take to their heels. They have set the meeting-house on fire, but the settlers put it out. Captain Samuel Ayer musters a company, follows Hertel, coming up with him and giving battle. Captain Ayer is killed; Hertel's brother is killed; and thirty others of the enemy. Sixteen of the settlers lay down their lives, and thirty-three are wounded or captured.

To strike a blow in return for all these attacks, a fleet sailed from Boston to Acadia and captured Port Royal, changing the name to Annapolis, in honor of Anne, Queen of England.

The next year the English Government sent a fleet under Sir Hovenden Walker, with an army, to capture Quebec; but the admiral was pigheaded and incompetent. Eight of his vessels were wrecked in the St. Lawrence, and nearly nine hundred men drowned; and the grand expedition came to an inglorious end.

For twelve years the war raged in Europe and in America, till, exhausted by the struggle, Louis XIV. consented to make peace, which was signed at Utrecht, April 11th, 1713.

CHAPTER XXVII.

MAINE AND NEW HAMPSHIRE.

ON the banks of the Kennebec, at a favorite fishing-place of the Indians, Sebastian Rale, Jesuit from France, built a chapel, and set up the cross and an image of the Virgin. Upon the chapel walls were pictures of his own painting, portraying the bliss of the redeemed and torments of the damned. The Indians were ever his children, and he their father. He was so kind that they regarded him as their true friend. If they went on a grand hunting expedition, Father Rale joined them; when they left their village at Norridgewock in midsummer for a sojourn at the sea-shore, he accompanied them. For twenty-five years he labored with untiring zeal to convert them to the Catholic faith. Such patience and energy brought its reward. The dusky warriors threw aside their "medicine" charms, and were baptized as Christians. Forty Indian boys in white gowns chanted the Sunday service. On gala-days they marched in procession, bearing banners and crosses. Those who had not been baptized still regarded him as their father. By acts of friendship, by untiring devotion and quenchless zeal, he made his power and influence felt among the Indians from the Hudson to the Gulf of Newfoundland.

At the beginning of Queen Anne's War, Governor Dudley, of Massachusetts, sent Colonel Hilton to seize the man who was wielding such mighty influence against the English. Colonel Hilton reached Norridgewock in midwinter, but did not find Father Rale, who had gone to Quebec. He burnt the chapel and returned.

When the war closed, and peace was signed at Utrecht in 1713, it was agreed that Maine, Nova Scotia, and Acadia should belong to England. The Indians met Governor Shute, of Massachusetts, on an island in the Kennebec, and promised to be faithful subjects of Great Britain; and agreed that the English might occupy the former settlements, and that they would not molest them.

The agreement was very distasteful to Sebastian Rale. He was a Frenchman, and he saw the few French settlers moving from the Penobscot, and Englishmen taking their place. They were at York, Saco, Wells, and Kennebunk. The smoke of their log-cabins was curling over the waters of Casco Bay. They were moving farther up the Piscataqua and Merrimac; soon they would be wanting the land at Norridgewock. What, then, would become of his flock?

The English were heretics, enemies of the Church. Had not Louis XIV. driven hundreds of thousands of them out of France! It was the duty of the Indians to resist the English. What right had the English to the land of the Indians? By subtle arts he influenced them against the settlers.

The Indians began a war on their own account by killing three men at Casco, and destroying the settlement, in August, 1720. "Rale is at the bottom of it," said the General Court of Massachusetts.

One hundred and fifty men marched to Norridgewock to seize the Jesuit, but he had gone to Quebec. The chief of the Norridgewocks, sincerely wishing to remain at peace with the English, gave up several warriors as hostages. Vaudreuil was Governor of Canada.

"Tell the Indians to drive out the English; I will give them all the assistance they want," said Vaudreuil to Rale.

"Norridgewock is within the territory of King George, and it is contrary to an Act of Parliament and a law of this province for any Jesuit or Roman priest to reside in any part of the British dominions," wrote Shute to Vaudreuil, and sent Colonel Westbrook to seize Rale; but the priest fled to the woods and escaped.

The Indians, to retaliate, fell upon the settlements at the mouth of the Kennebec, and captured their fishing-sloop. They attacked Fort George, on Arrowsick Island, burnt twenty-six houses, and destroyed Brunswick.

Father Rale in his chapel, in constant communication with Vaudreuil at Quebec, urged the Indians on; and all along the frontier, from the Connecticut to Nova Scotia, Indian bands prowled everywhere, falling upon the defenceless settlers. It was the same sad story everywhere—of surprises and ambushes—the shooting of defenceless men and women—taking their scalps—going as suddenly as they came; Father Rale and Vaudreuil ever urging them on. It was little use to chase the Indians, who in a few hours would be far away, to fall upon another settlement. A blow must be struck at the head-quarters: there could be no peace as long as Sebastian Rale could wield his power. Captains Moulton, Hanson, and two hundred men moved swiftly up the Kennebec.

It is August 12th, 1722. The men move in silence through the forest. They are near the Indian village; the party divide. They will not wait till nightfall, but push swiftly on.

"Take Rale prisoner. Let the Indians fire first," are the orders of Moulton.

He surmises that the surprise will so agitate the Indians that they will take poor aim.

The soldiers run toward the village. A wild cry rises from the wigwams. Sixty warriors rush out—fire; but their hands tremble, and not an Englishman is injured. A volley from the white men, and the Indians go down like grain before the reapers. Sebastian Rale fastened his house, and fired upon the invaders. Lieutenant Hanson burst open the door; Rale was loading his gun, and would ask no quarter. Hanson's blood was up. A flash from his gun, and the white-haired priest born amidst

VIEW FROM FORT GEORGE.

the vineyards of France—who had been a zealous missionary in the wilderness along the great lakes of the West, in Canada and the wilds of Maine, through whose pernicious influence hundreds of settlers had been slain—met his fate. The women and children escaped to the river, and many of the warriors; but the chiefs of the tribe, Mogg and Bomazeen, fell to rise no more. The chapel of the Jesuits was set on fire, and the expedition returned, having suffered no loss. It was a blow from which the Norridgewocks never recovered.

At the southern base of the White Mountains, where the River Saco winds through green meadows, was the home of the Pigwaket Indians. Their chief was Paugus. During the years of peace he visited the frontier towns of Massachusetts, and was well acquainted with the settlers; but his allegiance was to the French in Canada, at Montreal, where he could always obtain gunpowder and bullets. When the Jesuits stirred up the Indians of the Penobscot and Kennebec to make war upon the English, Paugus was ready to aid. It was a short march to the "Smile of the

Great Spirit," as the Indians called Lake Winnipiseogee; launching his canoe upon its peaceful waters, he could easily make his way to the Merrimac, and, descending that stream, fall upon the settlers of Dunstable, Bradford, and Haverhill.

There was a man in Dunstable who was as brave as any Indian, Captain John Lovewell. He could find his way through the forest as readily as the savages. He knew their haunts, their modes of fighting, their cunning.

In 1724 the Indians fell upon Dunstable, and killed two men. When the alarm was given, and eleven men started in pursuit, the Indians shot nine of them, took their scalps, and returned to the wigwams on the Saco, and held a great feast and dance over the success of their exploits.

"I will pay one hundred pounds for every Indian scalp," said the Governor of Massachusetts; and Captain Lovewell started with his soldiers to chastise the Pigwakets.

It was in December. The leaves had fallen, and there was snow on the ground, when Captain Lovewell with forty men marched up the Merrimac valley, and along the southern shore of Lake Winnipiseogee. They discovered tracks and followed them through the day, discovering, just at sunset, ten Indians sitting around a fire. At midnight there was a click of gun-locks, then a volley. The entire ten were killed. There was great rejoicing in all the towns—Dover, Newbury, Salem, and Boston—as Captain Lovewell and his men made their triumphant return, with the ten scalps dangling from a pole. There were ten Indians less. One thousand pounds prize-money! It was a quick way to get rich.

"We will attack the Pigwakets in their homes," said Captain Lovewell. His soldiers were eager to march. It was in April, 1725, when they started up the Merrimac, turning eastward, crossing the Winnipiseogee, leaving seven men who were sick; the others went bravely on to the boundary between Maine and New Hampshire.

It was Saturday morning. They were not far from the Indian villages. "We will leave our packs here," said Captain Lovewell, and the men threw them upon the ground.

Before starting, the chaplain, Jonathan Frye, offered prayer. While he was praying they heard a gun, and saw an Indian across the pond.

"We are discovered; shall we go on, or return?" asked Lovewell.

"We have come to find the Indians. We have prayed God that we might find them. We had rather die for our country than return without seeing them. If we were to go back, the people would call us cowards," said the men, and Lovewell moved on.

Suddenly they came upon a single Indian, who was killed by Ensign Wyman; but who, before falling, fired his gun at Captain Lovewell, mortally wounding him.

"We will go back to our packs," they said; but when they reached the place, found that the Indians had seized them. They were between 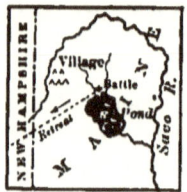 two little brooks, that meandered through the pine forest and emptied into the lake. Suddenly they found themselves confronted by nearly one hundred Indians, armed with new guns which they had obtained in Canada. They had gone past the Indian village, which was only a short distance away, and the Indians had cut off their retreat.

The terrible war-whoop rung through the forest. At the first fire seven English were killed and several wounded.

"Retreat to the shore of the pond!" shouted Lieutenant Wyman. He saw that the Indians were intending to surround them. By retreating to the water's edge, they would have no Indians at their back.

One cowardly man ran, at the first volley, back, to make his escape to the men who had been left behind on the march. The others retreated to the lake, sheltered themselves behind the trees, and resolved to fight to the last. All day long the fight went on, the Indians howling like wolves. Their medicine-man held a pow-wow—invoking the spirits to aid them; but Lieutenant Wyman put an end to it by sending a bullet through his heart.

"We will give you quarter," said the Indians.

"We ask for no quarter except at the muzzles of our guns!" was the defiant reply, and the battle went on until Paugus fell, shot by Lieutenant Wyman; then the Indians lost heart. When night came on, they stole away. Pitiable the condition of the English! The young chaplain, who had fought bravely—who, when wounded, still prayed for victory, was dead; Jacob Farrar was dying; Lieutenant Robbins and Robert Usher could not last many hours; eleven others were badly wounded. The Indians had seized their packs, and they were twenty miles from the seven men they had left at Ossipee.

"Load my gun, so that when the Indians come to scalp me I can kill one more!" said Lieutenant Robbins.

In the darkness of the night, the living, faint and weary, started. Four were so badly wounded that they could not travel. "Leave us; you cannot help us, and we shall hinder you," they said.

It was a brave parting; but if any were to reach home they must push

DEATH OF THE MEDICINE-MAN.

on. In war, necessity knows no compassion. They reached Ossipee, to find the seven men gone. The man who fled at the first fire had told a pitiable story—how all had been killed; and the soldiers, fearing that the Indians would soon be upon them, fled to Dunstable.

Weary the return. For three days they had only two ground-squirrels to eat; then they shot a partridge, caught some fish, and so sustained life until they reached home.

The Indians were weary of war. Their bravest warrior had fallen;

BUILDING SHIPS.

there was no longer a Father Rale to urge them on, and they made peace once more. So ended the war, which had been kindled wholly through the influence of the Jesuits.

Peace! how delightful it was! No longer were the people compelled to work with their rifles by their sides, ever on the watch for the lurking foe. The settlers went farther into the country. All the industries revived. Towns and villages sprung up. In Boston, on the Merrimac and Piscataqua, companies were building ships; and the colonies took on such vigorous life that George Berkeley, who had come from England to Rhode Island with his family, fired with enthusiasm to do something for education and religion in the Western World, and who gave his books to

FAMILY OF BISHOP BERKELEY.

establish the Redwood Library at Newport—looking forward, wrote this poetic prophecy of America:

"In happy climes, the seat of innocence,
   Where nature guides and virtue rules;
Where men shall not impose for truth and sense
   The pedantry of courts and schools—

"There shall be sung another golden age—
   The rise of empire and of arts;
The good and great inspiring epic rage;
   The wisest heads and noblest hearts.

"Not such as Europe breeds in her decay:
   Such as she bred when fresh and young,
When heavenly flame did animate her clay,
   By future poets shall be sung.

"Westward the course of empire takes its way;
   The four first acts already past,
A fifth shall close the drama with the day;
   Time's noblest offspring is the last."

CHAPTER XXVIII.

THE CAROLINAS.

THE men who had been instrumental in bringing Charles II. to the throne of England — Edward Hyde, whom Charles made Earl of Clarendon, George Monk, whom he made Duke of Albemarle, and six others—applied to him for a grant of land in America; and the frivolous man, who cared more for his pet poodle than all America, gave them the territory between Virginia and Florida, and extending west to the Pacific Ocean. They called it Carolina. It was a wilderness, except a small settlement near the Chowan River, made in 1653 by Roger Green and others, who had moved from Virginia to enjoy perfect freedom.

William Drummond was appointed governor; but what cared the people for him, or for Stevens, who succeeded him in 1667? Nothing. The men who built their rude log-cabins, with chimneys made of sticks and mud, who roamed the forest at will, living on wild turkeys and deer, snapped their fingers in the governor's face. They had suffered much under the arbitrary laws of Virginia; and in 1669 met in convention, and declared that there should be complete freedom of conscience; that there should be no taxes except what they themselves might impose.

Quite likely the earls and lords did not know what the settlers were doing: be that as it may, they employed the great metaphysician, John Locke, to plan a government. He knew very little of the influences at work in the New World—how men were being educated to think and act for themselves—but based his plan on Old World ideas; on a plan which Plato thought out among the olive-groves of Athens, when Greece was in her glory. He thought that there ought to be three orders of nobility—Landgrave, men who would own great tracts of land, like the earls of England and Germany; Cassiques, who were to be of a lower order; and Barons, who were to have a rank similar to the barons of England. The titles were to descend from the fathers to the eldest sons. They were to be exclusive owners of the land. They were to make and execute the laws. The people were to have no voice in affairs; they were to be only serfs.

John Locke, with all his learning, never mistrusted that the time had gone by for the establishment of such a government, for English-speak-

CAROLINA HOME.

ing people were in the Western World. The Frenchmen in Canada might consent to live under such a government, but Englishmen—never.

Neither the great metaphysician nor any one else in England took into account the distance of three thousand miles, the influence of the wilderness, the fact that there was little to interfere with the freedom of men. They did not reflect that men who could have venison, turkey, and fish on their tables the year round, who, by scratching the ground and putting in a few potatoes, could obtain sufficient food, were not likely to submit to such laws, or accept such a system as he had contrived.

The settlers cut gashes in the tall pines, and gathered the fragrant turpentine that oozed from the pores. The lords claimed the soil, and all there was on it; but when the tax-gatherer came to collect dues for the land and turpentine, they laughed in his face. Pay rents! Not they.

One of the governors which the lords sent over was not only governor, but secretary and collector, and attempted to carry things with a high hand, whereupon Jack Culpepper and a few others handled him so roughly that he was glad to get out of the colony. They ruled themselves for two years. In truth, they were a lawless set. They would not obey John Locke's laws, neither their own. Seth Sothel came from England to govern them; but he was a dissolute fellow, and they drove him out of the colony.

The settlements, up to 1670, were in the northern section of the territory; but in that year the earls and lords to whom Charles had given the land sent out a colony to develop the southern portion. The ships sailed into the harbor of Port Royal, and a beginning was made where Ribault

ON THE ASHLEY.

had established himself a century and a quarter before. It was called the Carteret Settlement, for Lord Carteret, one of the proprietors.

After the settlers had erected their houses, they remembered how the

Spaniards, in 1562, had massacred the Huguenots on that spot; and, fearing that they might come again, abandoned the place for one more secure,

YEAMANS HALL, GOOSE CREEK.

which they formed farther north, at the junction of two rivers, one of which they named Ashley, and the other Cooper, for Lord Ashley Cooper, one of the proprietors. They named the new settlement Charleston.

The eight men who had received the land from Charles never thought of purchasing it from the Indians—they appropriated it.

Buy land of the savages! Oh no. They were peers of the English realm, and the king had given them the land: why should they pay the Indians for it?

The colonists were charmed with the country, the winding rivers, the stately pines, the wide-spreading live-oaks, the jessamine and honeysuckle, magnolias, and azaleas filling the air with perfume. They cut down the trees, and opened plantations. Many of them were little better than slaves; for, having gotten into debt in England, they were put in jail, and were released only by selling their services to the proprietors, who charged high rates of interest for the money advanced.

In 1671 the lords sent out Sir John Yeamans to be Governor of South Carolina. One of the gentlemen accompanying him was from Drayton Hall, in Northamptonshire, who opened a beautiful plantation on the bank of the Ashley, above Charleston, and where his grandson reared a noble mansion, which is still standing.

The same year some negroes were brought to Charleston and sold—the beginning of negro slavery in South Carolina. It was a community of Cavaliers, Puritans, and Dutchmen. Few had money; many of them were struggling to get out of debt, and who found it all the harder after the introduction of slaves.

Huguenots came from France, driven from their old homes, from their mulberry orchards and vineyards, after the revocation of the Edict of Nantes by Louis XIV. They selected South Carolina as their future home. The mulberry and grape would thrive in its genial clime. They could feed the leaves of the mulberry to the silk-worm, reel the glossy fibre from the cocoons, spin and weave, and enjoy their religious belief unmolested by king or Pope, in their new far-off homes. Strange to say, the colonists wished they would stay away. Why should Frenchmen be

DRAYTON HALL, WESTERN FRONT.

allowed there? It was a revival of the old hatred between Englishmen and Frenchmen; but the Huguenots attended to their own affairs. They were peaceable and orderly. It was an infusion of some of the best blood of France. They soon forgot that they were Frenchmen. They became American citizens. The names of some of their descendants—Grimké, Huger, Legaré, Laurens, Marion—are inseparably connected with the history of our country.

The first settlers cared very little about building churches. The first —St. Michael's—was not erected until 1682. There were a few Episcopa-

PICKING FIGS.

lians, and some Dissenters; but most of the people did not care whether they had a church or not, or else were too poor to put forth any effort to build one.

The Earl of Albemarle sent over this order:

"The Church of England must be made the established church of Carolina."

Sir Nathaniel Moore, who had been appointed governor, issued an order compelling each colonist to pay thirty pounds annually for the support of a minister. The country was divided into parishes, and all who would not pay were disfranchised, deprived of holding any office of honor, trust, or profit. Quakers could not serve on a jury. The church-wardens, with two constables, every Sunday forenoon and afternoon visited all the grog-shops, arresting all idlers, and marching them to jail for not being in their places at church.

The laws were harsh toward those who had sold their services to the lords. Dennis Mahand attempted to escape to the Spaniards in Florida; but was caught, and had thirty-nine lashes put upon his bare back with the cat-o'-nine-tails. Many other settlers were whipped for attempting to escape.

Spain and England were at peace; but the Spaniards at St. Augustine suddenly fell upon the English settlement at Edisto in 1686, pil-

ORANGE FRUIT AND FLOWERS.

laged Mr. Marston's house, murdered the governor's brother, and carried off thirteen slaves. They destroyed another settlement at Port Royal.

The people of Charleston determined to have their revenge. Four hundred men were ready to march to St. Augustine; but just then Gov-

ST. MICHAEL'S CHURCH.

ernor Colleton arrived from England, and threatened to hang them if they attempted it.

In 1695 a vessel arrived at Charleston from Madagascar. Governor Smith went on board, and received a present from the captain of some rice, which he sowed in his garden. It was so luxuriant that he began its cultivation. His neighbors also cultivated it, and in a short time the colony not only supplied itself with rice, but sent ship-loads to England and to the colonies.

It was the beginning of a great industry. Governor Thomas Smith was born at Exeter, in England. He emigrated to South Carolina in 1671. He had a brother who emigrated to Boston, whose granddaughter, Abigail, married John Adams, the second President of the United States.

He built a country house on Back River, and made port-holes in the walls, so that it could be defended against the Indians, and dug a passage underground to the river, where he kept a boat concealed, so that, if not able to defend the house, he could escape by the secret passage.

When he was appointed governor, or landgrave, the proprietors gave him forty-eight thousand acres of land. He was a Puritan, clear-headed and honest; but there were so many quarrels going on between the colonists, between those who had sold their services and those who had bought them, that he became tired of being governor, and sent word to the proprietors that they must send over somebody else to take his place; as for being governor, he would not. While he was in office, the colony was divided into North and South Carolina.

It was Rev. Mr. White, of Dorchester, England, who started the Puritan emigration to New England; and the second party of emigrants from that town in 1630, settling in Massachusetts, named their new home Dorchester.

In 1696, a party of their descendants, hearing of the attractions of Carolina—the richness of the soil, the genial climate, where during sum-

LANDGRAVE SMITH'S BACK RIVER RESIDENCE.

mer and winter the flowers were ever in bloom—bade good-bye to their friends in Massachusetts, to start life anew amidst the live-oaks and magnolias of the South. They selected a site on the bank of the Ashley, and named it Dorchester. They were Puritans, and one of the first buildings erected was a church. They were hard-working, and Dorchester soon became a thrifty town. They established a market, and had fairs twice a year, which attracted people from all parts of the colony. They established a free school. "We have come," they said, "to encourage the promotion of religion."

From the banks of the Ashley, another colony went out in 1752 to Georgia, and started still another Dorchester. It was vigorous seed

OLD MEETING-HOUSE, DORCHESTER.

which Rev. John White sent out from that little fishing-town on the southern coast of England.

Dorchester on the Ashley has disappeared. Stately trees grow where the thrifty settlers once held their annual fair; and the azaleas, honeysuckles, and jessamine bloom where once they drove their teams. Everything has disappeared, except the old white church in which they worshipped.

In 1702, when war was declared between England and Spain, Governor Moore sailed, with several hundred men, to capture St. Augustine;

but he had no cannon, the Spanish fort was strong, and he accomplished nothing. The expedition cost six thousand pounds, and was the beginning of a great deal of trouble. There were only five thousand people in the colony, and their taxes were so great that they could not pay them. They accused Governor Moore of feathering his own nest—of purchasing supplies of himself, and in other ways. Two parties arose—the governor and his friends, who were Episcopalians, and the people, who were Dissenters.

The lords sent over Sir Nathaniel Johnson to succeed Moore. He was self-willed and obstinate. The colonists had had no schools, and very few could read. Those who lived in the backwoods had no churches—many had never heard a sermon. They knew very little about the Bible or anything else. They used very profane oaths, and Governor Johnson undertook to make them good church-going people by passing laws against swearing.

"Whoever blasphemes the Trinity, or questions the Divine authority of the Bible, will be sent to prison for three years." "Every citizen chosen member of the Assembly must partake of the Lord's Supper in accordance with the rule of the Church," was the law passed by the Assembly, which disfranchised all the Dissenters!

Though disfranchised, the people were patriots, and showed what good Englishmen they were when a frigate and four other French vessels appeared off Charleston to attack the place. The drums beat, and they came with their guns to resist the invasion. Governor Johnson built a fort on an island in the harbor, which still bears his name. He had but a few soldiers, but he would make the most of them.

Captain Le Feboner, who commanded the French, sent a lieutenant on shore with a white flag, demanding the surrender of the place. The lieutenant was blindfolded, and marched from place to place; but wherever the handkerchief was taken from his eyes, he beheld troops around him, and went back reporting that the English had a large army; whereas Governor Johnson had kept a company on the march ahead of the Frenchman, and he had seen the same troops all the time.

Captain Le Feboner was amazed. He sailed away, not daring to make an attack. Soon after he was gone, a French vessel, with ninety men and supplies, sailed into the harbor, and was captured.

The Tuscaroras were the most powerful Indian tribe in North Carolina. Settlers had taken their lands, stolen their corn and sweet potatoes, and were driving the game from the country. The Indians resolved to be revenged. They dipped a stick in blood, and sent it to the Yeamanes, in South Carolina, who joined the conspiracy, and sharpened their scalping-knives for the terrible work.

In the spring of 1715 the blow fell. Hundreds of settlers were killed; but Governor Craven defeated the Yeamanes near Port Royal with a terrible slaughter, and the Tuscaroras lost three hundred in a battle with the North Carolina settlers. They were so nearly annihilated that they fled North, and joined the Iroquois.

The lords who owned the land would not assist the colonists, who were ground down with taxes. There was so much trouble that Queen Anne bought back their territory, paying the proprietors twenty-two thousand five hundred pounds, and the attempt to establish a government on the plan thought out by John Locke came to an end in 1729.

The governors of North Carolina found so much difficulty in ruling the indolent people, that one of them, Governor Burrington, in 1731, wrote this to the Duke of Newcastle:

"The people of North Carolina are neither to be cajoled nor outwitted. Whenever a governor attempts to effect anything by this means, he will lose his labor, and show his ignorance. The inhabitants are not industrious, but subtle and crafty; always behaving insolently to their governor. Some they have imprisoned; driven others out of the country; and at times have set up a governor of their own choice, supported by men under arms."

Burrington was so distasteful to them, that they soon compelled him to leave. He was a wicked man, and in 1734 was murdered in a carouse in London.

The people loved liberty; but cared very little for those other qualities of character necessary for the building up of a thrifty State.

Governor Johnson, a Scotchman, appointed in 1734, was a good man. In his address to the Assembly he deplored the condition of affairs.

"The morals of the people are loose. There is no provision for education. Law is disregarded by the rich, and they oppress the poor, who have no redress."

He was wise and prudent, and had so much influence in Scotland that many people emigrated from that country, sailing up Cape Fear River, and settling on the high banks in the interior. They loved law and order, and were deeply religious. With their coming, North Carolina took on a new life.

Through the years in which New York and New England were struggling against the Indians—from the beginning of the eighteenth century to the time of the Revolution—there was very little occurring to disturb the Carolinas. The settlers of North Carolina made tar and turpentine, and the planters of South Carolina cultivated their rice-fields. Many ship-loads of slaves were brought from the West Indies and Africa. The planters grew rich on their labor, reared stately mansions in Charleston, and elegant residences in the country; living in princely style, riding in coaches, and attended by retinues of servants. They adorned their grounds with flowers, and entertained their friends with hospitality; but the poor people found themselves growing poorer. How could they get on where there were so many slaves? The planters regarded labor as degrading, and treated the poor whites with contempt. So it came about that there were wider distinctions in society in South Carolina than in any other colony.

CHAPTER XXIX.

GEORGIA.

THE jails of England were filled with men who could not pay their debts. Some were spendthrifts; others had worked hard; but the wolf was ever at the door, and they could not get on in the world. Hard-hearted creditors had thrust them behind the prison-bars. What hope for such a prisoner?

> "No grateful fire before him glows,
>   And yet the winter's breath is chill;
> And o'er his half-clad person goes
>   The frequent ague thrill!
>
> "Silent, save ever and anon,
> A sound, half murmur and half groan,
> Forces apart the painful grip
> Of the old sufferer's bearded lip;
> O sad and crushing is the fate
> Of old age chained and desolate!"

What could society do? It might have changed the laws, but did not. The large-hearted General James Oglethorpe, member of Parliament, forty years old, and who had fought the Turks in Hungary, who was in the great battles around Belgrade with Prince Eugene, conceived a plan for the relief of poor, deserving men — that of founding a colony in America, where, with a little help, they might start life anew. He enlisted some of the noblemen of England in his enterprise. George II. favored it, and granted them the country between the Altamaha and Savannah Rivers, for a colony to be named Georgia. Noblemen, members of Parliament, and kind-hearted people contributed to the enterprise; and in January, 1733, the ship *Anne*, with thirty-five families, one hundred and thirty persons, entered the Savannah River. Oglethorpe laid out a town, with streets running at right angles, with many pleasant parks, and named it Savannah. He held a feast the next Sunday after his arrival. Many of the South Carolina people were there; and altogether they devoured four fat hogs, eight turkeys, besides chickens and beef, drank one hogshead of punch, one of beer, and a vast deal of wine.

General Oglethorpe purchased the land of Tomo Chichi, one of the Indian chiefs. He hired the slaves of some of the planters of South Carolina to clear the ground and prepare it for planting. The emigrants worked with a will; and in a very short time the settlers were living in nice houses. The woods were full of game, and there were fish in the rivers; they were so near Carolina that they could obtain abundance of food, and none of the hardships were encountered which other colonies had endured.

OGLETHORPE.

Captain M'Pherson, with a company of Scotchmen, built a fort on the Ogeechee River, and named it for the Duke of Argyle. Other colonists came; and in two years there were more than five hundred settlers. Many of the emigrants were from Scotland. One party settled at Darien, on the Altamaha. They brought their bagpipes, and, when through with work for the day, passed the evening hours in playing the quaint melodies of the dear old land. They were industrious and devout.

The Salzburgers came; and who were they? They were descendants of the Waldenses, who lived in the beautiful valley of Vaudois, in Piedmont, who, away back in the twelfth century, wanted to read the Bible, which the Pope would not permit. Terrible the persecutions they endured.* Armies were sent against them, again and again; thousands were killed in battle or burnt at the stake; but nothing could quench the spirit of religious freedom in the Waldenses. Some who escaped the horrible massacres perpetrated by the armies sent by the Pope fled northward through Switzerland, crossed Lake Constance, and found refuge in Salzburg. For more than fifty years they lived in peace—so few in numbers that the priests took no notice of them; but they increased and held meetings of their own. That the priests could not permit. They were thrown into prison, and suffered the horrors of the terrible torture-chamber.

The jailer made them lay a finger or a thumb upon a post; he gently touched a spring—whack! down came a hammer like a gun-lock, driv-

---

* See "Story of Liberty," p. 304.

ing a sharp needle through the finger, and nailing it to the post! He put iron bracelets on their arms that came together with a spring, and driving pins like the prickles of a chestnut-burr into the flesh. He had an iron cap which he put upon their heads, with a lining of sharp knives that gashed the scalp. He stripped off their clothing, laid them upon a bench of corrugated oak, and kneaded them, as a baker does his bread, with a knobbed rolling-pin. He put them in a wide, deep cradle, the bottom and sides all knobs, rocked them to and fro until the flesh became like quivering jelly! He sawed their thighs to the bone with a string of iron beads; he thrust an iron ball into their mouths, pulled a string, and the ball blossomed into an iron lily—forcing open their jaws until they cracked in the sockets! A pair of pinchers clasped the tongue: one twitch, and it was torn out by the roots! They were led through dark and gloomy passages to a dungeon, to be embraced by a maiden—and who was she? There she stood—an iron statue, hooded, and wearing an iron ruffle, enveloped in an iron cloak. The jailer touched a spring, and the maiden clasped her victim in her iron arms. It was not a quick embrace; but one slow and long enduring, with needles of steel piercing the flesh, two iron spikes piercing the eye-balls. The jailer gave a turn of a screw, and the spikes went a little deeper; another turn, and deeper still. What ages of pain, fever, thirst, agony! Another turn of the screw, and closer the embrace. When death had ended all, a trap-door opens, and the maiden drops her victim. Down—down—down it falls, two hundred feet into a dark and gloomy cavern, upon the dying forms of those that had preceded it. No record, except in God's book of remembrance!

In 1728 the Archbishop of Salzburg set himself to eradicate the Protestants from his bishopric. In three years he drove thirty thousand into exile—to Prussia, Holland, and England, or where they could find refuge. They heard of America as a land for the oppressed, and fifty families started in 1733, dragging their goods in rude carts, carrying heavy packs, making their way to Frankfort-on-the-Main, and floating down the river in boats, sailing for Georgia.

They reached the promised land, worn, weary, and poor in everything except faith in the principles for which they had suffered. They loved the Bible and Prayer-book better than anything else. "Hitherto hath the Lord helped us," they said, and called the little settlement on the bank of the Savannah, Ebenezer.

The settlers were not all so sturdy in their religious principles as the Salzburgers; some of the English and Scotchmen quarrelled, or drank more rum than was good for them, and were put in the stocks. They were pleased with the country, and wrote home such glowing accounts of the delightfulness of the climate that many others came. Among the number were two young men, brothers—John and Charles Wesley—who had been educated at Oxford, and who were fired with religious zeal. They were the first Methodists. John visited the Indian chief, Tomis Chichi, and asked him to become a Christian.

"Me be Christian? Christians get drunk! Christians beat men! Christians tell lies! Me no Christian!" said Tomis.

John and Charles Wesley did not stay long, but went back to England. Another preacher, Rev. George Whitefield, visited Charleston and Savannah in 1738.

"Don't have anything to do with him," said Rev. Alexander Gordon, the Episcopal minister at Charleston, and preached a sermon from the text, "Those who have turned the world upside down have come hither also."

Instead of inducing the people to stay away from Mr. Whitefield's preaching, everybody wanted to hear him, and came in crowds. Mr. Whitefield loved a joke, and preached a sermon in reply, taking this for his text: "Alexander the coppersmith did me much evil."

Rum and negroes!—The laws passed by Parliament said that nobody should sell rum or hold slaves in Georgia; but men would have their rum, notwithstanding the law. General Oglethorpe saw that South Carolina was getting rich through the employment of slave-labor. General Oglethorpe was large-hearted; he established a home for orphans at Savannah, and begged money for their support in England. He discovered, also, a way to make it self-supporting. He was opposed to slavery on principle. The laws would not let him hold slaves in Georgia, but he might do it in South Carolina. Would not the nobleness of charity make it right for

JOHN WESLEY.

him to hold slaves? He thought it would, and bought a plantation and a large number of slaves. If the governor could do it outside of Georgia, why could not others, less scrupulous, hold slaves inside the boundary?

CHARLES WESLEY.

How could Oglethorpe prosecute them for doing openly what he was doing, as it were, surreptitiously? So, through the Jesuitical action of Oglethorpe, slavery was introduced.

Many of the negroes brought from Africa to Charleston by the slave-ships panted for freedom and fled into the forests of Georgia. Some reached St. Augustine. Spain and England were at war. The Jesuits at St. Augustine prevailed upon some of the negroes to return to South Carolina and stir up the slaves to revolt, and murder their masters. The slaves, not reflecting that they were weak and their masters strong, began an insurrection in 1740, which was quickly put down.

"Arrest any of the Jesuits or Spaniards you may find in Georgia," said Governor Oglethorpe, to the sheriff, who scoured the country with a *posse* of men.

Oglethorpe sent a letter to the Governor of New York and other colonies, informing them of what the Spaniards were doing, and the whole country was thrown into a fever of excitement. Oglethorpe made a settlement on St. Simond's Island, at the mouth of the Altamaha, with forts to protect it.

"An English settlement at St. Simond's — right under our noses!" The Spaniards at St. Augustine resented it. The Jesuits sent presents to the Indians to induce them to be their allies in sweeping the English into the Atlantic; but Oglethorpe, getting wind of the movement, made his way through the forests, threading thickets, crossing rivers, and enduring many hardships, to meet the Indians in a grand council, which assembled

GEORGIA.

at Coweta, three hundred miles north-west of Savannah, and was so influential that they agreed to be true friends of the English.

Thirty vessels were off St. Simond's, with the Spanish flag at their mast-heads, and cannon peeping out of the port-holes! Don Manuel de Montiama was commander, with five thousand soldiers. He would make ash-heaps of St. Simond's and Savannah.

Oglethorpe could muster only eight hundred men, with one merchant-vessel of twenty guns, and two schooners. He made a brave fight with his vessels; but the Spaniards obliged him to abandon them. Montiama sailed into the harbor of Frederica. The town was at the head of the bay. To get up to it the Spaniards must make a sweep around the "Devil's Elbow," a point of land on which Oglethorpe planted some cannon, which could give such a raking fire that Montiama, instead of attempting to pass it, landed his troops below to move upon the town. It would be an easy march along a sandy road, beneath tall pines and green palmettoes on one side, and a swamp on the other. Veteran troops of Spain, in light uniforms, banners waving, started at daybreak along the narrow way, putting to flight the few men which Oglethorpe had stationed to guard the road. The Spaniards pursued, but could not overtake them. The day was warm. They stacked their guns, threw themselves upon the ground to wipe the sweat from their brows, before marching across the plain to enter the town. They begin to prepare for breakfast.

Crack! crack! A volley! There was a flashing amidst the palmettoes. Some of the Spaniards lying upon the ground never rose again. Others, rising, went down, pierced by the bullets of a company of Scotch Highlanders. A panic seized the Spaniards; down the defile they fled, leaving their guns, knapsacks, everything—pursued by the Highlanders and the Indians, who were allies of the English. The Indians buried their tomahawks in the skulls of those they captured. The Spaniards did not stop until they reached the boats. Don Montiama had lost several hundred men; but he had still four thousand. He supposed that Oglethorpe had nearly as many, and was greatly surprised to learn from a deserter that the English numbered only eight hundred.

Oglethorpe knew that the men had deserted, and some plan must be contrived to deceive the Spaniards. What did he do but write a letter to the deserters!

"Persuade the Spaniards to believe that the English have only a few hundred men. Don't let the Spaniards know that two thousand men are coming from Charleston, nor that Admiral Vernon is on his way with a fleet to attack St. Augustine. If you are successful, a heavy reward will be paid you!"

Oglethorpe had taken some of the Spaniards prisoners. One of them was promised a great reward if he would deliver the letter to the deserters. Did the deserter receive the letter? Not by any means. It found its way, just as Oglethorpe expected it would, into the hands of Don Montiama.

"Sails!" "Sails!" There they were, white specks out upon the ocean. The Spaniards could see them. They must be a part of Admiral Vernon's fleet, bound for St. Augustine. There was a commotion in the Spanish camp—soldiers embarking in hot haste; and when they were on board, Don Montiama hoisted sail and hastened to St. Augustine, to defend it against Admiral Vernon. But the admiral never made his appearance: the vessels were merchantmen quietly pursuing their voyage to other ports. So, through the trick played by Oglethorpe, the Spanish invasion came to an inglorious end.

CHAPTER XXX.

THE NEGRO TRAGEDY.

IT was a foolish thing for Mrs. Hogg to do—open her money-drawer when a rascally young sailor, by the name of Wilson, was in her shop; for, having caught a glimpse of the silver, he walked down Broad Street to John Hughson's tavern, and told three negroes, Cæsar, Prince, and Cuffee, all about it. The next morning, when Mrs. Hogg opened her shop, she found that it had been plundered—that goods and money were missing. It was the spring of 1741. New York contained twelve thousand inhabitants, and in a short time everybody was talking about the burglary.

Some people cannot keep a secret. Cuffee could not, but showed a handful of silver to Mary Burton, who did chores in John Hughson's dirty tavern down by the North River. It was not a nice place for Mary, who was only fifteen years old, for the groggery was the resort of sailors and the scum of the town. Negro slaves bought their grog at Hughson's bar. Mary was bound out to the tavern-keeper, and quite likely heard much vile language. Cuffee gave Mary a piece of money, which she in turn showed to her playmates. The secret was out, and the constable marched Cuffee, Prince, Cæsar, an Irish girl named Peggy, and John Hughson and his wife to jail as robbers and accomplices.

"Fire! fire! The governor's house on fire!"

The people of New York were just finishing their dinners. They ran with pails, buckets, and ladders, but before they could put out the fire the governor's house, the secretary's office, and the soldiers' barracks were in ashes. A plumber had been soldering the tin on the roof of the governor's house, and a spark from his furnace had done the mischief. The loss was so great that everybody talked about it.

"Fire! fire! Captain Warren's house on fire!" It had caught from the chimney on the roof, but was quickly put out.

"Fire! fire! Van Zandt's storehouse on fire!" The storehouse stood down by the East River, and was filled with lumber and hay. A man had been smoking in the building; no one doubted that a spark from his pipe had started the flames.

"Fire! fire! Mr. Quirk's barn on fire!" Bells are ringing, and people are running to put it out. This the next day after Van Zandt's. The barn was on the east side of the town.

"Another fire over west." Ben Thomas's house, next to Captain Sarbay's. Two fires at the same time on Saturday. Ben Thomas owned a negro slave, and the fire started in his chamber over the kitchen, between two beds.

Coals near a hay-stack, close to John Murray's stables in Broadway— right in the heart of the town. That was what somebody discovered on Sunday morning. The coals had gone out, but there they were. Who put them there? That was the question.

"Fire! fire! Sergeant Burns's house is on fire!" That was the alarm on Monday morning. The people ran, but found that it was only the burning of soot in the chimney.

"Fire! fire! Mrs. Hilton's house, next to Captain Sarbay's—the roof in flames!" That was the alarm of Monday afternoon; seven alarms in two weeks. No doubt somebody was trying to burn the town. Who could it be? "The negroes—Spanish negroes!"

Who were they? Captain Sarbay owned one of them. They had been brought into New York from a Spanish vessel which had been captured.

"We are freemen in our own country," said the negroes; but the court had condemned them to be sold as slaves. It must be that they were taking their revenge. That was the conclusion arrived at, without thought or reason. There was no positive evidence that either of the houses had been set on fire. That in Ben Thomas's house was over the kitchen, and a spark from a crevice in the chimney might have set the straw-beds on fire. The coals by John Murray's hay-stack might have been extinguished before they were thrown there.

Mrs. Earle, who lived on Broadway, had a story to tell. Three negroes were going past her house. One said, "Fire! fire! scorch a little now; but by-and-by—" Then he swore.

Mrs. Earle's hair stood on end. Those words "by-and-by," did they not mean something terrible? She told her neighbor Mrs. George about it, and Mrs. George felt the cold shivers creep over her.

"There they are!" The two women looked out and saw the three negroes; one of them was Mr. Walters's Quaco. The women, with their hearts in their mouths, rushed out to tell their neighbors that there was a dreadful conspiracy among the negroes to burn the town. People lost their wits, became panic-stricken, and seized a large number of the negroes and thrust them into jail.

"What did you mean, Quaco, when you said, 'Scorch a little—but by-and-by?'"

"I meant that the Spaniards had got scorched by Admiral Vernon, and that they would get more by-and-by," said Quaco.

The news had just come that Admiral Vernon had captured Porto Bello, in the West Indies.

"To white people, one hundred pounds; to free negroes, one hundred pounds and pardon; to slaves, one hundred pounds, pardon, freedom!" That was what the governor offered to those who would tell what they knew about the conspiracy. He called out the troops to patrol the town. He called the Supreme Court together, and summoned the grand-jury. Every lawyer in New York offered his services to the governor to aid in ferreting out the conspirators. Governor, judges, sheriffs, grand-jury, lawyers, people—all were beside themselves. The entire community was panic-stricken. The soldiers marched the streets with their guns, the constables searched all the houses of the negroes who were in jail; but they found no evidence of any conspiracy or plan for insurrection.

April came, and the court sat to try the negroes; also John Hughson for robbing Mrs. Hogg, and Arthur Price for stealing goods when the governor's house was on fire. Mary Burton was the chief witness.

"Do you know anything about the conspiracy?" Mary bit her apron. "Tell us all about it, Mary; you can have one hundred pounds."

One hundred pounds! What a sum for a girl of fifteen! Mary hesitated.

"You must tell us; you must speak the truth. What a terrible sin if you do not! you will have to answer for it at the day of judgment. It will be a damnable sin laid at your door," said Judge Horsmenden.

She was in court. There sat the judges, wearing their big white wigs. There were seventeen of the coolest-headed men and most respected citizens of New York. Is it strange that a chore-girl of a dirty tavern, who had no education, no friends, who was little better than a slave, whose master and mistress were in jail for receiving stolen goods—is it a wonder that, with one hundred pounds before her, besieged by the governor, judges, jury, and all the lawyers, she should tell such a story as they wanted to hear—that there was a conspiracy among the negroes?

"Yes, there was a conspiracy; she had heard Cuffee, Cæsar, and Prince talk it over. They talked about burning the fort and the tavern.

They were going to do it in the night, and when the people came to put out the fires the negroes would kill them. John Hughson, Mrs. Hughson, and Peggy, an Irish girl, had promised to help them. Cæsar was to be governor, and Hughson king. There were thirty negroes in it. They had eight muskets, three pistols, and four swords!"

What a revelation! Judges and jury stood aghast! Every white man, woman, and child not in the plot to be murdered! They were so horrified that they could not see how absurd the story, and how great the improbability—that it was a lie from beginning to end. Thirty negroes, with eight guns, three pistols, and four swords, were to murder twelve thousand white men and women, and set up a government of their own!

"Go on, Mary. Tell us more."

And Mary went on, telling how they were to stand at the door of Trinity Church, and murder the people when they came out of meeting.

Arthur Price, who was in prison for stealing goods from the governor's house, saw that there was a chance for him to get clear, and have one hundred pounds besides. He swore that Mary had told a true story. Cæsar and Prince were condemned to be hung. "We are not guilty," said the negroes, as they stood with the halters around their necks. Nobody believed them, and the sheriff swung them off.

The governor appointed May 13th for fasting and prayer. On that day there was a fire over in Hackensack, and two barns burnt. Of course the negroes did it. Two were arrested, one confessed; both were tied to stakes and burnt to death.

Wilder grew the excitement. Mary Burton had more confessions to make; the judges and jury accepted every word of her statement as truth. John Hughson, his wife, and Peggy were hung.

"We are innocent; there is not a word of truth in Mary's stories," they said. But what were their protestations worth with people who were going crazy with excitement. There must be somebody behind the negroes.

A ship sailed into the harbor from Savannah, bringing a letter from Governor Oglethorpe, of Georgia, to Lieutenant-governor Clark. "I have some intelligence of a villanous design. The Spaniards have employed emissaries to burn all the magazines and large towns in America. Many priests are employed for the purpose, who pretend to be physicians, dancing-masters, and other such kind of occupations," wrote Governor Oglethorpe.

"The Spaniards! the Papists! the Papists!" The cry ran through the town. Who were the emissaries?

"John Ney, the school-master; he is a priest in disguise."

Poor John Ney, a quiet, inoffensive, retiring man, who had always minded his own business, and had eked out a scanty living by teaching school, was hauled up before the court.

"He has been often at our house," said John Hughson's daughter, Sarah, who also had been arrested, and who was thinking how she could save her own neck from the halter. "He used to draw a circle on the floor with chalk, and each negro put his foot in it and swore a terrible oath to kill all the white folks. He gave them the sacrament, and absolved them from all sin," she said, telling a lie which governor, judges, jury, and lawyers all believed; and John Ney, without a friend to utter a word in his defence, was taken out to the gallows.

"I never knew Hughson or his wife; never saw them. I have no knowledge of any conspiracy. I am not a Catholic, but a minister of the Church of England."

What was that denial to a panic-stricken court and people?

"He is a Papist—a conspirator. Hang him!"

The rope was put round his neck, the black cap drawn over his head, the rope cut, and his lifeless body dangled in the air.

Mr. Roosevelt's negro, Quaco, was charged with having set the governor's house on fire, when, before the panic, everybody was satisfied that the wind had blown a spark from the plumber's furnace, which had set the roof on fire.

"Burn him, if he will not confess."

Quaco was tied to the stake, and the fagots piled around him.

"Tell all you know about the conspiracy, and you shall be pardoned."

"I set the governor's house on fire. I took a coal from the kitchen and carried it up to the roof, but it didn't catch. I went up the next day, blew the coals into a flame, and kindled the fire."

"Burn him! burn him!" shouted the crowd, too crazy to see that Quaco's confession was a lie—that a brand would not hold its fire for twenty-four hours. "Burn him! burn him!"

The fagots were lighted, the flames curled around him, and his life went out amidst the hootings and maledictions of the demented multitude.

"White men who wore ruffled shirts used to come to the tavern. They sent letters to Hughson with money in them," said Mary Burton, inventing more lies.

White men with ruffled shirts! Who were they? Mary gave the names of some of the best men in New York.

Ah! Judge Horsmanden begins to see things in a different light. That cannot be. Mary is telling lies. The panic dies out as suddenly as it began.

The governor appoints a day of thanksgiving. For what? "To thank God for having delivered the colony from the execrable conspiracy;" so read the proclamation.

Conspiracy! There had been none. The negroes were innocent. John Ney was innocent. The Papists, the Spaniards, had laid no plans. The Pope had no emissaries in disguise. There was not a Catholic priest in New York. John Hughson, his wife, and Peggy were all innocent, except as receivers of the goods which Cuffee, Prince, and Cæsar had stolen. There was no evidence entitled to the court's credence that any fire had been set by design. The confession which Quaco had made was invented by the poor fellow in his fright—a vain effort to save his life. How sad the record! Nearly two hundred imprisoned; twelve burnt to death; eighteen hung; thirty-two transported and sold as slaves in the West Indies, and every one innocent!

How shall we account for such a craze? Governor, judges, the wisest and best men, the whole community, going mad, losing their wits, imprisoning, hanging the innocent, believing the stories of an injudicious chore-girl of a dirty groggery, rejecting the protestations of a school-master—a minister of the Church of England. Accepting lies for truth, and regarding the truth as lies.

The hanging of the twenty men and women at Salem was a ripple of the great wave of superstition that had been sweeping over Europe, sending hundreds and thousands to the stake and gallows. Popes, bishops, priests, Catholic and Protestant alike—good men in every country—believed that God had commanded them to put witches to death. There were tears upon the cheeks of the judges at Salem when they condemned Rebecca Nurse.

A half-century had rolled away since the delusion in regard to witchcraft; but suddenly, with no superstition of the ages to give it force, a wilder panic seized the people of New York. Everybody went crazy—governor, judges, jury, lawyers, ministers, people!

It is the most unaccountable event in the history of our country.

CHAPTER XXXI.

THE BEGINNING OF A GREAT STRUGGLE.

WHO owned the country west of the Alleghanies? "England owns it by priority of discovery," said George II.; "for Sebastian Cabot was the first to sail along the Atlantic Coast, and Sir Francis Drake was the first to visit the Pacific. England owns from ocean to ocean."

"It belongs to France," said Louis XV. "Champlain was the first European who visited the country of the Great Lakes."

Four years had passed since the signing of the treaty between France and England at Aix-la-Chapelle. It was only the laying down of the sword for a short time. Nothing had been said about boundaries in America, and anybody could see that the struggle sooner or later would begin again. During the year the Indians of Canada, especially of the St. Francis tribe, which were most under the influence of the Jesuits, were restless. They had made many forays in the past upon the settlements in New Hampshire, and were eager to be once more engaged in capturing English prisoners, and selling them as slaves to the French in Montreal.

In April, 1752, David Stinson, Amos Eastman, William and John Stark, paddled up the Merrimac in canoes. Twenty-five miles brought them to the frontier settlement at Boscawen. They pushed on up the winding river forty miles farther; entered Baker's River, a little stream which meandered through a lovely valley, built a camp, and set their traps to catch the beaver which were building their dams across the streams.

"There are Indians about. I have discovered their tracks," said one of the party.

"We had best take up our traps," they said, and John Stark went to take them up, when suddenly he found himself confronted by two Indians, who made him their prisoner. They did not know that there were more English near by, nor did John tell them.

"Why is John gone so long? Perhaps he has got lost," said the other hunters. They fired a gun. The countenances of the Indians lighted with joy. They stole through the forest with John, and came upon his three companions. Eastman was on the shore, William Stark and Stinson in the boat. They seized Eastman.

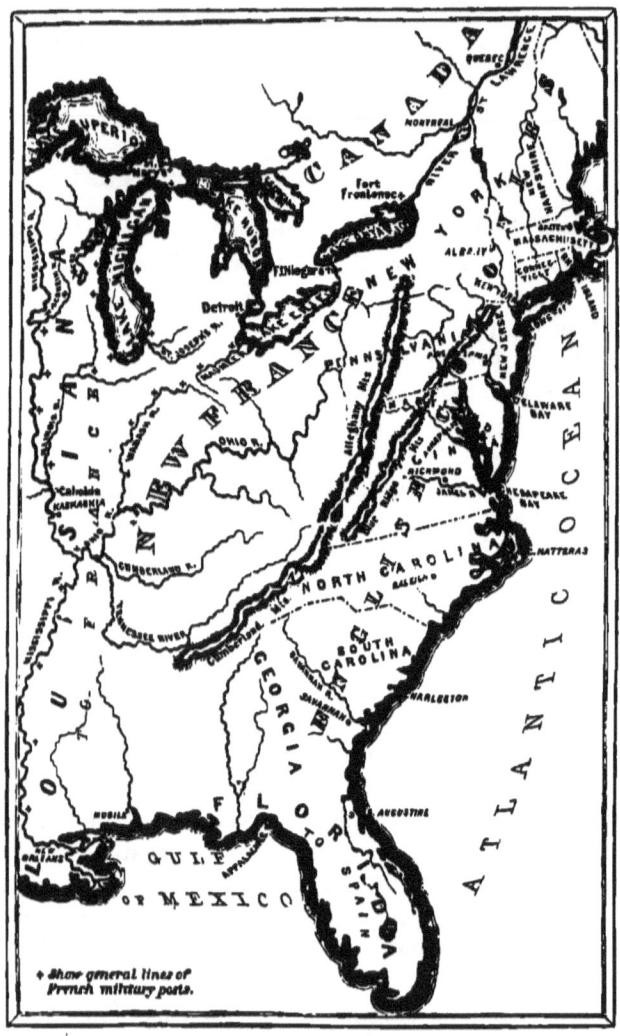

THE FRENCH FORTS.

"Pull to the other shore!" shouted John.

Crack! crack! went the guns of the Indians. Stinson fell dead, and a bullet split the paddle in William Stark's hand. He leaped to the

"CRACK! CRACK! WENT THE GUNS OF THE INDIANS."

other bank. Crack! crack! went the guns again. The bullets whistled around William, but he was a swift runner, and was soon out of sight. The Indians gave John a whipping for having shouted to William, loaded him with the plunder of the camp, and marched quickly to their canoes. They divided, one party going west over the Green Mountains with the furs which they had captured—going directly to Albany, because they could get better prices there than in Canada—and the other party, with their two prisoners, paddling up the Connecticut, carrying their canoes to Lake Memphremagog, descending the St. Francis River to their village on the bank of the St. Lawrence, half-way between Quebec and Montreal.

The village of St. Francis was a collection of miserable cabins. The Jesuits had built a chapel, where a little tinkling bell called the Indians to morning mass and evening vespers.

The whole population—warriors, squaws, and children—came out to receive the party returning from so successful a foray. True, there was no war between France and England, but what of that? Had they not made war on their own account? The Jesuit fathers had no rebuke for them. Were not the English all heretics? The prisoners must run the gauntlet. It is not quite certain what the word came from, but it means running between two rows of men armed with sticks, each Indian to give the prisoner a whack as he passed. Eastman was the oldest, and ran first. Whack! whack! fell the blows, beating his flesh black and blue.

"Your turn now!" said an Indian to John Stark.

He is thirty years old, tall, and broad-shouldered. His muscles are springs of steel. He has an iron will. He is quick to think and act.

The Indians grasp their cudgels in a firmer grip. Stark comes upon the run. Quick as a flash he wrests a cudgel from an Indian, swings it about his head with the strength of a giant, giving blows on their faces and on their foreheads. They go down as the Philistines fell before Samson. The Indians take to their heels to escape his mighty strokes.

"You hoe corn," they say, putting a hoe in his hands.

He strikes it into the ground a few times, hoeing up the young corn instead of the weeds, then flings the hoe into the river.

"Squaws hoe corn, braves fight!" he said.

Did they punish him? On the contrary, they patted him on the shoulder.

"Bono! bono!"—good! good! they said, greatly pleased at his spirit; they wanted him to be their chief.

Eastman got his freedom for sixty dollars; but Stark had to pay one hundred for being so bold and brave.

While the Jesuit Indians were making raids upon the Merrimac, Christopher Gist was crossing the Alleghany Mountains with eleven families, and making a settlement near Pittsburgh. Intelligence of what he was doing reached the Governor of Canada. The English were taking possession of Ohio! He would not permit it. He determined to drive them out. He sent a party of soldiers, who built a fort on the Alleghany at Franklin, in Venango County, in the territory which the Ohio Company had purchased.

Governor Dinwiddie, of Virginia, looked around to find some one to send a message to the French. There were many able men in the prime of life in Virginia, but he passed them all by, and selected a tall young man—only twenty-two years old—George Washington.

Who was he, and what had he done to commend himself to act as ambassador in a matter affecting the relations not only of the Ohio Company, but Virginia and all the other colonies? He was great-grandson of John Washington, who stood so staunchly by Charles I., who emigrated to Virginia when Cromwell came into power. He was born on February 22d, 1732, on the banks of the Potomac, in a little, old, low-roofed house, with a big chimney on the outside of each gable.

ARMS AND CREST OF THE WASHINGTON FAMILY.

Soon after his birth his father moved to Fredericksburg, and George went to school and studied arithmetic and grammar, and learned to write a clear round hand. His oldest brother, Lawrence, was sent to England to be educated. He came back in 1740. England and Spain were at war, and the English went on an expedition to the West Indies to capture the Spanish towns. Virginia raised some troops, and Lawrence Washington went as captain, and had a taste of fighting in an attack by Admiral Vernon on Carthagena. He was gone two years. His father died in 1743, leaving a great estate on the Potomac to Lawrence, which he named Mount Vernon, in honor of his commander, Admiral Vernon. He built a fine mansion overlooking the river, married Annie Fairfax, and lived in fine style, having a stable full of horses.

George was eleven years old, and was sent to Mr. Williams's school, where he studied surveying. He wanted to be a midshipman on one of Admiral Vernon's ships. A commission was obtained for him; but his mother asked him to give up the idea of being a sailor, and his affection for her was so tender that he did not accept the commission.

When he was fifteen years old he went to Mount Vernon to live with Lawrence, whose next neighbor was Lord Fairfax — a tall, gaunt, raw-boned man, with sharp nose, piercing eyes, sixty years old, who owned immense estates on the Potomac, and beyond the Blue Ridge along the Shenandoah, which he had inherited from his mother, daughter of Lord

MOUNT VERNON.

Culpepper, to whom they had been given by Charles II. Lord Fairfax had many horses. He was fond of hunting and riding at a breakneck speed, leaping fallen trees and high fences, in chasing deer and foxes with a pack of hounds and a troop of his neighbors. A fox-hunt in the early morning, when the air was fresh and invigorating, stirred the blood—the master of the band sending out blasts from his trumpet that echoed far over the valley, and singing a hunting song:

> "A southerly wind and cloudy sky
> Proclaim it a hunting morning;
> Before the sun rises, away we fly,
> Dull sleep and a downy bed scorning.
> Tantara! tantara! tantara!"

Of all the riders there was none bolder than George Washington. No untamed colt, no matter how high he might kick, could unseat the tall boy when he was once on the animal's back.

Lord Fairfax wanted his land in the Shenandoah surveyed, and engaged the sixteen-year-old lad to do the work. He rode on horseback up the valley of the Potomac, entered the valley of the "Daughter of the Stars," as the Indians called the beautiful Shenandoah. He laid off the wild land into farms, working hard all day with his compass, sleeping at night on the floor of a log-cabin, or wrapping himself in his blanket beneath the trees, earning five or six dollars a day.

He laid out a manor for Lord Fairfax, who built a great house, with numerous outbuildings, and who treated everybody with the greatest hospitality. He called his place Greenway Court. Squatters, negroes, Indians, always could have a meal of victuals at Greenway.

The Governor of Virginia appointed him public surveyor. The planters paid him liberally. They raised a great deal of tobacco, which they pressed into hogsheads, and which was rolled to Belhaven, on the Potomac, where they loaded it on vessels and shipped it to England.

Belhaven was a hamlet of a few houses; but Colonel Fairfax, Lawrence Washington, and a few of their neighbors, thinking it might be made a large town, purchased the land, and set the young surveyor to laying it out. They named it Alexandria. Whatever he undertook to do was well done. He wrote the notes of his survey in a clear round hand, easy to read as a printed page. He was so much respected that the governor appointed him a major in the militia when he was only eighteen. He took fencing lessons of Jacob Van Braam, a Dutchman, who had been with his brother Lawrence in the war against the Spaniards.

Governor Dinwiddie had tried in vain to find some one who would take a letter to the French beyond the mountains. Of all the brave and able men in Virginia, no one cared to go. There were terrible hardships to be encountered, to say nothing of the chance of a man losing his scalp.

"I will go, sir," said the young surveyor, twenty years old, and he was so self-reliant and capable that the governor intrusted him with the mission.

THE BEGINNING OF A GREAT STRUGGLE. 371

WASHINGTON SURVEYING LORD FAIRFAX'S LAND.

The leaves were falling from the elms and maples on the 30th of October, when he started from Williamsburg with Jacob Van Braam, who was to go with him. Eight men, with a tent and provisions, accompanied them on horseback. Two were Indians.

They rode up the valley of the Potomac to Cumberland, followed up a little stream called Will's Creek, climbed over the mountains, and reached the Monongahela. The provisions were put in a canoe and sent down the stream; but the men on horseback reached the Ohio before the men in the boats. While waiting for it, the young surveyor was making a map of the country.

"Here is a place for a fort, and it will be a city some day," he said, as he stood upon the point of land at the junction of the Alleghany and Monongahela, where now the smoke of thousands of furnaces of Pittsburgh darken the sun.

It was seventy miles up the valley to the first French fort at Venango. The French commander, Joncaire, had no authority to receive the letters. He must send Major Washington to his superior up French Creek, to Fort La Bœuf; but he treated the young officer from Virginia with great respect, entertaining him with wine grown in the vineyards of France.

"The country is ours, and we intend to hold it," said the French commander.

Four weary days through the snow, where now fountains of oil are flowing, brought them to Fort La Bœuf, fifteen miles only from Lake Erie. Washington presented his letter, was courteously entertained two days, and received a letter in reply, to be delivered to the Governor of Virginia.

Great were the hardships of the homeward journey. There had been heavy rains. French Creek was swollen. The canoes of the voyagers were in danger of being dashed upon the rocks. Many times Washington had to leap into the water to lift the boats from the rocks.

It was Christmas when they started from Venango. The pack-horses were broken down. Washington piled the baggage on his horse, and started on foot, dressed as an Indian. The snow was deep, and the rivers filled with ice. Washington and Mr. Gist, who was with him, left Van Braam and the others, and struck through the forest for the junction of the Alleghany and the Monongahela, taking an Indian for a guide; but the Indian was in the pay of the French, and led them a roundabout tramp through the woods. The Indian was in advance; suddenly he turned, raised his gun, and fired at Washington. He was not three rods away, but, strange to say, missed him. The Indian sprung behind a tree, and began to load his gun. Washington and Gist seized him.

"I'll put an end to the rascal!" said Gist.

"Oh no," said Washington; "we will set him adrift."

They gave him a piece of meat, but kept his gun. They travelled all night, going by the compass, and reached the Alleghany. The river was filled with floating ice. They had only one hatchet, but set themselves to work, taking turns in building a raft, which took them all day. They got on board with poles to push it across the stream. When halfway, a cake of ice struck Washington with such force that it knocked him from the raft; but he got on board once more. The ice was so thick that they could not push the raft to either shore, and landed upon an island. Night came on. They were drenched to the skin. Their clothes were coats of frozen mail. They nearly lost their lives from freezing; but when morning came the river was frozen from shore to shore, and they gained the land, pushed on all day, reached the cabin of a settler, and were saved from perishing.

Jacob Van Braam and the others of the party came; and with fresh horses they made their way over the mountains, reaching Williamsburg January 16th, 1754.

What was the reply of the French? That the letter of the Governor of Virginia would be sent to the Governor of Canada, the Marquis du Quesne.

CHAPTER XXXII.

DEFEAT OF GENERAL BRADDOCK.

"WE must secure the Ohio country in advance of the French," was the declaration of the Governor of Virginia.

The assembly voted ten thousand pounds. A regiment was raised. Joshua Fry was appointed colonel, and George Washington lieutenant-

THE LAND IN DISPUTE.

colonel. Two of the companies were sent to build a fort on the spot which Washington had selected. They made their way through the woods, down the Monongahela, and began to build the fort; but were suddenly interrupted by the appearance of sixty large flat-boats and three hundred canoes, bringing one thousand French and Indians, and eighteen cannon. Captain Contrecœur was commander.

"Surrender, or I shall fire upon you," he said.

There were only forty-one Virginians in the party, and Ensign Ward, who commanded them, was obliged to surrender, but was permitted to leave with his men. The French went to work with axes and spades, and erected a strong fort, mounted their cannon upon it, and named it Du Quesne, in honor of the Governor of Canada.

Ensign Ward reached Cumberland, and told Washington of what had taken place. Though the French had occupied the country in advance of Washington, he was not the man to turn back, but marched to Great Meadows, thirty-seven miles from Pittsburgh.

"The French are coming out to surprise you," was the word brought by an Indian.

Why not surprise them? He started at midnight and fell upon them. Their leader, Jumonville, was killed, and half the party captured. He returned quickly to Great Meadows, threw up a little fort, which he named "Fort Necessity," and sent a messenger for his re-enforcements to hasten; but before they arrived a large body of French and Indians were upon him, and he was obliged to surrender.

War had not been declared between France and England, but it had begun. It was not a struggle merely to determine to whom the country west of the Alleghany belonged; not a question of boundaries, but a conflict between two civilizations, two races, two religions.

The French were descended from people who spoke the Latin language. They were Catholics. Their rulers had always taught that government was paternal, and would take care of them.

The English had German and Norman blood in their veins. Their language was strong and vigorous. They did not regard the king as their father; they had protested against the claim of popes and priests to hold their consciences and intellects in their keeping. Government to them was not paternal. Men were individuals, and had a right to make their own laws, which the king himself was bound to obey.

The French and Jesuits were setting themselves to hold a vast territory, capable of sustaining millions of the human race. They intended to make the range of mountains, from the White Mountains in New Hampshire to Central Alabama, the boundary between the two civilizations, races, and religions.

The English colonies had a population of eleven hundred and sixty-five thousand whites, and two hundred and sixty-eight thousand negroes.

The French population of Canada was only about one hundred and twenty thousand; so there were fourteen people in the English settlements where there was one in Canada.

Why had not Canada grown faster? because the French did not like to leave their vineyards and their sunny homes, to live in a country where the snow covered the ground from November to May. The peasants of *la belle* France preferred to live where they could gather with their neighbors in the pleasant wine-shops of their native villages, and talk of what was going on, and have a dance upon the green in the calm summer evenings. Why should they leave such pleasures to live where the wolves and foxes were ever howling?

The Jesuits had done what they could to build up Canada. They had been very zealous for the Church of Rome and for the order of Loyola. There was scarcely a heretic in all that vast reach of country. Bitter their hatred; but hate and prejudice always make men blind, not only to what is right but to their own interests.

It was an irreparable mistake which the Jesuits made when they induced Louis XIV. to revoke the Edict of Nantes, and at the same time excluding the Huguenots from Canada.. The Huguenots were attached to France, and when they were in exile, when they were being burnt to death, sent up fervent prayers for the king. They would have emigrated to Canada, but the Jesuits kept them out. Canada and the whole of America between the Alleghanies and the Pacific Ocean was to be theirs. They were ever intermeddling with the Governor of Canada, and quarrelling with the fur-traders. The Governors of Canada were ever looking after their own interests.

One, who died just before George Washington made his journey to the Ohio, was feathering his own nest while managing affairs. The King of France allowed him thirteen hundred dollars salary, but he laid up sixty thousand livres every year by plundering the people. The example of the governor was followed by everybody else. Father Letour, a Jesuit priest, was so greedy of making money that he had a contractor murdered who stood in the way of his supplying a fort with provisions.

How could Canada grow when everybody in office was plundering the people? The Canadians lived by hunting and fishing. They loved the wild life of the woods. They planted but little. Why should they clear land and delve among the stumps with hoes, when the woods and streams were full of game?

Away back at the beginning of things, when Adam was in Eden, God told him to dress it and subdue the ground, and it should bring forth food. It is the subduing of the ground that is at the beginning of all progress. A people who live by hunting and fishing will always be poor and low down in civilization. It is digging the ground that produces wealth, and there is no end to the riches which men can accumulate if they begin in the right way.

The English in America, with sturdy blows, had been letting the sunlight in upon the wilderness—clearing farms, ploughing, sowing, reaping; the women spinning and weaving: wheels were humming and shuttles flying from morning till night.

Working with the hands sets the brain to work. Every town had its school, its church, a school-master, and minister. Men were thinking for themselves—upon government, upon individual rights, upon obligations to themselves, their neighbor, and to God.

Life, activity, energy along the Atlantic shore—on the Connecticut, Hudson, and Potomac; sluggishness and torpor on the St. Lawrence. The King of France and the Jesuits managed everything in Canada. The people had no voice in anything, while in the English colonies the people managed their own affairs.

Two frigates, the *Nightingale* and *Sea-horse*, commanded by Admiral Keppel, with sixteen merchant-vessels, sailed up the Potomac to Alexandria, bringing two regiments of British troops, commanded by Major-general Edward Braddock—haughty, proud, austere, who looked down with contempt upon the people of America.

There were stirring times in Alexandria—the king's troops landing, pitching their tents, appearing on parade. There was a gathering of governors—Shirley from Massachusetts, Delancey from New York, Morris from Pennsylvania, Sharp from Maryland, Dinwiddie from Virginia, with their secretaries. The rich planters came to pay their respects to the commander of the king's troops and the governors. There were grand dinner-parties and much ceremony. General Braddock took Colonel Carlyle's house—the best in Alexandria—for his head-quarters. It had been built two years before, in 1753, of stone brought from the Isle of Wight, in vessels that sailed to Virginia after tobacco. Men whose names are written large in the history of our country came to see General Braddock. Benjamin Franklin, who was the king's deputy-postmaster, came to make arrangements for sending letters. He knew more about public affairs than General Braddock and all the governors together. Horatio Gates came from New York, to tender two companies to General Braddock; Richard Henry Lee, captain of a company of Virginia troops, was there to offer his services. Hugh Mercer came with a company of volunteers from Fredericksburg. Daniel Morgan, a teamster from Occoquan, between Alexandria and Mount Vernon, was there to drive a wagon. He was accepted as a teamster, and for doing something which displeased Braddock was whipped. General Braddock and all the English officers had a good opinion of themselves, but thought very little of the "provin-

BRADDOCK'S HEAD-QUARTERS.

cials," as they called everybody who lived in America. No provincial general or colonel, commissioned by the governor, could hold any rank while serving with the officers commissioned by the king. Colonel George Washington was high-spirited enough to resent such an insult, and resigned his commission. General Braddock found that he needed the man who knew all about the Ohio country, and appointed him on his staff, and the Governor of Virginia appointed him commander of the Virginia troops which were to accompany Braddock.

Who should pay for the support of the troops—the king or the colonies? The question had been discussed among the king's ministers in Parliament; and now, on the 14th of April, 1755, the governors, with Gen-

DEFEAT OF GENERAL BRADDOCK.

eral Braddock and Admiral Keppel, meet in a secret congress to discuss and settle the question.

The king and his ministers and Parliament were taxing the people of the provinces in various ways; the governors were all getting rich by plundering them; and the Legislatures, ever watchful of their rights, were refusing to vote supplies, when they could have nothing to say as to how the money was to be expended.

The governors all sided with the king and the ministers. It was natural, for they were all appointed by the king. They resolved that the king's ministers ought to find out some method of *compelling* the people of America to supply the troops under General Braddock. It was a little cloud on the horizon, which became a thunder-gust in after years.

The people of Alexandria had swung their hats when Braddock came, but they were heartily glad when his troops were on their way up the Potomac; for there was bad blood between his soldiers, whose uniforms were bright and new—red coats with buff facings—and the Virginia soldiers, whose uniforms were home-made, and so short-tailed that the regulars called them "bobtails." With rum in abundance, with contempt

WASHINGTON'S TALK WITH BRADDOCK.

on the part of the regulars, and a resenting of insult on the part of the Virginians, there were many brawls and fights.

Braddock's whole force was twenty-one hundred men, including the eight companies of Virginians under Washington. The English general had fought on European battle-fields. He had marched on smooth roads, but knew nothing of the difficulties of getting through an American wilderness. He scorned advice. He was so punctilious and fussy, that the army only made five miles a day; and if it had not been for Benjamin Franklin, would not have gotten on at all for want of wagons and horses, but he obtained them from the Pennsylvania farmers.

The army reached Cumberland the first week in June. General Braddock accepted Washington's advice to leave the heavy baggage, and move on with twelve hundred men more rapidly.

It was a bright July morning. The army was approaching Fort Du Quesne; ten miles more, and it would be there. Proudly the soldiers moved along the valley of the Monongahela, wearing their bright red uniforms, their gun-barrels and bayonets glaring in the sunlight, drums beating, trumpets sounding, and their banners waving. Lieutenant-colonel Gage, with three hundred men, led the advance. He forded the river, crossed a plain, and ascended a hill. Mr. Gordon was in advance of all, with a company, marking out the road. General Braddock had no expectation of being attacked. He was to attack the French. Mr. Gordon beheld a man wearing a gray hunting-frock waving his hat. A silver gorget gleamed upon his breast. It was a French officer, Beaujean, who had come out from Fort Du Quesne with two hundred and thirty Frenchmen and six hundred and thirty Indians, to give General Braddock a little taste of fighting in the wilderness of America. From every tree there came a flash, and the head of Gage's column melted away; but the English fired a volley, and Beaujean and thirteen of his men went down.

Gage's artillerymen wheeled two cannon into position, and opened fire. The roar of the cannon echoed along the river, frightening the Indians, who started to run; but the French held their ground. The Indians came back, yelling the war-whoop.

"Vive le Roi!" shouted the French.

"Hurrah for King George!" cried the English.

Lieutenant-colonel Burton came up with a re-enforcement, but his troops were panic-stricken. General Braddock tried to rally his men. They loaded and fired at random; they saw flashes, puffs of smoke, but few of the enemy. There was firing in front, on both flanks and in the rear, where the Indians were shooting the horses of the baggage-train. The drivers fled. Men and officers were dropping all the time. Braddock was trying to form his men in platoons and battalions, after the

DEFEAT OF GENERAL BRADDOCK.

method laid down in all military books; while the Virginians, accustomed to the wilderness, sprung behind rocks and trees, or fell flat on the ground, and watched their opportunity to put a bullet through the head of a Frenchman or Indian. Braddock cursed them for not standing up in platoons, and struck them with his sword.

How preposterous! Whoever heard of a battle being fought in that way from behind trees!

Captain Waggener placed his company of Virginians behind a fallen tree, which served them for a breastwork, and poured a telling volley

"THEY SAW PUFFS OF SMOKE, BUT FEW OF THE ENEMY."

upon the French, but the next minute fifty of them were killed by the panic-stricken British, who had so lost their wits that they took them to be Frenchmen. The French and Indians aimed to pick off all the English officers. Sir Peter Halket, Braddock's second in command, fell dead. Shirley, Braddock's secretary, went down with a bullet through his breast. Colonels Burton, Gage, and Orme, Major Spark, Major Halket, Captain Morris, all were wounded.

Washington's horse was killed. He mounted a second; that, too, was shot. A bullet went through his coat; another, a third, a fourth; but his time had not come to die. God had a great work for him to do for the human race, and this was the beginning.

All through the afternoon, from two o'clock to five, the hurly-burly went on—the English huddled in groups or scattered along the narrow road, firing away their ammunition, seeing only now and then a Frenchman or Indian. The Virginians alone were cool, watching their opportunity, and sending their bullets through the skulls of the savages as they peeped from behind the trees.

It was five o'clock in the afternoon; General Braddock had had five horses shot under him; he was issuing an order when a bullet struck him, and he fell upon the ground. His troops threw aside their guns and knapsacks, then fled like a herd of frightened sheep. Washington tried to stop them. He begged, threatened, but in vain.

"Don't leave your general to be scalped!" shouted Colonel Orme. "I'll give you sixty guineas to carry him off."

What was Braddock or money to them? To escape was their only thought. Captain Stewart and another Virginian officer took the wounded general in their arms and bore him from the field. All through the night, all the next day, the English fled, the Virginians under Washington protecting the rear and carrying the wounded general.

The French and Indians made no attempt at pursuit; they had won a great victory, and were dividing the spoil—drinking the rum, eating the bacon, and counting their scalps in savage glee.

It was Sunday evening. The remnant of the defeated army was at Great Meadows. Braddock had issued his orders up to this time, but no other words had passed his lips. The death pallor was settling over his face. "Who would have thought it? We shall know better how to deal with them next time," he said. They were his last words; a few minutes, and the heart ceased its beating. Incapacity, haughtiness, pride, contempt of advice, had resulted in defeat and disaster.

Governor Shirley, of Massachusetts, was at Oswego, in New York, in-

DEFEAT OF GENERAL BRADDOCK. 383

tending to capture Niagara; but the news of the defeat of Braddock so disheartened his men and upset all his plans, that he did not make the attempt.

Another expedition, under General Johnson, started from Albany to capture Crown Point.

The troops were mostly from New England. The news of the dis-

BRADDOCK'S GRAVE.

aster to Braddock, instead of dispiriting them, only made them more resolute. One of the regiments was from New Hampshire, commanded by Colonel Blanchard. One of the companies of the regiment was called the "Rangers." The soldiers had rifles, and wore green frocks. They were commanded by Robert Rogers. John Stark was lieutenant. They built a fort on the Hudson, which they named Fort Edward.

General Johnson opened a road from the Hudson to Lake St. Sacrament. Johnson hated the name given by the Jesuits, and changed it to Lake George, for the King of England. No French or Jesuit names for

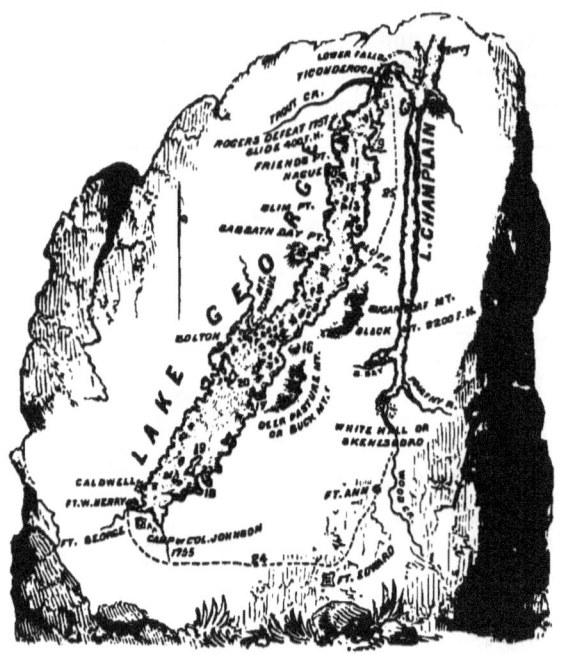

LAKE GEORGE.

him. Two hundred ship-carpenters went to work building boats, in which he intended to go down the lake, making his way to Ticonderoga, where he would build a fort which would command both lakes, and be a barrier in the path of the French. He had thirty-four hundred men. Hendrick, the Mohawk chief, joined him with two hundred warriors. General Johnson's son, Thayendanegea, or Joseph Brant, or "Bundle of Sticks," whose mother was one of Johnson's Indian wives, accompanied his father, although he was only thirteen years old.

Scouts brought word that the French were already building a fort at Ticonderoga. Baron Dieskau, the commander, was quick to act.

"Boldness wins," was Dieskau's motto.

Sometimes it does, sometimes it does not. He conceived a bold plan, that of marching past Johnson, capturing Fort Edward, and falling upon Albany. He had nine hundred French and six hundred Indians. Such a move would cut off Johnson, and carry consternation to the English everywhere. The Indians did not like to attack forts; they were afraid of cannon, and urged Dieskau to attack Johnson, who was encamped on the shore of the lake.

"The French are going to attack Fort Edward," was the word brought by scouts.

General Johnson called a council of war, proposing to send one thousand troops under Colonel Williams to meet Dieskau.

JOSEPH BRANT.

"What do you think?" he asked of the chief of the Mohawks.

"If they are to fight, they are too few; if to be killed, too many," said Hendrick.

Notwithstanding the advice, General Johnson ordered Colonel Williams to march. He was a brave officer. He had made his will when he was at Albany, bequeathing his property for the founding of a school, the beginning of Williams College.

25

Four miles out from Johnson's camp there was a swamp on one side of the road, and a low ridge on the other. The trees were tall, and the underbrush very thick.

What a place for an ambush! Dieskau posted his men, where they could sweep the road with their fire. The Indians threw themselves on their faces, or crouched behind the trees.

Into the trap marched the Mohawks—Hendrick in advance.

Nearly a century and a half had passed since that battle on the shore of the lake, a few miles further north, between the Iroquois and Algonquins—in which Samuel Champlain took part; and the enmity between the Indians was still the same.

SIR WILLIAM JOHNSON.

Colonel Williams, Lieutenant Whiting, and Lieutenant Israel Putnam, with the Massachusetts, New Hampshire, and Connecticut troops, were just behind.

A gun flashed, and the old Mohawk chief—ever the friend of the English—fell dead. The swamp and low ridge were aflame. The Mohawks fled. Colonel Williams was shot. Though the backwoodsmen of New England were confronted by troops who had fought on the battle-fields of France, they fought bravely, retreating in good order to the lake.

Boldness wins! Baron Dieskau had won one victory, and would quickly make an end of the English.

Johnson's troops were hard at work. They were all wood-choppers, and the trees were falling beneath their blows for a breastwork. The artillerymen were dragging the cannon up from the ships and putting them in position.

It was half-past eleven, when the English saw beneath the boughs of the trees the white uniforms of the French, who came on in platoons, firing volley after volley. The Canadian Indians poured in a rattling fire

HENDRICK.

from behind the trees, but were terribly frightened when Johnson's cannon began to thunder, and fled to a safe distance.

"Cowards!" cried Dieskau; but that did not make them brave.

The Mohawks had also skulked to the rear, but they took heart and returned. Johnson was slightly wounded at the beginning of the battle, and went to his tent, leaving General Lyman, of Connecticut, to command the troops. He was a brave, cool-headed man, and his men were as brave as he.

"They fight like devils!" said Dieskau. A bullet struck him, but he would not leave the field. Boldness wins! he would fight on. St. Pierre, his next officer, was killed. Another bullet strikes Dieskau; a third; but he will not leave the field. He sits upon a stump and coolly gives his orders.

The September sun wheels down the west. For five hours the battle goes on. The strength of the French is failing. The men of New England, defeated in the morning, can restrain themselves no longer. They leap over the barricade, fall upon the French, and strike them down with the butts of their guns, putting them to rout.

Seth Pomeroy, of Connecticut, comes upon Dieskau, who sits upon a stump, unable to move. Pomeroy does not understand French, nor Dieskau English. The French general puts his hand in his pocket to pull out his watch to present to his captor. Pomeroy thinks he is drawing a pistol, and fires, wounding the brave Frenchman once more; but he is kindly cared for by the surgeons, and lives to reach England.

The French and Indians flee. General Lyman begs Johnson to let him follow on and finish them; but Johnson will not permit him. He is afraid of a trap somewhere. But Captain McGninnes, with two hundred men from New Hampshire, has heard the firing at Fort Edward, and is hastening through the woods. He meets the fleeing French, and the battle begins again. McGninnes is killed; but his men avenge his death by putting the enemy once more to rout.

The sun goes down. Three battles have been fought between the trained troops of France and their Indian allies on the one side, and the men of New England, who have left their harvest-fields to become soldiers. Nearly four hundred of their number have fallen; but they have retrieved the disaster of the morning, and are victors on the field. The French have lost nearly half their number.

General Johnson has had little to do with winning the victory, but he reaps all the honors. The king makes him a baronet, and presents him with twenty-five thousand dollars. General Lyman, the brave, cool-headed man, who has directed affairs, gets nothing, and Johnson makes little mention of his services.

George II. and his ministers—the Dukes of Cumberland, Newcastle, Devonshire, and Bedford—opinionated, incompetent men, who were mismanaging the affairs of England, rejoiced when they heard of the victory; but they were not far-sighted enough to see what would be its influence—how it would lead the people in America to draw contrasts; that by every fireside men would talk about the arrogance, haughtiness, and incompetency of British officers and soldiers—defeated on the banks of the Monongahela, Braddock's army saved by the coolness and bravery of the young Virginian colonel and his soldiers; how the veteran soldiers of France and the Indians of Canada had been beaten by the men of New England and New York, and not a British soldier or officer present to help or hinder.

"We can manage our own affairs, and fight our own battles," was the conclusion they arrived at.

CHAPTER XXXIII.
THE EMPEROR OF AUSTRIA'S WILL.

CHARLES IV., Emperor of Austria, made his will, giving his empire to Maria Theresa, Queen of Hungary; but no sooner was the breath out of his body than a pack of hungry princes set themselves to get possession of portions of the territory, and in a short time all Europe was at

SITE OF FORT NUMBER FOUR.

war. It was a turmoil that reached eastward to the Ganges in India, and westward to the Hudson. Men were hacked to pieces by the sword on the plains of India, while the Indians of America buried their tomahawks in the skulls of men, women, and children on the banks of the Merrimac and Connecticut, in consequence of that act.

War was declared by France against Great Britain March 15th, 1744. The King of France sent a vessel across the Atlantic with orders to General Du Vivier at Louisburg, Cape Breton, to strike a blow upon the English. Du Vivier was quick to act. He sailed from Louisburg on the 15th of May with one thousand men, and captured the English fort at Canso, and its garrison of eighty men. He sent the prisoners to Boston. Not till the vessel bringing the prisoners entered the harbor did anybody know that war had begun.

Upon the breaking out of the war, all the Indians east of the Hudson, except the Stockbridge tribe in Massachusetts, hastened to Canada to join the French.

On April 17th, 1744, they struck their first blow at Gorham, in Maine, killing Mr. Bryant and several others. Another party killed Josiah Bishop in Boscawen, New Hampshire, on the Merrimac. Another party swept down the Connecticut to Charlestown, New Hampshire, to Fort Number Four, captured three men, took them to Canada, and sold them as slaves. No huntsman could go for beaver or deer now with safety. Indians were sure to be following stealthily upon their trail, to shoot them down and take their scalps.

On the eastern shore of Cape Breton, looking toward Newfoundland, was the great and strong fortress of Louisburg, which for thirty years the

CAPE BRETON.

French had been building. The walls were thirty feet high, built of stone. There were six bastions, with platforms for one hundred and eighty cannon. Outside the walls was a ditch eighty feet wide. On an island was a battery of thirty cannon; and there was still another fortification, called the Royal Battery, with thirty more cannon.

FOLLOWING A TRAIL.

Beneath the guns of the fortress the vessels of the French could find protection and shelter, or sail out to capture the fishermen of New England, or to harass and ravage the New England coast. France had erected it to command the entrance to the Gulf of St. Lawrence, and protect New France from hostile fleets.

Benning Wentworth, Governor of New Hampshire, lived at Little Har-

GOVERNOR BENNING WENTWORTH.

bor, near Portsmouth, in a spacious mansion that contained more than fifty rooms. One of his neighbors, Colonel Vaughan, unfolded to him a grand project—the capture of Louisburg. "It can be done!" said the colonel.

Governor Wentworth was so interested in the plan, that he sent him to Boston to confer with Governor Shirley, who saw what a grand idea it was, and laid the matter before the General Court.

"I propose that we send four thousand soldiers to capture Louisburg, and I ask you to keep the matter secret," he said to the members.

The members were astonished. What chance would four thousand men have against such a fortress, with French frigates in the harbor? Not any. It could not be done; we cannot think of it, was the decision. The members alone held the great secret; but one of them unwittingly made it known while he was praying one morning with his family.

"Let thy wisdom, Lord, guide us in the proposed great undertaking!" was his prayer.

What did he mean? What was the great undertaking? Perhaps his wife wormed the secret out of him; at any rate, a few days later, it was known that the governor had proposed to send an army to capture Louisburg, and that the General Court had refused to entertain the project. Capture Louisburg! The people caught the great idea.

"Let it be done!" urged the men of Marblehead, Salem, and Boston, sending letters to urge on the project.

"We will do it!" said the members of the General Court, deciding the

WENTWORTH HOUSE, LITTLE HARBOR.

matter by a single vote in the majority. A single vote does great things sometimes.

"I desire the assistance of your fleet," was Governor Shirley's message to Admiral Warren in the West Indies.

"We will send five hundred men," responded the Legislature of Connecticut.

"We will send three hundred," was the word from New Hampshire; and Rhode Island promised the same number. Who should command? In all New England there was not an officer who had seen fighting,

SIR WILLIAM PEPPERELL'S HOUSE.

except with the Indians. William Pepperell, of Kittery, had some excellent qualifications for a commander, for he was cool, self-reliant, and had made his mark as one able to win success. His father came, a poor boy, from England to the Isles of Shoals, and made money catching fish. He settled at Kittery. William had built ships, and sent them to Europe and the West Indies. He had sent to London for law-books, and was studying law. He was colonel of a regiment, and kept a sharp eye on the Indians. In all that he had undertaken he had succeeded; and he was so much respected, and people had such faith in him, that Governor Shirley appointed him commander.

"I am not capable of taking command," said Pepperell.

"As thy day is, so shall thy strength be!" answered George Whitefield, the great preacher, urging him on.

"*Nil desperandum, Christo duce,*" was the motto which Whitefield gave, to be placed upon his flag.

In less than two months all was ready, so great was the enthusiasm of the people. On the 1st of April a fleet of nearly one hundred vessels sailed out of Boston harbor and steered eastward. Admiral Warren came with five vessels, carrying sixty guns each, and six frigates.

Great the consternation at Louisburg on the 29th of April, 1745, when the French saw one hundred and twenty vessels in the harbor, and thousands of soldiers landing in boats on the beach. Near the Royal Battery was a long row of houses filled with barrels of pitch, tar, and oakum. Colonel Vaughan, of New Hampshire, with four hundred men, when night came on, crept up to the houses and set them on fire, which so frightened the Frenchmen holding the battery that they fled into the fortress, leaving all the cannon and ammunition.

"By the grace of God and the courage of thirteen men, I entered the Royal Battery about nine o'clock, and am waiting for re-enforcements and a flag," was the note which Colonel Vaughan wrote to General Pepperell.

Now came the hard work—the lifting of heavy cannon into boats, landing them on the beach, dragging them on sledges through the shallows, wading up to their knees in half-frozen mud—working from dark till sunrise, so that the French should not discover what was going on.

Colonel Gorham attempted to take the battery on the island; but the

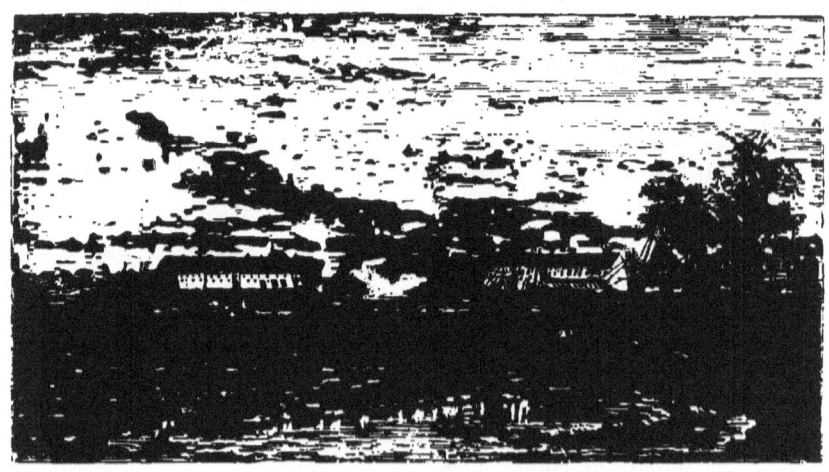

NAVY-YARD, KITTERY, MAINE.

wind was blowing a gale, some of the boats were swamped, and one hundred and seventy men were lost.

A French war-vessel, with sixty-four guns and ammunition, came sailing into the harbor, and fell into the hands of Admiral Warren. But day after day, night after night, the work of the siege went on. Sickness broke out; many soldiers died; but no one faltered. Great was the joy of the New Englanders when they discovered some cannon which the French had buried. Colonel Gridly soon had them in position, and the cannonade began—the solid shot banging against the stone walls, grinding the granite to powder, splitting it and making great gaps, and dismounting the cannon. The French commander was brave; but, seeing how it must end, hung out a white flag, and on June 17th the great fortress, with all its cannon and nineteen hundred soldiers, surrendered to the ship-builder of Kittery, and the brave men who, with undaunted enthusiasm, had obeyed his orders.

SIR WILLIAM PEPPERELL.

At daybreak on Tuesday, July 2d, 1745, Captain Bennett reached Boston with the news. Never was there such rejoicing—bells ringing, cannon thundering at Castle William, at the north and south batteries; bonfires on the Common, tents spread, casks of wine tapped; at night candles in every window, and rockets streaming up the sky!

"Before sunrise the streets were as thick with people as on election-day, and we had the finest illumination I ever beheld with my eyes," wrote Rev. Mr. Chauncy to Governor Pepperell.

At Portsmouth, Salem, Newport, New York, and Philadelphia the rejoicings were as great; and when the news reached England the guns in the Park and Tower thundered, and there was a jubilee all over the land. During the war, which lasted for years, the English won no other victory like it.

Who were the men that did it? "They were not," said the Rev. Mr. Chauncy, in the sermon which he preached—"they were not the scum of the land, idle, worthless creatures, but men who feared God, who feared an oath—men of life and spirit!"

The Governors of New York and Massachusetts met the Iroquois Indians in council, gave them presents, and sent them and the Stockbridge Indians against the Canadians. Parties of Mohawks captured prisoners under the walls of Crown Point; and on the banks of the St. Lawrence. So the bloody trail lengthened and widened year after year.

General Rigaud Vaudreuil, with eight hundred French and Indians, appeared before Fort Massachusetts, in which there were only twenty-two men, three women, and five children. Half of the men were sick. They had only four pounds of powder. The garrison saw that they could make but a feeble resistance against such odds, and were obliged to surrender.

But not so successful were the French and Indians at Number Four,

STOCKBRIDGE.

which the Indians tried many times to capture, but never succeeded. Captain Phineas Stevens, who commanded it, was ever on the watch.

"GUARDING THEIR WIVES AND CHILDREN."

He had a number of dogs, which always let him know when the Indians were near.

The settlers were on the lookout. On Sunday the men went to meeting with their guns, guarding their wives and children.

On June 19th, 1746, Captain Stevens went out with fifty men to work in the field. He sent his dogs into the woods, which soon came back with their hair on end, and growling.

"There are Indians about, and they will ambush us at the causeway yonder," said Captain Stevens. He sent a soldier ahead to reconnoitre, who discovered an Indian, and fired upon him. Instantly the woods were full of Indians. The fight began. Stevens's men leaped behind the trees. They killed twelve savages, and drove the others into a swamp, compelling them to flee. They left blankets, swords, and hatchets, in their haste to get away. None of the English were killed, and only seven wounded.

The next year several hundred French and Indians, under Debleine, attempted once more to take Number Four. They besieged it several days, watching in the woods for the English to show themselves, but the latter kept under cover.

"Burn the fort!" was the order of the French commander—an order more easily given than executed. The Indians tried to carry it out by smearing arrows with pitch, and shooting a flaming torch against the walls; but the women brought buckets of water, and the soldiers put out a fire as soon as it was kindled.

The Indians piled a cart with fagots, run out long poles in front, with pitch-knots at the end, all aflame; but Captain Stevens, anticipating such a mode of attack, had dug a trench around the fort with passages leading to it, and the soldiers, creeping through with buckets of water, extinguished the fagots.

"You shall have good quarters, and safe-conduct to Montreal, if you will surrender," was the message sent in by Debleine by a flag.

"I don't want any safe-conduct to Montreal; I shall hold the fort!" was the reply.

Debleine, having no cannon, and finding that he could not frighten the sturdy defender, went back to Canada, much chagrined at his failure. The brave defence caused great rejoicing, and Sir Charles Knowles, commander of the British fleet in Boston harbor, made Captain Stevens a present of a silver-hilted sword, in appreciation of what he had done. What brave boys and girls there were in those days!

Jacob Ames lived in Groton, Massachusetts. He went out one morning to catch his horse, and saw an Indian. He ran back to his house, and the Indian after him. His hand was upon the latch, the door partly open, when the Indian shot him. He fell across the threshold. Mr. Ames's son seized his gun and fired at the Indian, slightly wounding him. The Indian was half-way in the house, when the boy slammed the door against him, giving the savage a tight squeezing. His sister sprung to help him.

"Give me father's gun!" shouted the boy. His sister handed it to him, and he brought the breach down upon the Indian's foot with a whack that made him yell with pain and back out of the door.

Beautiful the green meadows, the surrounding hills, and the distant mountains forming the landscape in Walpole, New Hampshire, which Colonel Benjamin Bellows and John Kilburn gazed upon on the banks of the Connecticut River in 1749. They had built their log-houses with loop-holes in the walls, through which they could fire upon the Indians in case they were attacked.

Though peace had been agreed upon between France and England, the people who lived along the frontier felt no security, for the French in Canada were continually urging the Indians to commit depredations on the English. It was a short and easy journey from Crown Point, on Lake Champlain, to the valley of the Connecticut, and the Indians, who sold their furs to the French, were frequent visitors to the settlements along the Connecticut.

One of the Indians who visited John Kilburn was called Captain Philip. He had been baptized and christened by the Jesuit priest at the Indian village of St. Francis, on the bank of the St. Lawrence, half-way from Montreal to Quebec. The St. Francis tribe were called Christian Indians. There were rumors that war would break out again between England and France, and before war was declared hostilities began.

In the spring of 1755, Captain Philip made a visit to John Kilburn's house with some beaver-skins for sale. He wanted powder, bullets, and flint for pay. August came. The settlers heard that war had begun, and knew that the French and Indians might be upon them at any moment. They strengthened their block-houses. No one went into the field to work alone. They always carried their guns with them. They had some faithful watch-dogs, which always growled when Indians were about. There were nearly forty men in the settlement. They appointed Colonel Bellows their leader. He had a suspicion that they might be attacked. "We must have a supply of meal, so that in case we are attacked we shall have something to eat," he said.

The settlers filled each a bag with corn, shouldered it, and then, in single file, each man carrying his gun, they marched to the grist-mill which they had erected, ground the corn into meal, shouldered the sacks once more, and started homeward, their faithful watch-dogs trotting in advance, paying no attention to squirrels or partridges, or game of that sort. Suddenly the dogs came back growling, the hair on their backs in a ruff.

"There are Indians about. Throw down your sacks!" said Colonel Bellows. The men threw their sacks on the ground, dropped into the ferns, and looked to the priming of their guns. The ferns were tall, and completely concealed them. Colonel Bellows suspected that the Indians had laid an ambuscade in the path which they must pass. He crept slowly forward to see what he could discover, careful not to break a twig or make any noise. He reached the top of a little hill, peeped through the ferns, and discovered a great number of Indians, nearly two hundred, crowding behind trees or lying on the ground, waiting for the white man to enter the trap. He made his way back to his men, issued his orders in a whisper, and all crowded through the ferns toward the Indians till they were only a few rods from them.

All were ready. Every man sprung to his feet and yelled, as loud as he could, "Hi—ya—! Hi—ya—!" It was a terrible howl. The next moment not a settler was to be seen; all had dropped upon the ground and were concealed by the ferns. In an instant every Indian was on his feet, just as Colonel Bellows expected, not knowing what to make of it, firing their guns, but hitting nobody. There was an answering flash from the ferns, each settler taking aim; and the Indians leaped into the air, or fell headlong before the bullets.

The red men outnumbered the settlers five to one, but were so astounded by the surprise that, picking up the wounded, they made a hasty retreat into a swamp, and the settlers ran to their block-houses, anticipating an attack. Not one of them had been injured.

Captain Philip, with another party of Indians, was creeping stealthily through the woods toward John Kilburn's house. Mr. Kilburn and his son John, Mr. Pike and his son, were out in the field reaping wheat, their guns close at hand. Mr. Kilburn had trained his dog to scour the woods, and the faithful animal ever had his eyes and ears open, and was sniffing the wind if a wolf or bear was about. On this afternoon in August the dog came running in with his hair in a ruff, and growling.

"Indians!" said Mr. Kilburn. The men and boys seized their guns, ran for the house, and had just time to get inside and bar the door, when Captain Philip and nearly two hundred Indians made their appearance.

The Indians stand at a safe distance, and so did Captain Philip, though he came out near enough to talk.

"Come out, old John! Come out, young John! I give you good quarter!" he shouted.

There were only two men, the two boys, Mrs. Kilburn, and her daughter, in the house, with three hundred Indians attacking them; but John Kilburn was not in the least frightened. Neither was Mrs. Kilburn, nor her son or daughter. They had several guns extra. Mrs. Kilburn and her daughter knew how to load them, and they would rather die than be taken prisoners. The Indians had no cannon, and their bullets would not go through the stout timbers. Only by burning the house would they be able to get in.

"Get you gone, you rascals, or I'll quarter you!" was the defiant answer which John Kilburn shouted through one of the loop-holes to Captain Philip, who went back to the dark crowd of savages, who set up the war-whoop.

"They yell like so many devils!" said John Kilburn; but he was not in the least disturbed by the howling.

Then the bullets began to come through the shingles on the roof and strike against the timbers. The Indians surrounded the house; but there were loop-holes on each side. Mr. Kilburn and Mr. Pike took two of the sides, and the two boys the others. Bang! bang! went the guns of Mr. Kilburn and Mr. Pike. Bang! bang! went the boys' guns. They could fire at a rest, and take deliberate aim. The Indians could not see the muzzles of the guns, and the moment one of the red men peeped from behind a tree his skull was in danger. One by one they fell, which enraged them all the more; and they crept nearer, firing rapidly, riddling the shingles, hoping, quite likely, that a bullet might glance down from the roof and hit those inside. "The roof looks like a sieve," said John Kilburn, as he saw the holes. Mrs. Kilburn and her daughter were loading the extra guns the while, and handing them to the men and boys, who kept up such a rapid fire that the Indians came to the conclusion that there were large numbers of men in the house. "We shall soon be out of bullets," said Mrs. Kilburn.

A thought came. Why not catch the bullets that were coming through the roof? The balls had nearly spent their force when they came through, and they hung up a blanket with thick folds, which stopped them entirely; and the girl, gathering them as they fell harmlessly upon the floor, put them into a ladle, melted them, and run new bullets, which soon were whizzing through the air, and doing damage to the enemy.

THE INDIANS AIMING AT THE LOOP-HOLES.

All through the afternoon the fight goes on, the Indians aiming at the loop-holes. One comes in and inflicts a ghastly wound in Mr. Pike's thigh; but the Indians do not know it, and the brave defence is kept up until the Indians, foiled in all their efforts, set Mr. Kilburn's wheat on fire, kill his cattle, bury their dead and slink away, not having taken a scalp or a prisoner. They have only wounded one man.

When everything goes well with the Indian, he can be very brave; but when the tide is against him, he quickly loses courage, and becomes disheartened; and so Captain Philip made his way back to Canada, very much crestfallen at the repulse received at the hands of two men, a woman, two boys, and a brave-hearted girl.

Peace was patched up in Europe between France and England in 1748—England giving back to France the strong fortress of Louisburg, and restoring everything just as it was before the war.

CHAPTER XXXIV.

INCOMPETENT AND COWARDLY GENERALS.

THE incompetent Duke of Cumberland, and the other weak and feeble dukes, earls, lords, and marquises composing the king's ministry, were not only mismanaging affairs in England, but sent over men as incompetent as themselves to mismanage affairs in America. They sent the Earl of Loudoun to be commander-in-chief, and Major-general Abercrombie to command the troops in the field. Loudoun had a long string of titles to his name, and took pleasure, when writing a letter, in spreading them all out, as a peacock spreads his tail, for his own admiration. Colonel Bradstreet had been sent to Oswego with a large amount of supplies—provisions sufficient to last five thousand men six months, besides cannon and other military stores.

"A French army is getting ready to take Oswego," was the information he gave upon his return.

A remarkable man had arrived in Canada, the Marquis de Montcalm, forty-four years old, who had been in the army since he was fourteen, and had seen a great deal of fighting in Germany and Italy, in the war brought about by the determination of the Emperor of Austria to make Maria Theresa his heir. He was quick to think, resolute to act, and coolheaded. The King of France had chosen one of the best men in all France to carry on the struggle in America. No sooner had he landed in Quebec than he made all haste to Ticonderoga, to see for himself the situation of affairs on the frontier. While Loudoun and Abercrombie were idling away the bright days of midsummer at Albany, Montcalm was paddling in a canoe along the shores of Lake Champlain, and tramping through the woods to Ticonderoga, laying his plans. The English generals were asleep, he wide awake. He would strike a blow when they least expected it. He returned to Montreal, started three regiments of French soldiers and a large body of Canadians and Indians up the St. Lawrence in boats and by land to Fort Frontenac at Kingston, and paddled along the shores of Lake Ontario to Oswego.

INCOMPETENT AND COWARDLY GENERALS. 409

There were two forts at Oswego — one on each side of the river. Montcalm landed his cannon, mounted them at night and opened fire, compelling the rebels to retreat from

THE EXPEDITION.

Fort Oswego, on the east bank, to Fort Ontario, on the west bank. He took possession of the captured fort, and turned its guns upon Ontario. A cannon-ball killed Colonel Mercer, the English commander; and the garrison of sixteen hundred men, after losing forty-five, surrendered. What a prize! All the provisions, one hundred and twenty cannon, three hundred boats, six vessels on the lake, three chests filled with money!

OSWEGO IN 1755.

A week later Montcalm was back in Montreal with his army and prisoners, attending the *Te Deum* chanted by the Jesuit fathers in the churches, who erected a pillar, surmounted with the banner of France, with this inscription:

"THIS IS THE BANNER OF VICTORY; BRING LILIES WITH FULL HANDS."

Lord Loudoun had sent General Webb with several thousand men up the Mohawk to Oswego; but he moved so slow that before he reached Oneida Montcalm was master of the situation; and Webb, fearing that the French would be upon him, blocked the road with trees and turned back to Albany.

"What cowards the English are!" said the Oneida, Seneca, and Onondaga Indians; "they are like children." Montcalm's victory dazzled them, and a large number hastened to Montreal to receive presents, promising to take no part in the struggle.

"The French are flushed with victory; they will be upon us. Cut down trees, block the roads," was the order of the pusillanimous Loudoun, who expected that Montcalm would soon be showing himself at Albany, and who did nothing except write letters to England, complaining of the provincials.

FORT AT OSWEGO.

The troops of New England were dying of disease and inaction. They were ready to march against the enemy; but Loudoun made no movement, except to go to New York with some of the troops, sending a portion to Philadelphia to be quartered upon the people.

Robert Rogers, of New Hampshire, who had been fighting the French, persuaded Lord Loudoun to permit him to enlist a battalion of men to be called Rangers, who were to be under his command. He would scout the woods with them, and discover what the French and Indians were doing. The men were brave hunters. It was a service of hardship and privation. They would have to make long marches, and sleep on the ground; to endure great fatigues; brave the cold of winter; wrapping themselves in their blankets at night, and lying down, with the snow for their bed. They must be ever on the lookout for Indians. There would be times when they could kindle no fire to keep themselves from freezing; there would also be times when they would have little to eat. They would ever be in danger of losing their scalps.

Although the hardships would be so great, Robert Rogers had no difficulty in obtaining all the men he wanted. The settlers had suffered so much from their enemy that they were eager to take their revenge. There was a fascination in the service. How stirring the thought of stealing through the woods, making roundabout marches, shooting a deer or bear—eating the nice steaks—lying down to sleep beneath the trees; up again in the morning, coming upon the French and Indians unawares, pouring in a volley, killing the savages or taking them prisoners, and returning in triumph! The pulses of the young hunters beat more quickly at the thought. Major Rogers chose the man for captain who had knocked the Indians right and left when he was called upon to run the gauntlet—John Stark—who could follow a trail as well as any Indian; who was always cool and collected, and as brave as a lion. They wore green frocks, and, besides their rifles, each man had a long knife, which he could use in a close fight.

Winter came. Vandreuil, who commanded the French at Ticonderoga, knowing that there was a regiment of Irish soldiers and the Rangers at Fort William Henry, planned its capture. With eleven hundred French and four hundred Indians he made his way stealthily through the woods. It would have been easier travelling on the lake; but he intended to surprise the English, and would not expose himself to view upon the lake.

St. Patrick's-day came. "The Irish will all be drunk to-night, and we will march into the fort!" said Vandreuil.

The Irish were keeping St. Patrick's-day in fine style—drinking rum. Major Rogers was away, and Captain Stark was in command of the Rangers. He was cool-headed. He liked rum as well as his soldiers, but it would not do for everybody to be drunk at once.

"Who knows but that the French will attempt to surprise the fort to-night?" was the question he put to himself, and resolved that the Rangers should be sober.

"Will you not give us an extra allowance of grog?" the Rangers asked. He did not like to deny them. They were old acquaintances and friends at home; he would try and not offend them. He had sprained his wrist, and would use it as an excuse. "I cannot hold a pen to write the order on the commissary," he said.

It was past midnight. The regular soldiers, wearied with their revelry, were sleeping off their drunken stupor. The sentinels of the Rangers were pacing their rounds upon the walls. Looking northward toward Crown Point, they saw a dark mass of men moving down the lake. In a moment Stark and the Rangers are at their posts. Their rifles flash; Vaudreuil is chagrined. So, then, the English are not all drunk. Before he can get ready to attack with all his force, the drunken soldiers have been shaken by their commander, and are upon the walls ready to pour a stream of fire upon him. He sets the out-buildings on fire, and returns to Ticonderoga, foiled through the watchfulness of Stark.

FORT WILLIAM HENRY.

The ice on Lake George was thick and strong in March, 1757, when the Rangers, seventy-four in number, with iron spurs on their feet, several days' rations in their bags, their blankets rolled upon their shoulders, marching in single file, with trailed arms, Major Rogers at the head and John Stark in the rear, started from Fort William Henry to see what the French were doing at Ticonderoga and Crown Point. They carried snow-shoes for use in the woods. They made their way over the gleaming ice for two days; but on the third day they left the lake, put on their snow-shoes, entered the woods, marched past Ticonderoga, came out upon the western shore of Lake Champlain, and discovered a party of French with horses and sleds on their way from Ticonderoga to Crown Point. Stark, with a part of the Rangers, made a dash and captured seven prisoners. He did not see another party of French around a point of land in season to capture them; they escaped to Ticonderoga and gave the alarm.

Major Rogers knew that a large party of French and Indians would be sent out from Ticonderoga to intercept him, and at once started to return. It was a rainy day. The snow was damp and heavy. "We will go to our last night's camp and dry our guns," said he. They reached the camping-place, where the fires were still burning, dried their guns, put in new priming, and started once more, Rogers in front, Stark bringing up the rear. It was two o'clock in the afternoon; Rogers descended a hill, crossed a brook, and was picking his way up another hill, when he found himself face to face with more than two hundred Indians and French, the nearest not twenty feet distant.

A volley—Lieutenant Kennedy and John Gardiner fall dead; a bullet glances from Rogers's skull, for a moment taking away his senses; the blood flows down his face, blinding him. Several other Rangers are wounded.

"Form here!" Captain Stark issues the order, and the Rangers under his command take position on a little hill. The Rangers down in the valley fire a volley at the French, holding their ground till all the wounded can make their way back to Stark's position. Rogers wipes the blood from his face, and issues his orders.

"You are to command the centre," he says to Stark. He sends Sergeants Walker and Philips with eight men to the rear, to give notice of any attempt of the enemy to crawl round and attack from that direction.

"Don't throw away your ammunition! Keep cool! Don't expose yourselves!" are the orders, and each Ranger takes position behind a tree. They know that the enemy outnumbers them three to one; that they have had the advantage of the first fire; but each Ranger prepares to fight to the bitter end.

Round through the woods steal a part of the French and Indians, making a wide circuit. Major Rogers reasoned correctly, and placed the two sergeants in the right place. The eight Rangers pick off the French one by one, giving them such a warm reception that, instead of rushing on, they remain at a distance.

The other French, with a horde of Indians howling the war-whoop, begin the attack in front, the Indians, springing from tree to tree, getting nearer and nearer. But the Rangers are on the watch, and many of the savages leap into the air and fall dead, or crawl away, leaving bloody trails upon the snow.

"If you will surrender, we will give you good quarter!" shouted the French commander.

Major Rogers was faint from loss of blood, and at that moment was faint-hearted. He feared that the Rangers would all be picked off before the fight would cease. It would be three hours to sunset. Could

JOHN STARK.

they hold out till then? He had no thought of surrendering, but would it not be best to retreat?

John Stark's blood is up. "Retreat! No. That will be certain destruction. We can beat them here. I'll shoot the first man that attempts to retreat." It was bold language for him to use to his commander; but he knew that Rogers had been stunned by the bullet that had glanced from his skull, and was not quite himself.

The fight goes on—the Rangers taking sure aim, the French firing more wildly; but still, one by one, the Rangers drop. Captain Spikeman and Mr. Baker are killed. A bullet strikes the lock of Stark's gun, and renders it useless. He sees a Frenchman fall at the instant, springs forward, seizes his gun, returns to his tree, and renews the fight.

A bullet tears through Rogers's wrist, and the blood spurts out in a stream. It must be stopped, or he will bleed to death. Rogers wears his back hair braided in a cue. "Take your knife and cut off my cue," he says to one of the Rangers, who whips out his hunting-knife, cuts off the cue, and Rogers sticks it into the wound to stop the flow of blood.

All through the dreary afternoon the fight goes on. The snow is crimsoned with blood. The killed and mortally wounded lie where they fell. For the Rangers there is no escape; they must conquer, or die.

The shades of night steal on; the fire of the French and Indians has been growing less; the war-whoop dies away; the last gun is fired. The enemy, picking up their wounded, retire to Ticonderoga, leaving the Rangers victors. What a dear-bought victory! One-half of them killed or wounded. Of the enemy, one hundred and sixteen have fallen!

The Rangers were only four miles from Ticonderoga, and might expect to be attacked again in the morning. They were forty miles from Fort William Henry. They were weary and worn, but they must move on. They made litters for the wounded and started, marching all night, but making only a few miles. The rain had ceased; the air was chill. They must have help. John Stark, leaving them, started for Fort William Henry, reaching it at sunset. Soldiers with horses and sleds went at once, and John Stark with them, stopping not a moment to rest his weary limbs. At sunrise he was back to the Rangers with re-enforcements and supplies. The French had not followed them, and they made their way safely back to Fort William Henry, having fought one of the most obstinate, unequal, yet victorious battles recorded in history.

The ever-active and brave Montcalm came from Montreal, when spring opened, to take direction of affairs at Ticonderoga, determined to capture Fort William Henry. Everything was in his favor. He had six thousand Frenchmen and Canadians, and a great following of Indians. He had sent so many presents to the Iroquois, and had been so brave and successful, that many of the warriors had paid him a visit at the little fort of St. John's, on the Richelieu, and joined in the war-dances with the Algonquins—forgetting for the moment their old feud, and promising to take no part in the war.

The English general, Webb, was weak, incompetent, and a coward.

He had five thousand men at Fort Edward, and one thousand at Fort William Henry, most of them from New England—brave men, ready to meet the enemy. Webb, Abercrombie, and Lord Loudoun all looked down upon them; but there were hundreds of men in the ranks who could have managed affairs better than either of these three incapables sent over by the ministers of George II.

What a sight was that which Montcalm beheld on the last day of July, 1757, at Ticonderoga—the arrival of one of his officers, Marin, and a party of Indians, with the bleeding scalps of forty-two Englishmen, whom they had killed near Fort Edward! Montcalm was just starting to capture Fort William Henry; M. de Levy had gone with twenty-five hundred; and Montcalm followed the next day in two hundred and fifty boats. The rowers sung the songs of France, keeping time to the music with the dipping of their paddles as they moved past Paradise Bay, and the bold headlands and wooded islands.

On that same day General Webb, escorted by two hundred men under Major Israel Putnam, of Connecticut, was riding from Fort Edward to Fort William Henry.

"Go down the lake and make a reconnoissance," was the order of Webb to Putnam, who went half-way down the beautiful sheet of water, discovering the fleet of Montcalm, and returning with that intelligence.

"Montcalm with his whole army is coming!" said Putnam. He urged General Webb to order the whole force of the English at Fort Edward to hasten to the defence of Fort William Henry.

"No; they will get in our rear, take Fort Edward, and move on Albany. Keep your information secret," said Webb, as he leaped upon his horse and rode as fast as he could through the woods to Fort Edward. Upon arriving there, he sent Colonel Munroe, a brave provincial officer, with one thousand men, to re-enforce the garrison at Fort William Henry, remaining himself at Fort Edward, trembling and nervous, fearing that the French would be attacking him.

Montcalm sailed down the lake. The sentinels on the walls of the fort beheld the great fleet of boats filled with soldiers, wearing the bright uniforms of France, their banners waving above them. Montcalm kept on till he was almost within cannon-shot of the fort, and ran the boats upon the pebbled beach on the western shore. The troops landed, pitched their tents, dragged the cannon from the bateaux, threw up a bank of earth, and placed the cannon in position. The Indians and the soldiers under M. de Levy made a circuit through the woods, and took position south of the fort.

INCOMPETENT AND COWARDLY GENERALS. 417

PARADISE BAY.

Munroe had four hundred and fifty men in the fort. On the spot now marked by the ruins of Fort George were seventeen hundred and fifty men, protected by intrenchments. A messenger with a white flag appeared, with a letter from Montcalm demanding the surrender not only of the fort, but of all the troops outside of it.

27

"I will defend it to the last!" was the answer of Munroe, who sent to Webb, asking for re-enforcements.

"I cannot send you any," was the reply of the coward.

Montcalm's cannon opened. He had thirteen cannon and three mortars. For six days the artillery thundered, making very little impression on the walls; but Colonel Munroe's provisions were running low. There were abundant supplies at Fort Edward. Webb had four thousand men, and it would be easy for him to march through the woods and attack the French in the rear. The soldiers could hear the roar of the guns all through the day, and were eager to march; but no orders were issued. There is one enemy that the bravest soldier cannot conquer — hunger.

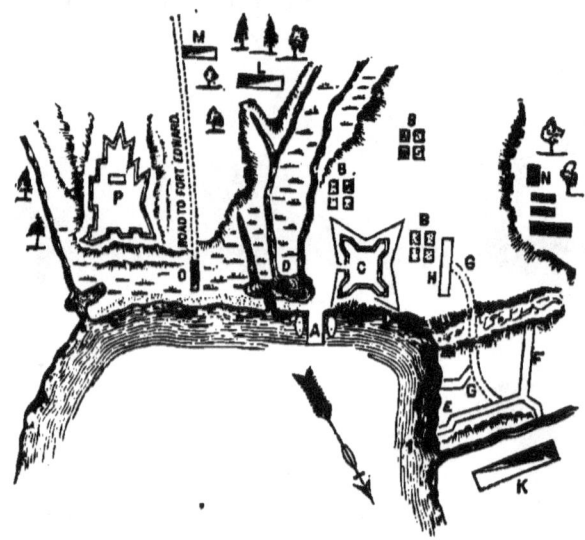

PLAN OF FORT WILLIAM HENRY.

A. Dock; B. Garrison gardens; C. Fort William Henry; D. Morass; E. Montcalm's 1st Battery of 9 guns and 2 mortars; F. Montcalm's 2d Battery of 10 guns and 8 mortars; G. Montcalm's approaches; H. Two intended Batteries; I. Place where Montcalm landed his artillery; K. Montcalm's camp, with the main body of the army; L. M. de Levy's camp—4000 Regulars and Canadians; M. M. de la Corne, with 1500 Canadians and Indians; N. English encampment before the retrenchment was made; O. The bridge over the morass; P. The English retrenchment.

When his provisions were all gone, when he saw that he could have no help from his pusillanimous commander, Colonel Munroe hung out a white flag, offering to surrender the fort on condition that he and all the soldiers should be allowed to march to Fort Edward, and be protected by the French while on the way. Montcalm agreed to the proposition, and promised not only to protect them from the Indians, but to take care of the sick; and when they recovered, they were to be allowed to return to their homes.

It was on the morning of August 10th when the garrison filed out of the fort and moved down the road toward Fort Edward.

Around them were the savages, brandishing their tomahawks and scalping-knives with hungry eyes. They had come to take the scalps of the English. Were they to be cheated? Not they. The English were unarmed, and could make no resistance. An Indian raised his tomahawk and brought it down upon a soldier's skull, and the bloody carnage began. The sight of the flowing blood made them demons. Howling like wolves, they rushed upon the defenceless men, women, and children, hacking them to pieces. Montcalm ran among them, seized their hatchets, and tried to stop them.

BLOODY POND.

"Kill me, but spare them!" he said. The other French officers tried to stay the fury of the Indians, but in vain. The terrible slaughter went on, till the fleeing fugitives found protection from five hundred troops sent out from Fort Edward to receive them.

Montcalm, having set the place on fire, taking all the cannon, went back to Ticonderoga, well satisfied with what he had done.

Major Putnam went up from Fort Edward after the French had departed, and wrote to Webb of what he saw: the bodies of the dead smouldering in the flames—among them the corpses of more than one hundred women, who had been butchered. The French had thrown many of the bodies into a little sheet of water, which since then has been called "Bloody Pond."

"We shall be attacked!" said Webb, who was inside of Fort Edward, pale and trembling. He was so frightened that he sent his baggage down the Hudson, and talked of abandoning the defences.

Governor Powell was as much frightened as Webb, and sent word to the people of the Connecticut Valley that they must drive in their cattle, and cut their carts to pieces, so that the French should not get hold of them. Lord Londonn, in New York, was most frightened of all, and prepared to encamp on Long Island, where the French could not get at him.

The year closed with the French masters of the Ohio Valley, Lake George, and Lake Champlain; they had won victory after victory, while the English, through the utter incapacity of Braddock, Loudoun, Abercrombie, and Webb, had suffered repeated defeats.

CHAPTER XXXV.

TWO CIVILIZATIONS.

THE great empire of New France, which Champlain had dreamed of, and which the Jesuits had labored so zealously to build up, was weak and feeble, and at a stand-still. It was the intermeddling of the Jesuits which more than anything else had retarded the growth. They wanted an empire in which they would have supreme control. All Protestants had been carefully excluded. Many of the eight hundred thousand Huguenots which had been driven from France would have settled in Canada, but no heretic could be permitted to find an asylum there. The French who had emigrated to Canada were, for the most part, weak and feeble. No great ideal had animated them. Many of them had intermarried with the Indians, and their children were half Indian, finding far more pleasure in roving the woods and hunting bears than in following the plough or bending down to the sickle in the harvest-field.

The government of Canada, all through the years, had been conducted on the idea of the feudal ages. The king was absolute; the Church had the control of every man's conscience; the people had no rights; they were only serfs. They had no manufactures—all their clothing, all their implements, and much of their food, came from France. Under such conditions how could Canada advance? The King of France, Louis XV., giving himself up to a round of sensual pleasure—balls and *fêtes* at Fontainebleau and Versailles—could not understand why New France did not keep pace with the English colonies. His ministers could not understand it. They had no comprehension of the spirit of liberty which was rising everywhere. They did not see that the time had come when old ideas were to pass away; that king, nobleman, priest—all were to go down before the people; and that the contest going on along the shores of Lake George and Lake Champlain was the beginning of a new order of things. There was one Frenchman who saw that, sooner or later, the lilies of France would give place to the cross of St. George in America—the Marquis de Montcalm.

William Pitt, Prime-minister of England, sent out a fleet of vessels to capture the fleets of France, to cut off the supplies of Canada. "New France needs peace," Montcalm wrote to the French minister. "Such are the number of the English, such the difficulty of receiving supplies, that sooner or later it must fall." His soldiers had only half a pound of bread per day. In the whole country there were but few sheep and cattle. The wars of previous years had told upon New France. Men had been fighting when they should have been following the plough; and now that the ships of England were everywhere capturing the French ships, the country was on the verge of starvation.

The Rangers of New Hampshire were keeping watch along Lake George and Lake Champlain. They made secret expeditions—dragging their boats from lake to lake, carrying their packs; going down Lake Champlain toward Canada, capturing boats laden with supplies for Crown Point—striking a blow, and returning to Fort William Henry.

The lake was frozen, and the snow four feet deep in the woods in March, 1758, when Major Rogers and one hundred and sixty-two men on snow-shoes started for Fort Edward, and made their way north to the Narrows on Lake George. They camped on the shore of the lake. At sunrise the next morning they were once more on the march, crossing to Sabbath-day Point. From the hills Major Rogers looked northward over the lake with a glass, but could see no signs of French or Indians. When night came, Lieutenant Phillips and fifteen men, laying aside their snow-shoes and putting on skates, glided down the lake, discovering a fire in the woods. They hastened back and reported what they had seen. The Rangers went on, reached the place, but no fire was burning. They did not know that the French had discovered them, and, putting out the fire, had fled to Ticonderoga, giving the alarm. At sunrise the Rangers left the lake and struck into the woods, marching until noon. They ate dinner, and started once more along the base of a mountain. It was toilsome travelling in the deep snow.

"Indians!" The advance-guard whispered it, and the word ran along the line; ninety-six savages had been discovered. The Rangers laid down their packs and prepared for battle. In silence they went on, concealed by a ridge. They were abreast of the Indians. Suddenly they spring to the top of the ridge and fire a volley, killing forty of the savages. The rest retreated, followed by a portion of the Rangers, who were exulting over their victory, but who found themselves confronted by six hundred French, Canadians, and Indians, who fired upon the Rangers, killing nearly fifty of them in a body. Major Rogers began a retreat, but discovered two hundred Indians climbing a hill to get in his rear; but Lieutenant Phillips, with eighteen Rangers, gained the top of the hill in advance, and drove them back. The French were creeping round on his other flank, but Lieutenant Craftons stopped them. The Rangers were outnumbered five to one. Nearer pursued the French, till they were not sixty feet distant. More than one hundred of the Rangers

DRAGGING THE BOATS.

had fallen, and they were dropping every moment, crimsoning the snow with their blood. More than three hundred of the enemy were pressing upon Phillips and his handful of men.

"Will you give me good quarter, if I surrender?" shouted Phillips to the French.

"We will," they replied. The men ceased firing; and a few mo-

LAKE GEORGE, FROM THE TOP OF ROGERS'S ROCK.

ments later were lying upon the snow, with their heads split open and their scalps torn from their skulls. The French were pressing upon Rogers. He climbed the mountain, which descends sharp and steep on one side to the lake—a bare ledge hundreds of feet high. He threw his rifle, and everything that could hinder him from walking, down the rocks. He saw them glide down the cliff, and out upon the gleaming ice. He stood upright on his snow-shoes, unbuckled the straps, turned himself round, and buckled them on again. It was the work of a moment. He walked back from the edge of the cliff into the woods, and disappeared from view just before the Indians came up, hastening to capture one who had done them so much harm. Now they were upon his track; they were sure of overtaking him. The foremost warrior reached the cliff. No Rogers there. Two tracks toward the cliff—none from it. He could not make it out.

Other warriors came and gazed upon the tracks. Had two Englishmen thrown themselves headlong over the cliff, to be dashed in pieces, rather than be captured?

Ha! ha! They hear a voice from below them, and behold Major Rogers, with his pack and gun, moving across the lake—hastening to join the others of his party who have escaped.

EARL OF BUTE.

Notwithstanding all these and other discouragements, Montcalm prepared to defend Canada to the last.

William Pitt was sick of Lord Loudoun, and the king ordered him to England. General Abercrombie was Lord Bute's particular friend; and at the solicitation of that nobleman, Pitt allowed him to remain in

America, but sent out the brave, active, intelligent young Lord Howe to give life to the army which was to take Ticonderoga. General Abercrombie had been in America two years. He was commander-in-chief. He had done nothing except to dig a ditch around Albany; but, having been in America so long, was supposed to know all about affairs.

There were lively times in New York when the troops from England

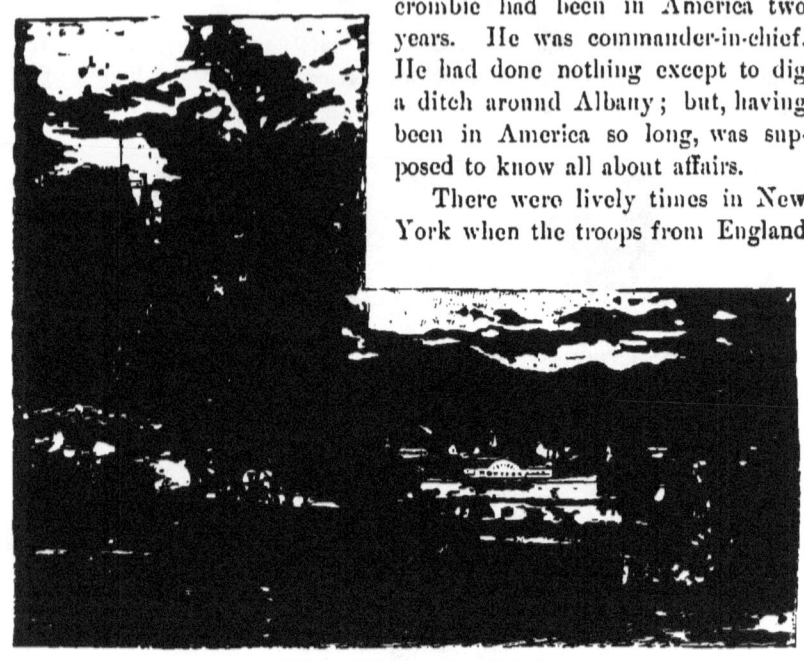

SOUTHERN END OF LAKE GEORGE.

and Scotland landed; livelier times at Albany, when the schooners and barges were discharging their supplies—boxes, barrels, cannon, ammunition; and still more lively scenes at the southern end of Lake George, around the ruins of Fort William Henry, where sixteen thousand men were in camp. There was no end of teams bringing supplies from Fort Edward. Hundreds of ship-carpenters were at work building boats, bateaux, and rafts. The shore of the lake was dotted with tents. Soldiers from Scotland, England, Ireland, New Hampshire, Massachusetts, Connecticut, Rhode Island, New York, and New Jersey were in camp, side by side. The Highlanders wearing their plaids, the Grenadiers, the light infantry, the artillery in their red coats, looked with contempt upon the men in homespun, who had left their ploughing and turned their cattle to pasture, and enlisted as soldiers for a three months' campaign. True, they had turned out once or twice a year and marched to the drum-beat on the village green; but what did they know about war?

The troops that had come across the Atlantic laughed at the ungainly ways of the provincials, who togged along like sheep, instead of marching in regular order; who had elected their officers, just as they elected their selectmen—in town-meeting. Little do the young lords and sprigs of nobility, commanding the troops of the king, know what sort of men these backwoodsmen are, or what they will do for the human race during the next twenty years.

Day breaks July 5th, 1758. The drums beat the reveille. Camp-fires are kindled; the blue smoke curls above the trees. The soldiers eat their breakfast. The carpenters have hewn their last planks, driven the last nail into the nine hundred small-boats and one hundred and thirty whale-boats, which are drawn up on the beach. They have completed their bateaux and rafts, upon which the artillery-men are to transport their cannon. At sunrise all are ready. The soldiers step into the boats, and the great flotilla moves away—trumpets sounding, drums beating, banners waving, arms gleaming in the sunlight—the dip of the rowers' oars keeping time to the music, the bright red uniforms and waving plumes reflected from the placid waters. Never before had such an army been seen in America—never before such a brilliant pageant on Lake George. The army reached Sabbath-day Point; the boats were run upon the beach, and the soldiers kindled fires and cooked their supper.

Upon a bear-skin within his tent lay Lord Howe—young, beloved by

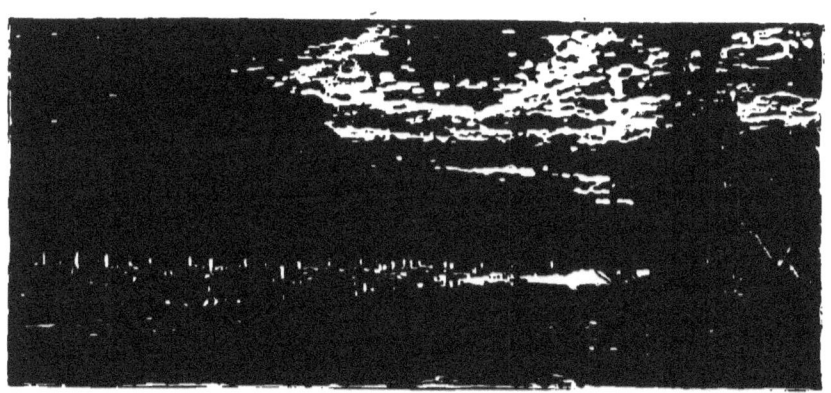

"THE GREAT FLOTILLA MOVES AWAY."

all for his kindness, energy, and tireless activity. By him are Major Rogers and John Stark, who know all the country around Ticonderoga and beyond to Crown Point. General Abercrombie and most of the officers commanding the king's troops are haughty in their deportment toward the provincials; but Lord Howe has discovered their worth, and made them his confidants and advisers. The Rangers inform him that the river between Lake George and Lake Champlain is four miles long, running south-easterly; that there are rapids and falls two miles from the fort, where the French have built a saw-mill. The fort stands on the point of land between the river and Lake Champlain. There are wet meadows directly north of the fort, and the only approach is from the north-west, over the strip of land between the river and the meadow.

Montcalm has made a line of breastworks across the point of land half a mile from the fort. His soldiers have been working like beavers, cutting down the tall trees outside the breastwork, felling them in such a way that they lie across one another, with their limbs interlaced. They

SABBATH-DAY POINT.

drive sharpened stakes into the ground, dig up the stumps and place them in line, with their gnarled roots sticking out in every direction.

Montcalm has only thirty-six hundred men, but he knows what to do with them. He inspires them with his own indomitable spirit and enthusiasm. Every man is at work with an axe or spade, or putting his shoulder to a log or stump to place it in position. He has sent out three hundred men to the saw-mill. There are three pickets still farther out, by a sheltered cove at the northern end of the lake. On the mountain overlooking the fort stands a sentinel, with a signal-flag, looking up the lake with watchful eyes to announce the coming of the English. At midnight the boats were once more in motion. Lord Howe, Colonel Bradstreet, and Major Rogers together in a boat, pulled by strong-armed rowers, pushing ahead to reconnoitre.

The morning sun throws its beams upon the lofty summit of Black

THE NORTHERN END OF LAKE GEORGE.

Mountain. The shadows lift from the lake. Montcalm looks up from the fort to Mount Defiance, and beholds a white flag waving in the morning air. The sentinel has caught the gleam of the sunlight on the bright bayonets of the advancing army. He can see the dipping of the oars. The thousand boats come into view, gliding amidst the islands. The Rangers leap on shore. They know the ground. The regiments disembark, and by noon the army is ready to march. The Rangers have been pushing so near Montcalm's lines that they can see the Frenchmen at work with axes and spades.

"If the English will but give us a little more time, we will beat them," Montcalm is saying to his men.

Lord Howe is eager to push on. The brigades form and move through the woods, Lord Howe in advance. The French from the saw-mill are making their way to the fort, but have taken the wrong path, and fall in with the troops under Lord Howe. There is a flashing of muskets. Some of the French fall; others leap into the river, to escape by swimming; one hundred and fifty surrender. A few English have fallen, and among the killed is Lord Howe.

The soul of the enterprise has departed. All is confusion. General Abercrombie has no plan, nor has any other English officer. The troops stop where they are till morning, sleeping on their arms, and then march back to the landing. There is a road from the landing to the fort, crossing the river twice, and the French have broken down the bridges; but Colonel Bradstreet, whom the English officers regard as a backwoodsman, sets his men at work, and has the bridges rebuilt before noon, and the army moves on, encamping within a mile and a half of the enemy's lines, upon the ground which the Rangers have been holding.

The chief-engineer, Clerk, accompanied by John Stark, reconnoitres Montcalm's position. The engineer has studied in the military schools. War is a science, in his estimation, to be conducted by set rules. He sees fallen trees, stumps, banks of earth, and stakes driven into the ground.

"Their works are flimsy," he says.

"I do not think so. I regard them as formidable," is the outspoken opinion of John Stark.

What does this country bumpkin know of war? Nothing, in the estimation of a learned engineer.

Some of the English officers shake their heads when they gaze upon the tangled mass of fallen trees, the line of stakes, rows of stumps, and breastwork of earth, every moment growing more formidable under the untiring activity of Marquis de Montcalm. Abercrombie does not go upon the ground. His tent is pitched at the saw-mill. He sees nothing, knows nothing: he accepts only the report of the engineer, that the defences which Montcalm has made are so weak that the British troops will tear them away in a twinkling. He has cannon, but they are at the landing; it will take time to bring them up, and he will order an attack at once. He does not expect much help from the provincials. They may clear the way, draw the first fire of the French, and then the troops of the king will go in and make quick work.

"If I were called upon to take Fort Carillon, I should only ask for

TWO CIVILIZATIONS.

two cannon and some mortars on yonder mountain," said Montcalm, looking up to the summit of Mount Defiance, and rejoicing to think that the stupid English were going to do just what he wished them to do—butt their heads against the stumps which he had placed in the lines of his defence.

"Let the attack be made at once!" was Abercrombie's order.

It was one o'clock in the afternoon when the sixteen thousand men, in three lines, moved toward Montcalm's breastworks—the Rangers on the left of the front line, the boatmen in the centre, the light infantry on the right. The second line was composed wholly of Massachusetts and New York troops; the third line of the king's troops. The rearguard was composed of Connecticut and New Jersey troops. Four hundred and forty of the Iroquois, under Sir William Johnson, hovered in the rear. If the English succeeded, they would be ready to scalp the French.

"Let there be openings between the provincial regiments, so that when the provincials have drawn the fire of the French, the king's troops may rush in with fixed bayonets," was the order of Abercrombie, who planned just how the battle must be fought, and remained in his tent, two miles away.

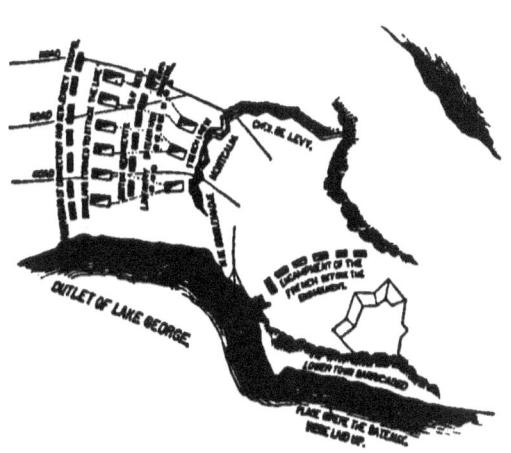

PLAN OF ATTACK BY GENERAL ABERCROMBIE AT TICONDEROGA, JULY 8TH, 1758.

"Let not a gun be fired till I give the order!" said Montcalm, walking along his lines in his shirt-sleeves.

Up to the fallen trees marched the Rangers, crouching close to the earth, sheltering themselves behind the logs. They know very well that there is serious work before them. The provincials follow their example. The king's soldiers, marching as if upon parade, move bravely on, scorning such unmilitary proceedings. They reach the fallen trees. The French lines suddenly are a line of light, cannon and small arms pouring a pitiless storm of leaden rain and iron hail upon the red-coated soldiers, stumbling and falling, in their efforts to get through the tangled thickets. The Highlanders are brave. The officers set them examples of courage;

"THE HIGHLANDERS ARE BRAVE."

but they fall by scores. Some of them get near enough to the breastworks to gaze into the eyes of the enemy, only to be shot down at last. The English endeavored to turn the French right; but Montcalm, watching every movement, threw in re-enforcements and drove them back. Again and again the English moved to the attack, centring all their force upon a single point; but the ever-watchful Montcalm was at hand to repulse them. After every repulse of the English Montcalm distributes refreshments to his troops, and praises them for their valor. Night closes upon the scene—with a great army in retreat, defeated, humiliated, having lost nearly two thousand killed and wounded.

The English still outnumbered the French fourfold. Not a cannon had been fired by them. The army was well supplied with provisions, but the pusillanimous and frightened general, who had not been within two miles of the battle-ground, gave orders to re-embark at once. When the morning dawned, the army was far on its way up the lake. Abercrombie reached the southern shore, sent his cannon and ammunition to Albany, for fear the French would capture them! He set the soldiers to work building a useless redoubt, which he named Fort George.

The man who had rebuilt the bridges broken down by the French, Colonel Bradstreet, had a plan which he wished to put into execution — the capture of Fort Frontenac, near the present town of Kingston, in Canada, on the northern shore of Ontario.

"We can do it," he said. He knew that there was but a small garrison to defend it, for Montcalm had gathered all the available soldiers to the defence of Ticonderoga. He persuaded General Abercrombie to call a Council of War, and obtained permission to carry out his plan. He went up the Mohawk with seven hundred men from Massachusetts,

FORT GEORGE.

eleven hundred from New York, made a speech to the Iroquois, and prevailed upon one hundred and fifty of the warriors to join him. He hastened in boats from Oswego along the lake shore, and on the 25th of August landed at Fort Frontenac. Some of the garrison fled; the few remaining surrendered themselves, and everything in and around the fort—thirty cannon, six mortars, nine vessels in the harbor, each carrying from eight to eighteen guns, and loaded with supplies for Fort Du Quesne. He destroyed the place, and returned with the prisoners and plunder, not losing a man. The country took notice that a backwoodsman had planned it, that Americans, without the lifting of a finger on the part of British officers or soldiers, carried out the undertaking.

A British fleet, under Admiral Boscawen, and an army under Generals Amherst and Wolfe, captured Louisburg in June, causing great rejoicing in England and in the colonies.

Another expedition was on the march westward over the Alleghanies toward the Ohio. General Joseph Forbes was commander; he was sick, slowly wasting away, and had to be carried on a litter. He had twelve hundred and fifty Highlanders, twenty-seven hundred and fifty Pennsylvanians, under John Armstrong, and nineteen hundred Virginians, under George Washington. With the Pennsylvania troops was a young man by the name of Benjamin West, whom the world afterward heard of as a great painter, and a boy thirteen years old, named Anthony Wayne, whom the world also heard from. General Forbes sent Colonel Boquet in advance to a place called Loyal Hanna.

"There are only five hundred French and three hundred Indians at Fort Du Quesne," said the Indian scouts to Boquet, who sent Major Grant to reconnoitre the fort. The Virginians and Highlanders climbed the mountains, and made their way stealthily through the forest. Major Grant was to reconnoitre, not to bring on a fight; but why not put his men in ambush, draw the French into it, cut them down, and make himself master of Fort Du Quesne? If he were to accomplish it, what honor! He sent a few men toward the fort — not knowing that four hundred Frenchmen under Aubrey had arrived to re-enforce the garrison. The French and Indians poured out of the fort, fell upon the first party, drove it back upon the second, fell upon that, killing, wounding, or taking prisoners two hundred and ninety. Grant himself was taken prisoner.

November came. There was snow upon the mountains, and winter would soon be setting in. Forbes was still fifty miles from Fort Du Quesne. "It is too late to go on; we cannot take Fort Du Quesne this year," said the officers in council.

TWO CIVILIZATIONS.   435

The council was in session when the scouts brought in three prisoners. "The garrison is weak. Colonel Bradstreet has captured Fort Frontenac and the provisions which were intended for Du Quesne," they said.

"Let us go on. Let me have twenty-five hundred picked men," was Washington's plea.

General Forbes granted the request. Washington did not select any of the king's troops, but strong men accustomed to climbing mountains and enduring hardships. The men filled their knapsacks with provisions. It was fifty miles to the fort through an unbroken wilderness. John

TAKING POSSESSION OF FORT DU QUESNE.

Armstrong was sent in advance, with one thousand men, to open a road. In five days they were within seventeen miles of the fort. On the 24th of November the whole army was only two miles distant.

The officers in the service of the King of France had planted their forts along the Ohio, the Illinois, and the Mississippi; they had done what they could to secure the vast empire for their sovereign, who was ever thinking more of his own personal comfort and pleasure than of the welfare of his people, or the building up of his empire; but, neglected and unsustained, they could no longer hope to keep back the wave of English civilization and power rolling over the Alleghanies. At the best they could make but a feeble resistance to the seven thousand English ready to encircle them; and the disheartened garrison, reduced to five hundred, setting fire to the fort and buildings, at midnight stepped into their boats and floated down the Ohio, abandoning forever the gate-way of the great West.

The English sentinels pacing their rounds saw the western sky aglow. On the morning of November 25th, 1758, the Pennsylvanians and Virginians reached the fort, whose walls were still standing, and John Armstrong raised the British flag above them.

"I re-name it Pittsburgh," said General Forbes—in honor of the far-seeing, clear-headed, resolute man, whose indomitable will and energy was making England supreme in the Western World.

CHAPTER XXXVI.

THE DESTINY OF AN EMPIRE.

WONDERFUL the powers of the human intellect and the human will! William Pitt was infusing every man in England with his own enthusiasm in carrying on the struggle against France. English cannon were thundering in Germany, in the West Indies, on the plains of India, and with the opening of 1759 the contest was to be renewed in America. He spread out the map of America, and himself planned the campaign. One army, under General Prideaux and Sir William Johnson, was to go west from Albany, to capture the fort which the French had built on the bluff below the Falls of Niagara, where ever since the day when La Salle sailed up the Great Lakes the flag of France had floated serenely in the air. By capturing that fort, all communication would be cut off between Canada and the chain of forts on the upper lakes, and along the Ohio and Mississippi. Its capture would paralyze the power of France in the Great West.

WILLIAM PITT.

The second army, under General Amherst, was to make one more attempt against Ticonderoga and Crown Point, and, capturing those places, was to move north to Montreal and strike at the heart of Canada.

The third army, under General Wolfe, was to sail from Halifax and Louisburg, up the St. Lawrence, to capture Quebec. A great fleet of war-ships, under Admiral Loudoun, was to accompany the army. If Quebec could be captured, there would be an end to French rule in Canada.

William Pitt was not only firing all England with his enthusiasm, but America. In every village in New England and New York were men ready to enlist—seven thousand in Massachusetts, five thousand in Connecticut, several regiments from New Hampshire, one thousand men from New Jersey. The people taxed themselves willingly, indulging the fond hope that the time had at last arrived when they could conquer Canada and put an end to the great struggle.

The Marquis de Montcalm, far-sighted, clear-headed, and brave, saw what great preparation England was making, and wrote pathetic letters to

MONTREAL, 1760. (FROM AN OLD PRINT.)

France calling for help. He had only thirty-two hundred French soldiers. Of the Canadians not more than seven thousand could be called into service. There were only about eighty thousand people in Canada, all told. The English were putting fifty thousand men into the field. He must have supplies. The fields were untilled. There were few cattle and horses to be had. The soldiers had not been paid. There was very little money in Canada; but promises to pay, printed on paper, to the amount of more than forty million livres had been issued. No one wanted any more paper-promises, which were not money.

"Without a good fortune, which I cannot expect, or unless the English make blunders, they will take Canada this year, or in the next campaign," wrote Montcalm to Belleisle, the Prime-minister of Louis XV., pleading for help.

The King of France was spending his money in other ways. What cared he for business? He was forty years old. Life had been a constant round of pleasure. Every sense had been indulged, until there was no enjoyment. The woman whom he had created Marchioness de Pompadour could wind him round her little finger. She was ever getting up new amusements for him—travelled with him from place to place. Their thoughts were of the little comedies which she got up in the Tuileries, the lawn-parties at Fontainebleau, instead of affairs of State. Madame de Pompadour was fond of porcelain, and persuaded Louis to establish a manufactory at Sevres. She loved magnificent houses, and the king built them for her with costly apartments, elaborately furnished. He could spend millions of livres to gratify this woman, but the bills sent from Quebec by Montcalm were all unpaid. The king could give breakfasts to the courtiers costing thousands of livres, but not a dollar to uphold the power of France in America.

The spring opened, and General Prideaux, with twelve hundred men, several cannon, and mortars, sailed from Oswego in schooners and boats along the south shore of Ontario, landing at a little inlet six miles from Fort Niagara. The troops marched through the woods and took position close to the fort, planted their cannon, and opened fire.

There were only a few French soldiers in the fort, but an army of twelve hundred was hastening to their relief. The French commander, D'Aubrey, had collected them from the forts along the Ohio, the Wabash, Detroit, and Mackinac. They came down Lake Erie in boats, landed above the falls, and hastened to attack the English. General Prideaux had been killed by the bursting of a cohorn, but Sir William Johnson posted his men to meet them. The Iroquois scouts told Sir William of all the movements of the French, who made their appearance on the morning of July 24th. The Iroquois and Algonquins came face to face. The Iroquois made a sign for a parley, which the Algonquins answered with a wild yell, and the battle began—the Iroquois running out on both sides of the French and firing upon them, while the English rushed upon them, pouring in a volley. The French had not looked for such an onset. They turned and fled, followed by the Iroquois, who shot them down in great numbers. In a few minutes the fight was over, but the pursuit was kept up until the Iroquois were out of breath, and returned to count their scalps and divide their plunder. No help could come to the garrison, which hung out a white flag and surrendered—six hundred in number—with all their cannon and supplies.

Once more a great army, numbering eleven thousand, with drums beating and banners waving, was making its way across the limpid waters of Lake George.

Montcalm was at Quebec, and General Bourlamasque, who had aided in the defeat of Abercrombie, was in command of the French. The lines of defence were stronger than ever, but the French general had few troops. Montcalm had none to send him. He might hold out for awhile; but there was little hope of maintaining the fortress against such an army and against such a general, who, though slow to move, was no coward, and who had captured Louisburg.

The English landed. Again there was a skirmish at the saw-mill, and the English lay at night on their arms. The French, all except four hundred, instead of preparing for battle, were stealing away in boats to Crown Point.

Morning dawned, and the English discovered that the lines which Montcalm had so bravely defended were deserted; but the French were still holding the fort, and as they advanced the cannon began to thunder. The English brought up their artillery, and all day long shot and shell were flying, and the roar of the cannonade echoing far way. Night came, and the uproar ceased; but the four hundred Frenchmen left behind in the fort were hard at work loading all the cannon on the walls to the muzzle, laying trains of fuses from gun to gun, and to the magazine, where there were many barrels of powder. All was ready. The soldiers stepped silently into their boats, which, one by one, glided away. One boat remained, one soldier still lingered in the fort. Ten o'clock. He lighted a fuse, leaped into the boat, and was gone.

What a cannonade was that which burst out from the ramparts of Ticonderoga! louder, more terrific than ever before, the air filled with shot and shell and bursting cannon, and then the walls of the fort rose, lifted far above the forest trees — timbers, stones, masses of rock and earth, cannon-balls, and bursting shells. Ticonderoga, built at such cost to France, defended so bravely by Montcalm, was a heap of ruins.

General Amherst despatched the Rangers of New Hampshire in pursuit of the French. Major Stark, with two hundred men, reached Crown Point, and found a lofty cross standing in the centre of the fortress, erected to commemorate the victory of Montcalm at Ticonderoga; but the fort had been destroyed, and the French were fleeing toward Canada.

How easy it is to miss a great opportunity! The French had abandoned their two strong fortresses at Amherst's approach. The way was open for his advance to Canada. The flotilla which had brought him to Crown Point would avail to transport him to St. John's. It was a short

THE DESTINY OF AN EMPIRE. 441

march from there to Montreal. It was midsummer; the troops were eager to move on. If he were to take Montreal his name would go down the ages.

"There is a tide in the affairs of men,
Which, taken at the flood, leads on to fortune."

General Amherst halted at Crown Point, and set the ship-carpenters to construct schooners and other vessels. He planned a new fort, with walls thirty-five feet thick, and twenty-five high, of solid masonry. August and September passed, the troops idling away their time. In October the vessels were ready, and sailed down the lake. The sailors disarmed the French vessels, drove them ashore, or sent them to the bottom of the lake. It was the middle of October—too late to move upon Montreal, General Amherst thought, and fixed his army for the winter at Crown Point. Through want of energy the great opportunity had passed by, never to return.

There was one man who was determined to make the most of this opportunity—James Wolfe, commander of the army sailing from Halifax and Louisburg to Quebec. It was an imposing scene—twenty-two ships of the line, twenty-eight frigates, and a great fleet of vessels carrying supplies and troops, moving up the St. Lawrence. The vessels came to anchor at the Island of Orleans.

WOLFE.

General Wolfe, standing on the deck of his vessel, looking north, beheld the Falls of Montmorency—a white sheet, two hundred and fifty feet high—flashing in the sunlight, the tide rippling upon the pebbled beach at their base, while above the water was pouring down a rocky gorge. Small pines and hemlocks—a thick, dense forest clothed the landscape in perpetual green. Up the river, eight miles away, he beheld the citadel of Quebec on the perpendicular cliff, rising two hundred feet above the river—the flag of France floating serenely above it. Between the cliff and Montmorency was a little stream—the St. Charles—joining the St. Lawrence from the north.

Upon the point of land between the two streams was the old town of Quebec.

Between the St. Charles and the Montmorency Montcalm had posted his army, with batteries along the shore, to sweep the English with grape and canister if they should attempt to land. The cliff was high, sharp, and steep above the town. The summit of the cliff was a level plateau—the Plains of Abraham. For nine miles above the city Montcalm had placed batteries and posted troops to protect any possible landing-place.

MONTCALM.

General Wolfe had ten thousand men and a great fleet. Montcalm had nearly as many men. The Canadians rallied at his call—old white-haired men, and boys of fourteen. Canada was their home. Their country, their religion—everything most dear was in danger, and they were ready to fight to the bitter end.

The English troops landed on the Island of Orleans, and on the southern shore opposite Quebec. The war-ships opened fire upon the town. Red-hot shot were sent whirling through the air, crashing into the houses, and setting them on fire.

Along the shore, under the cliff, Montcalm had a great fleet of boats, filled with pitch-knots and smeared with tar. At midnight the sailors of the fleet saw the boats all aflame floating down with the current upon them; but they leaped into their boats, pulled out to meet the floating flames, and pushed them aside with their boat-hooks, and not a vessel was harmed.

General Wolfe gazed upon the lines of Montcalm, seeking in vain to find a place where he could hope to land his army. July was fast passing away. He must strike somewhere. The white sheet of Montmorency was ever before him. He would land on the northern shore, and somewhere along its rocky bed he would find a place to cross that stream and fall upon Montcalm. The troops were taken to the landing-place in boats. There was a fording-place three miles from the St. Lawrence;

but Montcalm had posted troops to protect it. When the tide was out the beach was bare at this part of the falls. He resolved to have a portion of his men go across the narrow passage and secure a footing, while the remainder of the army would land directly from the boats. The troops were placed in position, the signal given. The air was filled with shot and shell—the war-ships running out their guns and opening fire upon the French lines; while Montcalm's guns, paying no attention to the vessels, swept the beach. Some of the boats were injured, others reached the shore. The troops landed. Some advanced before all were ready, and the French drove them back. The tide was rising. The enterprise had failed, and the English were obliged to retreat, losing nearly five hundred in the attack.

August came. General Murray, with twelve hundred men, went up the St. Lawrence in boats, trying in vain to land. He only captured a few sick soldiers left in a hospital, who had some news to tell—that the French had abandoned Ticonderoga and Crown Point.

Welcome the news to General Wolfe. Amherst soon would be at Montreal. Before long the thunder of his guns would be heard opening the way to Quebec. Days passed, but his ears detected no sound of distant cannon. Indians said that Montreal was still in the hands of the French. What should be done? September had come. Sixty days more, and the fleet and army must go, for winter would be upon them.

"I am at a loss what to do," were the almost despairing words written to Pitt.

The spirits of the French were rising. Montcalm had completely baf-

MONTCALM'S HEAD-QUARTERS.

fled the English. Nature had done so much, that his tireless activity and eternal vigilance had accomplished the rest. The spirit of Wolfe chafed under the disappointment; fever set in: his cheeks were hollow, but his soul was on fire. He gazed upon the high and rocky cliff. If he could but get his army up there. Ah! he sees a ravine—a cove—a foot-path winding up the cliff. Frenchmen and Indians now and then have climbed it; Montcalm's vigilance has protected it. Wolfe can see the white tents on the bluff—a company of soldiers guard it. Wolfe forms

ST. JOHN'S GATE, QUEBEC.

his plans. He will land at midnight in the cove, climb the bank, surprise the hundred men guarding the path. Before re-enforcements from Quebec can reach the spot the English will be strong enough to hold it. He will mislead Montcalm by making him believe that he is intending to land below Quebec.

What is it Montcalm sees, looking out from the low-roofed house in which he has established his head-quarters? English sailors are taking soundings on the mud-flats below the town; an officer is making notes. Does General Wolfe intend to land at night at the mouth of the St. Charles? Something is going on; boats are moving to and fro—there is a bustle of preparation. The sun goes down, and darkness settles over the scene. The French sentinels see a fleet of boats putting out from the vessels below the town, but they do not see the boats that have crept up from the English camp along the southern shore several miles above the town.

General Wolfe has laid his plans. He has passed the period of vexation, and his mind is tranquil.

James Gray, whose home is near the green meadow of Runnymede, where the barons compelled John Lackland to sign the Great Charter of Liberty, has just given to the world an exquisite poem—"An Elegy in a Country Church-yard." He recites the stanzas as the boats glide noiselessly in the stream—

"'The boast of heraldry, the pomp of power,
And all that beauty, all that wealth e'er gave,
Await alike the inevitable hour—
The paths of glory lead but to the grave.'"

"I would prefer being the author of that poem to the glory of beating the French to-morrow," he says. He has given his last instructions. The boats approach the cove. Some of them sweep past it; but the soldiers leap upon the pebbled beach. They climb the steep bank, seize hold of the roots of trees, those behind giving a lift to those in front. No one speaks. They climb in silence—broken only by the grinding of their boots upon the rocks, and by their labored breathing. "*Qui vive!*" It is the challenge of the French sentinel, "Who goes there?" England, a new civilization—the beginning of a new order of things for Canada go there! Too late the challenge. The one hundred Frenchmen awake from their sleep. A few muskets flash, and the French flee.

THE PLACE WHERE WOLFE LANDED.

The rising sun throws its gleams upon ten thousand Englishmen standing on the Plains of Abraham! A messenger rides in hot haste to Montcalm with the news.

"The English are on the Plains of Abraham!"
"Impossible!" said Montcalm.
"They are there, nevertheless, monsieur."
"They must be crushed at once."

The drums beat in Quebec, and the soldiers of France hasten out of the city westward. Montcalm has five thousand men; most of them are Canadians, who have left their homes to take part in the campaign. General Bourganville is above Quebec, with two thousand. Vaudreuil will soon be at hand with fifteen hundred; with these Montcalm will sweep the English over the bluff into the river. The armies stand face to face in the open field. The cannon which Montcalm has brought up open fire, and answering replies are sent back by the two small pieces which the English have dragged up the bluff with ropes. Two lines of men are about to fire in each others' faces in the open field. At Ticonderoga the French were behind breastworks and stumps, but now they must meet the troops of England face to face, with nothing to shield them.

BATTLE OF QUEBEC.

Montcalm forms his men. Fifteen hundred Canadians are to advance and begin the attack. Under cover of their fire he will advance rapidly, pour in volley after volley, and hurl the English over the cliff.

Calmly and silently the Highlanders and Grenadiers of England await the attack: Murray on the right wing, nearest the river—General Wolfe on the left.

"Reserve your fire until they are within forty yards!" is Wolfe's last order.

The French advance rapidly, firing wildly. A few men drop from the English ranks, but no one wavers. Nearer they come, Montcalm urging them on. The English raise their guns; there is a flash, a roar, and confusion in the French lines. Montcalm's ablest general falls; but Montcalm cheers his men, and the fight goes on. Another volley from the Highlanders and Grenadiers. The French lines waver.

"Charge!" Wolfe gives the order, and the English, with fixed bayonets, advance. A bullet tears through Wolfe's wrist, but it is nothing. He winds his handkerchief around it and leads on his men. Murray, his second commander, goes down with a bullet through his lungs. A second ball strikes Wolfe. He staggers. His aid springs to support him. "Let not any man see me drop," he says. A third strikes him in the breast. The soldiers carry him to the rear. He is faint, but drinks a glass of water, and revives.

The French are fleeing. "They run. Hurrah! hurrah!" The wild cheers of the English mingling with the uproar of battle reach the ears of the dying commander.

"Who run?"

"The French."

"God be praised! I die happy!"

It is scarcely fifteen minutes since the battle began, and it is over. The French are fleeing to Quebec; their brave commander has done what he could to save New France, but has lost the battle, and is borne from the field mortally wounded.

Fifteen minutes! It is a brief space of time, but long enough to decide the destiny of an empire!

While General Wolfe is taking possession of Quebec, General Amherst is sending Captain Kennedy, accompanied by a few soldiers, with overtures of peace, to the St. Francis Indians. It is the tribe which for a half century has been under the teachings of the Jesuits. They have a chapel. Morning and evening they meet at the tolling of the bell to say their prayers. They call themselves Christian Indians, but are barbarous and inhuman. They seize Captain Kennedy and his companions, tie them to stakes one by one, kindle fires around them, and dance with fiendish delight while they are burning. For a third of a century this tribe has massacred the people of New England, and General Amherst orders Major Rogers and the Rangers of New Hampshire to punish them.

The autumn leaves were falling and the nights were lengthening when the Rangers started in boats from Crown Point, one evening after sunset. They were two hundred in number, and started secretly, that no one might know whither they had gone. Before daybreak they landed, drew their boats on shore, and secreted themselves in the woods. No fire was kindled, so that no column of blue smoke would reveal their hiding-place.

They reached Missisquoi Bay, at the northern end of the lake; from thence it was seventy-five miles to the village of the St. Francis tribe, through a pathless forest. They must not only travel by the compass, but cross several large rivers, wade through terrible swamps up to their knees in water, their feet sinking into beds of moss and peat. There were places where hurricanes had swept down the tall trees, which blocked their way. There was little game to be had, and they must carry their provisions.

448   OLD TIMES IN THE COLONIES.

Quite likely the Indians would discover them, and they must be ever on the watch against surprise. They left their boats and marched northeast. On the fifth day some of their powder took fire; the explosion burnt several soldiers, and Major Rogers was obliged to send them back

BURNING THE PRISONERS.

to Crown Point, reducing his number to one hundred and forty-two Twenty-two days the party toiled through the terrible swamps.

"We must be near St. Francis," said Major Rogers. He climbed a tree and beheld the River St. Lawrence, and only three miles away the

A SCALP-DANCE.

Indian village — a street with rude huts and wigwams, and the chapel and house of the Jesuit priests.

The Rangers kept perfectly still till dark, and then Major Rogers and two others stole down to the village. They could hear the beating of drums and the whooping of the savages. Getting nearer, they could see the Indians holding a scalp-dance. The scalps which they had taken from time to time—more than six hundred in number—were suspended on poles. The savages were making the night hideous with their howlings. Major Rogers took note of all that he saw, and crept back to the main body of the Rangers, determined to make the Indians dance to another tune before morning.

Two o'clock. The howling had ceased; and the Indians, exhausted by their contortions in the dance, were asleep. The St. Lawrence was sweeping on calmly and silently to the sea. There was not a sound to break the stillness as the Rangers crept toward the village and closed around it. A dog barked; an Indian came out from a hut, but a rifle bullet brought him down. Surprised, amazed, the Indians rushed out, attempting to flee, but found themselves hemmed in on every side.

"Burn the town!" shouted Major Rogers.

The buildings, all except three, in which the Indians had stored their corn, were set on fire. The rifles of the Rangers and the devouring flames quickly did their work—wiping out the town and more than two hundred warriors. The women and children were spared. Five English captives were rescued.

"There are three hundred French and Indians only four miles from here, and you never will get back; they will soon be upon you," said the rescued prisoners.

Major Rogers knew that it was time for him to be moving; and before sunrise he was on his return—not to Lake Champlain, but toward the head-waters of the Connecticut. The French and Indians pursued, came up with a party of the Rangers, and captured them. The other Rangers suffered terrible hardships before they reached Charlestown, in New Hampshire. But they accomplished their work; and the Indians, who had filled so many homes with sorrow—the most savage and blood-thirsty in Canada—as a tribe, disappeared forever.

The struggle between France and England for the control of the Western Continent ended with the surrender of Montreal to General Amherst in 1760. It was in 1609 that Samuel Champlain, dreaming of establishing the Empire of New France, became the ally of the Algon-

WOLFE AND MONTCALM'S MONUMENT.

quins, and fired a shot on the western shore of Lake Champlain that made the Iroquois the enemies of France and the allies of England. One hundred and fifty years have rolled away since the firing of that gun. Throughout the period two civilizations have striven for mastery. France has been fighting to establish the ideas of the feudal period—the absolute authority of kings and popes over the bodies and souls of men. They are the ideas of a by-gone age. The thought never has dawned upon the dull intellects of the King of France and his ministers that the *people* are of any account; they do not know the meaning of the word. Not so the men of New England and New York marching to complete the conquest of Canada. Those citizen soldiers have been obtaining an insight into the rights which God has given to men—of individual liberty, of self-government. They make their own laws; they are their own masters. They will render allegiance to the king only as he himself shall respect their rights, and the laws which they may make.

Peace! How delightful it was! No more would the Indian steal upon the unsuspecting settler; no more the midnight alarm, the wild war-whoop, the gleaming scalping-knife, the massacre, or the captivity; no more weary watchings for the coming of the foe; but the farmer could follow the plough, or reap the ripening grain, or traverse the wilderness in safety and security.

Peace brings prosperity. Fifteen years pass, and the people of America, educated by influences and conditions all unknown on the other side of the Atlantic, announce to the world that all men are created free and equal, and endowed with inalienable rights. They give their honor, their fortunes, their lives in support of it. Victory crowns their efforts, and the colonies become a nation, independent, powerful, and teacher of all the nations, by the power of an illustrious example in defence of Justice, Liberty, and the Rights of Man.

INDEX.

A.

Abercrombie, General, 408, 426, 430.
Acadia settled, 58.
Alexander, William, settles Newfoundland, 148.
Amuret IV., Sultan, visited by Mary Fisher, 45.
Andros, Sir Edmund, 266.
Annapolis captured, 327.
Arbitrary rule in Massachusetts, 267.
Argall, Samuel, 96, 107.
Armada, Spanish, 73.
Austin, Anne, 219.

B.

Bacon's Rebellion, 261.
Baltimore surveyed, 206.
Barneveld, John, 100, 113.
Bastwick, Rev. Mr., 206.
Baxter, Richard, 305.
Bendle, Thomas, 311.
Bellows, Benjamin, 403.
Berkeley, Sir William, 259, 260.
" Bishop, 336.
Berwick attacked, 320.
" destroyed, 327.
Billington, John, 118.
Blackstone, William, 168.
Block, Adriaen, builds the *Onrust*, 99 ; in Holland, 101.
Bloomaert, Samuel, 145.
Bogardus, Dominie, 197.
Boleyn, Anne, 51.
Bomazeen, 320.
Boquet's expedition, 434.
Boscawen, Admiral, 484.
Boston settled, 169.
Braddock, General, 377.
" army of, 380.
" defeat of, 382.

Bradford, William, 126, 129.
Bradley, Isaac, 280.
Bradstreet, Colonel, 428, 433, 435.
Brant, Joseph, 385.
Brewster, William, 121.
Brittany fishermen, 38, 39.
Brookfield attacked, 244.
Brown, John and Samuel, 164.
" Thomas, physician, 305.
Bunyan, John, 236.
Burden, Anne, 219.
Burgesses of Virginia, 108.
Burial Hill, 125.
Bute, Earl of, 425.

C.

Cabeza de Vasca, 28-31.
Cabot, John and Sebastian, 17, 21.
Calvert, George, 293.
Calvin, John, 155.
Canada, Civilization of, 421, 428.
" settled, 43.
" government, 255.
Cancella, Louis, 30.
Canonicus, 180.
Carolina officers, 337.
Carteret, Philip, Governor of New Jersey, 292.
Cartier, Jacques, discovers Canada, 29.
Carver, John, Governor of Plymouth, 117.
Casco attacked by Indians, 321.
Casimir, Fort, 224.
Cat-skin caps, 40.
Cavaliers, 211, 213, 260.
Champlain, Samuel, first visit to America, 59; settles Acadia, 59; visits the St. Lawrence, 66; joins the Algonquins against the Iroquois, 71; plans the empire of New France, 102; expedition to Lake Huron, 104; battle with the Iroquois, 105.

Charles I., King of England, 152; arbitrary acts, 158; conflict with Parliament, 159; establishes monopolies, 162; struggle with Parliament, 207; execution, 213.
Charles II., times of, 234.
" IV. of Austria, 389.
Charter of Connecticut, 229, 269.
" of Massachusetts, 266.
Christmas at Plymouth, 134.
Christiansen, Hendrick, 100.
Church, Benjamin, 325.
" Captain, 248.
Clarendon, Earl of, 327.
Clark, Thomas, mate of the *Mayflower*, 121.
Coddington, William, settles Newport, 190.
Colbert, 252.
Conant, Roger, 156.
Connecticut settled, 172.
Conquest of Mexico, 24.
Controversy in Massachusetts, 193.
Copper ore in New Jersey, 291.
Coronado discovers California, 30.
Cortez, Hernando, 23.
Cotton, Rev. John, 165.
Cradock, Matthew, 165, 166.
Cranmer, Archbishop, 303.
Crashaw, Rev. Mr., 91.
Cromwell, Oliver, 207, 219.
Crown Point abandoned by the French, 440.
Crusaders, 39.
Culpepper, Governor, 262, 369.

D.

Dare, Virginia, 35.
Davenport, Rev. John, 183.
Davis, Captain, carried to Canada, 281.
Deerfield attacked, 322.
Defence of Fort William Henry, 411.
De Guast, Pierre, 58.
De Guercheville, Madame, 92, 94, 95.
Delaware, Lord, 91.
" settled, 145.
De Lamberville, Jean, 254.
De la Motte, Jesuit, 96.
De la Roche, Marquis, 55, 56.
De Monts, 58, 62.
Denonville, Governor of Canada, 256.
De Rouville, 279, 322.
De Saussage, 94.
De Soto, Ferdinand, 29, 30.
De Thet, Father, 96.

De Vries, Captain, 195.
Dieskau, Baron, 384, 385, 387.
Dinwiddie, Governor, 368, 370.
Dominic de Gourges, 33.
Dominican priests, 30.
Dorchester, Georgia, 346.
" merchants, 156.
" Massachusetts, 345.
" South Carolina, 343.
Dover, New Hampshire, 142, 249, 273.
Drake, Sir Francis, 33.
Drayton Hall, 340, 341.
Du Quesne, Marquis of, 373.
Dustin, Hannah, 285.
" Thomas, 285.
Duxbury settled, 139.
Dyer, William and Mary, 219.

E.

Eayers, Mrs., conceals Goff and Whalley, 239.
Eelkins, Captain, 196.
Edge Hill, Battle of, 210.
Eliot, John, 159.
" " missionary to Indians, 243.
Emigration to Connecticut, 174.
" to Virginia, 214, 264.
Endicott, John, 157, 178.
Exeter settled, 193.

F.

Fairfax, Lord, 369, 370.
Fenwick, Alice, 176.
Fire in London, 233.
Fisher, Mary, 218, 219.
Fisheries of Newfoundland, 21, 33, 37.
Florida discovered, 23.
" settled, 31.
Flotilla on Lake George, 427.
Fort Du Quesne, 375, 435.
" Frontenac captured, 439.
" George, 142.
" Good Hope, 172.
" La Bœuf, 372.
" Necessity, 375.
" Niagara captured, 439.
Forbes, General, 435.
Fox, George, 52, 53, 216.
Fox-hunting, 369.
Francis I., King of France, 24.
Franklin, Benjamin, 377.
Frontenac, Louis, 251, 252, 254, 277, 278.

INDEX. 457

Fry, Colonel Joshua, 374.
Fur trade, 40, 41, 146, 148, 252.

G.

Games in England, 83.
Gates, Thomas, 89.
Georgia settled, 350.
Gilbert, Sir Humphrey, 83, 84.
Gist, Christopher, 372.
Godyn, Samuel, 145.
Goff, John, 236, 248.
Gold, Thirst for, 60.
Gomez, Stephen, 25.
Gorges, Fernando, 62, 64, 141.
Governors, Gathering of, 377.
Gulf-stream, 19.
Gunpowder Plot, 75.
Gustavus Adolphus, 199.

H.

Habeas Corpus Act, 85.
Hakluyt, Richard, 57.
Hale, Sir Matthew, 305.
Hampden, John, 162.
Hampton settled, 91.
Harding's, Stephen, fight with Indians, 322.
Harvard College established, 187.
Haverhill attacked by Indians, 281.
Hawkins, John, 46.
Heard, Elizabeth, befriended by an Indian, 274.
Hendrick, 386.
Henrietta Maria, 152.
Henry IV. of France murdered, 88.
    " VIII. of England, 51.
Hertel, François, attacks Haverhill, 326.
Higginson, Rev. Francis, 163.
High Commission, 85.
Highlanders at Ticonderoga, 426.
Hilton, Colonel, 328.
    " William and Edward, settle Dover, 142.
Hollis, Denzel, 159.
Holmes, William, settles Windsor, Connecticut, 172.
Honfleur fishermen, 37.
Hooker, Rev. Thomas, emigrates to Connecticut, 175.
Hopkins, Matthew, witch-finder, 304.
    " Stephen, 130.
Horsmenden, Judge, 359.
Hosset, Gillis, 145.
Houghton Hall, dinner to James I., 78.

Howe, Lord, 430.
Hudson River visited by Stephen Gomez, 25.
    "   " visited by Henry Hudson, 71.
Hughson, John, 359-361.
Huguenots, 30, 148, 341.
Hunt, Captain, sells Indians into slavery, 98.
Hutchinson, Ann, 192, 205.
    " Lucy, 80.

I.

Inquisition, 352.
Ironsides, men of Cromwell, 211.
Iroquois Indians, 53, 69, 256, 257, 258.

J.

James I., King of England, 74; dines at Houghton Hall, 78; decree in regard to sports, 79; entertains the King of Denmark, 84; sends thieves to Virginia, 107; death, 152.
James II., 232, 265, 270, 271.
Jamestown, settlement of, 63; confusion at, 90; cattle sent to, 91; settlers purchase wives, 109; first slaves bought, 109; massacre of inhabitants, 110; destroyed, 262.
Jesuits founded, 49; influence in the world, 51; hated by the people of England, 72; connected with Gunpowder Plot, 76; connected with murder of Henry IV., 88; far-reaching plans, 93, 94; interfere in Canadian affairs, 147; efforts to convert the Iroquois, 254; influence the Indians of Maine, 273; mission to St. Francis Indians, 320; Father Rale and the Norridgewock Indians, 329, 330.
Johnson, General, 387.
    " Isaac, 165.
    " Lady Arabella, 165.
Jonson, Ben, poet, 82.

K.

Keezar, John, 281.
Kempthorn, Simon, 218.
Keppel, Admiral, 379.
Kieft, William, 198-201.
Kilburn, John, 403.
King Philip's War, 241.
    " William's War, 271.
Kirk, David, captures Quebec, 148.

L.

Labor in South Carolina, 349.
La Montagne, Doctor, 198.
Lane, Ralph, carries tobacco to London, 44.

Las Casas, Bishop, 45.
Laud, Archbishop, 207, 209.
Leet, Governor, 238.
Legacy of Blood, 318.
Lent, 37.
Locke's, John, plan of government, 337.
London Company, 63.
Londoun, Earl of, 408, 410, 419.
Louis XIV., 254, 319.
Louisburg, 391, 396, 407.
Lovewell's expedition, 331.
Loyola, Ignatius, 49.
Lyford, John, 156.
Lyman, General, 387.

M.

Manhattan settled, 143.
Marston Moor, Battle of, 211.
Maryland settled, 294.
" officers, 295.
Mason, John, 141, 179.
Massachusetts Company, 162.
Massacre at Fort William Henry.
" at Jamestown, 110.
" of Huguenots, 32.
" of Indians by the Dutch, 203.
Massasoit visits Plymouth, 122, 131.
Mather, Cotton, 313.
Maverick, Samuel, 168.
May-poles, 206, 235.
Membertn, 62, 89.
Merry Mount, 137.
Ministry of George II., 388.
Minuet, Peter, 143, 144, 200.
Mississippi River discovered, 28.
Montmorenci, Duke of, 146.
Montreal attacked by Iroquois, 258.
Morgan, Daniel, 378.
Morton, Thomas, 137.
Moulton, General, accused of being a witch, 309.
Munroe, Colonel, defends Fort William Henry, 418.
Murray, General, 443.

N.

Narragansett Bay discovered, 24.
Naseby, Battle of, 212.
Neff, Mary, 286.
Negro tragedy, 357.
New Albion, 33.
" Amsterdam, 231, 233.

Newbury settled, 173.
New Hampshire settled, 142.
" Haven settled, 183.
" Jersey settled, 291.
Newport settled, 190.
New York settled, 142.
Ney, John, burnt, 361, 362.
Nicot, Jules, carries tobacco to France, 44.
Nicholson, Sir Francis, 263.
Norridgewock expedition, 328.
Northmen, 18, 21.

O.

Oglethorpe, General, 350, 351, 353, 355, 360.
Oldham, John, killed by Indians, 177.
Oswego captured, 409.

P.

Pamphilio Narvaez, 25.
Parliament under Charles I., 159.
Parris, Rev. Mr., 310, 312, 313, 314.
Parsons, Hugh, 309.
Patroons, 145.
Penn, Admiral, 198.
" William, 297-299, 301, 302.
Pepperell, William, 395.
Pequod Indians, 176, 179, 180.
Philadelphia settled, 298.
Philip, King, 241-245, 248, 249.
Phipps, William, 290.
Pigwaket Indians, 330.
Pilgrims, 111-140.
Pitt, William, 422, 425, 437.
Pittsburgh named, 436.
Plains of Abraham, 446.
Pomeroy, Seth, 387.
Ponce de Leon, 22.
Pontrincourt, Baron, 58.
Pope Alexander VI., 17, 303.
Pope's Day, 77.
Popham, Lord John, 64, 65.
Population of Canada, 375.
Portland attacked, 280.
Port Royal, Nova Scotia, 59, 290.
" " South Carolina, 30, 339.
Porto Rico, 35.
Prayer-book, 164, 268.
Priest, Degory, 120.
Pring, Martin, 57.
Printing in Virginia, 259.
Prynne, William, 206.

Punishments in time of James I., 85, 152-183, 345.
Puritans, 51, 84.
Pym, John, 208.

Q.

Quaco, Burning of, 361.
Quakers, 216-227, 299, 342.
Quebec, 30, 66, 146, 441-444.
Quo warranto, 265.

R.

Raleigh, Sir Walter, 35.
Rale, the Jesuit, 328.
Randolph, Edmund, 265.
Rangers, 383, 413, 427, 444.
Ravaillac, the Jesuit, 88.
Revelry at Court of James I., 82.
Revolution in Boston, 269.
" in Virginia, 261.
Rhode Island settled, 190.
Ribault, John, 30, 31.
Rice brought to South Carolina, 344.
Richelieu, Cardinal, 148.
Roanoke Island settled, 35.
Robinson, John, 51, 115.
Rogers, Major, 383.
" Robert, 411, 422, 424.
Running the gauntlet, 365.
Rupert, Prince, 209.

S.

Sable Island, 56.
Sainte Hélène, 278.
Salem settled, 157.
" witchcraft, 310-317.
Salmon Falls attacked, 279.
Salzburg, Archbishop of, 351.
Samoset visits Plymouth, 122.
San Salvador discovered, 17.
Sante Fé, 30.
Savannah, 350, 355.
Saybrook settled, 176.
Schenectady attacked, 277.
Schools in Massachusetts, 187.
Schuyler, Arent, 291.
Separatists, 51.
Sewall, Samuel, 316.
Shawmut settled, 169.
Ship-money, 162.
Shirley, Governor, 382.

Ship *Abigail*, 157.
" *Anne*, 350.
" *Arbella*, 166.
" *Archangel*, 61.
" *Concord*, 56.
" *Eagle*, 165.
" *Fortune*, 133.
" *Half-Moon*, 71.
" *Hesperus*, 167.
" *Jonas*, 46.
" *Lyon*, 167, 169.
" *Mayflower*, 116, 124, 125.
" *Naseby*, 234.
" *New Netherlands*, 142.
" *Onrust*, 99.
" *Rose*, 269.
" *Royal Charles*, 233.
" *Solomon*, 46.
" *Sparrow*, 136.
" *Swallow*, 46, 218.
" *William*, 196, 298.
" *Zouterberg*, 195.
Smith, John, 90, 97.
Soap-makers' Company, 160.
South Carolina, 24, 347.
Southwick, Lawrence and Cassandra, 219.
Spaniards attack Savannah, 355.
" in Florida, 343.
Spotswood, Archbishop, 304.
" Governor, 264.
St. Augustine, 33, 347.
St. Botolph's church, 165.
St. Croix settlement, 58.
St. Francis, 102.
" " Indians, 320, 365, 402, 449.
St. John's destroyed, 33.
St. Patrick's Day, 411.
Stafford, Earl of, 208.
Standish, Miles, 118, 121, 127, 135, 138, 139.
" Rose, 122.
Stark, John, 363-365, 411, 414, 427, 430.
Stevens, Phineas, 398.
Strawberry Bank, 57.
Stuyvesant, Peter, 224, 230.
Sunday sports, 79.
Swedish settlements, 199.

T.

Tadousac settled, 66.
Taxes in Virginia, 263.
Thanksgiving, 133, 169.

INDEX.

Theatres in time of James I., 80.
Thompson, David, 142.
Titubu, 310.
Ticonderoga, 426, 428-431, 440.
Tobacco, 43, 263.
Tribute paid by Indians, 198.
Trinidad discovered, 21.
Tuscarora Indians, 348.

U.

Underhill, John, 178, 179.
Universal Suffrage, 183.
United Colonies, 194.
Utrecht, Peace of, 327.

V.

Van Braam, Jacob, 373.
Van Rensselaer, Jeremias, 230
Vane, Sir Henry, 192.
Vasco da Gama, 21.
Vasquez D'Ayllon, 24.
Vaudreuil, General, 398.
Vaughan, Colonel, 393, 396.
Ventadour, Duke of, 147.
Vernon, Admiral, 355, 359, 368.
Verrazano, John, 24.
Virginia settled, 63.

W.

Waggener, Captain, 381.
Walking Purchase, 301.
Waldron, Major, 249, 274.
Walloons, 141.
Walpole attacked by Indians, 402.
Wampanoag Indians, 241.
Wampum, 133.
War between England and Holland, 232.

War between France and England, 390.
Warren, Admiral, 394.
Washington, George, 368-370, 372.
" Lawrence, 369.
" Sir John, 215.
Washer-women, 161.
Webb, General, 410, 415, 416.
Wentworth, Benning, 393.
" Thomas, 209.
West India Company, 142, 230.
Wesley, John and Charles, 353.
Weston, Thomas, 115, 116, 133, 134.
Weymouth, Captain, 61.
" settled, 134.
Whalley, Edward, 236, 248.
Wheelright, Rev. John, 192, 193.
White, John, 35, 156.
Whitfield, Rev. George, 353.
Whittaker, Joseph, 281.
William and Mary College, 263.
" of Orange, 271.
Williams, Ephraim, 385.
" Roger, 170, 187-189.
Winslow, Edward, 122, 129, 172.
Winthrop, John, 165, 168, 169.
" " Jr., 227, 228, 237.
Witches, Chapter XXV., 300.
Wives for Virginia settlers, 109.
Wolfe's, General, death, 447.
Wollaston, Captain, 137.
Wouter van Twiller, 195-197, 224, 230.

Y.

Yeamans, Sir John, 340.
Yeardly, Sir George, 107.
York, Duke of, 231.

THE END.

INTERESTING BOOKS FOR BOYS:

BOUND VOLUMES OF HARPER'S YOUNG PEOPLE for 1884, 1885, 1886, and 1887, Handsomely Bound in Illuminated Cloth, $3 50 per vol. *Bound Volumes for 1880, 1881, 1882, and 1883 are out of stock.*

THE BOY TRAVELLERS ON THE CONGO. Adventures of Two Youths in a Journey with Henry M. Stanley "Through the Dark Continent." By THOMAS W. KNOX. Copiously Illustrated. 8vo, Cloth, $3 00.

THE BOY TRAVELLERS IN THE RUSSIAN EMPIRE. Adventures of Two Youths in a Journey in European and Asiatic Russia. With Accounts of a Tour across Siberia, Voyages on the Amoor, Volga, and other Rivers, a Visit to Central Asia, Travels among the Exiles, and a Historical Sketch of the Empire from its Foundation to the Present Time. By THOMAS W. KNOX. Copiously Illustrated. 8vo, Cloth, $3 00.

THE BOY TRAVELLERS IN SOUTH AMERICA. Adventures of Two Youths in a Journey through Ecuador, Peru, Bolivia, Brazil, Paraguay, Argentine Republic, and Chili. With Descriptions of Patagonia and Tierra del Fuego, and Voyages upon the Amazon and La Plata Rivers. By THOMAS W. KNOX. Copiously Illustrated. 8vo, Cloth, $3 00.

THE BOY TRAVELLERS IN THE FAR EAST. By THOMAS W. KNOX. Five Parts. Copiously Illustrated. 8vo, Cloth, $3 00 each.

> PART I. ADVENTURES OF TWO YOUTHS IN A JOURNEY TO JAPAN AND CHINA.—PART II. ADVENTURES OF TWO YOUTHS IN A JOURNEY TO SIAM AND JAVA. With Descriptions of Cochin-China, Cambodia, Sumatra, and the Malay Archipelago.—PART III. ADVENTURES OF TWO YOUTHS IN A JOURNEY TO CEYLON AND INDIA. With Descriptions of Borneo, the Philippine Islands, and Burmah.—PART IV. ADVENTURES OF TWO YOUTHS IN A JOURNEY TO EGYPT AND PALESTINE.—PART V. ADVENTURES OF TWO YOUTHS IN A JOURNEY THROUGH AFRICA.

THE VOYAGE OF THE "VIVIAN" to the North Pole and Beyond. Adventures of Two Youths in the Open Polar Sea. By THOMAS W. KNOX. Profusely Illustrated. 8vo, Cloth, $2 50.

HUNTING ADVENTURES ON LAND AND SEA. By THOMAS W. KNOX. Two Parts. Copiously Illustrated. 8vo, Cloth, $2 50 each.

> PART I. THE YOUNG NIMRODS IN NORTH AMERICA.
> PART II. THE YOUNG NIMRODS AROUND THE WORLD.

WHAT MR. DARWIN SAW IN HIS VOYAGE ROUND THE WORLD IN THE SHIP "BEAGLE." Illustrated. 8vo, Cloth, $3 00.

FRIENDS WORTH KNOWING. Glimpses of American Natural History. By ERNEST INGERSOLL. Illustrated. 16mo, Cloth, $1 00.

BY CHARLES CARLETON COFFIN. Five Volumes. Illustrated. 8vo, Cloth, $3 00 each.

> THE STORY OF LIBERTY.—OLD TIMES IN THE COLONIES.—THE BOYS OF '76 (A History of the Battles of the Revolution).—BUILDING THE NATION.—DRUM-BEAT OF THE NATION.

Interesting Books for Boys.

CAMP LIFE IN THE WOODS; AND THE TRICKS OF TRAPPING AND TRAP MAKING. By W. HAMILTON GIBSON, Author of "Pastoral Days." Illustrated by the Author. 16mo, Cloth, $1 00.

HOW TO GET STRONG, AND HOW TO STAY SO. By WILLIAM BLAIKIE. With Illustrations. 16mo, Cloth, $1 00.

"HARPER'S YOUNG PEOPLE" SERIES. Illustrated. 16mo, Cloth, $1 00 per vol.
 THE ADVENTURES OF JIMMY BROWN. Written by Himself, and Edited by W. L. ALDEN. —THE CRUISE OF THE CANOE CLUB. THE CRUISE OF THE "GHOST." THE MORAL PIRATES. By W. L. ALDEN.—TOBY TYLER; OR, TEN WEEKS WITH A CIRCUS. MR. STUBBS'S BROTHER: A Sequel to "Toby Tyler." TIM AND TIP; OR, THE ADVENTURES OF A BOY AND A DOG. LEFT BEHIND; OR, TEN DAYS A NEWSBOY. RAISING THE "PEARL." SILENT PETE. By JAMES OTIS.—THE STORY OF MUSIC AND MUSICIANS. JO'S OPPORTUNITY. ROLF HOUSE. MILDRED'S BARGAIN, AND OTHER STORIES. NAN. By LUCY C. LILLIE.—THE FOUR MACNICOLS. By WILLIAM BLACK.—THE LOST CITY; OR, THE BOY EXPLORERS IN CENTRAL ASIA. INTO UNKNOWN SEAS. By DAVID KER.—THE TALKING LEAVES. An Indian Story. TWO ARROWS: A Story of Red and White. By W. O. STODDARD.—WHO WAS PAUL GRAYSON? By JOHN HABBERTON, Author of "Helen's Babies."—PRINCE LAZYBONES, AND OTHER STORIES. By Mrs. W. J. HAYS.—THE ICE QUEEN. By ERNEST INGERSOLL.—WAKULLA: A Story of Adventure in Florida. THE FLAMINGO FEATHER. By C. K. MUNROE.—STRANGE STORIES FROM HISTORY. By GEORGE CARY EGGLESTON.

THE STARTLING EXPLOITS OF DR. J. B. QUIÈS. From the French of PAUL CÉLIÈRE. By Mrs. CASHEL HOEY and Mr. JOHN LILLIE. Profusely Illustrated. Crown 8vo, Extra Cloth, $1 75.

FROM THE FORECASTLE TO THE CABIN. By Captain S. SAMUELS. Illustrated. 12mo, Extra Cloth, $1 50.

MICROSCOPY FOR BEGINNERS; OR, COMMON OBJECTS FROM THE PONDS AND DITCHES. By ALFRED C. STOKES, M.D. Illustrated. 12mo, Cloth, $1 50.

MARY AND MARTHA. The Mother and the Wife of George Washington. By BENSON J. LOSSING, LL.D., Author of "Field-book of the Revolution," "Field-book of the War of 1812," "Cyclopædia of United States History," &c. Illustrated by Facsimiles of Pen-and-ink Drawings by H. Rosa. 8vo, Ornamental Cloth, $2 50.

THE HISTORY OF THE UNITED STATES NAVY, FOR BOYS. By BENSON J. LOSSING, LL.D. Illustrated. 12mo, Half Leather, $1 75.

THE ADVENTURES OF A YOUNG NATURALIST. By LUCIEN BIART. With 117 Illustrations. 12mo, Cloth, $1 75.

AN INVOLUNTARY VOYAGE. By LUCIEN BIART. Illustrated. 12mo, Cloth, $1 25.

ROUND THE WORLD; including a Residence in Victoria, and a Journey by Rail across North America. By a Boy. Edited by SAMUEL SMILES. Illustrated. 12mo, Cloth, $1 50.

THE SELF-HELP SERIES. By SAMUEL SMILES. 12mo, Cloth, $1 00 per volume.
 SELF-HELP.—CHARACTER.—THRIFT.—DUTY.

POLITICS FOR YOUNG AMERICANS. By CHARLES NORDHOFF. 12mo, Half Leather, 75 cents.

THE CHILDREN OF OLD PARK'S TAVERN. A Story of the South Shore. By FRANCES A. HUMPHREY. 16mo, Cloth, $1 00.

Interesting Books for Boys. 3

STORIES OF THE GORILLA COUNTRY. By Paul B. Du Chaillu. Illustrated 12mo, Cloth, $1 50.

THE COUNTRY OF THE DWARFS. By Paul B. Du Chaillu. Illustrated. 12mo Cloth, $1 50.

WILD LIFE UNDER THE EQUATOR. By Paul B. Du Chaillu. Illustrated 12mo, Cloth, $1 50.

MY APINGI KINGDOM: with Life in the Great Sahara, and Sketches of the Chase of the Ostrich, Hyena, &c. By Paul B. Du Chaillu. Illustrated. 12mo, Clot $1 50.

LOST IN THE JUNGLE. By Paul B. Du Chaillu. Illustrated. 12mo, Cloth, $1 5

THE BOYHOOD OF GREAT MEN. By John G. Edgar. Illustrated. 16mo, Clot $1 00.

THE FOOTPRINTS OF FAMOUS MEN. By John G. Edgar. Illustrated. 16m Cloth, $1 00.

HISTORY FOR BOYS; or, Annals of the Nations of Modern Europe. By John Edgar. Illustrated. 16mo, Cloth, $1 00.

SEA-KINGS AND NAVAL HEROES. A Book for Boys. By John G. Edgar. Illu trated. 16mo, Cloth, $1 00.

THE WARS OF THE ROSES. By John G. Edgar. Illustrated. 16mo, Cloth, $1 0

UPLAND AND MEADOW. A Ponetquissings Chronicle. By Charles C. Abbott, M.I pp. x., 398. 12mo, Ornamental Cloth, $1 50.

STORIES OF THE ISLAND WORLD. By Charles Nordhoff. Illustrated. 12m Cloth, $1 00.

THE THOUSAND AND ONE NIGHTS; or, The Arabian Nights' Entertainment Translated and Arranged for Family Reading, with Explanatory Notes, by E. V Lane. 600 Illustrations by Harvey. 2 vols., 12mo, Cloth, $3 50.

HENRY MAYHEW'S WORKS. 4 vols., 16mo, Cloth, $1 25 per vol.
    The Boyhood of Martin Luther.—The Story of the Peasant-Boy Philosopher· Young Benjamin Franklin.—The Wonders of Science.

SCIENCE FOR THE YOUNG. By Jacob Abbott. Illustrated. 4 vols.: *Heat.—Light.- Water and Land.—Force.* 12mo, Cloth, $1 50 each.

OUR CHILDREN'S SONGS. Illustrated. 8vo, Ornamental Cover, $1 00.

THE HISTORY OF SANDFORD AND MERTON. By Thomas Day. 18mo, Hal Bound, 75 cents.

YOUTH'S HEALTH-BOOK. 32mo, Paper, 25 cents; Cloth, 40 cents.

STORIES OF THE OLD DOMINION. From the Settlement to the End of the Revolu tion. By John Esten Cooke. Illustrated. 12mo, Cloth, $1 50.

THE LIFE AND SURPRISING ADVENTURES OF ROBINSON CRUSOE, of Yorl Mariner; with a Biographical Account of Defoe. Illustrated by Adams. Complet Edition. 12mo, Cloth, $1 60.

Interesting Books for Boys.

THE HISTORY OF A MOUTHFUL OF BREAD, and its Effect on the Organization of Men and Animals. By JEAN MACÉ. Translated from the Eighth French Edition by Mrs. ALFRED GATTY. 12mo, Cloth, $1 75.

THE SERVANTS OF THE STOMACH. By JEAN MACÉ. Reprinted from the London Edition, Revised and Corrected. 12mo, Cloth, $1 75.

FRED MARKHAM IN RUSSIA; or, The Boy Travellers in the Land of the Czar. By W. H. G. KINGSTON. Illustrated. Small 4to, Cloth, 75 cents.

SELF-MADE MEN. By CHARLES C. B. SEYMOUR. Many Portraits. 12mo, Cloth, $1 75.

THE SWISS FAMILY ROBINSON; or, Adventures of a Father and Mother and Four Sons on a Desert Island. Illustrated. 2 vols., 18mo, Cloth, $1 50.

THE SWISS FAMILY ROBINSON — Continued: being a Sequel to the Foregoing. 2 vols., 18mo, Cloth, $1 50.

DOGS AND THEIR DOINGS. By Rev. F. O. MORRIS, B.A. Illustrated. Square 8vo, Cloth, Gilt Sides, $1 75.

TALES FROM THE ODYSSEY FOR BOYS AND GIRLS. By C. M. B. 32mo, Paper, 25 cents; Cloth, 40 cents.

THE ADVENTURES OF REUBEN DAVIDGER; Seventeen Years and Four Months Captive among the Dyaks of Borneo. By J. GREENWOOD. 8vo, Cloth, Illustrated, $1 25; 4to, Paper, 15 cents.

WILD SPORTS OF THE WORLD. A Book of Natural History and Adventure. By J. GREENWOOD. Illustrated. Crown 8vo, Cloth, $2 50.

CAST UP BY THE SEA; or, The Adventures of Ned Grey. By Sir SAMUEL W. BAKER, M.A., F.R.S., F.R.G.S. 12mo, Cloth, Illustrated, $1 25; 4to, Paper, 15 cents.

HOMES WITHOUT HANDS: Being a Description of the Habitations of Animals, classed according to their Principle of Construction. By the Rev. J. G. WOOD, M.A., F.L.S. With about 140 Illustrations engraved on Wood by G. Pearson, from Original Designs made by F. W. Keyl and E. A. Smith, under the Author's Superintendence. 8vo, Cloth, $4 50; Sheep, $5 00; Roan, $5 00; Half Calf, $6 75.

THE ILLUSTRATED NATURAL HISTORY. By the Rev. J. G. WOOD, M.A., F.L.S. With 450 Engravings. 12mo, Cloth, $1 05.

CHAPTERS ON PLANT LIFE. By Mrs. S. B. HERRICK. Illustrated. Square 16mo, Cloth, 60 cents.

FLY-RODS AND FLY-TACKLE. Suggestions as to their Manufacture and Use. By HENRY P. WELLS. Illustrated. Post 8vo, Illuminated Cloth, $2 50.

NEW GAMES FOR PARLOR AND LAWN. New Games for Parlor and Lawn, with a few Old Friends in a New Dress. By GEORGE B. BARTLETT. 16mo, Cloth, $1 00.

INDIAN HISTORY FOR YOUNG FOLKS. By FRANCIS S. DRAKE. With Colored Frontispiece, Numerous Illustrations, and a Map of the United States, showing the Locations and Relative Sizes of the Indian Reservations. Square 8vo, Ornamental Cloth, $3 00.

PUBLISHED BY HARPER & BROTHERS, NEW YORK.

☞ HARPER & BROTHERS *will send any of the above works by mail, postage prepaid, to any part of the United States or Canada, on receipt of the price.*

www.ingramcontent.com/pod-product-compliance
Lightning Source LLC
Chambersburg PA
CBHW031954300426
44117CB00008B/759